LAND, LABOUR AND DIET
IN NORTHERN RHODESIA

D1483290

OXFORD UNIVERSITY PRESS
AMEN HOUSE, E.C. 4
London Edinburgh Glasgow New York
Toronto Melbourne Capetown Bombay
Calcutta Madras
HUMPHREY MILFORD
PUBLISHER TO THE UNIVERSITY

Bemba village—Nkula, 1930.
(Ethnographer's tent on left.)

LAND, LABOUR AND DIET IN NORTHERN RHODESIA

AN ECONOMIC STUDY OF THE BEMBA TRIBE

BY

AUDREY I. RICHARDS

M.A. (Cantab.), Ph.D. (London)

*Senior Lecturer in Social Anthropology
at the University of the Witwatersrand
Johannesburg
Sometime Lecturer in Social Anthropology at the London School of Economics*

Published for the

INTERNATIONAL INSTITUTE OF
AFRICAN LANGUAGES & CULTURES

by the OXFORD UNIVERSITY PRESS

LONDON   NEW YORK   TORONTO

1939

PRINTED IN GREAT BRITAIN

TO
LORNA GORE-BROWNE

FOREWORD

IN the case of an African tribe on which little has been published, the simplest procedure for a field-worker is to write an outline account of the social structure and the chief activities of the people, and afterwards, if the material warrants, to produce more detailed studies of special aspects of the culture. This procedure I have reversed by publishing the present book. I did so for a practical reason. While I was in the midst of writing an introductory monograph on the Bemba of North-Eastern Rhodesia I became a member of the Diet Committee of the International Institute of African Languages and Cultures, a small group of anthropologists, medical and nutritional experts set up in 1935 to discuss the possible contribution of the ethnological field-worker to the study of nutrition among various African tribes.[1] This was a practical problem for the Institute since it had recently sent out a number of trained anthropologists to make comparative studies in different parts of Africa (Sierre Leone, Gold Coast, Nigeria, Kenya, Uganda, Nyasaland, Rhodesia, and the Union) and it had been suggested that these field-workers, all living in intimate personal contact with the village life of the natives, might be asked to collect quantitative data on the diet of particular African peoples which would be of more value to nutritional science than the purely descriptive material so far recorded.

Research schemes are always difficult to formulate in the abstract, and for this reason it was decided to use as a basis for discussion some data on the diet of the Bemba which I had recently collected under conditions very similar to those we had in mind. The figures were admittedly inadequate, and had never been intended as part of a piece of nutritional research, but other quantitative surveys of the diet of African natives living under tribal conditions practically did not exist, and we had therefore to treat these

[1] The committee was composed as follows: Miss K. Abrahams (Dietician to University College Hospital, London); Miss D. G. Brackett (Secretary of the International Institute of African Languages and Cultures); Dr. R. Firth (Reader in Social Anthropology of the London University); Dr. J. L. Gilks (lately P.M.O., Kenya Colony); Dr. F. Kelly (Assistant Director, Imperial Bureau of Animal Nutrition); Dr. R. McCance and Dr. E. M. Widdowson (Pathological Department, King's College Hospital, London); Dr. E. B. Worthington (African Research Survey), and myself.

preliminary observations on the Bemba dietary as a basis for our discussions of possible methods of field-research.

To this end some Bemba foodstuffs were sent home to England for analysis, and Dr. McCance and Dr. E. M. Widdowson kindly undertook this work at King's College Hospital. Through joint work with them on this concrete data the possibilities of co-operation between anthropologists and nutritional research workers began to take shape. Dr. Widdowson estimated the composition of the Bemba diet roughly on the basis of my preliminary notes,[1] and she has generously allowed me to draw on her work right through this book. Our results are not conclusive as a final statement on Bemba diet problems, but the data revealed certain salient characteristics of primitive dietaries as distinct from our own, and suggested some of the main requirements of nutritional research among peoples living under these particular conditions.

It became evident to us, for instance, that the information required by the nutritional expert was far too detailed for an anthropologist to be able to collect in the course of his general study of tribal organization. It needed long periods of continuous observation, besides special training in methods of weighing and dispatching samples of foodstuffs for analysis. On the other hand I became impressed during two years' work on this committee, and a shorter period serving as a member of the Nutrition Committee of the Economic Advisory Council, with the importance of social and economic factors in determining native diet, especially in the case of societies in which tribal institutions had virtually collapsed in contact with European civilization.

Again and again it appeared in particular cases that methods of storage or distribution, tribal systems of production and co-operation, economic incentives, or traditional attitudes and values in relation to foodstuffs, were at the root of special deficiencies in diet.[2] Anthropological studies of native food habits and their methods of consuming and producing seemed to be essential in any dietetic investigation that might be planned. Yet it was just this type

[1] Already published as an article, 'A Dietary Study in North-Eastern Rhodesia', *Africa*, vol. ix, 1936.

[2] Cf. the work of Fellows of the Institute, e.g. M. and S. L. Fortes, 'Food in the Domestic Economy of the Tallensi', *Africa*, vol. ix, 1936; M. Read, 'Native Standards of Living and African Culture Change', Supplement to *Africa*, vol. xi, no. 3, 1938; also work so far unpublished by Kalervo Oberg among the Banyankole, H. Kuper in Swaziland, and E. H. Ashton in Basutoland.

of material that was least available to those considering nutrition from a practical point of view. Each African Government has its medical, agricultural, and veterinary advisors, but as yet few have appointed departmental experts on the anthropological side.

This shortage of anthropological data seemed to the Committee to be serious in view of the number of nutritional surveys of African peoples then being planned.[1] It was therefore suggested that it would be instructive if I wrote a short book describing, in the case of one particular tribe, the different sociological factors which directly determined the food-supply. The book grew after the fashion of its kind. I was obliged to include introductory, historical, and general material that should have been published in a preliminary monograph. The value of the work seemed to me to lie in its comprehensive treatment of the subject and the evidence that could be given from any one area of the variety of different factors, whether economic, political, legal, or religious which actually affected the people's diet. The result is in effect a description of the whole economic life of the tribe. I have therefore tried to include such information of the sociological type as the anthropologist will require for comparative purposes, together with data on different activities, such as cooking and gardening, which are more detailed than usually given in ethnographic monographs but which, I think, will be useful to the specialist on the nutrition side. To venture like this on the border-line between two different sciences, biological and social, is an ungrateful task. What pleases one set of experts displeases the other. But if the book gives a broad idea of the extent and variety of nutritional problems in one African society it will have achieved its aim.

From the theoretical point of view the book is an elaboration, on the basis of my own field material, of an earlier student thesis compiled from written documents, in which I tried to prove that hunger was the chief determinant of human relationships, initially within the family, but later in wider social groups, the village, age-grade, or political state. But the emphasis is rather different. In the first book I described the fundamental urge for food as shaping human institutions, and in the second I have given concrete material to show how the biological facts of appetite and diet are themselves shaped by the particular system of human relationships and traditional activities which are standardized in a social group—

[1] Under the stimulus of the Colonial Office inquiry described on p. 2.

in other words the cultural mechanisms for producing, preparing, and dividing food.

I have gained much since writing the earlier book from recent developments of Professor Malinowski's type of functional analysis of institutions, and in particular his treatment of agriculture in his last book (*Coral Gardens and Their Magic*, 1935). The practical bent of the present work also has led to frequent comparisons between traditional tribal economics and the new products of European industrial organization, and hence to the type of anthropological problem known as 'culture contact' on this side of the Atlantic, and 'acculturation' on the other. On this aspect I also owe much to the stimulus of Malinowski's recent work and to that of many of the Institute Fellows who have tackled similar questions in the field.[1] The American concept of 'culture patterns', with its emphasis on the comparative view-point I have found very stimulating, more especially as outlined recently by R. Linton, R. Benedict, and M. Mead. I cannot accept the criteria used by the last two writers to describe the culture patterns of particular societies, but I hope later to present the main body of my Bemba material in a form which will serve as a basis for comparative work of a rather different type, and in the meantime I have tried in this book to indicate the 'orientation' or 'pattern' of Bemba interests and activities as they affect the consumption or production of food.

The expeditions on which this material was collected were financed by several different Foundations, and to these I must tender very grateful thanks. For my first trip (May 1930–July 1931) grants were made by the Board of Bantu Studies of Capetown University, the Rhodes Trustees, and the Percy Sladen Trust. On my second tour (January 1933–July 1934) I had a fellowship from the Rockefeller Foundation. To this last body I also owe thanks for assistance in working up my material at the London School of Economics—in particular for the help of Miss Pauline Blackmore, who died tragically of a sudden illness in the middle of the work, and that of Miss Phyllis Kaberry, herself a fieldworker with Australian experience, who gave me much expert aid.

In Northern Rhodesia my work would have been quite impossible without the hospitality I was continually given. Miss H. Eastland, the Government native welfare officer at Kasama, let

[1] Cf. *Methods of Study of Culture Contact*, International Institute of African Languages and Cultures, Memo XV, 1938.

me make her house my home. I stayed a month at the White
Fathers' Mission at Cilubula where I received endless kindness,
and Mr. E. Munday, then District Commissioner at Chinsali,
gave me every conceivable help at the most difficult initial period
of my work, as also the Rev. and Mrs. Maxwell Robertson of the
Church of Scotland Mission at Lubwa. To the multitude of others
who gave me help and hospitality I must return collective thanks.

I am grateful also for much anthropological information. The
Government of Northern Rhodesia have given me permission to
use the tribal map at the end of the book and to quote from the
report of their Diet Committee. The members of the White
Fathers' Mission helped me much in my early struggles with
Bemba language and custom, particularly Bishops Roy and van
Sambeek, Fathers Étienne and Guillermé, and Mother Séraphine.
The Rev. R. MacMinn of the Church of Scotland Mission has
always answered my questions most generously and lent me for
some weeks his clerk, Paul Mushindo, whose real linguistic gifts
were of great service. Many members of the administrative,
educational, and agricultural services of Northern Rhodesia have
given me very useful information, particularly the late Mr. E. B. H.
Goodall, whose knowledge of Bemba custom seemed to me wider
than that of any other European I met, Mr. Christopher Bell, Mr.
Vernon Brelsford, and Mr. Douglas Miller. Mr. Godfrey Wilson,
lately appointed Director of the Rhodes-Livingstone Institute, has
checked up a number of points for me recently. Mr. T. Fox-
Pitt has always given me most ungrudging help, and he and Dr.
Haslam, Mr. Unwin Moffat, Mr. C. G. Trapnell, and Mr. Gerald
Wilson have all read parts of the book and made most valuable
criticisms on it. Father Tanguey very kindly corrected some
native texts for me and sent alternative translations.

But my greatest debt of all is to my friends, Colonel and Mrs.
Gore-Browne, who allowed me to make their house, Shiwa Ŋandu,
a centre of work for so many months on both trips. Their keen
interest in anthropological and other scientific investigations in
the country made it a pleasure to be with them. Mrs. Gore-
Browne stayed with me for some weeks in two different native
villages where her knowledge of the language and her quick
powers of contact were invaluable. On many aspects of Bemba
cultivation she is much more qualified to speak than I am. She has
sent me material constantly, and read and criticized most of this

book. It stands in her name because she made so much of my work a delight.

The orthography of the Bemba language has undergone many changes. The old *w* is now written *b* so that the 'Awemba' of the old maps is changed to 'Babemba'. The hard *ch*, formerly written *k* or *ch* (as in 'Chitimukulu') is now more usually expressed by the *c* symbol. The sound represented first by *shy*, then by the phonetic *ʃ*, is now written *sh*. The alternative use of the vowels *u* or *w*, *y* or *i* and the principles of word division are still controversial subjects. I have tried to follow the most recent recommendations of the Government Language Committee but am aware that there are many inconsistencies in the spelling of native words in my text.

AUDREY I. RICHARDS

UNIVERSITY OF THE WITWATERSRAND,
       January, 1939

CONTENTS

LIST OF ILLUSTRATIONS

LIST OF MAPS

INTRODUCTION

Some Characteristics of Primitive Diet.

IT was long assumed that the 'savage' selected his food under the guidance of some superior natural instinct denied to his civilized fellows, and that he lived on food which was more 'natural' and therefore more healthy than our own. For over two hundred years dietetic theorists have begged us to copy his choice of victuals—to eat our vegetables raw as he is supposed (quite erroneously) to do, to bake with flour as coarse as that produced between rough grinding stones, or to live on fruits and nuts.

But increasing medical knowledge has shown us the extremely wide prevalence of malnutrition, deficiency diseases, and a general lack of resistance to infection in just those areas inhabited by peoples whose 'natural' and healthy life has been envied. Reports from the British Colonies alone show the frequent incidence of such diseases as beriberi, pellagra, anaemia, goitre, night blindness, tropical ulcer, dental caries, and a high rate of tuberculosis and pulmonary infections in general.[1] The literature on the subject is so far scanty, but such reports come from areas as widely distant as Nigeria, Kenya, the South African Protectorates, Zanzibar, and Melanesia. The benefits of a primitive diet are evidently not so great as it once seemed.

From the little material available it appears that these diets show very similar deficiencies. A seasonal shortage, amounting sometimes to starvation, is a regular occurrence among some of these peoples. Many of them have to rely on the bush to supply them with vegetables and small game—often a valuable source of supply, but always an uncertain one. Fruit-growing practically does not exist. Fresh vegetables may only be available for a few months of the year, especially in tropical regions where the rainfall is limited to one season. Transport difficulties often prevent the effective distribution of supplies. For instance, the Government Reports from most African territories constantly comment on the limited areas of consumption of particular foods, such as fish. The inhabitants of a lake district or the sea-shore may live on this valuable foodstuff, while the peoples a short distance inland are

[1] Cf. *Nutritional Research in the British Colonial Empire*, Imperial Bureau of Animal Nutrition, Technical Communication No. 8.

dangerously short of animal protein just through the want of an
organized system of markets or trade. Apart from the annual
shortage, most primitive diets have other features in common.
For instance, there is usually a reliance on one type of foodstuff,
with the resultant dangers of lack of balance in the dietary; and
as regards specific constituents, the shortage of animal proteins,
fats, fresh vegetables, and mineral salts is commonly reported.
Milk, the food recommended by scientists as containing all the
elements necessary to health, is of unexpectedly limited distribution. Among the agricultural peoples of Africa and Melanesia,
for instance, it is quite common for natives to get no milk at all
from the time they are weaned until their death.

Disclosures such as these raise important medical and administrative problems, and the new science of nutrition is now being
applied to the study of the feeding of the so-called backward
peoples for the first time. One by one the great Colonial Powers
have shown their interest in the diet problems of the primitive
races under their rule.[1] A recent circular issued by the British
Colonial Office made a specific demand for information as to the
state of diet research in all the British Colonies and stressed
the triple importance of medicine, agriculture, and economics in
the solution of problems of health.[2] The nutrition committee
of the Economic Advisory Council just referred to was set up
in 1937 as the direct result. Scientists working in eastern
countries—Japan, China, India, Malay, and Ceylon—have also
been trying to estimate the special nutritional needs of peoples
living under the particular environmental conditions of the tropics.
In 1937 a special Inter-Governmental Conference of the Far-
Eastern Countries dealt specially with the question of diet in
relation to health in that part of the world.[3]

The African Problem.

To turn to Africa alone—the area dealt with exclusively in this
book—it is probable that here many primitive peoples have existed
for centuries, on diets which would be considered insufficient

[1] 'The Food and Nutrition of African Natives', Institute of African Languages
and Cultures, Memo xiii, 1937. *L'Alimentation dans les possessions tropicales*,
H. Labouret, *Africa*, vol. xi, April 1938; 'Problemes de l'alimentation au Congo
Belge', Trolli et Bigwood, *La Science de l'alimentation en* 1937.

[2] Colonial No. 121, 1936.

[3] Report of the Inter-Governmental Conference of the Far-eastern Countries
(Bandoeng, August 1937).

according to European and American standards. The question is now whether they can be allowed to continue at this level of development. In this continent it is obvious that the close economic interdependence of black and white has altered the whole nutritional situation for the native peoples. A diet which may have been adequate to the old village existence is plainly not sufficient to allow the African to advance or to permit him to adapt himself to the new industrial and agricultural conditions in which he finds himself. Men who worked an intermittent three or four hours a day in their tribal reserves are now asked to do a regular eight or ten hours under white supervision on the big plantations or in industrial concerns. In these circumstances, it is not surprising that they need more food and that the great mining companies, whether in South Africa, the Rhodesias, or the Belgian Congo, have found it necessary to keep their new recruits on special light duty and very good rations before they are considered fit to undertake the heaviest work under-ground. They do not hope to maintain their level of production unless they feed their labourers on a diet which is sometimes twice as ample as that usually eaten in the native village, as well as being much better balanced.[1] The biggest industrialists have in fact abandoned perforce the old European theory that natives need nothing but mealies in order to be able to work.

Apart from the feeding of African labourers, there is the far more urgent question of the nutrition of the population as a whole. It is an unfortunate fact that the diet of many primitive peoples has deteriorated in contact with white civilization rather than the reverse, and that in many parts of Africa the difficulty of the administrator is to ensure that the people live on as good a diet as formerly, let alone a better one. In urban areas the new use of European foods, white flour or unpolished rice, have robbed the people of many of the most valuable constituents of their former diet. The sudden development of industrialization in Africa, as in India and elsewhere, has invariably led to a lightning growth of the town populations, inadequately accommodated, cut off from contact with their land and the educational agencies to which they were formerly subject, and existing in conditions of extreme poverty. In the rural districts the diet situation is equally alarming.

[1] Cf. the comparison between the mine and village dietaries in N. Rhodesia given on p. 40.

In many parts of Africa the natives are trying to produce the same amount of food as they did formerly from lands that have been cut down to a fraction of their original size, and are thus heavily over-stocked and often badly eroded. Their nutritional habits and economic ambitions make some of them unwilling to slaughter their beasts or to adopt modern agricultural methods which might enable them, temporarily or permanently, to make an adequate living on the smaller acreage available to them. Others have not the necessary knowledge to enable them to do so. The male labour supply of tribes in many rural areas of Nyasaland, Northern Rhodesia, and the Union has been halved by constant migration to and from the mines and the towns to the country, and in such cases agricultural production has inevitably decreased. The desire for money and European goods has destroyed the old incentives to food production. Small wonder that the medical officers report that the physique of natives, whether in the town or the country, is actually deteriorating and that the proportion of definite malnutrition is on the increase.[1] This is a situation which is already acute in South Africa and likely to become so in other parts of the continent. Hence the demand for nutritional research among African peoples conducted on broad general lines.

The chemical analysis of different native foods has been begun in laboratories at Johannesburg, Nairobi, Dar-es-Salaam, and Lagos, and one or two nutritional surveys have been carried out.[2] But at present we have practically no intensive studies of the diet in particular tribes and the economic conditions responsible for the food supply.

[1] Vide the statements made by the Deputy-Chief Health Officer of the Union in evidence before the Native Labour Committee at Pretoria, e.g. '15 years ago district surgeons and health officers in the native territories and country areas hardly ever mentioned malnutrition and tuberculosis, but today their reports mentioned an increase year by year' (Cape Times, 4.ii.38), and that the percentage of recruits rejected annually by the mines was on the increase: and his statement at the Health Conference at Johannesburg that 'Native recruits to the mines are mostly starved of vitamin C' (Cape Times, 15.ii.38). Also the report of the Medical Superintendent of Victoria Hospital for natives at Lovedale that malnutrition was the prevalent feature of 1937' (Cape Times, 2.ii.38); and the Annual Report of the Dept. of Public Health, 1937 which states (p. 90) that scurvy, pellagra, and gross vitamin deficiencies are to be found in most native territories. Cf. also Africa Emergent, by W. MacMillan, 1938, p. 45.

[2] e.g. Orr, J. B., and Gilkes, J. L., The Physique and Health of Two African Tribes, Medical Research Council Special Rep. Ser. No. 155, 1931; McCulloch, W. E., 'An inquiry into the dietaries of the Hausas and Town Fulani', W.A. Medical Journal, 1929–30, vol. iii.

The Difficulties of Primitive Diet Research.

Any attempt to study the diets of primitive peoples will be fraught
with difficulties at the first. The whole field is as yet unmapped.
The actual composition of many of the tropical foodstuffs is still
unfamiliar to the nutritional expert, and we have little idea of the
immense variety of different foods on which human life can be
sustained. Experts distinguish between the nutritional habits of
one European country and another, but in fact all these people
are living on mixed diets of a very similar kind, and their composition shows nothing like the range of difference that is found
among tribes which are reduced by the nature of their environment, almost entirely to one type of foodstuff. To take a few
examples only: the Somali live on camels' milk, dates, and a
little rice. They neglect green vegetables almost entirely and have
a genuine contempt for eggs. They can apparently subsist for at
least three months, leading an active nomadic life on milk alone,
drinking about ten pints a day.[1] Among the Bahima, the Hamiti-
cised pastoral element of the Banyankole culture (Uganda), the
women also take little but milk, drinking three or four big calabashes a day:[2] while the young men of another pastoral people, the
Masai of Kenya, live for many years of their life on milk, meat,
and fresh blood drawn from the jugular veins of their cattle, and
take practically no vegetable food on account of certain magico-
religious beliefs. A still more curious diet is that of the Elmolo, a
dwindling race inhabiting the rocky shores of Lake Rudolf, where
no meats, cereals, grain, vegetables or fruit exist, and the people
live from month to month on fish, crocodiles and turtles, and
drink only the water of the Lake.[3] Such wide variations cannot
and do not exist in a civilized world, and no scientist would dare to
reproduce them under hospital or laboratory conditions for experimental purposes. Hence the enormous range of nutritional problems which remain to be dealt with in the case of some of these
primitive peoples.

[1] Reports to the Nutrition Committee of the Economic Advisory Council,
1937.

[2] Unpublished material by K. Oberg.

[3] See Fuchs, V. E., 'The Lake Rudolf Rift Valley Expedition, 1935', *Geographical Journal*, vol. lxxxvi, 1935, pp. 114–42, in which he describes the
curious physical deformity common to this tribe, believed to be due to dietary
deficiency—a deformity which 'may make walking a difficulty and gives the leg
the appearance of having a second knee somewhere above the ankle'.

From the practical point of view there are further difficulties owing to the great seasonal changes in these diets. To make a diet survey in any one area, accurate quantitative records would have to be made in sample communities over a period of at least a year, and this has never, to my knowledge, been done. Again the observer would be dealing for the most part with illiterate peoples unable to co-operate in the experiment, and he could not esti-mate the consumption of his sample families by means of weekly budgets, as is done in the course of American or European research. The calculation of the daily intake might be made very difficult by the customs of tribal hospitality and the people's habit of sharing food among a wide and constantly varying circle of relatives. The single family with a fixed membership round a common 'table' is rare.

As a further problem the observer would be dealing with peoples whose living conditions are entirely unfamiliar in most cases —their housing and eating customs, their methods of producing and distributing food, and the ideas and beliefs that make them choose one foodstuff rather than another. The English housewife may be supplied with pamphlets on the calorie values of different dishes, and listen to radio talks on the best and most economical use of her resources, but when she shuts the book or switches off the wireless, she has actually to produce a meal on a limited budget, in a particular kitchen and as part of a fixed routine of life —house-cleaning, laundry, and shopping, the hours of school or her husband's work. She actually knows how to cook relatively few dishes and nutritional habits limit her to a still smaller selec-tion of these, whatever her class. The habit of eating is very largely fixed and traditions of housecraft correspond to it. The French woman would be ashamed to serve some of the meals an English woman does, and the German will take trouble over dishes that neither of the others will prepare. Eating and drinking are social institutions, too, in any community and this determines the use of a people's resources. Some English families spend a lot on the traditional Sunday dinner and the Saturday pub, and go short the rest of the week: others think it important to eat the same each day. Some can buy economically in bulk, some cannot. All grade their foods according to a definite social scale. Whatever the nutritional value of tripe and onions, there are situations when it cannot be eaten and people who do not care to serve it. Besides all these limiting factors, we each of us have some kind of theory or belief, based on traditional teaching, childish memories or personal experience, as to what will do us 'good', suit us, slim us, make our children grow, or 'last' us when at work.[1]

Even in modern society our knowledge of the chemical properties of different foodstuffs, and their effects on the animal organism far exceeds the data so far collected on these cultural factors determining diet. But among the simpler peoples living in the more remote parts of the earth we often do not know the simplest details of daily life, let alone the fact that in many primitive societies edible objects become the centre of social, religious, economic, and even political ambitions, as well as their primary use in satisfying hunger. Herds of stock or grain bins may be the people's chief or only material possessions, the measure of their health and status and the most important prerogatives of political authority. Foodstuffs may be used as forms of currency, as a means of fulfilling legal contracts or of making gifts. All these values affect their alimentary use. The European farmer may hold a different opinion from that of his veterinary expert as to the treatment of his cattle, but both agree that the chief use of raising stock is to produce a supply of beef or milk. Among a number of African peoples this is definitely not so. It is well known that in the Nilotic area, for instance, where cattle are the object of a sacred cult, the natives have sometimes suffered hunger rather than kill an animal for food, and among most of the pastoral Bantu animals are slaughtered chiefly for sacrificial purposes. To the inhabitants of Malekula, in the New Hebrides, pigs are the centre of life, the means of social progress and of power. The people give pigs for wives, accumulate, exchange and raise credit with pigs, and not, it is to be noted, those animals which provide the most pork, but those with their tusks curled, through the removal of the canines, so that they grow up and round and down, till they pierce the lower jaw-bone and make two or three complete circles.[2] Many other Melanesians produce yams and taro in surplus quantities in order to exchange them ritually, or even to allow them to rot as a form of display. Others gather food over a long period for the purpose of biennial or quadrennial feasts

[1] The variety of such prejudices in different parts of England are as yet unknown I think. Dr. O. A. Oeser found that the poverty-stricken boys of Glasgow refused to drink the free school milk on the grounds that it was 'girls' food', and the girls because they were afraid it would make them fat.

[2] Cf. *Savage Civilization*, Tom Harrisson, 1937, pp. 23–9.

with religious or social functions, and then consume huge quantities of victuals in a few weeks. These secondary values associated with different foodstuffs are sentiments rooted so deeply in the economic, political, and religious life of a people as to require a detailed anthropological study for their investigation.

Primitive theories of diet are equally important. The English woman is daily assured in newspaper advertisements that her dullard son, her laggard lover, or her mediocre husband can be changed to her heart's desire in a few weeks by adding an extra plate of cereals to his diet, or taking a nightly hot drink. But the so-called savage also has his magic beliefs. He eats one food and despises another because of the valuable qualities he thinks he can attain by these means, or alternatively the drawbacks he feels he can avoid. Many Melanesians for instance chew the burning ginger root to give them courage, and it is common belief all over the world that the strength or the cunning of an animal may be acquired by eating a part of it. Peoples of certain ranks, or passing through particular states, such as pregnancy, mourning, or initiation also frequently keep taboos on different foodstuffs to give them magic protection, and in many societies whole social groups, clans, sexes, or age-grades for example, permanently abstain from one type of food—thus possibly affecting considerably the composition of their diets.[1] The study of all these magico-religious attitudes to different foods must be an essential part of any nutritional survey as well as a record of the people's digestive theories and their beliefs as to the correct feeding of infants and the sick.

But if social values and nutritional dogmas shape a people's food habits, it is their economic institutions that enable them to produce their supplies. Here again the anthropological approach to diet problems is seen to be a very important one. Agricultural and pastoral activities are governed by cultural rules, some based on empirical knowledge and some on magico-religious beliefs. These vary from tribe to tribe, even in areas where environmental conditions are very similar. Food is everywhere produced by co-operative action and it is on the success of their social organization that different peoples' diets depend. Man works to produce sufficient or surplus victuals under the urge of a number of economic incentives and these are culturally defined in each tribe. Distribution is a question of the utmost importance among peoples

[1] Cf. my *Hunger and Work in a Savage Tribe*, 1932, chap. vii.

living for the most part on perishable foods, and it is their different legal systems and principles of social grouping that enable them to share their supplies between the different members or classes of the community. All these social and economic factors directly affect the production and consumption of food in a native area, although unfortunately in many parts of Africa we have not got even preliminary social and economic studies of the kind described, let alone more detailed investigations of the technical aspects of agriculture or animal husbandry such as would be necessary before any practical improvements in native diets could be planned.

Thus our discussion of the special problems of primitive diet research seems to have led us to two conclusions. In the first instance quantitative studies of native dietaries require the development of new techniques, in particular special methods of estimating the consumption of food and the standards of living among peoples not living on a money economy[1] and also of recording the seasonal changes in diet in those many areas where the alterations from month to month are very great. These are difficulties that will have to be faced, but it is not surprising in the particular circumstances that so few quantitative studies of native dietaries have yet been made, and that most of the nutritional investigations of the African peoples so far published should have been based on the data obtained in hospitals, mining camps, and schools rather than on that collected in the tribal areas themselves.

Secondly, if changes are to be made in diets that are obviously deficient a general knowledge of the tribal structure of the different African peoples is essential as well as more detailed investigations of their economic activities and ambitions, their beliefs, and their habits of using food. This information is for the most part not yet available. To carry out a thorough nutritional survey would therefore require a full team. To the medical, nutritional, agricultural, and other environmental experts, an anthropologist should be added as well. This is a type of joint field-work that has never yet been tried but one which would lead, I think, to the most valuable results.[2] It is for this reason that I publish this book.

[1] Cf. Margaret Read, *Native Standards of Living and African Culture Change*, Institute of African Languages and Cultures Memorandum XVI, 1938, for suggestions along these lines.

[2] Since writing, an experimental expedition of this type composed of a doctor, a nutritional expert, an agricultural officer, and an anthropologist has set out to make a comparative study of the diet and nutritional problems of two Bantu

It is an attempt to describe in the case of one particular African people—the Bemba of North-Eastern Rhodesia[1]—the different cultural factors that combine to influence the production, distribution, and consumption of food. It is an account of the foodstuffs of a given area, the use the people put them to, their eating customs and prejudices, and their methods of growing, storing, and dividing food. It thus contains an outline of the type of material an anthropologist considers necessary for the study of primitive diet.[2]

The Present Study.

The material for the present study was collected during two expeditions to North-Eastern Rhodesia (May 1930–July 1931 and January 1933–July 1934). In both I was engaged on a purely anthropological investigation, but since agriculture is the chief economic activity of the Bemba, and gardening and food their principal topics of talk, it was natural that I should have found myself constantly considering the question of the people's food supply. The social and economic changes in this area produced by the new calls on its labour also necessitated a detailed study of native agricultural methods and domestic economics, as these were affected by the absence of so large a proportion of the adult males. I made constant observations of the people's economic activities, as well as their cooking, distributing, and eating customs, as part of my study of their whole domestic life, and added to the general outline study, which must occupy any anthropologist during the first months of a field trip, many of the detailed observations used in this book. I took daily records of the food eaten by sample families at different times of year,[3] and made notes on the types of cultivation in a great number of individual gardens. I also kept daily calendars of the work of the men and women in two

tribes in Nyasaland under the auspices of the International Institute of African Languages and Cultures and the Medical Research Council.

[1] Formerly written 'Awemba'. *Vide* Gouldsbury and Sheane, *The Great Plateau of Northern Rhodesia*, 1911.

[2] It is hoped that this work will be read in conjunction with the report of the Government Ecological Survey of this area now in progress, and that a medical survey of the physique and health of the natives living on this diet may be undertaken later.

[3] With the help of Mrs. Gore-Browne in the first two cases. These records have been published jointly with Dr. E. M. Widdowson, in the article already referred to. 'A Dietary Study in Northern Rhodesia', *Africa*, vol. ix, no. 2, 1937.

particular villages and timed their different activities (cf. Appendix, Table E).

The conditions of work in this area were particularly favourable from some points of view. The Bemba live in communities of thirty to fifty huts. These are not surrounded by any kind of enclosure and most of the cooking, eating, dancing, quarrelling, and children's play take place out of doors. Hence by placing my tent in the middle of a village, I could watch the people's activities going on around me. I never slept in a native hut but think I observed as much or more from my point of vantage. Kinship patterns and the interplay of individual character—factors that also influence economic co-operation and food distribution—stood out clearly in settlements of this size. I reckoned to spend three to six weeks in each village. The type of chieftainship—the dominant institution in this culture—necessitated my travelling rather extensively from district to district in order to complete a study of ritual and political forms. These visits to different villages from one end of the country to another were valuable from an agricultural point of view since they showed me the range of local variation in cultivation and gave me comparative material on the social and economic changes introduced into Bemba villages by European contacts of different types.[1] But a nutrition expert making a quantitative study of diet would probably have collected more valuable material by staying in one village throughout the whole year.

I worked throughout in the native language as this was essential in this particular area. I therefore had to give up a month entirely to linguistic work on my arrival, and spent at least three before I was able to question informants with any success.[2] The actual

[1] Cf. my 'Anthropological Problems in North-Eastern Rhodesia', *Africa*, 1932, vol. v, and 'The Village Census in the Study of Contact Problems', ibid., 1935, vol. viii.
Longer visits were made to villages selected from four different administrative districts, i.e. visits of one to two months in the following: Chiefs' villages—Citimukulu, Mwamba, Nkula, Candamukulu, Matipa on Cilubi Island; and commoners' villages, *Chinsali district*—Pambalasa, Kachienja, Kasaka, Kasakatula; *Mpika district*—Shilusuko; *Kasama district*—Kungu, Mubanga, Kampamba. Visits of one week to three weeks: Chiefs' villages—Makassa, Nkolemfumu, Mwaba, Lucembe, Shimwalule, and commoner's villages, *Mpika district*—Kapongolo; *Kasama district*—Cimba, Citikafula, Molema.
[2] Some grammars and vocabularies exist. W. Lammond, *A Short Grammar of Chibemba*, 1926; *Bemba–English Vocabulary*, 1926; E. B. H. Goodall, *Some Wemba Words*, 1921; P. Guillermé, *Dictionnaire Français–Chibemba*, 1920.

weighing of food and other records of the same type could no doubt have been made with the aid of an interpreter, but the general anthropological study, on which I was principally engaged, necessitated considerable linguistic knowledge, and on the nutritional aspect I had to be able not only to question natives but to listen to their talk when eating and drinking, and to participate in their domestic life.

I travelled with two servants, both members of the tribe, a cook and a small boy, and occasionally invited notables, royal women or members of the chief's council to go on journeys with me to make contacts easier.[1] I moved by bicycle and carriers, but dismissed the latter on arrival at each village in order not to disturb the ordinary course of village life more than necessary. It was superficially easy to mix with the people and join in their activities, since they are naturally courteous and have a great tradition of respect for authority. I was evidently considered an economic asset to a village[2] and a source of amusement and interest in a rather uneventful life, and was therefore tolerated, and even welcomed, from the start, in huts and on expeditions to gardens or fishing pools. The women, with whom I spent the greater part of the day, were far less in awe of the European than the men, who had so much more practical experience of the white man's power. But time served to show the deep reticences of the people, especially with regard to their ritual life. I was only able to attend religious ceremonies after considerable difficulties, and when I had finally won the confidence of the Paramount and other chiefs. These difficulties do not concern us, however, in the present book, since when discussing their foods and their gardens the people were ready and even enthusiastic informants. But there is no doubt that in an area where the only white people consist of three main classes—Government officials, missionaries, and traders—and where the tribe itself is organized on an autocratic basis, the anthropologist will find it impossible to be treated as an equal by the natives. I was able to

---

[1] I believe educated natives could have been used to keep many of the records, but the standard of education is backward in this area compared to that in S. and E. Africa, and I was only able to find one who could help me for two or three months.

[2] I never paid for information, but I bought native produce, employed people occasionally, distributed snuff, meat, and occasionally beer, and also gave elementary medical help, and presents to chiefs or headmen as tribal etiquette demanded.

avoid identifying myself with either of the three classes of Europeans referred to, and in some ways it was easier for a woman anthropologist to do so than for a man. I gradually established a role as an inquirer into native customs, with the taking of notes and photographs as my 'work', and many elderly men and women were actually interested in 'teaching' me, but I was always treated as a person in authority however little I tried to exert that power. I was referred to as 'chieftainess' or even 'chief', as are most Government officials, and finally found it best to adopt the speech patterns of the Bemba royal family when addressing commoners, and to accept as much deference as they did. This position of prestige prevented my attaining any real position of equality with the people but was an advantage in carrying out village censuses when it was helpful to be able to exert a certain amount of authority.[1]

To these preliminary statements I should add the fact that I have never lived in a European agricultural community, and it is therefore possible that some of the customs of cultivation which I describe as 'primitive' exist among peasants in this continent. I have had a general biological training but know nothing of medical and agricultural science or of ecology, and was unable at the time to get any practical co-operation from experts in these fields.

To describe a culture the anthropologist has to draw upon notes of personal observations, native texts, and concrete documentation in the form of daily records, plans, and descriptions of individual cases. It has not been possible to get a tenth of this material *into* a book of this size, and much of it cannot be summarized in statistical form. I have therefore given concrete cases here and there as illustrative material only, indicating where I could whether such incidents were common. Where I have used the phrase 'The Bemba say ...', I mean a statement regularly made in answer to a question, or a formalized utterance in the shape of a proverb or saying. Different points of view as occurring between

[1] Cf. also M. Herskovits' use of the term 'social visibility' in relation to a white anthropologist in Africa, *Life in a Haitian Valley*, 1937, pp. 322-23. My friend E. J. Lindgren has pointed out to me how important it is for the ethnologist to describe his role in a native community and has stressed the very different attitude of the Asiatic peoples of N. China to the visit of a European anthropologist from that of the Africans and Melanesians. *Congrès international des sciences anthropologiques et ethnologiques*, 1934, Section B. Cf. also O. A. Oeser's 'Methods and assumptions in field-work in Social Psychology', *B. Journal of Psychology*, 1937, vol. xxvii.

the various sections of the community I have tried to specify. Sentences given in quotations are actual native texts translated freely, but where some doubtful meaning might occur or an English figure of speech has been used, I have added the translation of the relevant passages in the Bemba tongue. I have used the word 'native' as synonymous with Bemba throughout the book.

PART I

THE PEOPLE—THEIR COUNTRY AND DIET

CHAPTER I

THE BEMBA PEOPLE AND THEIR COUNTRY

Origin.

THE Bemba are the largest and most highly organized tribe in North-Eastern Rhodesia.[1] They are a warrior people of Congo origin which apparently invaded their present territory at the end of the seventeenth or the beginning of the eighteenth century. Moving eastwards from the banks of the Kasai, they eventually reached the great Luapula river which forms the western boundary of this part of Northern Rhodesia. They passed north of the Bangweolu swamps, according to most traditions, travelled up the Chambesi in a north-easterly direction, and finally established their Paramount chief, the Citimukulu, in the centre of this Tanganyika plateau not far from the present Government station of Kasama. From this point they gradually expanded, pushing back earlier immigrants of the same origin, such as the Bisa, either in a west and south-westerly direction into the swamps of Lake Bangweolu, or eastwards to the borders of the Luangwa valley. They also drove wedges into the territory of the Lungu, Itabwa, and Mambwe to the north. Hence numbers of scattered tribelets came to acknowledge the rule of the Citimukulu and paid him tribute, and groups of his chosen followers were settled in the outlying districts to exact these dues. His power seems to have been still further consolidated by the arrival of Arab traders in the middle of the nineteenth century, since they brought him guns, of which he kept complete possession, in return for ivory and slaves. In fact before the coming of the white man at the end of the century it seems that the Citimukulu held sway over the whole of the district between the four great lakes, Tanganyika, Nyasa, Bangweolu, and Mweru, and south into the present Lala and Lamba country. With the

---

[1] J. Moffat Thomson gives the following figures for the biggest tribes of NE. Rhodesia: Bemba 114,274, Cewa 78,400, Ngoni 53,991, and none of the other tribal groups number more than 30,000. N. Rhodesian Government 'Memorandum on the native tribes and tribal areas of N. Rhodesia', 1934.

establishment of the British South Africa Company at Kasama in 1899 the military conquests of the Bemba suddenly ceased. The Citimukulus of to-day rule over their own territory only. It stretches from 29° west to 32·5° east and from 9° north to 12° south, and covers the whole of the administrative district of Kasama and most of those of Mpika, Chinsali, and Luwingu, an area rather larger than that of Ireland. It includes much of the Bisa and Lungu territory occupied during the last century and now predominantly inhabited by them, and the Bemba are still regarded as the dominant tribe in the district by members of other groups.

According to their own traditions, and those of the surrounding peoples, the Bemba were originally an offshoot of the great Luba tribe which inhabited the Katanga area of the Congo east of the Kasai river, and their invasion of their present territory seems to have been one of a series of immigrations of which the Bisa were apparently the first to arrive, the Bemba the second, and the Lunda, now inhabiting the region round Lake Mweru, the third.[1] The swamp-dwelling peoples of the Bangweolu district—the Ushi, Unga, Bena Ngumbo, Bena Cishinga, &c.—have also a tradition of Congo origin, as have the Lala and Lamba peoples to the south, and the Kaonde in North-Western Rhodesia, to mention only a number of the bigger tribes. Whatever the date and order of their arrival it is sufficient for our present purposes to state that all these tribes have certain features in common. The languages they speak are sufficiently alike for them to be grouped for administrative purposes as 'Cibemba-speaking people'.[2] They are all predominantly agricultural as are the kindred peoples in the Congo.[3] Descent,

---

[1] J. C. C. Coxhead notes that Lacerda visited the Lunda kings in the region in 1798, and deduces that this tribe arrived some sixty years earlier, i.e. in 1740, and the Bemba a generation or two earlier still. *The Native Tribes of N.E. Rhodesia; their laws and customs*, R.A.I. Occasional Papers No. 5, p. 3. Verhulpen considers that 'Babemba' was the name given to the Lunda people when they had crossed the Luapula into their present territory. Op. cit., p. 391. The Bemba themselves are emphatic that they arrived with the Lunda and parted with them just south of Lake Mweru.

[2] Cf. tribal map at the end of the book. Members of all these tribes are described as 'Bemba' by compound managers on the N.R. copper belt.

[3] A few cattle and sheep are kept by the tribes in the Bangweolu swamps, such as the Ushi, Bisa, &c., by the Cewa on the Nyasaland border (A. Hodgson, *J.R.A.I.*, 1933, p. 152) and the Lunda in N.W. Rhodesia (Smith and Dale, op. cit., vol. i, p. 131), and a certain number of the Kasai tribes give a marriage payment in sheep and goats, such as the Songe (Van Overbergh, *Les Basonge*, 1908, p. 215), and Luba (Verhulpen, op. cit., p. 262), or even in cattle among the

clan affiliation, and succession to office follow the matrilineal line, *Marriage* and marriage is matrilocal with service performed by the bridegroom for his father-in-law as the essential element in the contract, not the transfer of goods. Associated with the marriage rites are girls' initiation ceremonies without any corresponding ritual in the case of boys. All these Bemba—Bisa—Lunda—Lala —Lamba peoples recognize themselves as being closely akin, and many of their clan names are found widely distributed over the whole area. They are sharply distinguished from the tribes on the Nyasaland border of Northern Rhodesia which have been dominated by the invasion of the pastoral, patrilineal Ngoni, who broke off from the main body of the Zulu, trekked north, crossed the Zambesi in 1835, and settled in the country of the matrilineal Cewa, Tumbuka, and Senga. They are also differentiated from those tribes of North-Western Rhodesia which were originally conquered by invading peoples from Bechuanaland (Ruhutse) and later from Basutoland (Kololo) to form the present Barotse kingdom, and from the Ila-speaking peoples in the Kafue valley, who also show strong southern influences, keep cattle, and combine patrilocal marriage and patriarchal authority with matrilineal descent. These Bemba-like peoples must also be reckoned in a different category from the cattle-owning tribes, mostly patrilineal, on the northern border of Bembaland, such as the Lungu, Itabwa, and Mambwe, which resemble more closely Eastern Bantu groups like the Nyamwesi to the north-east of Lake Tanganyika. For all these reasons we are justified in regarding the Bemba, Lunda, Bisa, Lamba, Lala, and even the Kaonde peoples, to take only the most prominent of these Northern Rhodesian tribes, as ethnically akin and possessing many characteristics in common. Of these the Bemba themselves are the largest and most homogeneous group and can be taken as representative.

Mode of Life.

As regards their general mode of living and economic activities the Bemba are, broadly speaking, typical of the Central Bantu, and it

Nyubunga (L. Lietard, 'Étude sommaire sur la tribu des Lualua-Kasai', *Bull. Soc. Royale Belge de géographie*, 1929, pp. 40–3), but none of these tribes can be reckoned as pastoral peoples proper. In fact the exclusion of the Congo tribes from the E. and S. African cattle-complex is used by Herskovits to demarcate them as a separate culture area. 'The Cattle-complex in E. Africa', *American Anthropologist*, N.S., vol. xxviii, 1926, pp. 640–4.

is important to state at the outset how far any conclusions reached in this book are likely to apply to contiguous areas. Briefly then the Bemba live in small communities, the average village consisting of 30 to 50 huts, while that of the present Citimukulu numbers 150, and in the old days chiefs' villages reached higher figures still.[1] Each village is a kinship unit under the rule of a headman who is appointed by the chief of the district and responsible to him. It changes in composition from time to time, as well as shifting from site to site. The settlements are widely scattered and the density of the population never reaches a greater figure than 3·9 per square mile.[2] This system of local grouping resembles that of the kindred peoples of North-Eastern Rhodesia, but is in marked contrast to that of the Eastern Bantu tribes such as the Ganda, Chagga, &c., who live in isolated homesteads, from the smaller family kraals composed of a man, his wife, and his sons common in South Africa, or the larger Bantu settlements numbering as many as 10,000 inhabitants found, for instance, in Bechuanaland.

The Bemba have already been described as an agricultural people, though, like most of the Bantu, they are fond of hunting and fishing and rely on the bush for many of the wild plants and fruits used for food.[3] Their chiefs used formerly to capture cattle from the surrounding tribes, and kept these sporadically, but the Bemba lack entirely the pastoral tradition. Only a third of the Province is free from fly, and to-day neither chiefs nor commoners own more than a few goats or sheep, and occasional cattle in urban areas.[4] The people are shifting cultivators, that is to say, they clear

---

[1] Here as in other parts of Africa the establishment of European rule and the prevention of war has led to a far greater dispersion of the people than was possible in the old days when they tended to group themselves under the protection of their chiefs in large stockaded villages. At the present day the Bemba villages divide and subdivide as often as possible within the limits of the Government minimum of ten adult males.   [2] 1·86 in the Mpika area.

Hunting &
Congolese

[3] Herskovits considers that the predominance of hunting, associated with special guilds of hunters, and a well-marked type of ritual are characteristic of the Congo peoples, and this ritual, according to Maes, becomes more complex farther and farther west from L. Leopold. Herskovits, cf. footnote, p. 17; Maes, 'Notes sur les populations des bassins du Kasai', &c., Mus. Congo Belge, 1924, vol. i, pp. 74–82. In N. Rhodesia, the Ila and the Lunda of the N.W. province have hunters' guilds and the latter give hunters a special burial. Smith and Dale, The Ila-speaking Peoples of N. Rhodesia, 1920, vol. i, p. 168; F. H. Melland, In Witchbound Africa, 1923, p. 267. The Bemba had formerly specialist elephant hunters, and now carry out ritual hunts, but it is not an important economic activity in this area, cf. Chap. XVI.

[4] There are 354 head of cattle in the Kasama area now, but these are chiefly

a fresh strip of the bush each year to make their gardens, and when the forest land round their villages has all been used (four or five years) they move to a fresh site a few miles away, build themselves new huts, and start cultivating again. This general type of agriculture is practised over most of Northern Rhodesia, the Belgian Congo, large parts of Nyasaland, Tanganyika, and the less highly developed areas of Uganda and Kenya, everywhere giving place to fixed cultivation of an elementary type with the introduction of European cash crops, shortage of land, or urban development. But a recent intensive study of native agricultural methods in one area—North-Western Rhodesia—shows that the term 'shifting cultivator' can cover the greatest variety of methods of utilizing bush land.[1] The Bemba cultivate by clearing the undergrowth, pollarding the trees over a strip of bush, and burning the branches and brushwood so obtained on a small space in the centre of the cleared patch to make an ash-fertilized bed on which the seeds are sown broadcast without further hoeing. In subsequent years the gardens are dug up into mounds on which other crops are grown. This method, known from the earliest days of the British occupation as the *citemene* system after the native name for a cut garden, is practised all over this part of North-Eastern Rhodesia, and by some of the Lamba-Kaonde and Lunda-Luba peoples on the northern plateau of North-Western Rhodesia. It is reckoned as one of the most primitive forms of bush cultivation, everywhere associated with poor soil. As we shall see, the Bemba show great ingenuity in the alternation of crops and the use of the fertile soil of old village sites, yet as a whole their cultivation is much less complex than that of a number of the neighbouring tribes. They do not hoe their ash-beds before sowing as is practised by the Ila-Tonga group, use green manuring as do the Mambwe, or cultivate mixed crops in a series of specialized gardens and grassland fields as do some of the Sikololo-speaking peoples.[2] In fact, from an agricultural point of view they are reckoned as among the more backward of the Northern Rhodesian tribes.

kept by members of other tribes or Bemba who have learnt cattle-keeping in other territories. They are kept in this area since the sale of milk to Europeans is profitable.

[1] *The Soils, Vegetation and Agricultural Systems of N.W. Rhodesia*, Report of the Ecological Survey by C. G. Trapnell & J. N. Clothier, 1937. (Subsequently referred to as Report of the Ecological Survey.)

[2] Ibid. *Vide* also Unwin Moffat, *Native Agriculture in the Abercorn District*, Bulletin, Dept. of Agriculture, N. Rhodesia, 1933.

The aboriginal crops in this part of the country seem to be finger millet, Kaffir corn, bulrush millet, Kaffir beans, Livingstone potatoes, and numerous cucurbits—pumpkins, edible gourds, cucumbers, melons, &c. Ground-nuts, maize, cassava, sweet potatoes and yams, all grown widely in Central Africa, are of New World origin, apparently introduced by the Portuguese in the seventeenth century. Bemba tradition confirms this classification. They declare that their first ancestor, Citi Muluba, travelled from the Luba country carrying in his hair the seeds of Kaffir corn, finger millet, Kaffir beans, cow peas, pumpkins, and the small wrinkled cucumbers known as *amankolobwe*. Their most important economic rites centre round the cultivation of Kaffir corn, now less often grown, quick-growing finger millet, cow pea, Livingstone potato, pumpkin, maize, and *amankolobwe*, and the ritual associated with any particular crop has often been reckoned as an index of its age.[1] Bemba maintain that they have grown maize and ground-nuts 'for a long time', that sweet potatoes were introduced by Swahili traders in the reign of a chief who lived at the end of the nineteenth century, while the Bisa, the neighbouring tribe to the west, taught them how to grow cassava.

Of all these crops their staple is the finger millet, a coarse tufted grass about 3 feet high bearing fine grain of the size of bird-seed on five or six radiating finger-like spikes.[2] This is a hardy plant specially suited to poor soils, but its distribution in Central Africa seems to show that Kaffir corn is grown in preference wherever the soil makes this possible, and that it has been ousted from its position as a staple crop by cassava and maize in all the more fertile environments. In North-Western Rhodesia, the only area in which native agricultural methods have been surveyed, the Lamba-Kaonde live on Kaffir corn and have relegated finger millet to a subsidiary position; among the Lunda-Luba in the same province cassava has taken its place as the staple crop.[3]

In the Bangweolu swamps cassava is the staple food, and on the Nyasaland border, the Cewa, Tumbuka, and others live chiefly on maize. Cassava is now the chief food cultivated in the Belgian Congo and only a few tribes such as the Yeke and

Staple food in Congo.

---

[1] Junod, *Life of a South African Tribe*, 1927, vol. i, p. 395.
[2] *Eleusine corecana.* This is the *mufhoho* of the High veld tribes of the N. Transvaal and the *popoko* of the High veld Mashona. In both latter cases it is grown for beer only.   [3] Report of the Ecological Survey, p. 25.

Bunda apparently still live on finger millet.[1] Maize is the staple crop of most of the Southern Rhodesian tribes. In many other parts of Africa the finger millet is now cultivated entirely for the purpose of brewing beer, for which it seems specially suited, and is grown in this way in Southern Rhodesia, Tanganyika, the Congo, Uganda, and Kenya. Thus in their almost entire reliance on finger millet the Bemba are now in rather an unusual position as regards the composition of their diet. They grow less Kaffir corn than before because of the lack of suitable soil and the labour to protect it from birds. It is sometimes described as a chief's crop on the latter account. Maize gives a poor yield in this district, and sweet potatoes and cassava have only been grown widely during the recent locust raids in response to direct Government pressure.

Material Culture and Economic Organization.

The material equipment of the Bemba is of the simplest. It consists of four implements, (*a*) a wedge-shaped axe blade (*isembe*, plur. *amasembe*) forged locally, fixed into a wooden haft, and used to clear the bush, to cut poles for fencing, hut-building, and simple furniture such as beds or storing racks, to hollow out tree-trunks for canoes, to fashion logs into drums, stools or mortars, or to hammer out bark-cloth; (*b*) a hoe (*ulukasu*, plur. *amakasu*), the only instrument used exclusively for cultivation, formerly traded from the Lungu and other more skilled iron-workers to the west and now bought at European stores; (*c*) a spear (*ilifumo*, plur. *amafumo*) forged locally and used for war, hunting, fishing, and protection against wild beasts; (*d*) a bow (*ubuta*, plur. *amata*) formerly used in war and hunting and important as a family heirloom, but rarely made nowadays.[2] All these implements are of the simplest kind, neither carved nor ornamented, and all arts and crafts are extremely poorly developed in this district compared to the contiguous areas. Iron-work, which reached such

---

[1] e.g. among the Kongo (J. H. Weeks, *Among the Primitive Bakongo*, 1914, p. 86), the Shongo, Songomeno, Nkutsu (Torday and Joyce, *Les Bushongo*, 1925, pp. 131, 122), the tribes of the Kasai and L. Leopold (J. Maes, op. cit., vol. i, p. 6), the Ngala (Van Overbergh, *Les Basonge*, 1908, p. 197), the Luba (Verhulpen, op. cit., pp. 200, 307) and Torday and Joyce, *Notes ethnographiques*, p. 316).

[2] Small wedge-shaped razors, reaping knives, and flat 8-inch needles for threading mats form additional implements.

a high perfection among peoples like the Shongo, Kuba, and Luba, and is practised to a greater or less degree among the Kaonde, hardly exists among the Bemba. Wood-carving, the great art of the Congo tribes, is limited among the Bemba to the adornment of the simplest and most utilitarian objects such as stools and drums. Bark-cloth was made formerly, but it has now been practically ousted by European cloth. Weaving as practised by the Shongo, Songe, Kuba, Luba, Pende, and other kindred tribes is unknown; and though baskets and mats are made, they are of the simplest possible design, and the Bemba are prepared to buy a better type of basket made by the Nsenga rather than attempt to learn the art themselves. Cooking- and eating-pots are made all over the plateau.

The economic organization of the Bemba is not a complex one. The strongest ambition of the old Bemba chiefs seems to have been the conquest of territory and the exaction of tribute from the surrounding tribes rather than the accumulation of material goods. Wealth among the Southern Bantu consisted in herds of cattle, which marked a man's status, enabled him to marry, to pay his fines, to make offerings to his chief or ancestral spirits, and to carry out all his kinship obligations, but the Bemba had few material possessions that could be accumulated as capital or used as any form of currency. Ivory tusks were the monopoly of the chiefs of each district and used for display, or traded for Arab goods, such as bales of cloth or guns, with which faithful warriors and subjects were rewarded. Beyond this the wealth of a Bemba chief consisted in the amount of service he could command as agricultural labour or military force, and the number of slaves, whether of his own tribe or conquered peoples, he possessed. Marriage contracts and most other kinship obligations were fulfilled by the giving of service, not goods, and enslavement was often enforced in lieu of a fine. No organized system of barter or exchange existed. Salt and hoes seem occasionally to have been traded, but regular markets which are a prominent feature of tribal life among the Eastern Bantu, and in such Congo tribes as the Shongo and Kongo, were quite unknown among the Bemba. We are dealing with a warrior people in which the whole economic system was dominated by the political relationship of subject and chief, and the organization of labour founded on it.

As regards its present economic position Bembaland must be regarded as a labour reserve. No economic crop has been found

for this people owing to the poverty of the soil and the prohibitive
cost of transport either to Abercorn, at the base of Lake Tanganyika, or to Broken Hill, the nearest station on the railway line.[1]
For the same reasons white settlement practically does not exist,
except in the region round Abercorn. Thus wage-earning possibilities are scanty for the natives of this area,[2] and to pay their
Government tax, now 7s. 6d. a year, and to purchase the European
goods to which they have become accustomed, large numbers of
the adult men of the tribe—from 40 to 60 per cent.—are obliged
to leave the territory annually to look for work, mostly in the copper mines of Northern Rhodesia, but also in the Katanga mines,
Southern Rhodesia, and even South Africa. It is rare to find a
man who has never left his country to work abroad, and the
majority migrate to and fro between the mines and the villages
and only finally settle in their home districts in their old age.
Thus in this respect many of the food problems of the Bemba are
typical of those that exist in all such manless areas in Africa,
whether in Rhodesia, Nyasaland, or the Protectorates. That is to
say, we shall have to describe an agricultural system in which most
of the old incentives to work have disappeared, the male labour
force is nearly halved, and the system of economic co-operation
broken down.

Social Structure.

It is impossible to describe in detail the tribal structure of the
Bemba, either as a preface to this special study, or from a comparative point of view. There are, however, certain main principles of
their social organization which are absolutely fundamental to an
understanding of all their organized activities and forms of co-
operation, and give the direction to their interests. Of these the
dominant institution of the Bemba is their highly complex political
system and the particularly autocratic character of the chieftainship on which it is based. Allegiance to a common Paramount—
the Citimukulu—is the main tie uniting the members of a tribe
that is scattered very thinly over a wide area. It determines their
local grouping, and is the basis of the traditional pride of this
warrior people and its distinction from neighbouring tribes.

---

[1] 3¾d. per lb. from Kasama to the rail-head at Broken Hill.

[2] It was estimated in the Kasama district in 1934 that about 30 per cent. of the
adult males could have earned their tax locally. (Provincial Commissioner's
Report.)

On a man's relationship to his chief depends his residence, his use of land, the economic group he works with, the way in which his food is distributed, the religious and magic beliefs that sustain him in his work, and his social ambitions. Thus without understanding the political organization of the Bemba it is impossible to describe their system of food production.

Briefly, then, this political system consists of a Paramount chief, the Citimukulu, a hereditary ruler with a fixed title, drawn from the royal clan—the *Benayandu* or 'Crocodile' people—who traces his descent in the matrilineal line for more than twenty-five holders of the office. The Citimukulu rules over his own district, the centre of the Bemba country—Lubemba—but also acts as overlord to a number of territorial chiefs, who govern districts similar in size, succeed to fixed titles, and are drawn from the same clan, and in fact the same lineage group, as the Paramount himself.[1] Each of these territorial chiefs has one or two subchiefs under him, these again being drawn from the royal clan, but in some cases from more distant branches of the family which have become localized in one particular area.[2] Sisters and maternal nieces of the chiefs are reckoned as chieftainesses, *Banamfumu*. They succeed to titles, and rule over villages, while the chief's mother, the Candamukulu, has a small territory of her own, and plays an important part in tribal councils. Beneath the chiefs come the heads of villages (*mwine mushi*, plur. *bene mushi*) appointed by them. A particular feature of this political system is the hierarchy of the 40–50 officials, *Bakabilo*, many of them also of royal descent, who succeed to fixed titles, and perform ritual duties at the court, take charge of the chief's complex mortuary and accession ceremonies, and act as a council for the whole tribe.[3] Besides these hereditary priests and councillors attached to the Paramount's court, though not resident at it, each chief and subchief has his own councillors (*bafilolo*), with legal and executive functions, living at his court and appointed by him, and in the

[1] The most important of such territorial chiefs are the Mwamba, Nkolemfumu, and Nkula, and at the moment the first two are own brothers to the Citimukulu, and the last a first cousin.

[2] e.g. Mwaba is a sub-chief of Nkula, but this title has become associated with another branch of the Crocodile clan.

[3] Autocratic chieftainships, associated with hierarchies of hereditary court officials, are found among the contiguous tribes in the Congo, e.g. Luba (Verhulpen, op. cit., pp. 55, 186), Shongo (Torday, *Causeries congolaises*, 1925, p. 55), Kongo (J. H. Weeks, op. cit., p. 37).

old days had captains of his army, executioners, and other court dignitaries as well. The complexity of this political organization form an interesting contrast to the simplicity of the people's economic system. Such a centralized form of government is not found among the surrounding tribes.

The power of the chief rests ultimately on his people's belief in his supernatural powers over the prosperity of the land and the welfare of his individual subjects. By his inheritance of the guardian spirits (*umupashi*, plur. *imipashi*) of the line of dead chiefs, and his possession of the sacred relics (*babenye*) of the tribe, he has power of approach to the tribal deities and he is responsible for the economic rites on which the food-production of these people is thought to depend.

Besides their supernatural powers the chiefs formerly based their apparently unchallenged authority on the physical force they could exert. They controlled and armed their warriors, and had power of life or death over their subjects, whom they could kill, enslave, or sell, and in the case of women, bestow in marriage. Their legal system gave them the right to mutilate those who offended them, and it put them in supreme charge of the poison (*mwafi*) ordeal. The land theoretically belonged to them, and they exacted tribute in labour and kind from those who cultivated it, and maintained monopolies over ivory and salt. No Bemba could reach a high social status or obtain economic privileges unless related to the royal family or a personal favourite with them. Thus it is impossible to study land tenure, leadership in economic enterprises, incentives to agricultural labour, the distribution of land and goods, or exchange, without bearing the political system of this tribe in mind. Linton has recently used the word 'Orientation' to describe for comparative purposes the chief focus of the interests and social institutions of any particular people under review. In this sense military ambition under an autocratic chieftainship is the orientation of the Bemba tribe.[1]

It is obvious that chiefs of this type who relied on the use of military force, tribute labour, and slavery for their supremacy, but did not accumulate material possessions or possess any valuable economic resources in their territory, are in a particularly poor position at the present day. The Bemba chief receives a small subsidy from the Government—£60 a year in the case of the

[1] Cf. R. Linton, *The Study of Man*, 1936.

Paramount chief and less for the territorial chiefs—and therefore earns annually about the same amount as a clerk. Rich African rulers such as the Nigerian emirs, the Barotse king, or some of the South-African potentates, do not exist in this area, and hence one of the important practical problems to discuss is the effect of this poverty of the Bemba chiefs on an economic system which is as closely linked with the political organization as is theirs.

White Contact.

Permanent contact between Bemba and Europeans dates from 1890, when the White Fathers built a station at Kayambi on their north-eastern border and entered the country two years later. The British South Africa Co. established a post at Abercorn in 1893 and at Mirongo, near the present Government station at Chinsali, in 1896. These stations were built to put an end to slave raids in this area, but two years later (1898) the Administration intervened in a disputed succession to an important chieftainship and established themselves at Kasama, now the Provincial head-quarters, in the centre of the Bemba country, while the White Fathers, who entered the district more or less simultaneously, built their big station at Chilubula, twelve miles off, now the chief centre of the Diocese. There are at present Government stations at Kasama, Chinsali, Mpika (the site of a large aerodrome), Mporokoso, and Luwingu—to mention only those in the Bemba country proper. Most of these stations consist of a couple of houses built for the Government officials, an office, and a store, but Kasama is a bigger centre and has a white population of 54. Catholic influence is predominant in the heart of the Bemba country and the White Fathers have now built over ten stations in the tribal territory, mostly distributed in key situations near the villages of big chiefs. They also have a teachers' training school at Rosa to the north-east of Kasama. The Church of Scotland Mission has a big teachers' training-school at Lubwa to the south-east of the district, and stations near the borders of the Bemba country at Mwenzo and Chitambo. The London Missionary Society also has seven mission centres in or near Bemba territory including Senga, Mporokoso and Mbereshi. There is one Government School at Kasama. There is only one big European plantation, Shiwa Ŋandu, to the south-west of the area which produces essential oils. Three European trading companies have native stores at most of the Government centres.

Thus the Europeans in Bemba country are exceedingly few in number,[1] and are limited to Government officials—administrative and medical—missionaries, and a few traders. In remoter parts of the country, e.g. the Chinsali or Mporokoso districts, many natives probably only see a white man in their villages once or twice a year when the District Officer is on tour or a European hunter travelling in the area. But in villages on the motor-road or near a Government station or mission, the contact between the two races is constant, and for this reason I shall distinguish these two types of village by using such terms as 'remote', 'distant', or 'old-fashioned' for the first, i.e. for communities more than two days' walk from a white settlement, and 'modern' or 'Europeanized' for the second.

As regards their material culture European goods have been adopted wherever financially possible. The younger men mostly wear shorts and such tattered remnants of shirts as remain to them. The others stick to the old fashion, a strip of cloth—ankle-length, worn high beneath the armpits with one end tucked in over the breast. This falls to the feet when walking about the village, but is hitched up short when the wearer is working. Women wear European dresses near white settlements, but otherwise find cloths more serviceable as they tear less easily. The old bark-cloth is rarely seen nowadays. Pottery is giving place to enamel ware and petrol tins round the white stores, but not in the ordinary villages. Some of the huts near Kasama are built with sun-dried brick and filled with home-made European furniture, but beyond this narrow radius the native hut is practically unchanged. There were 6081 native-owned guns, shot or muzzle-loading in a population of 84,645 taxable males in the Northern Province in 1934.[2]

The proportion of literate natives is exceedingly low, and few speak any English except the clerks or the domestic servants of the white man. Even on mission estates the number of people educated two generations back must be as yet very small. There is one Government doctor at Kasama in charge of a district nearly as

---

[1] 289 Europeans in the total Northern Province of N. Rhodesia, which far exceeds the Bemba territory, in 1934. Native Affairs Report 1934, p. 39.

[2] Ibid., pp. 41, 45.

big as Wales, and here a small native hospital has been built. There is also a Mission doctor and hospital at Lubwa. Bemba agricultural methods are practically untouched. There are now two Government agricultural officers devoted to research in native agriculture, but during my visit there were none at all.

Character.

The temperamental characteristics of a primitive people are as important as their environment and social organization in determining the nature of their food-production, and to some extent, of course, each is a function of the other. But unfortunately it is just these temperamental traits that are so difficult to describe objectively. Until some more scientific criteria have been evolved the observer is bound to rely on his personal judgement and impressions. He thinks probably in terms of crude contrasts between the behaviour common in his own culture and that in the society he is studying, or if he is lucky enough to have a wide experience of a number of tribes in one area, he can make what are probably more fruitful comparisons between the reactions of each different people to a common situation, such as their behaviour towards the European or their power of adaptation to our civilization. Such broad comparisons are, I believe, the best way of describing the temperamental traits of a particular tribe at the present time. I shall therefore limit myself here to a summary of the comments usually made on the Bemba by Europeans who are familiar with several different tribes in this district, and add my own comparative observations of Bemba and Bisa characteristics made during a short visit to the latter people.

Moffat Thomson in his survey of the tribes of this area describes the Bemba as cheerful and light-hearted, and the same traits are mentioned by Gouldsbury and Sheane, but gaiety has for so long been considered a characteristic of the negro race in general that it is difficult to regard this as a specifically Bemba trait, although I admit that my first impression of a Bemba village was one of constant vivacity, chatter, and quick laughter, and it remains to this day my most permanent memory. It was rare to see a nervous worried face, although as many African observers have noticed, the old people when in repose sit for long periods in silence with a fixed expression of extreme sadness and almost disillusion.

More interesting from a comparative point of view are the

statements of missionaries in charge of boarding-schools which
take pupils from different tribes, or from compound managers in
charge of mixed compounds on the copper belt. These seem to
agree that the Bemba are bad at hard, continuous work, but good
at tasks for which daring or sudden exertion is required. Among
the highly paid employees on the more dangerous underground
work at Wankie coal-mine, Bemba-speaking natives are in the
predominance. In urban areas they are football enthusiasts, almost
maniacs, but whether in mine or in school they are said to lose
interest in any task at which steady day-to-day work is required.
Whether this is an innate temperamental trait or whether it is
a habit of mind dependent on strong warrior traditions it is impossible to say, but it certainly affects the whole nature of this
people's agricultural work, as will be seen. (Cf. 'The will to work',
Chap. XIX.)

In their relations to others the Bemba are considered to be
touchy and quarrelsome. At Luanshya mine, to give only one
instance, it has been found necessary for the Bemba wives to
draw their rations in a separate queue in order to avoid disputes
with the women of other tribes. This reputation for quarrelling
may be due to the quickness with which the Bemba seem to flare
into rages and then suddenly cool, but it is also probably associated
with their strong tribal tradition of superiority to the other
tribes on the plateau. This expresses itself in countless ways. On
one occasion the boys at Lubwa training school left in a body for
their villages, because they discovered they had been ranked after
one of the 'subject' tribes in a competition for tidy dormitories.
At the mines trouble is caused by Bemba hurling too freely the
epithet of 'slave'. But besides their aggressive attitude to members
of other tribes, the Bemba are quick to take offence amongst themselves. They are obsessed with problems of status and constantly
on the look-out for their personal dignity, as is perhaps natural in
a society in which so much depends on rank. All their human
relationships are dominated by the rules of respect to age and
position, and I should hazard a guess that more quarrels were
caused by imagined slights than by material damage of any kind.
It is probably this universal acceptance of the rights of rank that
makes the Bemba appear so submissive and almost servile to the
European compared to some of the more democratic tribes such as
the Bisa or the Inamwanga. Arrogant towards other tribes, and

touchy towards their fellows, they seem to endure in silence any kind of treatment from a chief or a European.

To my mind their most attractive characteristics are quick sympathy and adaptability in human relationships, an elaborate courtesy and sense of etiquette, and a great polish of speech. A day spent at the Paramount's court is apt to make a European's manners seem crude and boorish by contrast. In ordinary intercourse the Bemba strike one as more sophisticated and civilized than the neighbouring Bisa, but much less sensible, hard-working, and efficient in managing their practical affairs.

Country and Climate.[1]

A glance at the Tribal map will show that the Bemba proper only inhabit the central portion of the country over which the Cibemba-speaking peoples are scattered. The natural boundaries of this Greater Bembaland are: Lake Tanganyika on the North, Lake Bangweolu to the West, and the escarpment of the Luangwa valley rift to the East. Only to the South is there no geographical boundary and the same type of forest extends almost uninterruptedly from Mpika to Broken Hill, 350 miles away.

The Bemba country is generally described as the 'Great plateau' of Northern Rhodesia. Crossing the country from the west to the east one seems to be moving over a series of tablelands tilted and bent into different shapes. Two or three days walk from the main escarpment to the East the general undulating character of the 'plateau' comes to an end in a succession of lesser scarps until one descends to the Luangwa escarpment proper. Natives are so impressed by this terrific natural boundary that they have been known to make a special journey to gaze down on the Luangwa valley from the *Mucinga Lubemba*—the 'great wall of the Bemba country'.

The country is very well watered. The divide is on the Northeastern side of the area. Streams to the east of this flow into the Zambesi, by way of the Luangwa, those to the west belong to the Congo system. The Chambesi, a broad still river that crosses the Bemba territory from the Northern border to the South-west is the most significant landmark in native eyes,

---

[1] Mrs. Gore-Browne drafted these first four paragraphs for me. *Vide* also A. G. Ogilvie, 'Co-operative Research in Geography; with an African example', *British Ass. for Advancement of Science*, Section E, 1931.

a centre of historical associations and valued for its fish. To the South-west of the territory the plateau ends imperceptibly, and rivers running parallel to each other open out into ever widening grassy courses till they become merged in the Bangweolu swamp itself. These wide grassy margins which Europeans call *dambos* are characteristic of the rivers in this region. It is not unusual to plod half a mile of water-logged country to find perhaps a five-foot stream in the centre.

Forest trees cover the whole of the 'plateau' except where bare ridges, protruding in many places, show that the main rock floor is never far underneath. From the air the country has the appearance of an endless expanse of trees broken by numberless watercourses and dotted here and there with clusters of native huts and the small circular patches that represent their millet gardens. Natives distinguish three types of forest. First, the prevailing rather monotonous, semi-deciduous, bush forest, which they regard as their garden land: next the less common, tall, 'old forest' land, the relics of a more temperate climate. Here the trees of the upper story are perhaps twice as high as that of the ordinary woodland, so great is the contrast between the old and the newer forest. Lastly, when overlooking this country, one picks out deep patches of green along some of the river courses. These are '*mushitu* forests,' evergreen groves usually treated as sacred and often kept as the burying places of dead chiefs. They are peculiar to this country and are again survivals of a once ubiquitous forest evergreen.

These *umushitu* forests are the only parts of the countryside which do not change with the seasons. Immediately the rains are over— that is to say at the beginning of April—the grass begins to dry and turn brown. By July when the cold weather has well set in the leaves begin to come off the trees. By the end of August spring has come and with it the new leaf growth. As a natural protection from the hot sun, which immediately follows the month of early spring, the new leaves sprout in various shades of scarlet, turning to brilliant green as they grow. Each species changes at a slightly different time, and by mid-September the woodland is a mass of vivid colours of varying shades. This is cut short by the forest fires, and in a day the gay tints of spring and early summer are changed to blacks and browns. Even before the first rains of November the new green grass begins to shoot up along the river margins and the trees that have not been checked by the late fires continue to put on new green leaves. By mid-rains grass and undergrowth has sprung up higher than a man's head and the bush looks quite impenetrable a few yards ahead. Young shoots stand a foot or two high all over the motor tracks. With the turn of the cold weather the country dries up once more. Dust lies six inches deep along the roads and coats the leaves and branches of the trees about 500 yards each side.

Access to the Bemba country has always been easy, at any rate along its western and southern borders. The history of the country is one of a series of invasions from the Katanga Basin to the west up the big rivers such as the Luapula. One of the main Arab trade-routes also passed across the district from north-east to south-west, and this fact materially influenced the history of the people during the nineteenth century. Although the railway line bends N.W. at Broken Hill, four hundred miles to the south of the district, the Cape to Cairo motor route passes right across it, and the natives have easy access to the mining districts of Northern Rhodesia and the Congo. Motor roads (earth tracks would be a better description) serve to connect the head-quarters of the district. But the life of the country still moves in a single file along the native paths, except where a few big rivers and swamps make it possible to use dug-out canoes.

The climate is of an inter-tropical type. The country lies south of the equator, but the plateau stands at an average height of 4,000 ft. above sea-level and the nights are almost invariably cool and even cold, whatever the temperature by day. The seasonal variations in climate are very marked. In the hot season of the year, which falls between August and November, the temperature varies from an annual average minimum of 61° to a maximum of 89°. Between 1925-31 the highest temperature reached was 108°. In the hot months the weather is oppressive, ending in heavy thunderstorms. At the end of this time the ground is hard and impossible to cultivate, and the forest fires have swept the country. The rivers are low and in some cases dried up.

The rains break at the end of October or the beginning of November, and the maximum rainfall—is usually experienced in December. The average annual fall varies from three inches in November to over nine inches in December and January. There is occasionally a temporary break (*icilala*) in the weather at the end of January, but the rains continue unabated until the end of March or April. The rain is usually ample for cultivation purposes, although the heaviest fall may come at an inconvenient time for the Bemba staple crop.

The wet season is followed by a dry and windy season which lasts from April to July. During these months dry, gusty winds blow almost continuously, and the temperature falls to a minimum in July (between 51° and 77°). The nights are unpleasantly chilly, with ground frost in specially high districts. The rivers begin to recede. These are the harvest months, and the season in which the new millet gardens are prepared.

Bemba cultivation is entirely dependent on this type of rainfall and is limited in most cases to the production of one crop a year instead of two as in those parts of Tanganyika where there is a double rainy season.

CHAPTER II

THE BEMBA DIET

Available Data.

A LIST of the chief Bemba foodstuffs is given at the end of this book (Appendix A). It will be seen that their environment provides them with a variety of foods—cereals, roots, pulses, green vegetables, fruit, honey, meat, fish, and salt, and they lack only one important constituent of our own dietary, namely, milk and all its products. But such a table of foodstuffs tells us very little about the diet itself. To study its composition we must know the quantities of each particular constituent the individual Bemba eats in an average day or year, and this information is not yet available. The records already published of the food eaten by sample families in different villages[1] were based on rough approximations, and on observations made during a few weeks only of the year—a serious drawback where the seasonal variations are so great. Since that date Mrs. Gore-Browne has calculated the average yearly supply of the staple food available for each individual by measuring the contents of a number of granaries at harvest-time and she has also estimated the probable average consumption of one or two other foods.[2] But these calculations refer to one area only and to a limited number of foodstuffs. The data is obviously insufficient on which to base accurate generalizations as to the composition of the Bemba diet. These pages will therefore be limited to a description of the salient features of the dietary as a whole. Some of these are characteristic of the feeding habits of primitive peoples in general and are of interest by way of broad comparison with our own; others are limited to this particular area, and even to the tribe concerned.

All Bemba individuals can be reckoned as eating, roughly speaking, the same type and quantity of food. Class distinctions practically do not exist in this respect. Chiefs certainly have a much more regular supply of food than commoners and drink very much more

---

[1] A. I. Richards and E. M. Widdowson, op. cit.

[2] This experiment covered 15 villages with a total population of 777 men, women, and children, and was made from July to January 1935–6. Report to the Diet Committee of N. Rhodesia, 1937 (unpublished).

beer. In fact they often subsist entirely on the latter to the complete exclusion of solids. Their wives, children, and courtiers also eat on the average more than the ordinary family, so much so that natives describe especially lavish hospitality as 'housekeeping after the fashion of the capital' (*umusango wa ku musumba*). But the difference is one of certainty of supply rather than of greatly increased consumption per day, and a small class of individuals only are affected. Otherwise the rich man and his poorer neighbours eat very much the same throughout the year.

Sex distinctions are not marked either. The man gets a larger share of meat or any favourite relish, but there are no foods specially tabooed to women, and I do not think the inequality is any greater than that common in many working households in this country. Age distinctions in diet are not pronounced. Young boys between 10 and 16 are probably the worst-fed section of the community since they have to forage for themselves and have no regular portion allotted to them, but even then the difference is not a striking one. Geographical variations in the food-supply certainly exist, but they are limited chiefly to differences in the amount of meat and fish consumed and not to the staple food. Therefore for all general purposes the following account may be taken as applying to the population as a whole.

Variations from Hunger to Plenty.

The most pronounced feature of this dietary is its alternation between hunger and plenty, a characteristic common to African peoples in areas where the distribution of rain allows only one season of cultivation a year, and where one staple crop is relied upon. In this territory the existence of a definite scarcity is noticed at once by the most casual observer. The Bemba constantly talk about 'hunger months' as distinguished from food months. At the end of the rainy season they regularly expect a shortage, whether it is severe or not. When the scarcity becomes marked the whole appearance of village life is changed. For adults meals are reduced from two to one a day, and beer is rarely if ever brewed. Children who seem to munch extras all day long in the plentiful season (April to October) are reduced to a single dish late in the day. In one bad year I saw cases of elderly people who ate nothing during the course of a day, and though this is not common, most adult natives can remember occasions when they went two days without food, and 'sat in the hut and drank water and took snuff'.

These extreme cases of hunger are admittedly rare, but it is a fact that when the supply of the staple millet is at an end, the Bemba are reduced to foods with a much lower nutritive value. The millet, of which, as we shall see, their diet is mainly composed, lasts on an average for nine months of the year only (April to November or December). Chiefs reckon to make their supply last till the new harvest and even later. In a good year some commoners would be able to do so, but I should doubt if this number ever reached more than half of the villagers in any one settlement.[1] When the staple food runs low, the only other cultivated crops available in the scarce season are edible gourds, which are largely composed of water, and small quantities of maize. Otherwise the natives rely on the bush, which provides fungi and caterpillars during these months.[2]

Thus the existence of a pronounced hunger season can be established without making any elaborate quantitative investigation. It is correlated with changes in the social life of the people which are equally marked. All activity is reduced to a minimum when food is short, and in a specially bad year garden work tends to be skimped. The direct effects of the shortage on the people's work output was illustrated in striking fashion during the recent locust raids (1933-4), when the gardens of some villages were destroyed and others less than a day's journey off escaped. For instance, at Candamukulu in April, where the people's gardens had escaped damage—they rose at six, cut trees to clear their gardens, rebuilt their houses, and gave an impression of constant activity and busyness. Sixty miles off, at a settlement that had empty granaries and ravaged gardens, the people had not yet started the work of the year at all.

---

[1] e.g. in Jan. 1934 at Kampamba, near Kasama, 9 out of 18 granaries were empty = 50%.

In Jan. 1934 at Mubanga, near Kasama, 20 out of 37 granaries were empty = 54%.

In Feb. 1934 at Kungu, near Kasama, 26 out of 29 granaries were empty = 89%.

The remaining granaries were nearly empty in each case.

[2] In one of the villages observed in February 1934, one family lived six days on gourds, while in another a woman who was nursing a baby fed herself and three children on mushrooms only for two days. At a third village in April of the same year, one family lived on wild spinach only for five days.

Other activities are also affected. There is little or no dancing in the hunger months, partly owing to the absence of beer.[1] Few journeys are planned, and the children tend to play listlessly. Usually more good-tempered than the average English baby, they whimper at the slightest provocation. I found it difficult to get informants to concentrate for more than short periods at this time of the year.

The physical effects of a seasonal shortage of food on the health of a people and the growth rate of their children has not yet been investigated, but from a sociological point of view there are other effects to be considered besides the lowering of energy due to actual under-feeding which the natives themselves recognize and describe (cf. p. 50). In a society in which people regularly expect to be hungry annually, and in which traditions and proverbs accustom them to expect such a period of privation, their whole attitude towards economic effort is affected. In some primitive tribes it is considered shameful for an individual or a whole community to go hungry.[2] It is something unexpected, and to be resisted with energy. Among the Bemba scarcity is within the ordinary run of experience, and accepted as such. This fact has a subtle but very powerful effect on their ideas of wealth and their incentives to work (cf. Chap. XIX).

Composition of the Diet.

The Bemba diet is in a sense a simple one since it is composed very largely of one cereal food—the finger millet already described. The bulk of each meal consists of a porridge made of this flour, and the subsidiary foods, meat or vegetable, are eaten with it in small quantities only (about half a pound of the latter to five pounds of the former). For their nutrition the Bemba depend almost entirely on the amount of millet they are able to get, and the seasonal variations from hunger to plenty consist in effect of the shortage or absence of this particular grain.[3]

[1] No ceremonies such as initiation rites or the founding of a village are carried out in the last moon of the rains, *Kutumpu* (March), probably for this reason. But it is also interesting that the people give ill health and bad luck as reasons for not holding ceremonies in this month. They say: 'March is an unlucky month. Look how many people fall ill at that moon.'

[2] Cf. Malinowski's account of the Trobriand islanders, who consider hunger shameful and give all their efforts to displaying food and producing it in excess. *Coral Gardens and their Magic*, 1935, vol. i, p. 227; *Argonauts of the W. Pacific*, 1922, p. 109.

[3] Dr. Widdowson calculates that the Bemba gets 75 per cent. of his calories

As a staple food, finger millet has a high nutritive value compared to other cereals used in this area. It is far superior to cassava in protein, fat, and mineral salts, and to the white millet of East Africa both in fat and minerals. Though inferior to maize in protein and fat, it is only very slightly so, and is again superior in minerals (iron, calcium, and phosphorus). On the other hand, as has been pointed out, the supply of millet as produced by the Bemba only lasts some nine months of the year, whereas the cassava roots remain in the garden beds throughout the year and are used a little at a time as wanted, so that people like the Bisa, who live on this crop, have a regular diet throughout the year. Sweet potatoes also can be eaten at most seasons, except during the rainy months. Millet has a further drawback in that it is used for beer as well as for porridge, and though the former evidently provides a valuable source of vitamin B contained in the germinating grain, yet it is an extravagant way of using the supplies, and the Bemba are in a worse position than peoples who grow a separate cereal for the purpose of brewing.

Their next most valuable foodstuffs are the pulses, ground-nuts, ground-beans, Kaffir beans, cow-peas, &c., commonly grown by most of these Bantu peoples. These are a valuable source of protein and fat, ground-nuts being particularly rich in the latter, and this adds to their importance in a diet in which fats of all kinds are very deficient. In fact, Trapnell suggests that the nutritive value of most of these simple cereal diets of Northern Rhodesia depends largely on the amount of the subsidiary pulses grown in addition to the main cereal crop.[1] In the case of the Bemba this supply of pulses seems to be far from adequate.[2] The store of dried beans and peas lasts only a few months of the year.

For their animal protein the Bemba depend on game, fish, caterpillars, wood-lice, &c., obtained from the bush, but game is very scarce in this area, is only easily hunted at certain seasons

from this carbohydrate food, and about 5 per cent. from fat, whereas we get 40–50 per cent. from carbohydrates and 30–40 per cent. from fat. Cf. op. cit. *Africa*, vol. ix, no. 2, 1936.

[1] Report to the Diet Committee of the N.R. Government, 1937.

[2] Mrs. Gore-Browne reports that in 15 villages visited from July to January 1936–7, no householders had any cow-peas left and only one any ground-nuts. In granaries I examined in a village in the same area in September 1933, 6 out of 14 householders had a few ground-nuts, beans, and dried potatoes. In the Kasama district in January 1934, 25 out of 37 householders had no store of pulses left at all.

of the year, and in some districts is hardly obtainable at all. Of fifteen villages visited by Mrs. Gore-Brown in 1936, four had eaten no meat at all during the seven months under observation, although these communities were settled in reputedly good hunting country. In the remaining 11 villages such totals as 13, 5, 9, and 25 small duiker had been divided. In another village where the reckoning had been made for a period of a year 40 duiker had been killed.[1] Of the three villages in which the diets have been analysed (Appendix C), it will be seen that no animal protein of any kind was eaten during the two weeks of observation in the case of one: in another it was very low.

In the ordinary Bemba village a little fish is caught in the small rivers at certain months of the year when the waters are flooding the banks or are falling again, but fish cannot be reckoned as an important article of diet except among the peoples who live on the banks of big rivers such as the Chambesi. Caterpillars are obtainable everywhere during the wet season, and make a quite considerable contribution to the animal protein of this diet.

Of the other subsidiary food, green leaves, either cultivated or wild, which form the main source of vitamin C, are obtainable for six or seven months of the year (April to September), while fruits are limited to two months (October and November). The edible gourds and mushrooms eaten as subsidiary foods in the hunger months of the year have little nutritive value.

Salt is not easily obtained (cf. p. 55). When available, about a teaspoonful a day would be spared for cooking, but it is not uncommon to find households that have been some weeks without any salt at all, and which have not been able to make good this deficiency by eating meat.

As far as it is possible to speak of the composition of the diet as a whole, generalizations based on figures collected in three villages at different seasons of the year show that the average calorie intake is 1,706 per man value per day, i.e. just over half that which is considered adequate in England and America. The fat is only an eighth as much as is usually eaten on our mixed diets. The intakes of calcium and phosphorus compare very favourably with those in England and America. Salt is exceedingly deficient at all seasons of the year. While it is impossible, for want of further information, to make direct comparisons with English scales of diet, it is

[1] A duiker might be reckoned the size of a small goat.

interesting to compare the minimum ration scales laid down by the Government for native employees in industrial undertakings, and the improvements on these latter scales worked out by such big mining companies as the Rhokana Corporation, to whom an increase in the annual output of work is of such importance as to justify the spending of large sums of money on better diet for the workers.

The comparisons given in the tables below are admittedly very rough ones, since Columns 2 and 3 give accurate weights of different foodstuffs and Column 1 approximations only, based on Mrs. Gore-Browne's granary measurements, but as regards the cereal food which forms the main part of each diet, there is not likely to be a serious inaccuracy as to the estimate for the daily intake of the village native, since the figure given (0·9 lb. a day), does not vary substantially from that obtained by the method of weighing in three villages in three different areas in another year (i.e. 0·7 lb., cf. Appendix C.). The figures for the calorie value of the village diet were obtained from the latter data and the average figure for an 8-months period.

Foodstuff	Bemba village diet	Government scale	Rhokana Corp.: proposed scale
Cereal[1] . . . (Maize or millet)	12·8 oz./day	24 oz./day	16 oz./day
Wheat bread .	. .	. .	6·0 oz./day
Pulses (various) .	0·016 oz./day	4·0 oz./day	4·5 ,,
Ground-nuts .	0·016 ,,	1·0 ,,	1·0 ,,
Green vegetables .	Not estimated	5·0 ,,	6·7 ,,
Meat . . .	0·25 oz./day	4·6 ,,	12·0 ,,
Fat . . .	. .	0·5 ,,	0·7 ,,
Salt . . .	Occasional	0·5 ,,	0·5 ,,
Beer . . .	8 oz./day	. .	20·0 ,,
Total calories per day	1,706	4,313	3,663

(Calorie value of typical European or American diet = 3,000)

[1] It is interesting to note that the Rhokana Corporation has been attempting to introduce an improved diet by reducing the number of calories obtained from meal and increasing those obtained from meat, even at a cost of reducing the total number of calories, i.e. Old scale: Total calories 4,313·7 with 2,544 from meal and 222 from meat. New Scale: Total calories 3,663 with 1,696 from meal and 425 from meat. The management believed that the increased output of work obtained from this diet would repay an increased annual expenditure of £7,526 on the new diet. (Figures from Report to the Diet Committee of the Government, 1937.) The results of this experiment are not yet published.

Seasonal Changes in Diet.

It is obvious, however, that the seasonal changes are so marked in this area, as in most other African tribes, that such figures of 'average' daily intake do not represent the actual situation at all. In effect the people have a harvest season from May to September

Chart showing Seasonal Changes in the Food Supply of the Bemba

————supplies plentiful.   - - - - - - supplies scarce.

The lines indicate the length of time the average Bemba uses each foodstuff, either because it ripens during that particular month, or in the case of game and fish, can be trapped then, or because he has only planted sufficient for the supply to last for a given number of months. For instance, maize could be made to last for 12 months of the year, but the ordinary Bemba only grows enough to use it fresh during 2, and therefore this period only is shown by a line. Dried relishes are not shown. Caterpillars swarm at different periods in different districts and hence are marked from November to April.

	WET WEATHER			COLD WEATHER				HOT WEATHER			WET WEATHER	
	Jan.	*Feb.*	*Mar.*	*Apr.*	*May*	*June*	*July*	*Aug.*	*Sep.*	*Oct.*	*Nov.*	*Dec.*
Gardens:												
Millet												
Maize												
Kaffir corn												
Cucurbits												
Ground-nuts												
Legumes (fresh)												
Legume leaves (fresh)												
Sweet potatoes												
Bush:												
Wild spinaches												
Mushrooms												
Orchids												
Fruit												
Meat												
Fish												
Caterpillars												
Ants, &c.												
Honey												

in which millet, beer, green food, ground-nuts, pulses are plentiful, and meat in some areas, and the diet is therefore ample and probably varied. This is followed by a dry season (October–November) in which millet and beer are still available but green vegetables scarce or non-existent. The wild fruits are much liked, but only last about a month or six weeks. Meat and fish are obtainable in these months also, but only in certain districts. At the beginning of the rains, November and December, the diet changes. Millet is already beginning to be short, and mushrooms and caterpillars are the main standby as additional relishes. In the late rains millet is practically non-obtainable, and gourds and occasional maize-cobs are often the only available foods. Thus the diet changes completely in composition from one season to another—a characteristic feature of primitive societies, of which the effects have not yet been investigated. Such essential constituents as are provided by the green vegetables, fruit, meat, and fish, given in the Appendix I, are only available for short periods of the year.

To conclude, it can be said that most constituents considered essential to a balanced dietary are present in the Bemba environment, with the important exceptions of sufficient animal protein, fat, and salt. There is an absolute shortage of millet reckoned either by the figures of the amount available annually or from the obvious seasonal scarcity, and the natives' reliance on this one staple makes this lack a dangerous one. The most valuable accessary foods such as the pulses only last part of the year, and the supply of green vegetables is limited to a few months. Milk is never obtainable. Except in the case of meat and milk these deficiencies appear to be due to difficulties of production, storing, and exchange rather than to any particular environmental defects.

Physique and Energy.

It is impossible to describe the physique and output of energy of the natives living on this diet, as no medical examination of the people for this purpose has been made. Certain superficial observations may, however, be included for general interest.

Compared to the surrounding tribes the Bemba are tall and muscular, but it is exceedingly rare to find any member of the tribe who is fat.[1] Girls between 16 and 18 are often quite plump, but they soon lose the extra fat and take on the angular figures of their mothers. Members of the royal family tend to be taller than the commoners, but it is not usual even to find a chief who is fat as compared with photographs of kings and notable personages among the Zulu and other pastoral tribes. Babies are usually plump and well covered before they are weaned, but after that their arms and legs become skinny and their abdomens bulge in the manner common to so many African children.

---

[1] It has been found recently that the average weight of 589 adult males *accepted* for mine work at Nkana was 127·65 lb. (9 stone 1 lb. 10 oz.), and that 83 per cent. weighed under 140 lb. (10 stone). This lightness in weight as compared to the European averages may, of course, be a racial characteristic.

Rainy weather. The girls of the village off to gather mushrooms.
Men make the carrying-baskets.

It is difficult without further data to compare the energy expended by these natives with the work done by different classes in this country. These Bemba are great walkers and can cover distances which surprise the white man new to the country. They are also trained from the earliest youth to carry heavy loads. Men employed as carriers will walk an average of 15 to 20 miles with 50 lb. loads on their heads daily for a fortnight or so, and women commonly go two- or three-day journeys with a 50 lb. load and a two-year-old baby in addition on their backs. On the other hand, the people do not often do more than a five-hour day in their gardens, the heaviest work being reckoned as hoeing and felling trees (cf. Chap. XVIII). The women probably expend more energy, since they thresh and grind corn on their return from their gardens. The Bemba will dance for an hour or two, but do not seem to be able to keep going for a whole afternoon and evening with the energy of the swamp-dwelling Bisa who live on fish. They seemed to me to work in sudden spurts and then to collapse into complete inactivity, were prostrated by the cold of a June or July dawn, and allowed the least interruption to put them off their work (cf. the calendars given in Chap. X; but in all these cases it is difficult to distinguish physiological from psychological factors (cf. Chap. XIX 'The Will to Work'.

After this preliminary descriptive account of the Bemba environment and foodstuffs, we must turn to the more directly anthropological aspect and consider the eating customs, prejudices, and ideas of these people, as these determine their use of different foods.

PART II

FOOD AND DRINK

CHAPTER III

NATIVE VIEWS ON FOOD

Food as a Centre of Interest.

FOOD and beer are without doubt the most exciting and interesting topics of native conversation, with the exception of
money, in areas affected by white contact. Any one who can follow
the ordinary gossip of a Bemba village will be struck at once by the
endless talk shouted from hut to hut as to what is about to be
eaten, what has already been eaten, and what lies in store for the
future, and this with an animation and a wealth of detail which
would be thought quite unusual in this country. It is, of course,
natural in an area where the supply is never constant from day to
day that the daily meal should be a subject of vivid interest. For
those who are accustomed to buy food ready prepared, it is difficult
to realize the emotional attitudes to foodstuffs among peoples
who are directly dependent on their environment for their diet.
Most of their food the Bemba grow, and hence they view their
fields and gardens concretely in terms of their future prospects of
food and drink. These they constantly discuss. I timed two old
women talking over an hour on the single topic of the probable
order of ripening of the pumpkins in three gardens, and the way
in which they were likely to be distributed. The question evidently dominated their imagination. I have visited millet fields,
near harvest time, and heard the owner exclaim ecstatically, 'Just
look at all that beer!' Foods collected from the bush, animal or
vegetable, are perhaps of even greater interest because of the element of luck in their discovery. A sudden find of caterpillars or
mushrooms, or a fish caught by hand in the reeds of a swamp, will
be discussed all over the village that night.

The European notices, too, that the natives tend to describe
their actual environment and the passage of the seasons in terms
of the dietetic changes associated with them. They talk of different
parts of the country according to their food deficiencies as 'where

they only eat pumpkin leaves', i.e. where game is short and the people have to rely on vegetable relishes. They refer to a visit to a village on a big river as, 'He has gone to eat fish with So-and-So.' The fortunes of each district are discussed year by year and villages described as 'with hunger' (*pa nsala*) or the converse, 'with beer' (*pa bwalua*), i.e. with so much grain that they can make beer frequently. The seasonal changes in food, and the stages in its production, give their names to the periods of the year. While a definite calendar of moons exists (cf. Chap. XVIII) the Bemba more often time events as having taken place 'in the hunger months', i.e. the last months of the rains when the millet supply is low; or 'when we were eating mushrooms', 'when the *mupundu* fruit was ripe', and 'when we were reaping, sowing', &c., and the ages of babies are usually reckoned by dating their births in this manner.

The position of the Bemba traveller, dependent as he is on the hazards of hospitality, provides a further element of uncertainty. The correct greeting to one who has returned from a journey is *Mwalyeni bwino*, 'Have you eaten well?' To which the courteous reply is *Kulila mulelya*, 'Provided you have eaten well yourself', or *E Mukwai kufipwishya*, 'Yes, sir, I eat everything up completely', or else *Fia kwa cilime bafipwa kano wa kulapo ŋanda*, 'It would have been impossible to finish up all the crops unless you had built a house alongside', i.e. it was so plentiful. There is a regular form of magic used to ensure a guest's arrival before a meal has been finished and not after. A knot tied in the grass with the right formula repeated will secure this result, and I found my staff even performed this rite on my own behalf if at all doubtful as to my reception on a visit to unknown English hosts.

Besides this direct interest in the food he is going to eat in the day, or the beer he may have the luck to come in time for, the secondary values acquired by food give it an added emotional interest to the Bemba. It must be remembered that there is no other way of accumulating wealth in this area except by acquiring sufficient food to feed many followers. The giving or receipt of food is a part of most economic transactions, and may come to represent a number of human relationships whether between different kinsmen or between subject and chief. For this reason the whole question of handling or dividing food acquires tremendous emotional significance for the native, and discussions of personalities or legal relationships tend to be ultimately expressed in this idiom. To speak of a chief is to mention before the end of the conversation his reputation for generosity or meanness in the giving of porridge and beer. To describe an attitude to any particular kinsman leads almost invariably to a comment, for instance, on the food in his granary, the number of relatives he supports, the share of meat he has asked for, or the amount of beer he contributed at the marriage of his daughter or the visit of an elder. In daily life the women, whether at work in the kitchen or sitting gossiping on their verandas at night, exchange interminable criticisms as to the way in which some particular dish of food has been divided, or the distribution of the four or five gourds of beer made at a brew. These casual observations of native life are significant. For us it requires a real effort of imagination to visualize a state of society in which food matters so much and from so many points of view, but this effort is necessary if we are to understand the emotional background of Bemba ideas as to diet.

The Perfect Meal.

To the Bemba each meal, to be satisfactory, must be composed of two constituents: a thick porridge (*ubwali*) made of millet and the relish (*umunani*) of vegetables, meat, or fish, which is eaten with it.

(*a*) *Ubwali*. *Ubwali* is made from coarse-ground flour[1] poured into boiling water, stirred until the mixture is stiff, and then kneaded and patted with a strong wooden blade—the Bemba spoon (*miko*)— and served in the open eating-baskets which the natives call *icipe* (plur. *ifipe*) in warm brown lumps that are round in shape. There is no comparable English dish. *Ubwali* is commonly translated by 'porridge' but this is misleading. The hot water and meal are mixed in proportion of 3 to 2 to make *ubwali* and this produces a solid mass of the consistency of plasticine and quite unlike what we know as porridge.[2] *Ubwali* is eaten in hunks torn off in the hand, rolled into balls, dipped in relish, and bolted whole.

Millet has already been described as the main constituent of Bemba diet, but it is difficult for the European, accustomed as he is to a large variety of foodstuffs, to realize fully what a 'staple crop' can mean to a primitive people. To the Bemba, millet porridge is

---

[1] Usually finger-millet, but *ubwali* may also be made with Kaffir-corn or cassava flour.

[2] The exact proportions in one sample (examined by Mrs. Gore-Browne) were—water 62 per cent. to flour 38 per cent. The word 'porridge' seems, however, preferable to 'mush' used in some Bantu grammars.

not only necessary, but it is the only constituent of his diet which actually ranks as food. All other foodstuffs, whatever their nutritive value, he considers merely as additions to the essential *ubwali*, as snacks to be eaten before the main meal is prepared, or as substitute foods during the hunger months. In fact, there are very few types of food which he eats without porridge, except the various gourds and pumpkins on which he is forced to live when his grain is exhausted, or sweet potatoes—a fairly recent introduction—maize, honey, and fruits of the bush. All these may be eaten freely, but are simply not considered to make a meal. I have watched natives eating the roasted grain off four or five maize cobs under my very eyes, only to hear them shouting to their fellows later, 'Alas, we are dying of hunger. We have not had a bite to eat all day'. This attitude is in complete contrast to that of most of the Southern Bantu, who live almost entirely on maize.[1]

The importance of millet porridge in native eyes is constantly reflected in traditional utterance and ritual. In proverb and folktale the word *ubwali* stands for food itself. When discussing his kinship obligations, a native will say, 'How can a man refuse to help his mother's brother who has given him *ubwali* all these years?' or, 'Is he not her son? How should she refuse to make him *ubwali*?' In fact, he uses the word as we do 'bread' in such phrases as 'daily bread' or 'working for our bread and butter', but more constantly, and really with better reason.

In Bemba ceremonial *ubwali* stands for food and indirectly for ordinary daily intercourse. Millet flour, meat, and salt represent the essential foodstuffs in the girl's initiation rite (*icisungu*), and at the founding of a chief's village, when small portions of each are buried beneath the walls of the Sacred Kitchen of the tribe.[2] At marriage a ceremonial exchange of dishes of *ubwali* between the relatives of the bridegroom and the bride occurs at one stage of the proceedings. A tiny lump of the porridge, made with special ritual precautions, is used to touch the lips of any individuals coming to an end of a ritual fast, whether during initiation, marriage, inheritance, &c. Further, an individual may himself announce that he is going to abstain from *ubwali* in order to show that he wishes to put himself in a special class apart from the ordinary activities of his fellows. Men or women

---

[1] Eaten, of course, in larger quantities and prepared as flour—'mealie-meal'.
[2] Cf. p. 48.

who believe themselves to be possessed by the spirits of dead
chiefs (*ngulu*) start their vocation by sleeping apart from the rest
of the community, and giving up porridge in favour of 'cold
food'[1] (*ifyatalala*). Later, when their reputation is assured, their
passage from ordinary life to the trance of possession is always
marked by abstention from *ubwali*, and this fact is commented on
excitedly by the rest of the villagers in some such terms as 'Look!
He has stopped eating. He is only eating cold things.' It is also
not uncommon for an individual who feels himself to be hurt or
insulted, to register his protest against his neighbours by refusing
porridge in the most ostentatious way possible. There is no need
in this case for him to starve completely, but merely to abstain
from the staple dish. For instance, a girl, jilted by my cook in
specially humiliating circumstances, ate nothing but pumpkins and
gourds for four days. This was described to me impressively as,
'Look! Grief has caught her by the throat. She is refusing food.'[2]
It was considered the correct conduct for a woman in such circumstances, and I have notes of similar instances on other occasions.
All such examples show the extent to which, in ritual as well as
fact, *ubwali* stands for 'food' in this particular tribe; and in this
emotional attitude to their staple crop I think the Bemba resemble
the majority of primitive tribes.

(*b*) *Umunani*. But the native, while he declares he cannot live
without *bwali*, is equally emphatic that he cannot eat porridge
without a relish (*umunani*), usually in the form of a liquid stew.
Both constituents of the meal are essential.

About two pounds of *umunani* would be reckoned as sufficient to
eat with five pounds of *ubwali*, and in fact the amount of porridge
prepared varies with the supply of relish available. 'When we have
little *umunani*, then we cook little porridge', a woman said, and on
days when no relish was procurable, it sometimes happened that
no porridge was prepared all day (cf. pp. 178–83).[3] Thus it will be
seen that to improve the food-supply in this area by increasing the
production of millet would be useless without at the same time
ensuring an adequate supply of vegetable crops for relish.

The term *umunani* is applied to stews—meat, fish, caterpillars,

---

[1] This taboo is also connected with the ritual attitude to the handling of fire
and the Bemba beliefs as to the impurity caused to food by polluted fire.

[2] *Moneni apa! Cikonko camuikata pa mukoshi! Akane cakulya.*

[3] Men travelling are, however, sometimes forced to do without *umunani* and
this is described by a special term *ukutula*.

locusts, ants, vegetables (wild and cultivated), mushrooms, &c.—
prepared to eat with porridge. The functions of the relish are two:
first to make the *ubwali* easier to swallow, and second to give it taste.
A lump of porridge is glutinous and also gritty—the latter not only
owing to the flour of which it is made, but to the extraneous matter
mixed in with it on the grindstone. It needs a coating of something slippery to make it slide down the throat. Dipping the porridge in a liquid stew makes it easier to swallow. Thus the use of
umunani, which to European eyes adds valuable constituents to the
diet, is defended by the native on the ground that it overcomes the
purely mechanical difficulty of getting the food down the throat.
Some of the relishes are themselves difficult to swallow, in particular the wild forms of spinach (*umusalu*), which are stringy and
often bitter. These the natives cook with ground-nut sauce
(*ntwilo*) (cf. p. 95). To the European this seems to add a valuable
constituent to the diet—fat—of which the supply is short in this
area, but the Bemba himself explains that the sauce is not food.
It is used to make the relish soft. It prevents the food 'coming
back'. Meat and vegetable stews are cooked with salt whenever
possible, and there is no doubt that an additional function of the
relish in native eyes is to give the porridge taste and to lessen the
monotony of the diet. Ground-nut sauce is also praised as bringing
out the taste of a number of different relishes such as mushrooms,
caterpillars, &c.

In general, only one relish is eaten at a meal. The Bemba do
not like to mix their foods, and despise the European habit of
eating a meal composed of two or three kinds of dishes. He calls
this habit *ukusobelekanya* and one said, 'It is like a bird first to
pick at this and then at that, or like a child who nibbles here
and there through the day.'[1]

This habit of eating one relish at a time can probably be
accounted for by the fact that there are few available choices of
dish in any one day, and that the Bemba, with their traditional
customs of hospitality, finish up all they cook. They do not keep
a little bit of stew in a larder for to-morrow. It would be eaten
by a passing relative. Nor do they plan several days' menu ahead

---

[1] But it is clear that the Bemba are not here implicating any modern dietetic
theory, such as the principle advocated recently by Dr. Hay, that protein and
starch should not be eaten together, for their favourite meal is porridge and
meat.

and so have two or three dishes on tap. Whatever the origin of
the prejudice, they stick to it fairly constantly even when adopting
European foods. Natives, and in particular children, who have
the opportunity to buy groceries in urban districts, will sit down
at a counter and eat half a pound of sugar at a time, not keeping
it to sprinkle over other foods. It remains to be seen how long
this habit will last in contact with civilization.

Bemba Dietetic Theory.

Besides their general ideas as to what a meal should consist of,
the Bemba have definite views as to the effects of eating and
drinking. Savage theories of digestion probably vary from area
to area as widely as do their ideas regarding procreation, although
we have little comparative information on the subject at the
moment. The Trobriand islanders, according to Malinowski, eat
for the pleasure it gives them, and are entirely unaware that their
health and strength depend on the process.[1] The Bemba are more
realistic. They are quite convinced that food is eaten to give them
physical energy, and recognize the weakening effects of any deficiency. Accustomed to an annual seasonal shortage, they reckon
to postpone certain heavy agricultural tasks until they feel they
have recovered from the previous weeks of underfeeding, and the
greater the scarcity, the longer the delay. Natives whom I asked
in June why they had not yet started to clear the bush for their
gardens[2] answered, 'We are waiting till the millet is ripe and we
have begun to eat again—until our arms have grown strong.' A
young man whom I had laughed at for not weeding his garden
in the early spring shrugged his shoulders, and merely answered
in explanation, 'February'. Shortage is so commonly expected at
this time of year that the mere mention of the name of the month
was considered quite a sufficient excuse for the lapse. The connexion between diet, and diet of a particular sort, and energy is

---

[1] B. Malinowski, *Coral Gardens and their Magic*, 1935, vol. i, pp. 226–8, also
Argonauts of the Western Pacific, 1922, pp. 168–72. It is significant that this is
an area where food is plentiful, and where its accumulation and exchange is one
of the chief economic and social ambitions of every man in the community. 'We
shall eat, and eat till we vomit', the Trobriander's dream of contentment, has
therefore particular sociological significance in this society. The situation is
different among the Bemba.

[2] April or May would have been the more usual time to start this work. It
will be seen from Chapters XV and XVIII that the hardest agricultural work
actually coincides with the end of the hunger months.

not likely to pass unnoticed in an area in which seasonal changes are so pronounced. There are also a series of words, such as *lushingwa*, 'the giddiness of a man who is hungry', which describe the different effects underfeeding is recognized as producing.

The relation between food and a fat body is dimly recognized, although it has been stated that very few Bemba put on much weight except adolescent girls and some old chiefs. I have heard one or two natives say that food made flesh and that a man who drank much beer would grow fat, but I do not think that diet alone is held responsible for such a condition. A fat body is considered a sign of prosperity and also a state of good luck. Wasting (*ukuonda*) is recognized as a form of illness, but there is nearly always the assumption that this state is due to witchcraft or the revenge of a haunting spirit, whereas a fat and shining body shows the reverse. It betokens the man of substance and success who has kept the forces of darkness at bay, as well as the man who is well fed. There is, therefore, a definite association between the idea of plenty, a well-covered body, and the protection from sorcery. (Cf. also foot-note, p. 58.)

Most natives will give quite a full account of the digestive system. Their theory is based on anatomical knowledge derived from cutting up animals, plus their own subjective sensations during and after eating. Thus they will describe the passage of food from the mouth to the stomach (*icifu*), the intestines (*malo*), the rectum (*inufwinga*), and its ejection as faeces (*amafi*), although they are unaware of the functions of the liver or the pancreas. But in speaking of the digestion of different foods they lay the greatest stress on the factors of which their direct personal experience has made them aware. These are chiefly three: the ease with which the foods are swallowed; the sensations they produce in the stomach, i.e. whether they melt quickly inside (*ukusunguluka*) or remain hard (*ukukosa pa munda*) or give a pain (*ukukalipa pa munda*); or whether they have good lasting power, that is to say, whether a long time elapses between the meal and the next pangs of hunger. Foods recognized as being slow to digest or 'remaining hard in the stomach' are often described as having greater lasting power than those which 'melt' quickly.

All Bemba grade their different foodstuffs in order of preference, and it is probably the habit of eating one relish at a time which enables them to do so with such clarity. The European cannot

easily describe what he feels after eating peas, as distinct from
beans, or how long each particular food will last him, but the
Bemba in many cases can. After a complete change of diet, for
instance, two days of meat-eating after a long period of vegetable
food, he will give a most concrete and convincing account of what he
believes to be going on inside him and state whether he appreciates
the concomitant sensations or not. Thus a man praising porridge
made of millet flour often says, 'If you have eaten your fill with
ubwali you do not get hungry quickly again as with other foods.'
He seems to appreciate the feelings in his stomach and elsewhere
which the eating of porridge gives. Any one who habitually bolts
the coarse heavy millet *ubwali* at the rate which the Bemba do,
probably becomes accustomed to a particular sensation of tension
inside. To the European this would amount almost to a pain, but
it is evident that the Bemba want to feel full in just this particular
way, and do not feel satisfied unless they have reached this state.
Other flours, such as maize or cassava, produce a different sensation according to him. They are softer and 'melt quicker inside'.
They are more suitable for invalids, but they do not give a man
strength (*amaka*) or prevent hunger from seizing him quickly after
the meal. Bemba, after leaving their country to work in urban
areas to the south, say they find it difficult to adjust themselves to
the maize flour 'mealie meal' they are given there. One old man,
probably too fixed in his gastric habits to become adapted to town
life, said, 'Yes, first I ate through one bag of flour and then a
second. Then at last I said, "Well, there it is! There is no food
to be found among the Europeans. Their foods are light"' (lit.
'small').[1] In the same way the Bemba representative sent over to
England recently for the Coronation ceremony declared himself
delighted by London, but complained that he had never felt full
during the trip, in spite of the fact that he was housed at an army
barracks and presumably ate ordinary army food. The reverse
phenomenon is seen in the case of a Bemba child born in the
copper belt and brought home to his mother's village in the
country at about five years old. He refused the *ubwali* they gave
him for several days, crying because it was tasteless, but also
because it was rough and gave him a pain.

The accessory foods are also valued according to their lasting
qualities. If maize is not considered as satisfying as millet, it is

_____
[1] *Kanshi tapali fyakulya pali Basungu. Filyo fyabo fili finono.*

said by natives to be far superior to the various gourds and pumpkins which form the alternative food at the same season of the
year. Of a daughter who returned ill from a visit to relatives where
grain was scarce, her mother said, 'Yes, of course she is tired.
Hasn't she been sitting munching pumpkins with her grandmother?' Sweet potatoes are ranked after maize, but above
gourds. Of the legumes, ground-nuts and ground-beans are
described as having 'strength which exceeds that of other seed',
and mushrooms and other relishes cooked with ground-nuts are
said to last longer than when eaten alone. Neither mushrooms nor
wild spinach are thought to give much energy. 'A man can't dig
on mushrooms, can he?' I heard a man explain to a critic of his
gardening activities during the months when these were the chief
form of food available. The cow-pea is supposed to last longer
than the bean, which in its turn is better than the European pea.
Peas are described as tasting nicer than beans, 'but you get hungry
again before three o'clock if you have eaten at midday'. Leaf
relishes (*umusalu*) are all reckoned less nourishing than dried beans
or peas. One of the best ways of staving off hunger is to eat the dish
known as *icitata* (cf. Appendix A) a hard dry cake made of various
legumes. Mothers say that if they give this to a child during the
hunger season and then ask it to drink water so that the 'food
swells inside', it will not feel the pangs of hunger for a long time.
This statement illustrates clearly the Bemba theory as to what
may be considered a nourishing food.

Like a number of other African peoples the Bemba have a
prejudice against eating raw vegetables, and only cook fresh greens
during a few months of the year.[1] They eat nothing raw except the
small indigenous cucumbers (*ifibimbi*) and sometimes *umupundu*
and *umusuku* fruits, and teachers in European schools have found
it difficult to introduce the eating of raw lettuce and tomatoes.
This prejudice seems to be based partly on habit among a people
who are prevented by the shortness of the annual rainy season
from eating fresh food all the year round; partly also they have a
definite feeling that cooked food is superior to raw. Such an
eating habit seems to be very persistent. Dr. Monica Hunter
tells me that the Nyakusa tribe in Tanganyika generally eat their

---

[1] Cf. the experience of the Rand mine managements that it is necessary to
chop up vegetables very finely indeed and mix them in a stew in order to avoid
their removal by the native employees.

vegetables fresh since they live in an area with a more or less
continuous rainfall. On the other hand, one of the neighbouring
groups, a branch of the Ngoni tribe which trekked up north to
this district from a rainless area in South Africa, continues to dry
and store most of their vegetables although it is plainly no longer
necessary for them to do so.

A good many foods are recognized as causing digestive troubles,
but not necessarily avoided on that account. Hiccoughs, heart-
burn, sickness, stomach pains, and diarrhoea are all considered
possible results of wrong feeding, although these symptoms may
point to other troubles as well. For instance, forms of syphilis
(*akaswende*) are believed to be due to 'things that are bad and black
in the stomach' (*ifintu fibi fyafita ku munda*), and thought to be
cured by strong emetics which cause the patient to vomit up
the evil matter. But in so far as diet is responsible for ill health,
a native will admit in cold blood that bad food, sour porridge, a
sudden excess of meat, or fresh maize eaten off the cob, will produce 'pain over the heart', even though when the time comes he
will not be proof against the temptation to eat them. In most
cases he may have nothing better to eat, or may feel loath to throw
away anything remotely speaking edible. Even an educated Bemba
defended the use of putrefying meat by saying, 'Yes, it will give
me diarrhoea, but that will be better than throwing the meat
away'. When the new maize ripens, the people bolt the cooked
grain, stripping four or five cobs at a time. I have seen them sit
rocking to and fro with indigestion saying, 'Yes, it hurts on the
heart, but we are glad because we are saved from hunger. The
new food has come.' Natives say that sick people and children
should be given gruel (*umusunga*) and soft food instead of *ubwali*,
but the latter at any rate eat what they want. Gastric troubles
are bound to be received with greater resignation than in our
community in an area where alternative diets for weak digestions
practically do not exist.

Tastes, Cravings, and Preferences.

Apart from grading their foodstuffs in the order of what they
believe to be their nutritive value, the Bemba recognize linguistically certain tastes, and also definite cravings for specific foods
probably associated with the deficiencies in their diet.

(*a*) *Tastes.* Bemba foods are not highly flavoured. Of some dishes they use the word *ukukauka*, meaning to be sharp and acid, like lemon-juice, in the mouth,[1] but very few acid fruits were eaten before the introduction of different citrus trees by the white man. Children eat lemons unsweetened and enjoy the bite of the acid, unlike most Europeans. The word *ukusasa* is used of foods that have gone sour or fermented, like beer a few days old, while *ukulula* describes the bitter taste of some of the wild spinaches which the women try to make more palatable with the addition of potash salts (*ifishikisa*) prepared from bush plants or ground-nut sauce. Sweet foods, in the sense of those with a sugary taste, are rare, though honey is sometimes found and is considered a great delicacy, and the stalk of the sweet sorghum (*icisale*) is chewed by children. The fruit of the *umupundu* and the *umusuku* trees are also sweetish. But sweetness in the sense that we understand it is not a term that could be applied to any Bemba dish, and the word *ukuloa* which is used to translate the English 'sweet' really means to be pleasant or palatable. Sugar becomes almost a necessity when natives have become accustomed to it, and the children brought up in urban areas where it is the fashion to use it, find it impossible for a time to eat *ubwali* without it when they are sent back to their own villages.[2] Strong tastes such as ginger root, peppermint, aromatic or hot flavours apparently do not exist, except for the pepper known as *mpilipili*, which is occasionally dried and used as a relish and described as making the mouth hot.[3] In fact, strong tastes are definitely not characteristic of Bemba diet.

(*b*) *Salt hunger.* Of the special cravings recognized by the Bemba the longing for salt is probably the most pronounced. Salt has always been hard to get in this country, and meat and other foods richly supplied with it are rare. In the old days the natural salt found in the pans at Mpika[4] and crystallized out into roundish lumps was among the few goods traded about the country. These salt balls were valued so highly that they were used as tribute to be given to chiefs, who themselves distributed them as rewards to faithful followers. To a certain extent they do so still. The process of evaporating salt from river grasses is

---

[1] E. B. H. Goodall adds 'salty': *Some Wemba Words*, p. 44.

[2] It is interesting to note that honey is considered bad for a sick person because it 'makes the heart beat fast'.

[3] This is in marked difference to W. African diets, where most dishes of stew are highly seasoned with peppers of different kinds.

[4] Cf. Appendix B for composition.

laborious and the product bitter to the taste. European salt is much better liked, but it is hard to get except in districts near white stores. In distant parts of the country both European and Mpika salt are used for barter, and the traveller will notice as he gets farther and farther away from civilization that the purchasing power of salt goes up and that of money goes down. The white man's carriers are given salt in part payment for their work so that they may buy their provisions with it, and women prefer it to any other form of payment for small services. I have often found that children would rather be given a little European salt than a sweet, and they eat it neat. At Katenda's village during a period of shortage (March 1933) some children, who had been living for some weeks chiefly on gourds, picked up grains of salt from the floor of my tent with moistened fingers. Their avid faces were striking.

The craving for salt is so strong that the word itself (*umucele*) has come to have figurative meanings. In proverbs and folk-tales the husband goes to fetch salt from distant places, and this represents the fulfilment of his duties as a husband. In the girls' initiation ceremony the woman who dresses up as a mock bridegroom at one stage of the ritual, carries an imitation lump of salt over her shoulder, and small pieces are included among the sacred objects (*mbusa*) presented to the girl during the rite. In the ceremonial of founding a chief's new village, salt, together with flour and meat, are buried in the foundations of the ruler's hut. Nowadays, too, the word *umucele* is sometimes used as a generic term for European goods as being the most highly valued of these. Two old women who came to live near Kasama because of the shopping facilities there, described their motive as, 'We came to lick a little of the white man's salt'.[1]

(c) *Meat*. The natives' longing for meat is also almost a craving. Meat and fish are considered the *umunani par excellence* and a special word *ubukashya* is used to describe the hunger for meat as distinct from other foods. The supply of game has probably always been inadequate in this area, but the situation is considerably worse to-day. I have noticed that natives returning from the copper field, however sceptical they may be of the other advantages of civilization, are all unanimous that 'It is fine to get so much meat.' In his own country it is no exaggeration to

[1] *Twaisako kumyanga tumucele.*

say that a native would give anything he possessed or do anything
he was asked simply in order to get a piece of meat. White men
get carriers easily if they are reputed to be good shots. A chief is
readily supplied with tribute labour if he has a hunter able to
get him meat. Each kill is the subject of universal conversation for days. Every atom of a killed beast is devoured down
to the ultimate entrail, in whatever state of decay. Small shreds
of flesh are dried over the fire and lovingly stored in a corner of
the owner's hut, whatever the smell. Different parts of the animal
are regularly graded in order of preference and are distributed
according to rank or position in the kinship group. Choice morsels
are strapped on bicycle carriers and carried long distances in
scorching sun as presents for chiefs. I timed a three-year-old girl
during the hunger season, crying for nearly two hours 'just for a
little piece of meat', but it must be admitted that this was in a
village near a white settlement where she must have known that
meat could have been got if her parents had had the money to pay
for it.

Fish is not valued so highly as meat, but it certainly ranks as
the next favourite relish and it is more easily obtained. Caterpillars, which form a very common relish during the rainy season,
are not considered as meat, nor do they form a favourite relish,
although they must certainly be reckoned as providing animal
protein.

This attitude to meat shows in a striking fashion the way in
which a physiological craving easily accounted for in an area of
pronounced shortage of animal protein and salt, becomes associated
with all sorts of social and psychological desires. Meat is not only
good to eat but it is so rare as to make a break in the daily monotony
of food and life. It is a sudden unexpected stroke of good fortune
and therefore means that the spirits are on the mortals' side. It
means plenty and the royal way of living at the chief's court. It is
an occasion for a feast. For all these reasons a village sometimes
reacts to the presence of meat in a way that is quite out of keeping
with its purely physiological value. This is specially the case
when the supply of meat is unusually large. When a buck has been
distributed in a small village, the natives claim that it is the meat
itself which makes them feel strong, and keen to dance all night
and to work next day. But in reality it is probably their excitement at the sudden change of diet, their pleasure at the sight of

so much food in one community, and their relief at the unexpected appearance of relish got without the usual effort and calculation of ways and means that causes such dramatic outbursts of energy.

For instance, at Kasaka village (September 1933) I shot a large roan antelope which was divided among twenty-two adults and forty-seven children in a community where there had not been much meat available recently. There was probably more than 2 lb. of meat a head on this occasion. Now meat takes some hours to digest, but the energy (or *amaka*, i.e. strength) which the native claimed that the food gave him was shown not only before the food was digested, but before it was cooked! During the division of the animal the excitement was tense. Men and women gathered round shouting and talking. Before the meal there was a buzz of expectation. Women ground extra flour with enthusiasm, 'Because we have so much meat to eat with it.' Every one sang at their work. Young men ran sky-larking round the village, like a set of English schoolboys in a playground. Directly after the meal, the women gathered near me talking in loud voices. They kept describing with ecstasy how full they felt. 'Our stomachs are rammed tight' (*munda uauma ndi! ndi! ndi!*), said one with enthusiasm, showing with a gesture a closed fist ramming down material hard. 'Yes,' said another, 'we shall all fall asleep at once (*ukulalafye nku!*), not toss or wake at night as we usually do.'[1] A mother, pointing to a baby of two sprawling, legs wide, replete by the fire, exclaimed, 'Yes, look at him, he is so full he cannot sit up straight.' Others pulled down their cloths from their breasts to display their bellies with delight, and indeed there seemed to be quite a visible swelling of the stomach. Part of the excitement seemed connected with the fact that there was not only enough meat for that day, but that it would last till the morrow. The food was so ample that all usual rules of courtesy were put aside. 'There is so much meat that you need not wait for an invitation to join a group of your friends round a basket,' said a young woman, 'you can just swoop down like a vulture and snatch what you want and no one will care.' An old couple sitting together on the veranda of their hut, repeated with quiet satisfaction over and over again, 'Yes, and there is just as much left for to-morrow.' Another old lady

---

[1] Mr. G. H. Wilson suggests to me that peaceful sleep is associated with the blessings of the spirits. There may be an association between plenty of food, sleep, removal of the fear of witchcraft, &c.

cried light-heartedly, hitting her stomach, 'I have been turned into a young girl, my heart is so light.'[1]

In an hour or so men and women gathered on the village square and burst into spontaneous dancing of a type I had never seen in ordinary life. Young men charged arm in arm up and down in lines singing Bemba and European songs. They imitated mission drilling and play-acting. Young girls played singing games amid screams of laughter. Drums beat, and the older women and babies clapped and shouted. It was like some wild Dionysiac rabble, and indeed these people might have been taken for drunkards, except that they were better tempered, more energetic, and showed more initiative in inventing new games. The next day, they went to work early, declaring that their arms were strong. The excitement on this particular occasion was admittedly unusual, but I have described it as an example of the extreme delight of the Bemba in the sight of meat, and of meat in such profusion that it could be used for once in an utterly reckless way.

(*d*) *Other cravings.* Old men who have become accustomed to drinking beer say that they feel their stomachs asking for beer. Elderly people also long for snuff and will go to any lengths to get even a small pinch. *Kuba no mupatikishya ku fwaka* means 'to be in a state of begging for snuff', but I do not know if this craving has any correlation with dietetic deficiencies. Pregnant women are expected to be liable to pika hungers and are said to 'ask their husbands suddenly to get them such and such'. They regularly pull lumps of clay from the walls of their huts to chew, and declare their mothers taught them this custom. I have heard that some children also eat clay, but I never saw this done.

(*e*) *Monotony and diet cravings.* Most Bemba seem to be specially liable to sudden cravings for different foods during the season of shortage. Whether this is due to definitely physiological reactions or to the excessive monotony of the diet at this season I do not know. To the European Bemba meals seem insipid and tedious at all seasons of the year. The foods available are not numerous, and even then they cannot all be used at any one time (cf. Chart on p. 41). There are a number of variations in the methods of cooking known, but, as in England, many of these require too much time for their preparation as a general rule. In one village

[1] *Nasanguka naba mukashyana ico mutima uayanguka.*

records taken during a plentiful season showed that only five different relishes were used on an average during a period of twenty-three days. Only one cultivator had stored or gathered as many as nine different forms of *umunani*, and he was a man of unusual intelligence. At another village in the hunger season four out of six families ate mushrooms only with their porridge for five days out of six, and this was considered usual at that time of year. Mrs. Gore-Browne states that in the thirty-two villages she visited between July and January *katapa*, the relish made from cassava leaves, was practically the only food eaten. Whether the Bemba really suffer more severely from monotony of diet than the average English working-class family I do not know. Bread, butter, jam, tea, meat, and vegetables probably recur with the same frequency in such households as do millet, porridge and relish in that of the Bemba. Nor is it easy to know whether a monotonous diet is harmful in itself if it is well balanced, but it is certainly in times of shortage of millet that the native complains of the lack of variety. At this season I have seen Bemba pay quite exorbitant prices for dried fish bought from a passing trader 'because we are so sick of eating pumpkin'. It would seem that a kind of despair had set in, and in this mood they were willing to pay anything to get a change of food, however bad the bargain they were making.[1]

(*f*) *Foods and social status.* Finally, the Bemba, like ourselves, have attached a kind of snobbish value to different foodstuffs. This is roughly correlated with the traditional beliefs in the strength and staying power of the dishes, but not entirely. As presents of honour, beer may be given, unthreshed millet, meat, fish, or honey. But it is almost an insult to give a man of rank a basket of maize. I once saw the late Nkula presented with such food by some villagers when travelling round his district, but he gave it contemptuously to the children of his retinue. Citimukulu also passed through a village where I was staying during a month of scarcity after locust raids. The people knew he was short of relish for his followers but did not dare to offer him caterpillars— their only supply that day—in public. His wives had to beg surreptitiously behind closed doors.

Roughly speaking, uncultivated plants are less highly thought of than cultivated. Some of the wild leaf relishes really are

---

[1] Cf. also Chap. XII on trading habits.

stringy and bitter to the taste, but the fact that these plants grow wild also tends to make them despised. For instance the wild orchid (*icikanda*) gathered by the children in September is considered with special contempt. A passing Lunda bragging to some Bemba villagers about the superior wealth and civilization of his own people, clinched the argument by saying, 'In our country we just divorce our wives if they serve *icikanda* relish, whereas yours have to cook it every day.' The burrowing cricket (*nyense*) and the mice, moles, or small birds which little boys trap are also despised. 'Food for children and for women in the hunger months' is an expression often used of such foods with an expression of contempt.

European foods are used only in the villages round white settlements and then apparently entirely for their kudos value, or else their ease in preparation.[1] Such articles are chiefly limited to tea, coffee, sugar, bread, and sardines. They seemed to me to be eaten as extras, used for purposes of entertainment or display, rather than an essential part of the diet, but the habit may have become more common since my visit to the area in 1934. Then clerks and native storekeepers in the Kasama townships used to be carried trays of tea in the middle of the morning by their wives, and in a neighbouring village I have seen four young men, after eating their ordinary meal of porridge and relish, sit down to share a tin of sardines on a table spread in full view of the community and ornamented with empty whisky bottles. They were described as having a 'sundowner'. In the same year a successful dance club run by an enterprising native returned from the mines, sold lemonade at 3*d.* a glass (i.e. a whole day's wages) and scones made from white flour in preference to supplying beer. It is purely want of money which prevents the extension of such customs in the modern type of village.

Magico-Religious Attitudes to Food.

(*a*) *Food taboos.* The whole question of food taboos has bulked very largely in anthropological literature from the earliest days. Such ritual restrictions on diet seem to have struck the attention of European observers immediately, and there is no doubt that where a particular class of food is tabooed permanently to a whole community or to a large section of it, such as a clan, age-grade, or

---

[1] Bread is liked chiefly for the latter reason I think.

to the different sexes, the matter becomes important from a nutritional point of view.

It may be said at once that the food taboo proper is not widely observed among these Central African people. The Bemba tribe is divided into clans named after various animals or plants, but in no case are totemic food taboos kept. In fact, in some cases the clan name is that of one of the staple foods of the tribe (Besa— an archaic name for millet; Boa, or 'mushroom'). Nor does there seem to be any food tabooed to one sex or the other, or considered appropriate to any particular time of life. Certain individuals regularly abstain from one or more types of relish. Such restrictions may be the result of an order given by a native doctor who may make a cure conditional on the regular observance of a food taboo, or it may follow the individual's own conviction that a particular food eaten on some memorable occasion has brought him ill luck and is therefore likely to do so again. In some cases one whole family (*ulupwa*) may avoid one type of relish, but it is impossible to decide in these instances whether the individuals have a natural antipathy to one food or the other, or whether the taboo is based entirely on magic grounds.

Another set of taboos are observed by chiefs, in this case entirely on animal food, and dependent on the belief in the magic properties of the animal. Animals with prominent lower teeth are unlucky. They are known as *ifinkuli* (sing. *icinkuli*)—the name given to children whose lower teeth have come through before their upper, and who used to be destroyed on this account. Such animals include the bush-pig, the wart-hog, the zebra, and the eland. The bush-buck is also taboo to a chief because it has a mottled skin and makes a choking noise, and is therefore believed to bring danger or leprosy and bronchial troubles. The flesh of the bush-pig is also considered unsuitable since it darts from side to side, and this it is said might disturb the judgements of the chief. For similar magic reasons, pregnant women must avoid the flesh of the bush-buck, 'Because it is mottled. Does she want her child to be striped?'[1] But it must be stated at once that the pregnancy taboos are not nearly so numerous as among other African and Melanesian peoples, and both the taboos observed by the chiefs and by pregnant women are restrictions not on one type of food— vegetable or animal—but on one particular species of vegetable

---

[1] She must also avoid the *ifinkuli* and the wild cat.

or animal. They can therefore have little appreciable dietetic importance.

(b) *Domestic animals.* We have seen from this account that ritual avoidances of food do not seriously affect the diet of large sections of the Bemba community. On the other hand it is not true to say that all available sources of food in the environment are exploited. The Bemba are not a pastoral people and could not keep cattle in large numbers because of the tsetse-fly. On the other hand sheep and goats are quite widely distributed in certain areas, and most households keep chickens and some pigeons. All these domestic animals are called *ifitekwa* or 'things kept', but in no case are *ifitekwa* kept primarily for meat or bred for that purpose. Goats or sheep may be given as a present to a chief or a European; dedicated to an ancestral spirit after successful recovery from illness; or given as compensation to an injured person for the loss of a limb or an eye. They may be killed and used as meat, but always on some such ceremonial occasion, never in case of pure hunger. Chickens are more numerous and less valuable, but even then a chicken is never killed 'just for food', even in the hunger season. Fowls are the ordinary present of honour for a chief or visitor of high status, and provide the ceremonial meal at a marriage or initiation ceremony. While there is no particularly sacred attitude towards chicken, a man will say, 'If I kill a chicken just to eat, I shall soon have none left.' That is to say he does not breed poultry scientifically, put down sittings of eggs, or calculate the number of chickens he may expect to get; nor does he make any attempt to feed them. Hens run about the village and lay their eggs wherever they please, and some of these sittings are finally hatched. But each new brood is regarded, with some justification, as a separate piece of good fortune for which the owner is not responsible, and which he is never certain will be repeated.[1] It is for this reason that he considers chickens should not be wasted or 'just eaten' and he will not part with eggs unless he can get money from a European for them. Teaching of scientific rearing of poultry would overcome the reluctance to use eggs. There is no fundamental magic belief at stake.

The Bemba attitude to pigeons is characteristic. These birds

---

[1] A number of magic rites are associated with the care of poultry such as the disposal of the eggshells at the crossroads, &c., and these may be taken as an indication of the measure of uncertainty the native feels on the question.

are kept by one or two men in most villages and housed in elaborate pigeon houses built with considerable trouble and protected
with magic rites. But they are hardly ever eaten because 'People
want to keep many pigeons, so they are afraid to waste the seed'
(i.e. to reduce the stock). They like to see the birds flying about
the village. They are things kept as a sign of rank. They just
flutter and flutter about. They show the rank of the owner of the
pigeon house.'[1] A common saying is 'The domestic animals of
rich people cause admiration like pigeons'[2] i.e. they wander here
and there and give the effect of countless numbers.

Goats and sheep also add to the reputation of their owner. The
reluctance of the Bemba to kill and use them for ordinary purposes
seems to be based on two different attitudes. On the one hand
these people are as ignorant of methods of rearing stock as they
are of poultry breeding. They lack completely any pastoral tradition, and the way in which goats, for instance, are treated, makes
it little short of miraculous that any survive. The Bemba children
do not herd them or look after them, and it is not uncommon for
the owner to forget to let his goats out of their pen to feed. A man
buys a goat or sheep as a sort of gesture, probably because he
wants to acquire possessions, and he puts it in a shed, but he
never seems to have any idea of building up a herd or relying
economically on the sale of meat. The milk is never used. Added
to this the killing of so large an animal as a goat or a sheep has a
particular significance for the native, and this makes him unwilling
to slaughter except for some special ceremonial reason. A goat is
something approaching a human being, and is used nowadays as
a substitute for human sacrifices. It can also serve as a compensation for some serious bodily injury, in which case it will
probably change hands but not be killed. It is interesting that the
Bemba, who have substituted money payments for many of their
old religious dues, feel that a financial compensation would be
unsuitable in such a case. 'It is right to give a goat because it is
a man who has been hurt.' There is even some indication that the
Bemba believe that to kill a domestic animal might bring dangerous
consequences, just as the murder of a man would. In this tribe
the belief that the spirit of a murdered man returns as a haunting

[1] *Fitekwa fya bukankala. Fyakupukapuka: filelanga bukankala bwa kwa
cibinda ca nkunda.*
[2] *Fitekwa fya bakankala fyakukumukapo fye nge nkunde.*

ghost is very strong. In the case of a dangerous animal like a leopard or a lion special ceremonies are performed to prevent the return of its spirit. In the old days the killing of an ox, I was told, was accompanied by the words, 'Kampinda (a name for the High God) who gave us this beast, now go out of it. Go and settle in that one', pointing to another animal. I never heard this said, but to this day the Nkolemambwe, the hereditary official responsible for killing most of the beasts slaughtered at the Paramount chief's court in connexion with various rites, describes himself as being 'fierce' (*umukali*) on this account, and as doing specially dangerous work for the community requiring subsequent purification. I have heard a native say that it is bad to kill a dog because its spirit could return. 'White men are cruel the way they shoot sick dogs. It is better to tie them up in the bush and walk quickly away and let them die.' Children are sometimes afraid to kill a chicken. One said, 'It is a frightening thing to watch the breath flutter away'.[1] This attitude towards the killing of domestic animals is interesting in an agricultural people in which the ritual attitude towards cattle has not been formalized in different institutions and religious ceremonies as it has among the pastoral Bantu. It amounts to a reluctance to treat goats and sheep merely as stock to be bred and killed, combined in this case with a lack of scientific knowledge of how to do so.

Conclusion.

To summarize the Bemba views on food it must be admitted that they grade their different victuals according to fairly crude criteria, such as their lasting power, and ease of swallowing. Also habits developed in early infancy have made them used to experiencing particular sensations after eating, such as the feeling of fullness after a meal of *ubwali*. Hence other types of dishes have ceased to seem to them to be 'satisfying'. On the other hand, most of their prejudices appear to be extraordinarily sound in the particular environment in which they live. Their preference for millet flour as against cassava meal is an extremely sensible one as the chart of comparative values of finger millet, cassava, and maize given

---

[1] *Pakuloleshyo muntu apo umweo uleputuka cakutina.* This fear seems to be combined with a definite desire to watch pain inflicted. Most natives consider it the treat of treats to see a sacrificial animal killed, and I have always noticed that children swarm to watch a goat killed and rather enjoy a long-drawn-out death.

on p. 409, Table B, shows. It will be seen that the millet has a protein value of 33 as against 7 for cassava and a much higher proportion of fat, thus making the former a much more suitable cereal in an area where animal and vegetable fats are so short.[1] Their scorn of maize is not, however, justified from a nutritional point of view, since it has a higher protein and fat content than the favourite millet. Habit and the additional difficulties which the cooking of maize involves probably influence them in this prejudice. The general order in which they grade their accessory foods, i.e. describing maize as giving more strength than gourds, legumes than green or dried leaf relishes or mushrooms also seem to correspond roughly to the nutritive values of these foodstuffs as shown in the Appendix B, as also their statement that ground-nut sauce, the most important source of fat in this diet, gives the food 'strength' (*amaka*). Cravings for salt and meat would probably be prophesied from a descriptive account of the deficiencies of the diet.

They do not make use of eggs and chickens, as they could do, but otherwise there are few of those ritual restrictions which limit the diet of a number of primitive tribes. The Bemba have also clearly a realistic outlook on the importance of food in relation to health and power of work. It remains to be seen whether the urban natives, under the stress of new economic and social ambitions lose this shrewd empirical sense.

[1] Compared to the Bangweolu area where the cassava-eating peoples have an ample supply of fish and hence a more adequate amount of fat in their diet.

CHAPTER IV

EATING AND DRINKING

Infant Feeding.

THE dietetic prejudices of any people must have their basis in their methods of infant feeding, and it is probable that the most characteristic distinctions between the Bemba attitude to food and our own are occasioned by differences in early training. Unfortunately, it is just on this aspect of Bemba nutrition that it is most difficult to collect accurate information. Babies are suckled at any hour of the day or night, whenever they cry. As they grow older, they are carried about the village on their elder sisters' backs, and seem to be given choice morsels by admiring or affectionate relatives at every hut. When food is plentiful, children under three nibble at something wherever they go. Throughout childhood it is therefore almost impossible to keep any quantitative record of diet. Certain broad facts, however, stand out in contrast to our own methods of infant feeding, and Bemba theory is interesting in this respect.

As in most other African communities, babies are suckled until they are between two and three years old. There is a strong taboo observed by all except urbanized natives on the conception of a new child before the weaning of the last. When the child is four months old, a special rite, 'the taking of the child', *ukupoko mwana*, is performed by the father and mother, and after this ceremony, *coitus interruptus* may be allowed between the parents, but it is considered very dangerous for the mother to become pregnant before her first baby has been successfully weaned. The child will fall ill of a particular disease, *ukulwale lunse*, of which the symptoms are coughing, wasting, or diarrhoea. Even in urbanized districts where the taboo is less rigidly observed, mothers are still uneasy. If a child has been hurriedly weaned to make way for a successor, and later falls ill, the parents are charged with the trouble. Neighbours shake their heads, and if the illness is fatal, whisper that the child has been killed by the mother's folly. There is no doubt that early weaning is still largely prevented by the fear of endangering the baby's life.

It is difficult to know whether the mother, at the end of this long

period of suckling, is able to give her child any nourishment at all.
Two or three years after the birth of the baby her breasts have
begun to hang down like wrinkled leather bags. But natives say
that the glands go on secreting as long as the child sucks the breast.
'On the first day nothing comes from the breast but a fluid like
water. On the second day, in the evening, the breasts are full
(*ukusaka*) with a white liquid.' After some months they say the fluid
is less, but that the secretion may continue for most of a woman's
life. If the mother dies the baby is suckled by its grandmother,
either as a form of consolation, or actually in the belief that it is
getting food. I know a case of a woman who had suckled seven
children of her own, evenly spread at about three years apart, and
who then began to nurse the baby of her eldest daughter, who had
died in childbirth.

It seems obvious that with a woman of this age, the baby is
dependent on comfort and caresses from its grandmother rather than
actual nourishment, and this is probably largely the case with the
two- or three-year-old child just before it is weaned. I have already
described the way in which Bemba babies cling to their mother's
breasts if frightened or distressed, or demand to be suckled long
after they have been weaned, at moments of illness or misery.[1]
In fact I have wondered whether the natives regard the mother's
milk as primarily a food at all. On the one hand they recognize
that lactation depends upon what the mother eats. I have heard
women say on different occasions, 'You can't suckle a child on
mushrooms without porridge', 'Her breasts are full as she ate meat
last night', 'If she doesn't eat how can she feed the child?', or
'Of course my baby is defecating all day long since I am eating
nothing but pumpkins'. On the other hand no woman I questioned
would definitely commit herself to the statement that the mother's
milk was food. A term for 'milk' does not exist among these agricultural people. The word *umukaka*, used of cow's milk drunk by
Europeans, is borrowed from Nyasaland. One woman described
the mother's milk as *amafina*,[2] the general term for any kind of
secretion, whether from the nose or ears. Another said, 'It is
water. Well, really, it is just the breast', and a third quite definitely, 'It is water only, not food. To suckle is not to appease
hunger. You give the child the breast perpetually to quieten him,

---

[1] *Hunger and Work in a Savage Tribe*, 1932, p. 44.
[2] Distinguish from *amafi* = faeces. Cf. p. 51.

not to feed him.'[1] Statements which would readily account for the
suckling of children by old women. In these circumstances it is
not surprising that the act of suckling has become symbolic of the
mother's generosity in Bemba literature and daily speech. Speaking of the son-to-mother relation men say in sentimental tones,
'How should a mother refuse her child anything when she has
suckled him with her breasts'? Praying to his great ancestress
Bwalya Cabala, Chief Mwamba said, 'You who suckled us and
carried us on your back in a skin'. The legal dues of the mother's
family are sometimes based on this service the woman has done
for the child, and only a sister can act·as a substitute for a dead
mother.

The belief that the breasts give comfort rather than nourishment
is correlated with the practice of feeding infants with supplementary foods, The Bemba deny entirely that a baby can live even for
a few weeks on its mother's milk alone. From the third or fourth
week the infant is fed with a thin milk gruel known as *umusunga*.
This is made in the first place by stirring a little flour into warm
water[2] held in the hollow of the hand, and later by throwing a
small handful of flour into boiling water and stirring until a smooth
paste of the consistency of gruel results. It is often sour since it is
considered bad to throw away remains of gruel blessed by the
spirits. This *umusunga* is literally rammed down the baby's throat
in spite of its protests. However the child may scream, splutter,
or cough up the food, it is relentlessly forced down again, pushed
with the mother's fore-finger or held in the baby's mouth while
the food is stroked down his throat, as a European may force a dog
to swallow a pill. This behaviour of the mother shows how important she considers the additional food. In every other respect she
indulges every whim of her baby, suckling him whenever he wishes
and giving him whatever he cries for, but on this one point she is
firm. 'How can the child get strong if he has nothing but the
breast?' parents will say indignantly. They criticize severely
European mothers, who suckle their babies for six months without
additional food: 'Look at those white women! They have their
cupboards full of tins of sugar and flour, and yet they grudge the

---

[1] *Amenshi fye epela! Kuonka te kuikuta yo! Kumupela ibele pefye ni kumunashya
ku mutima epela!*

[2] Not boiling water for fear lumps would be formed. Girls at Lubwa training
school are taught to simmer the gruel a little.

baby a little food.' I noticed, in fact, that in a native family where the father had been taught at a Mission School that it was wrong to feed a new-born baby on gruel, he yet insisted that his child should have condensed milk as well as the breast. He was as convinced as the rest of his fellows that the child would not grow up on the breast alone, and did not want people to say that he grudged his baby anything needed for its health.

Thus the native's dependence on millet porridge is a habit literally forced on him from his earliest days, in fact before he has acquired the necessary ferments for digesting the starch at all. By three or four months he has become entirely used to the gruel, and by eight or nine months he is being given small lumps of *ubwali* to eat by himself. This system of cramming the infant's stomach is considered by most Europeans to be harmful, and to be responsible for the protruding abdomens of all Bemba children, although these latter may be due to enlarged spleens as well as to unsuitable diet. The mortality of children between the ages of one and three is enormously high, for a variety of reasons, not only those connected with diet. It is impossible to be dogmatic on this point without further information. But it must be admitted that the Bemba infants cry less and have a more contented appearance than the children of the same age in this country.

When a child has reached the crawling age he is allowed and even encouraged to eat everything he can. I never heard a mother trying to restrict a small child's diet, but always boasting proudly about what a lot the child knew how to eat. He is given small handfuls of food in all his relations' houses, toddling from one hut door to another. Small children are always given the remains of food not thought good enough for grown-ups. Infants of under a year are fed with the beer dregs from last night's party, mothers saying with satisfaction: 'Look at that child. How strong he is! He likes beer already,' and any account of Bemba dishes includes a list of foods which 'no grown-up person would touch. Only children eat that.' In this way, therefore, the Bemba mother differs from the European with her more rigid ideas as to the digestive powers of her children.

To conclude, the characteristics of the Bemba system of infant feeding are three. First the length of the suckling period, and the complete freedom of the infant in feeding, both of psychological importance to the baby as well as nutritional, and valued by the native for the former reason only; second, the use of a supplementary cereal practically from birth, and the mother's absolute insistence on the necessity of this food, in every case the staple millet; third, the irregularity of infant feeding from the first days of life till the third or fourth year—a point which we shall have to develop further.

Eating Customs.

In this country medical practitioners tell us that digestion is affected by the rate at which food is swallowed, the temperature at which it is served, the proportion of liquid to solid, and the size and spacing of meals. Mothers of all classes are taught to suckle their babies at regular intervals. In well-to-do nurseries it is considered of the utmost importance that food should be served punctually and that, roughly speaking, the same amounts should be eaten each day. Children are constantly instructed how to carry out such an apparently instinctive act as putting food into their mouths. They are told not to eat 'so fast', or alternatively not to 'dawdle', to chew their food longer, to drink at special times, or to eat either more or less than they apparently seem inclined to. In all these matters, the mother is guided, partly by the theories she has acquired as to what is best for the child's digestion, and partly by her conception that eating a meal is a definite social activity in which the young must be carefully taught to play their part. Eating takes place at fixed intervals in the day's routine, often in special rooms allotted for the purpose. To eat at a different speed from others, to demand more or less than they do, to sit in a different manner, or talk in a different way is a breach of etiquette. Later, in an industrial country, the child is caught in the grip of the economic machine. He sits down to his midday dinner when the siren hoots, and to his evening meal when he comes home from work. For the greater majority of people in this country, it is rare for meals to vary in time more than from half an hour to an hour, or to eat food that differs from day to day in amount and composition. The whole complex of behaviour patterns that we roughly call 'eating customs' depends not only on physiological factors, but on the type of food eaten by a people, the material apparatus used for cooking and serving it, the system of housing, the rules of division observed by the community, and the routine of economic activities into which the preparation and consumption of meals has to be fitted. Among primitive peoples, these facts stand out more clearly perhaps than in our own.

To the Bemba the meal is, in a sense, the climax of the day. Cooking is a long and tedious process, as will be seen (Chap. V). The whole series of activities involved in fetching fuel, drawing water, preparing flour and collecting relish must be begun afresh each day, and can be reckoned to take at least 3 hours out of that day. But the time and nature of the meal is fixed by the type of agricultural work in hand.[1] This fact accounts for two of the chief characteristics of Bemba eating custom: the concentration on a single daily meal, and the irregularity of that meal. Although the Bemba may take some snack in the early morning such as cold *ubwali* left over from the night before, or some sweet potatoes or ground-nuts, it is quite impossible for the women to prepare a dish of porridge and relish more than once a day unless they are free from other work. Men and women are accustomed to go to their gardens in the early morning to do the bulk of their work on what we habitually describe as 'an empty stomach'. They return to the village at about noon, when the whole community waits for the evening meal. This habit of eating late in the day seems to have become fixed. Natives working in European employment tend to keep to it. Loaded carriers seem to prefer to walk their daily fifteen miles or so before eating, and labourers on European farms usually do the morning shift, from 6 a.m. to noon, without a 'breakfast'. In at least one Mission school, where the young native teachers were offered food before morning classes, they refused, saying they would not be able to work properly if they ate so early in the day. It is difficult to know whether such preferences are due entirely to habit, or whether the type of meal eaten by the Bemba actually takes a long time to digest. It is interesting to note that the compound managers of the copper mines at the Roan Antelope and Mufulira considered that the natives worked better if they had eaten a breakfast before going on shift, and made this practice compulsory, but the meal was not the heavy porridge in this case, but cocoa and white bread.

This concentration on a single meal is a habit to which the children are only accustomed gradually. Bemba infants, as we saw, are suckled whenever they wish, and in early childhood they eat all day long if possible. Natives recognize that small children

_____
[1] Cf. pp. 73, 104 and Chap. XVIII.

cannot go so long without food as their elders and cook them extras when they can. Women who stay at home in the village all morning roast ground-nuts for the little children, or bake them sweet potatoes in season, while all the young people forage for what they can get from various relatives, or look for fruits in the bush. Mothers going to work may be seen carrying smouldering embers on a bark holder, ready to make small fires to roast maize cobs if they happen to be ripe in the gardens. But when food is short the children have to go without and expect to do so, and as they reach adolescence they begin to adopt the tribal belief that it is childish and undignified to be eating at all hours of the day. They finally express the ordinary adult preference for a meal late in the day rather than early. Some natives comment half disparagingly on the frequency of the white man's meals, although of course they admire the riches of a European who is constantly able to entertain his friends. The white man, chiefly the government official in this area, has now become a standardized figure in a series of folk-tales, and in these he is always represented as stopping constantly in the middle of any activity to take breakfasts or to drink tea. I once listened to some small boys playing at being Europeans—a very favourite game. The boy who was acting as the district officer sat lounging in an imitation chair made of branches and bark rope and repeatedly called, 'Bring food'. At last one of his fellows, acting servant, said aside in an aghast whisper, 'You can't ask for food again. We've only just brought it to you.' The 'white man's' answer was immediate. 'You know nothing about Europeans! That is just what they do all day—just sit and call, Boy! Bring me food.'

The chief meal of the Bemba varies tremendously both as to its time, its size, and the accessory foods that may be added to it during the day. These changes depend chiefly on the nature of the women's agricultural work from season to season, the monthly changes in the types of food available, and the time taken to cook them. For instance, at Pambalasa village (September 1930), the women were working late into the day to finish piling the branches for burning in their gardens. They were back late to the village, and got the single meal ready at about five. There was no early morning snack for most of them. At Candamukulu's village (April 1931), the women were harvesting, but at this time of the year the maize was ripe, and a few cobs could be quickly roasted at about 8 a.m. as well as the evening meal, which varied in individual cases from 2 p.m. to 5 p.m. At the court of the Paramount chief I have noticed during several visits paid at different times of the year that the wives of the Citimukulu, who had very few agricultural duties, cooked small dishes of porridge for themselves twice a day, at about 10 and 4 p.m., while continuing to prepare the one big evening meal for the chief's labourers. The more detailed daily records kept at Kasaka village (September 1933) (pp. 178–83) show a decided variation in individual cases in this respect. These examples show clearly the extent to which economic routine and the seasonal changes in the food-supply alter, not only the time of the main meal of the day, but the actual daily intake of each individual in the form of extra snacks. These variations would upset many European digestions, but natives are either so used to delay that they do not feel discomfort, or else they resign themselves to the inevitable. I never heard a Bemba husband complain that his meal was late. On return from work the men sit about in their club-house, an open shelter called *nsaka*, for several hours, gradually growing more listless if the delay has been prolonged, and talking in a more desultory way. They seem able to eat more at a time than we could most of us manage, and to go longer periods without. Some carriers of mine took 50-lb. loads 15 miles a day for two days eating a few gourds one day and nothing but wild fruit the next, but after this effort they lay down and rested for a few days, and presumably ate all they could get. Another set of carriers similarly burdened ate 10 lb. of cassava each in $2\frac{1}{2}$ days (average ration about a pound a day), and then walked another 42 miles on about 4 dried fish apiece. They explained their action by saying, 'Our loads were so heavy that we thought, "Let's carry our food in our bellies".'[1] Such a method of dividing up a ration would probably be inconceivable to the average Englishman who is intellectually convinced of the advisability of eating the same each day, and has been accustomed in most cases to do so. It is an interesting illustration of the way in which the environmental limitations of a people's food supply, the methods of cooking they practise, their hospitality rules and general system of distribution, all act in concert to condition their appetites and digestive habits.

It remains to describe the actual consumption of a Bemba meal. To the casual observer the most characteristic feature of their

---

[1] *Twatile fipe nafifina, katusenda munda!* Information sent me by Mrs. Gore-Browne.

manner of eating is its speed and almost complete lack of ceremony. It is true that there is a certain amount of etiquette prescribed before the meal is actually started. Invitations must be issued respectfully for instance, and water brought to wash the hands of the guests. But once the company, whether of men or women, is gathered, there is no further delay. The five or six eaters squat round the vessels of food, and bolt the meal silently and swiftly. Lumps of porridge are torn off and swallowed apparently almost whole, and two or three pounds of *ubwali* disappears in as many moments. The eaters rise, turn on their heels and leave. Plenty of food is the *sine qua non* of gaiety and social activity in Bemba society, but eating itself is never considered a recreation. Meals are not times for rest, or chat, or merriment. In fact, it might be said there was almost something furtive about the group of eaters bowed over a porridge basket, and it is considered rude to address or to look at anyone during their meal. It would be equivalent to asking for a share.

These customs, which obviously affect the digestive habits of the people, are directly correlated with their material culture. Bemba who share food sit round one basket, and each tears off porridge from one lump. In these circumstances it is impossible to linger. While the man who eats faster than his fellows causes resentment, the one who eats too slowly goes hungry. For an eater to pause to tell an anecdote, as we might do, secure in possession of our own plate, would be fatal. It must be remembered, too, that Bemba houses have only one room, in or near which the women eat. Men take their meals in the full publicity of the whole village, hence there is a certain amount of hurry and shame attached. People do not like to eat when others are not doing so.

The usual meal of porridge and relish is served hot, but the temperature does not seem to be a matter of great importance to the natives. If the men are late, their porridge stands about gradually chilling, and is not put back to keep hot on the fire. Natives will eat lumps of cold porridge left over from the night before, and small pieces are carried while travelling. Water is not often drunk with meals, for fear it should make the porridge swell. A man may wash out his mouth with water before eating—*ukufumya malima*—'to remove the stickiness of the night', or he may drink after specially good food that has 'left itself in the throat'. He will only drink during a meal with a bitter food that 'makes our mouths dry as if there wasn't any saliva in them'.[1] It is very important to natives to get the right proportion of relish to porridge. Every one wants to get as much relish as possible, and here the rules of procedure are fixed. An old man may tear off a lump of *ubwali* and make it into a hollow spoon. This he will dip into the liquid relish and then pick up as much relish as possible (*ukuleme nkondwa*). The child, or inferior, may only just dip the porridge into the relish to moisten it (*ukutumpika*), and thus the proportion of vege-table varies very much according to age. A young man will not dare *ukuleme nkondwa* until he is given the permission by his father, said to be granted when the boy is able to do a full day's work in the gardens. A girl should wait the invitation of her mother before trying to take an adult portion of relish, and on the few occasions when a wife eats with her husband, in the privacy of their hut at night, she is supposed merely to dip her porridge in the stew like a child, until she reaches middle or old age when, among the Bemba, all sex disabilities seem to disappear.

Bemba eating customs can therefore be said to differ consider-ably from our own, both as regards the rhythm of meals, the regularity of daily intake, and the serving and rate of consumption, but in each case the manner of eating is just as precisely defined by cultural rule and related as strictly to the general economic system and social grouping of the people concerned. Even the proportion of liquid to solid, or relish to porridge, is prescribed by etiquette.

Beer Drinking.

Bemba beer (*ubwalua*) is one of their most important foodstuffs. It is made from the staple cereal itself.[2] It is a valuable source of vitamin B in which the diet is otherwise deficient.[3] On the day when it is drunk very few natives eat any other form of food, and some individuals, mostly chiefs, subsist on it entirely from day to day. But *ubwalua* is far more than a mere food. It is the people's only kind of entertainment, the chief break in the monotony of

---

[1] Information collected by Mrs. Gore-Browne.

[2] The Bantu peoples make beer from a number of different sources according to their environment, eleusine, Kaffir-corn, maize, cassava, bananas, honey, and, in the Congo, wine from palms and sugar-cane. The Bemba preference for millet beer is shared by a number of people such as the Bisa (of the swamps), or the Venda of the Transvaal (H. Stayt, *The Bavenda*, p. 35) who grow the cereal specially for the purpose.

[3] Kaffir beer is included as part of the rations issued to mine-workers on the Rand scale chiefly for this reason.

their village life, and, as in most other Bantu societies, the common, and sometimes the essential way of fulfilling social obligations. Beer is the present of honour between kinsmen. It is carried to chiefs as tribute, used to reward labour, or given as an offering to spirits. Nowadays, it may be one of the few ways by which a woman, left deserted by her husband, can make money for clothes.[1] Men cultivate extra ground in order to have enough millet for brewing. Abundance of beer is the glory of a commoner's hospitality, or a chief's court. Without it tribal councils cannot be held, and marriage or initiation ceremonies do not take place. For all these reasons it is impossible to describe the physical effects of native beer-drinking without knowing the part it plays in the Bemba's whole social life. *Ubwalua* is served in big calabashes holding about 2 or 3 gallons, or in disused petrol tins. It consists of a thick brown sludge to which hot water is added constantly throughout the evening so that the brew gets gradually weaker and weaker.[2] It is drunk through a hollow reed two or three gulps at a time. It is a cloudy fluid, often full of gritty particles, with a clear sharp taste not unlike the bitter flavour of English beer. Most natives become positively lyrical as to its qualities. They say it makes them rejoice (*ukusansamuka*) and that it warms their hearts (*ukukafyo mutima*)—the ordinary phrase used for getting excited and also angry. Old councillors at the chief's court who have become used to a regular supply of beer, complain bitterly if they are deprived of it. They say that it is bad for them to eat 'cold food', i.e. ordinary meals, and that they need something to 'burn their stomachs just there' (with a hand laid on the spot), and in fact beer must be much easier to digest in old age than most other Bemba foods.

Beer is recognized as making a man more talkative, liable to quarrel, or indulge in illicit love-making, and men whose hearts get hot quickly, to repeat the native phrase, are avoided at beer-drinks, if possible, because they may involve their friends in legal liabilities. I have even heard of cases where Bemba refused to marry into families with a reputation for becoming excitable when drunk. But drunkenness itself is not despised. In fact the drunkard

---

[1] The sale of beer is illegal in this district, but it is practically impossible to prevent the trading of small quantities.

[2] In samples taken at the beginning and at the end of an evening respectively, Dr. Widdowson found that the alcohol content varied from 4·44 per cent. to 2·10 per cent. (I am indebted to Mr. Douglas Miller of the Education Department for dispatching these samples.)

is regarded with a kind of laughing tolerance or envy and, as will be seen, the tribal drinking customs make it impossible for any one except a chief to become a regular drunkard. A commoner may brew beer more often than his fellows, or feel its effect quicker, but it is difficult for him actually to get much more to drink than they do. In any case, the drunkard is regarded generally as an irresponsible individual, and of anybody who commits adultery or assault when under the influence of drink, the phrase 'an affair of beer' (*umulandu ua bwalua*) is used quite tolerantly.

Some of the deleterious effects of alcohol are recognized. I never heard any complaints or jokes about double vision made, but have several times seen natives refuse to go out tree-cutting the morning after a beer-drink because of 'beer before the eyes' (*ubwalua pa menso*), meaning, I think, fear of giddiness or lack of co-ordination. Headaches are quite common the day after a big beer party. To the European, the remarkable thing about native drinking is the speed with which the people seem to get excited and garrulous. The percentage of alcohol is probably rarely more than 4 per cent., and many of the company get very little to drink during an evening. But it must be remembered that the *ubwalua* is drunk hot which may increase its potency, and also that it is drunk very much less regularly than in this country. The Paramount Chief told me that a great ruler should drink beer every day without exception. Otherwise, if he drank only once or twice a week, he would become drunk like a commoner and stagger about and give bad judgements in court. 'His chieftainship would suffer' (*ukuti bufumu buonaule*). This was obviously in the nature of a 'rationalization', but it is true that chiefs who drink regularly seem to get bemused, but never violently drunk as commoners occasionally do.

But it is probably the fact that beer-drinking is such a social event that accounts for the people's quick sense of exhilaration and even intoxication. Natives gather together from surrounding villages to drink at their relatives' huts and exchange gossip, and this is in itself an interesting occasion in a society in which the local group is so small. Further, beer is drunk by the maximum number of people who can crowd into one hut. At an average brewing three or four calabashes might be available for distribution, and of these one would be given to the headman to share with the elders of the village, another might be given to the son-in-law of the brewer to drink with the younger men of the village, and a third kept in the owner's hut for his near family or special friends. But in each case, after the formal drinking has begun, the original guests are joined by others who enter with a polite salutation, take a short pull at the beer, and stay for a short talk. When there is only one calabash to be divided in the village, each inhabitant will probably join the crowd in the hut at one time or another in the evening. Thus there is a constant coming and going of men and women, and the children who are too small to be left at home. Dancing nearly always accompanies the drinking. In these circumstances it is not surprising that there should be the maximum amount of excitement with the minimum of alcohol consumed. Old women usually drink with the men. It is considered bad form for young girls to do so, and women nursing small children are afraid to join in for fear that the baby might be harmed by contact with a hearth touched by some one ritually impure during the confusion of the evening's drink. Where there is enough beer therefore the women have a calabash of their own.

The guests come together in a condition of pleasurable anticipation. They crowd into a hut about eight feet in diameter and sit huddled on the floor side by side in the closest possible physical contact. The heat is terrific, as the fire is piled high to keep the water boiling and to give light to the company. Sweat pours down naked shoulders. Sometimes singing begins, and the whole company rock to and fro clapping their hands, or they may be wedged still tighter against the wall, and a space cleared for a solo dancer and a couple of big drums. The watchers sway, tap with their feet, and clap the rhythm. At other times the drums stand outside in the village square, and young men and women stream out of the hut to line up for the big round dance—*icila*, or the line dance—the *ngwai*. In these conditions the excitement of social intercourse is probably at least as potent as the influence of alcohol.[1] Real drunkenness, in the form in which we know it, is more often to be found in the modern villages where a man can 'drink alone', or with a few friends and when dancing does not accompany the drinking.

It is difficult to estimate the quantity of beer drunk by the Bemba during a year or an average night. In the harvest months—May to

[1] A compound-manager at Wankie Mine told me that he had found the same amount of intoxication produced among the mine employees at a Christmas beer-drink with an alcohol content of about half that which was usual. He explained it by saying, 'I think they had been expecting to get drunk at Christmas for so long.'

July or August—I should say that beer was brewed in most villages
about once a week. In the subsequent months the supply would be
less frequent, and during the scarce season at the end of the rains
ubwalua would only be found regularly at a chief's court. If asked
how often a woman should brew a year, the answer was anything
from four to six times, which, reckoning about 80 lb. of millet to one
brew, would mean an annual expenditure of about 400 lb. of millet
on beer.[1] Ten brews in one year was described to me as excessive,
with the added criticism: 'That is a woman who likes beer.' But
there is no doubt that in villages near white settlements, people
brew much more often than this because of the profits they hope
to make from the sale, and they even buy grain for the purpose.[2]

On any one night, the amount drunk per head is limited by the
rules of social etiquette. Under village conditions drinking follows
a definite order of precedence. The guests usually arrive between
four and five in the afternoon, after the day's work is done. They
enter one by one shouting: '*Hodi?*—May I come in?' at the door
and crouch on the newly cleaned floor side by side. Water is
bubbling in a big pot over the fire in charge of the woman of the
house, and the calabash, or sometimes more than one, stands ready
on the floor, for water may not be poured on the drink (*ukubiko
bwalua*) until the honoured guests are assembled. The owner then
rinses out his mouth with water and spits on the ground calling
a blessing of the ancestral spirits (*ukupala mate*) for a peaceful
beer-drink. He then hands round the drinking reed ceremoniously
to the eldest man present, who sucks the first draught, pronounces
on the quality of the beer, and hands the reed back to the host.
Drinking then follows in order of age and status. The old men
near the calabash talk and take long pulls at the *ubwalua* in turn,
while the elder women, if present, sit farther off, and rise occasionally to take a couple of drinks and then return to their place. Young

---

[1] Out of an annual production of roughly 2,400 lb. of grain per family (from
U. Moffat's report to the Diet Committee of N. Rhodesia, 1933). It must be
remembered, however, that the woman does not usually cook on the same day
as she provides beer and that she is brewing for the whole village and not for her
household alone.

[2] At Kasaka village during the months succeeding the harvest (1933) out of
11 women, 3 had brewed once; 2 twice; 2 three times, 2 four times, 1 five
times, and 1 six times. In the figures collected by Mrs. Gore-Browne 15
villages had brewed on an average 10 times each in 6 months from June to
January, using 9,400 lb. of millet, but figures are difficult to verify and the pro-
hibition on the sale of beer makes women reluctant to tell the truth on this point.

men come up to the pot later and kneel to take a short draught, usually in silence. Boys might be invited to take a drink as a joke by one of their elders, but they would never stay in the hut all the evening. Young girls chiefly drink at special women's beer-drinks, but on a general occasion they sometimes sit outside in groups of four or five and dare each other to go in to the drinking hut, with much giggling and jokes. I never saw them stay more than about a quarter of an hour. But all such additions to the circle take place later in the evening when the beer is already weak. It is clear in fact that with the formality practised under village conditions, the bulk of the three or four calabashes brewed at one go (*amatimba*) is distributed through the whole community but that the elder men and women have the largest proportion of this supply, the young men a smaller share, and the young women and boys an occasional drink in between dancing. Thus it might be estimated that the average consumption on any one night would be somewhere near $1\frac{1}{2}$ pints per head for an older man or woman, 1 pint for a younger, and about $\frac{1}{2}$ for a young girl.

Under modern conditions these rules of etiquette are often broken. There is apparently little obligation to share beer that is bought with money, and even when the owner has brewed her own supply there is a tendency for it to be shared with four or five people only, or even for it to be drunk alone. In such cases natives will start drinking in the morning and sit at it all day. The formalities of polite invitation and the order of drinking all go by the board, and in the circle of villages round a town like Kasama it would be fair to say that a large proportion of the younger men are regularly drunk every Saturday and Sunday in a way that is quite unlike the slight intoxication of an ordinary village beer-drink. On the other hand, in one or two modern communities, i.e. those on the grounds of some of the protestant missions or in the near neighbourhood, a large percentage of teetotallers is common, since the pledge is taken by many church members. But at present no other substitute form of entertainment seems to have been discovered for the Bemba, since tea is a prohibitive price in this area and the various non-alcoholic drinks made of millet, such as have been issued from time to time by different mining companies, are not commonly made. The drinking of beer, therefore, besides providing a valuable addition to a poor diet, continues to be essential to a normal existence in this tribe.

Beer essential.

G

CHAPTER V

GRANARY AND KITCHEN

Bemba Methods of Storage

BEMBA methods of storage are important from the nutritional point of view. In a tribe with little or no system of trade or barter the diet depends very largely on the amount and types of different foodstuffs that can be successfully stored. Efforts to encourage increased production of native crops are almost useless without a detailed study of their methods of preservation. This chapter, therefore, describes which foods the Bemba are able to store, how they do so, and also, an equally important question, the native system of estimating the amount of food he has available for any given period of time. The accumulation of food as a measure of wealth, legal rules of ownership, and the magico-religious beliefs regarding storage, will be dealt with in a later section of the book.

Storable Foods

1. Grains.

Millet is the only food stored in large quantities. In fact the word *ubutala* (plur. *amatala*) means essentially a millet granary. The grain is stored in the head, dried first in the sun. It is apparently possible to store millet for three or more years, although the natives' supplies are rarely sufficient to enable them to do so. Millet more than a year old is known as *comba*, and is said to be better for brewing beer than for making porridge, but I do not know whether this change in the quality of the grain could be prevented by better storing. As it is, a careful housewife will keep the older grain apart from the new, and at a chief's court it is common to find a half empty granary of *comba* kept entirely for beer. But in the case of a commoner the amount of grain actually stored from one season to another appears to be very small in this area.[1] This question may become of greater practical importance if the natives' ideas of accumulating food should change in the future.

Kaffir corn does not keep well as it appears to be attacked

[1] Cf. p. 36, for figures.

by small insects. This may be one of the reasons for the ousting of what is apparently the older Bemba crop by the more easily stored red millet,[1] and the small quantities of Kaffir corn grown nowadays are usually reaped head by head as it ripens and eaten at once.

Maize is also eaten fresh for the most part. A basket of 30 or 40 cobs may be kept in the granary for the few dishes of dried maize eaten, or they may be hung outside the walls, or on a tree.[2] I only saw one maize granary in the territory, and that had been built by a native who had had experience of cultivation in a European plantation in Southern Rhodesia, and was experimenting with ploughed fields of maize.

2. Ground-nuts.

Every Bemba reckons to store ground-nuts, however small a quantity, since they are such an essential element of his diet. Men of substance build small separate storing bins about half the height of ordinary granaries, while others keep their nuts in carrying baskets with the millet crop. The ground-nuts are always stored in the shell, which probably preserves their freshness, but they are first dried in the sun. Natives make a great distinction between the fresh nuts (*shya shibishi*) and the stored nuts, which are not so succulent and juicy.

3. Other Foodstuffs.

The other foodstuffs used by the Bemba are only stored in small quantities of 50 lb. or less in small containers inside their granaries. The seeds of late sowings of beans, sugar peas, and cow peas are left to shrivel up completely in the sun on the garden beds and then carried home in baskets and stored. *Legume leaves*[2] to be used for storing (*ayanakila*) are cut while the plant is still green, any time from February to April. They are then left to dry in the full sun for a day or more, when the shrivelled remains are stored in gourds or leaf containers. It will be noted that the exposure to the sun is as prolonged as possible by this method of

---

[1] In 1933–4 I found three chiefs with separate Kaffir corn granaries, and, as we saw, this crop is used ritually in some of the ceremonies performed at the capital, but only one commoner had a separate supply of this grain. I never saw more than about 200 lb. stored. Mr. C. G. Trapnell tells me Kaffir corn is quite commonly planted in some other areas I did not visit.

[2] The peasants of the Austrian Tyrol always store their maize in the open air.

drying—a process which is believed to destroy the vitamin content of vegetables.[1]

Gourds, fruit, &c. Gourds may be kept a few months, but not pumpkins. I once saw a small temporary granary of *mpundu* fruit, but I think this is very rare.

Roots, mushrooms, &c. Sweet potatoes, mushrooms, and caterpillars are preserved by a process of parboiling (*ukufubula*) and subsequent drying in the sun. These foods are used during the hunger months but are declared to be insipid.

Cassava is not stored, but eaten from the beds as wanted.

Meat and fish are not preserved in large quantities, because the supply is very scanty, but in each case the raw flesh is smoke-dried over the open fire. There is some trade in dried fish preserved in this way.

Granaries and Storing Vessels

The approach to a Bemba village is usually up a narrow, overgrown path, winding through untidy beds of pumpkins, beans, or maize. On the outskirts, the first buildings that catch the eye are the village granaries—lath and plaster cylinders with thatched roofs ranged in an irregular circle round the dwelling places. These grain bins are of varying sizes, but measure usually about 10 feet high and 20 feet in circumference, and are raised on uprights about a foot from the ground. Each granary stands as near as possible to its owner's hut, the majority round the outside of the village, but a few scattered here and there inside. To European eyes, they are often untidy and inefficient looking constructions. The supports are sometimes unevenly placed, so that the whole structure seems to tilt to one side. The walls may be whitewashed and painted with red, yellow, and black earth, but more often they are just roughly daubed with clay which cracks in the sun. The grass used for thatching is never cut evenly or bound round the edge, and therefore hangs in wisps of different lengths. But these granaries, though they do not conform to our artistic standards, are nevertheless the measure by which the prosperity of a village is very largely judged. Many huts with few grain bins mean few adult male householders in the community. Cracking walls, or

---

[1] Cf. the statement that the women of Nigeria dry their leaves in the shade in order to preserve their food value, quoted E. B. Worthington, 'Food and Nutrition of the African Native', *Africa*, vol. ix, 1936, p. 158.

Building a Bemba granary.

Plastering the granary walls.

Climbing the granary ladder to get out supplies.

uprights eaten by white ants show that supplies are running low. From a cursory glance from the outside, a native will tell you whether a granary is likely to be full or empty. 'Her food will last her till the cold weather', an observer will remark. 'If she had more than a couple of baskets of millet left, she would get her husband to mend the roof again.' And, in fact, this rough and ready means of estimating the well-being of a village probably does not fall far short of the mark.

The *ubutala* is made by tracing a circle from 16 to 20 feet on the ground, sinking a set of uprights to about 9 inches and binding them together with pliable withes (*ulubango*, plur. *amabango*) inside and out and lashed about 1½ feet apart. A rectangular opening about 2 feet by 1¾ feet is cut at the top of the wall to allow the owner to crawl in and out of the granary, and a platform built for a floor raised at about 2 feet from the ground. The wall is then mudded in, and dries in a smooth hard surface in the sun.[1] The roof is built separately on the ground, thatched, and then lifted into position. Subsequently it can be raised up and down at will to allow for the filling of the granary. Two logs (*amapunga*) wedged in position at the bottom of the window level act as a platform on which to stand baskets and other receptacles.

The capacity of such granaries varies. The average circumference of 15 grain bins in one village was 21 feet, the height of the walls to the window level 6 feet, making an average capacity of 661 cubic feet. Chiefs' granaries are bigger, and the four I measured had a capacity more than four times this size.

The millet in such granaries is protected from the heavy rain, but not from the damp. White ants attack the uprights, especially those that support the floor, and this gradually causes the granary to tilt over to one side or the other and finally to collapse. A thick layer of cinders soaked in castor oil is sometimes placed beneath

[1] Measurements of a small granary built at Citimukulu's village (June 1934) were as follows: Number of uprights used, 86. Height of uprights, 9 ft. Circumference of granary, 16 ft. Height of floor from ground, 10 in. Height of first transverse binding (*Lubango lua cishingo*), 1 ft. 10 in. from floor. Height of second transverse binding (*Lubango lua cibilibili*) 3 ft. 5 in. Height of third (*Lubango lua mapinga*) 4 ft. 8 in., forming the level of the window. Height of fourth (*Lubango lua kakolubanga*) was 8 in. above the window level, and the topmost withe (*Lubango pa mutwe*) was 1 ft. 6 in. above it. The measurements of the 'window' were 20 in. by 18 in. The whole took two men three days to build.

the *ubutala* to ward off ants, but more often than not the life of a granary is only two to three years. Nor can rats be kept outside for long.

Filling the granary. All food is dried in the sun before storing. Drying-racks (*icintambi*, plur. *ifintambi*) are built outside each village. These are rough platforms about 6 feet by 2 feet across, raised on uprights 8 feet high, and reached by a notched climbing-pole. On it are piled heads of millet, sorghum, or other crops to be dried before storing. The millet harvest is sometimes put temporarily in a rough field granary (*nkoloso*), usually made of plaited reeds, before it is carried into the village. As the gardens are often eight or more miles from the village, the convenience of this arrangement is obvious. Later the millet is carried into the village by the women in the big round baskets (*umuseke*, plur. *imiseke*) which contain 40 to 50 lb. The roof of the granary is lifted off and each basket is emptied in one at a time, with the appropriate magic of food-preservation (cf. pp. 206–8). When the whole supply of grain has been emptied into the bin, it must be trodden down hard (*ukushindaila*), a process which the natives consider very important for the preservation of their crop. Next, the roof must be raised into position, and the entrance barred with transverse logs.

To take out the grain, the owner leans a primitive ladder of notched logs (*umutanto*, plur. *imitanto*) against the granary, clambers up, removes the barricade across the entrance, squeezes through the narrow aperture, sometimes raising the roof as she does so, and swings herself down into the dark interior of the bin by the platform bars.

Precious seeds or dried legumes are often kept in a clay water-pot (*umutondo*) or gourd, the mouth of the vessel being plastered over with a layer of clay (*ukumashila*). This is apparently an efficient method of storage, and protects all crops except Kaffir corn from rats and insect pests. Another method of storing legumes or ground-nuts is to make one of the grass carriers known as *umubamba* (plur. *imibamba*). It is common to see natives going about the country carrying round egg-shaped bundles of grass tied with a net-work of bark strands, and containing a hundred pounds or so of seeds. The European is at a loss to understand how a ball about 2 feet in diameter can be made of unplaited grass, and how the beans are inserted in the middle. In fact, the method is ingenious. A round or oblong hole about 18 inches across and a foot deep is dug in soft ground. Strands of bark are laid criss-cross over the hole, sometimes with short sticks beneath to strengthen them. A bundle of grass is then spread out on top of the bark fibres and the ground-nuts or beans poured into the lined hole. More grass is then laid on top of the pile and the bark strands beneath pulled up and knotted firmly on top of the bundle, the projecting ends of grass being cut off smooth. The *umubamba* is then complete, light and easy to carry, but giving no protection against mice or white ants. The same is true of the smaller balls, made on the same principle with broad leaves instead of grass (*icifunda*, plur. *ififunda*), which are often used.

Gourds, baskets, or *imibamba* are usually kept inside the granary, balanced on the two transverse rods that make its top platform. Sealed pots of food are sometimes kept in the owner's hut. The *ubutala* platform has, in fact, a haphazard 'untidy' appearance to the European eye—the very reverse of what a well-stocked store-room should be.

Here the European is led to ask whether there is any special value in storing food in vessels of symmetrical shape or size ranged in a given order, as is the custom in the European store-cupboard, or whether the haphazard collection of receptacles found in a Bemba granary are just as efficient. It is obvious that the tins and bottles of the English housewife serve partly to keep air, damp, and animal or insect pests from the food, a function which is fulfilled fairly well by the Bemba granary and sealed jars, less well by the grass bundles and open baskets. But they also help the housewife to keep different foods separate, to save her time in searching for them, and to keep her aware of the quantities of food she has available. Her jars provide her with a rough system of measurement. Now, time is not a valuable commodity in Africa, and the Bemba housewife is quite prepared to sort out three types of relish kept in one vessel. But there is no doubt that the paucity of containers used by the Bemba often causes them to keep seeds for sowing and seeds for eating in the same receptacle, sometimes with unfortunate results. A woman with small supplies of beans, cow peas, or sugar peas seals them up in the same vessel and takes out a handful rather at hazard to cook or to sow. I have known families to eat their next year's seed in this way. Others may be more careful, select their seeds with discrimination and keep them apart, but in any case it is difficult to calculate the quantities of food stored in irregular-shaped vessels like gourds of different sizes. It is not impossible that any educational authority which gave time to the invention of separate storing vessels, roughly speaking of the same size, might gradually improve the process of seed-selection in this area, and also the power of the housewife to calculate the amount of food she has stored.

The problem of estimating the amount of millet available at any period of the year is another difficulty. From the outside the Bemba grain bin is simply an opaque lath and plaster cylinder, through which the height of the grain cannot be measured. Crawling through the entrance at the top, the housewife descends on to the flat surface of the millet. Its level can be roughly measured by the circular withes (*amabango*) described on p. 85, and the woman will say of her millet at the beginning of the season that it is 'up to the second or third withe'. But these bands are very irregularly placed, varying from 15 inches to 2 feet apart, and the builders seem to make no effort to measure the distances more equally. Very few natives seem to count the number of baskets of millet they put into the granary at harvest time, although the men, at any rate, are prepared to have a shot at the figure when asked. It did not usually tally with the rough estimate I made by measuring the circumference and height of the pile of grain. One man guessed 10 baskets, i.e. 500 lbs., whereas the weighed contents proved to be 350 lbs.

The problem, then, is whether the householder knows how much grain he has in his granary, say as compared with what he had last year, and whether his wife is able to calculate how long her food will last and to apportion it accordingly. The answer can only be reached by observing her methods of taking grain from the bin. The woman describes the process of taking out millet from the granary (*ukubansa*) as a very difficult task. 'Only old women know how to look after the food' (*ukutentembe filyo*— to care for or to plan out supplies).[1] To take out the grain, the housewife does not fill her basket from the top, as we might have expected, but scoops out the millet round each side until a column of grain is left standing in the middle of the granary. This may be a half cone leaning against one wall (*cinsenene*), or the pile formed by cutting off segments of the circle each side (*yombe*), or

---

[1] Cf. The slow process of education of the girl described in Chap. VIII.

a central column (*mushinge*). Having reached the floor, the housewife stands on the cleared space and very slowly scrapes down
the millet heads into her basket a few handfuls at a time, taking
care not to shake the main pile of grain. It is very important
not to trample on or disturb it in any way.

At first it seemed impossible to get from the women any explanation of why this procedure was considered so necessary.
I imagined the clearing of a space round the walls kept the grain

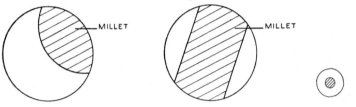

Kubansa cinsenene.   *Kubansa ŋombe.*   *Kubanse mushinge.*

from the damp, and that the method allowed air to reach the whole
of the column. This is probably so, but I never got this answer
from the women themselves, who only replied again and again,
'It is our way of making the food last', or 'A woman who takes
grain from her bin carelessly (*cibansebanse*) will find she has none
left in the rainy season'. They would not, or could not, explain
more clearly. The facts seemed to them to be obvious to the
meanest intelligence and to need no elaboration. At last some of
the men, more able to understand the European's constant pre-
occupation with the measurement of quantities, whether of size or
weight, provided the solution. It appeared that, besides avoiding
trampling and disturbing the grain, the native method enables the
housewife to calculate the amount of her supplies. It gives her,
in fact, a column of grain she can see instead of one she cannot,
and through a slow process of learning, season after season, the
elder women gradually acquire the power of estimating how long
a pile of grain will last, and how often it is safe to brew beer. She
never expresses her calculation numerically in terms of the number
of baskets of grain available in relation to the number of mouths
she has to feed, but she will say, for instance, 'This food will last
till the pumpkins are ripe', and she is usually right! There is no
doubt, however, that a type of granary which allowed for more
exact reckoning of its contents, either by means of more careful

inside marking, or widespread education in counting the number of baskets put in and taken out, would make foresight more possible, and probably act indirectly as an incentive to increased production.

To conclude, the Bemba system of storage[1] allows them to keep their staple crop for a period of about a year, but is hardly efficient enough to make it possible to accumulate for longer periods. Their type of granary, combined with their system of calculation, prevents them from estimating with European precision the size of their crop. They know methods of preserving most of their accessory foodstuffs, however tasteless the results of the process. But in actual fact only very insignificant quantities of legumes and other vegetables are stored, and the people are still largely dependent on the bush for relishes, except in the months immediately after harvest.

The Bemba Kitchen

Bemba methods of cookery depend on their type of fire-place and their cooking vessels. All heating is done over an open wood fire burning slowly on the floor of the hut with no chimney to draw up the smoke. The cooking vessels are placed directly over the fire supported on three conical clay stands (*amaphwasa*) about 1 foot high and 9 inches in diameter cemented on to the floor.

Bemba cooking vessels consist of open earthenware pots of various sizes and shapes which the enamel saucepans of the Europeans are only gradually beginning to oust. The largest pot used for making *ubwali* is known as an *inongo*. It is a big round vessel with an open mouth about 2 feet in diameter, but narrowing in slightly to form a neck. Each housewife reckons to have two or three *inongo* for cooking, but they are too heavy to carry to the river for water. For this purpose she uses a smaller pot with a narrower neck known as a *umutondo*. She may also cook stews in such a pot or in the little bowls about 9 inches in diameter known

---

[1] Other methods of storage are found among a number of the Central African tribes, e.g. the Ila build granaries on the walls of their huts with clay grain receptacles on the platforms (Smith and Dale, op. cit., vol. i, p. 121). Some of the Luba tribes in the Congo also build grain stores inside the hut, but keep maize and legumes outside on platforms on trees in grass containers (P. Colle, *Les Baluba*, 1913, p. 133). The Akele also store food in bundles tied to high platforms built in the centre of the village and thus protect the food from rats and mice (*Les Bushongo*, Torday and Joyce, 1925, p. 91).

The Bemba hearth.
(Photograph posed in roofless house.)

Making a cooking-pot.

The finished pot set to dry before firing.

as (*tunweno*, sing: *kunweno*) in which relish is also served. None of these pots can be covered during cooking, although the process of evaporation can be diminished slightly by covering the food with leaves in some cases. European saucepans are appreciated because they quicken cooking, but even these do not seem to be used with lids.

From a dietetic point of view a knowledge of native methods of cooking is of interest, since it should enable us to tell the extent to which the people either preserve or, alternatively, destroy the nutritive value of their foodstuffs by their methods of preservation, and also the variety in diet they are able to secure. To the sociologist cooking is a traditional art requiring more or less individual skill for its performance, learnt by a special educational mechanism, treated as an honoured calling or else as a menial task. It is also one activity of the many that go to make up the routine of the day or the month. Here it may be said at once that none of the Bemba methods of cooking appear very difficult to acquire or are governed by very precise rules as to quantities, &c. They are nearly all very lengthy however and require considerable energy and pains if they are to be successful. Domestic ability is admired and cooking is considered the centre of the woman's social life, but a comparison of Bemba cooking recipes with those of the Ngoni of Nyasaland or many of the Mashona peoples seems to show that the former are in some ways less ingenious in their use of the different foodstuffs available.

Porridge.

The preparation of porridge (*ukunayo bwali*) is obviously the most important task of the Bemba cook. Porridge is the essential element of any meal, and the time taken to cook it determines the whole routine of eating, and indirectly the tribal practices of hospitality.

To make the porridge, grain is threshed separately each day. The work is exhausting, and it is very rare for a housewife to grind a two days' supply. The millet heads must first be pounded (*ukutwa*) to free the fine grains from the stalks. The Bemba use high wooden mortars (*amabende*, sing: *libende*) from 2 to 3 feet high, in which they stamp the millet with stout poles about 3 feet long. Sometimes the woman stands to pound her grain, stamping rhythmically up and down with hands placed wide apart on the pestle. Sometimes she sits on a stool grasping the mortar with her legs. Another method is to pound the grain in a hollow in the ground. Two women then sit opposite each other with legs apart and pound alternately, singing to keep time. Each holds a flail with one hand, and with a quick movement of the other sweeps fresh heads of millet into the hole in the ground. This last method is probably less efficient, but it is more companionable and preferred by young people. The pounding is exhausting work. The women's bodies steam in the sun and the village resounds with the regular thud of the flails.[1]

The grain has now to be sifted from the chaff (*ukuela*). Winnowing consists in sending the grain swirling with a circular motion of the big open basket (*ulupe*) which sends the chaff to the surface where it can be scooped off while the grain remains beneath. It is then pounded for a few moments again (*ukusokola*) and then winnowed again (*ukupunga*). The chaff is emptied on the garden beds around the village and to this the natives attribute the greater fertility of this land. (Cf. p. 281).

It now remains to grind the flour (*ukupela*). Against the wall of the veranda of each house is a small circular platform, about 9 inches from the ground, worn into a smooth groove with much grinding. In front of this the woman kneels, and on it she places the handfuls of grain which she grinds beneath a small stone. This task is reckoned very hard work and the women sing to lighten their labour. The rhythmic to-and-fro of the grinding stone, and the notes of a song, falling flatter and flatter, are the common sounds in a village in the late afternoon.

The flour so produced is of a coarse quality, and careful housewives sometimes grind it fresh before making the thin gruel (*umusunga*) with which a small baby is fed.[2] Some species of millet are distinguished as being easier to grind than others, and the flour is graded according to its whiteness, Kaffir-corn flour being the lightest.

To cook the porridge, the flour is merely tipped from the basket into water boiling in a big *inongo*. The process of gauging the

---

[1] The conception that the African woman is an overworked drudge is probably derived from the sight of the housewife threshing, but I must add that on the occasion when I was myself most overcome with pity at the sight of the women pounding millet I overheard this remark from one victim to another in reference to myself: 'I don't know how these white women stand it. I should think her neck must ache bent over her writing all the morning.'

[2] Vide, p. 69.

right proportion of flour to water is apparently gained by experience, and no woman could give me a clear account of her reasons for measuring out what she did. To stir the porridge one of the big flat spoons (*miko*), about $2\frac{1}{2}$ feet high, is first dipped in hot water, and then plunged into the seething mass of porridge. It must be held with two hands, the left at the top and the right near the blade, so that the heavy mass of porridge is moved with the whole weight of the body. This is arduous work and the interior of the porridge is sometimes hardly cooked, especially when a young girl cooks for large numbers. The process is complete in two or three minutes, and great lumps of *ubwali*, now brown and smooth and solid, are scraped off the *miko* into the eating baskets. Here they should be patted smooth with the stirrer into balls like plum puddings (*ukumeta*), a point on which the housewife prides herself.

The process of preparing maize flour is very different and reckoned by the Bemba as a troublesome one. The maize cobs must be pounded for long periods in a mortar before the grains become detached. They are then repounded and the product finally ground into flour with the grindstone. This is the ordinary method used by the women of most of the Nyasaland tribes and in Southern Rhodesia, who never seem to complain of the work. The fact that the Bemba are reluctant to use maize flour probably depends on a number of different factors, viz. their preference for porridge made of millet, the low yield of maize on this particular soil, and the unaccustomed nature of the work, rather than its inherent difficulty.

The preparation of cassava flour is a three- or four-day process and therefore alters the whole household routine. To make cassava flour the roots are dug from the beds as they are wanted and roughly peeled so that the shells come off, much of the vegetable being wasted by the Bemba in this way.[1] The inner part of the root must now be soaked. The bitter cassava contains, as is well known, hydrocyanic acid, but the natives do not apparently recognize the plant as being poisonous. Bemba say that some roots taste bitter, and that these are dangerous, but that it is one particular plant at fault, not the rest. Children are often given cassava to chew raw and no ill results are expected. In fact, among the neighbouring Bisa, unsoaked cassava (*kapango*) is sometimes

[1] Bisa scrape it more economically.

pounded and added to the flour made from soaked cassava (*bwabi*) and no evil results apparently follow.[1]

Cassava roots are put to soak in streams or rivers 'until they are soft', i.e. usually two days in hot weather and four days in cold. The roots are then taken home in baskets, chopped, and dried in the sun. After this the lumps of cassava must be pounded in mortars into flour.

This detailed account of the making of different types of flour has a certain practical importance. In any society, living on a subsistence level, the preparation of the staple food must determine the routine of the household. The baking of bread was once the most important activity in our own kitchens and the work of the week was organized round the baking days. It is obvious that the Bemba method of making millet porridge fixes cooking on a day-to-day basis, and these people only use cassava flour as an extra or substitute. But among the Bisa and other neighbouring tribes, cassava is the staple food and household routine is therefore fixed on a four- to six-day basis to allow of the soaking of the roots. Thus the cassava user must look ahead. She must always have some roots soaking, others drying, others being pounded into flour. She must calculate for the probable arrival of visitors. The Bemba cook is not used to planning ahead. No wonder she considers cassava flour unsatisfactory as a staple food.

Relishes.

The Bemba have a number of different ways of cooking relishes and these are listed at the end of the book (p. 406, Table A). As we have seen, the kitchen equipment of the native woman only permits her to boil or stew, and the different dishes used as relish, which she distinguishes with separate names, usually have the same composition but are stewed for a shorter or longer time, or with the addition of more or less water. *Ukuipika*, the word for

---

[1] Mr. T. S. L. Fox-Pitt tells me that the Balunda of Mwinilunga district, N. Rhodesia, recognize a poisonous variety of cassava, i.e. *mulunga*, and say that if roots taste bitter when raw it must not be eaten. Otherwise drunkenness, staggering, and then vomiting will result. Death follows if the man has not been able to vomit up enough of the poison. The Baunga of Luwinga district state that some wizards can bury a medium (*amakayi*) in the centre of a cassava garden and so produce withering and decay of limbs in those that eat the roots from that patch. The leaves of cassava are eaten by Bemba and Bisa and some cases of illness have been reported among the former as the result.

'stew', is, in fact, the general term used for cooking. The chief
methods used are the following:

1. *Stewing (ukuipika).* By this method the food is placed in cold
water in an open earthenware vessel and left to simmer from three
to six hours over the fire, with additional water added if necessary.
Meat and fish are stewed till the flesh falls apart from the bone and
a rich gravy (*umuto*), considered a great delicacy, has been formed.
Green vegetables are also stewed, fresh peas and beans to form the
dish known as *imifoba*, and also the green leaf relish, whether the
wild spinaches or the cultivated plants such as cassava leaves,
bean, cow-pea, pumpkin, &c., leaves, which form the very common
Bemba dish known as *umusalu*. Gourds of different kinds are also
boiled in water until they are soft, and sweet potatoes cooked
similarly with broad leaves put to cover the pot so as to prevent
evaporation. Maize cobs are also most commonly boiled (*kunwe-
nena*).

Dried foods such as beans and peas are usually stewed four or
five hours over a low fire until a sort of puree or paste is formed
(*mintipu*), or the same dish may be dried still harder and patted
into a solid cake known as *citata*, which is an unpopular kind of
food only prepared in the hunger months when it is eaten in the
absence of porridge.

2. *Stewing with ground-nut sauce (ukusashila).* The art of good
cooking among the Bemba is to have sufficient ground-nut sauce
(*ntwilo*) to add to other relishes to make them palatable. To make
the sauce the nuts are pounded into shreds in a mortar (*ukutwila*)
and these shreds constantly taken out in the hand and squeezed
into a small bowl of water, so that the white oil from the nuts
makes a milky fluid. The residue is then returned to the mortar
and pounded again until the last drop of oil is extracted and a
thickish cream results. The *ntwilo* is then ready for use. It is
poured on to any cooked relish, and the whole stewed up again
for a short time with the addition of salt. *Ntwilo* is thought to
make meat or fish stews specially nice, and to be appetizing with
stewed spinaches, locusts, or caterpillars, but with the tasteless
dried leaf relishes and mushrooms it is considered almost essential.
Hence the insistence of the Bemba cultivator that he must grow
at least one patch of ground-nuts every season, although in
actual practice he rarely succeeds in producing sufficient to last
through the year.

3. *Roasting (ukuoca) or dry cooking (ukusalula)*. The Bemba have
no real method of baking or roasting, but they occasionally cook
foods in the ashes of open fires, and prepare sweet potatoes, maize
cobs, or meat skewered on sticks in this way when on a journey.
Another method of cooking is to put the food on an open potsherd
over the fire with just sufficient water to prevent scorching (*ukusalula nkwangwa*). It is one of the few quick ways of preparing a
relish. Fat meat is sometimes cooked in this manner, fresh green
legume pods, ground-beans, ground-nuts, or dried spinaches
softened with a little potash salt (*ifishikisa*). But this latter dish is
only used as a last resource. Natives say it is so dry and hard
'You eat it and it goes crack, crack, crack in your mouth' (*mulelya
muleti kwa kwa kwa!*).

4. *Seasoning*. It is interesting that salt, that scarce commodity,
is only used for the most tasteless foods, i.e. spinaches, dried
potatoes, or mushrooms (*fyafubulula*), the wild orchid (*cikanda*),
and the dried cakes made of legumes (*citata*). It is also used to
bring out the flavour of the ground-nut sauce. It is invariably
added after the cooking. The use of a potash salt (*ifishikisa*) made
from the bark of certain trees, to soften dried spinaches, is an
interesting adaptation to the environment.

Various fruits: Amankolobwe. This is a little cucumber with
a hard, wrinkled skin which is used either as a relish or to be
eaten alone during the hunger months. It may be boiled whole
and the contents sucked through a hole at one end, or it may be
stewed until soft, pouring off the juice to make a hot drink 'just
like tea'. Another way is to pull off the outer skins and to cook
them with *ifishikisa* as a relish in the hunger months. The leaves
provide an unpalatable relish and the seeds are sometimes used to
make a sauce similar to the *ntwilo* made from ground-nuts, 'But',
said a native, 'many people will never eat *amankolobwe*. It is only
fit for a time of starvation. It is a thing to eat when a man is really
hungry'—an interesting statement since this crop was evidently
one of the earliest Bemba foods.

There are several wild fruits eaten by the Bemba. The chief
varieties are the *mpundu*, the *masuku*, and the *umufungo*. These
are eaten raw. In addition a sweet drink is made in the hot season
by pounding both the *umpundu* and *umufungo* fruit with pestle and
mortar, leaving the mixture to stand for about a quarter of an hour
and then squeezing with the hands. This is known as *lumembwe*.

The liquid can be used to cook gruel with millet or Kaffir-corn flour. *Umusuku* fruits can be squeezed with the hands to make a similar drink.

Beer-making.

The process of beer-making (*ukulongo bwalua*) is the longest and most skilled operation the Bemba housewife has to undertake. The brewing may take anything from four to seven days, and the varying temperature and moisture of the air affect its success, so that with the most experienced brewer there is always an element of luck. No housewife could give me exact instructions as to the quantities of grain used and the time taken, but was apparently guided by a judgement based on long experience, or as she herself would express it, with vigour: 'Young girls can't make beer. Only we elders know how to brew.'

The process can be best understood by a description of a concrete case. On this occasion two carrying baskets of unthreshed grain (about 80 lb.) were taken from a granary early in the morning and the whole quantity was threshed. This was heavy work and took most of the morning. In the evening the brewer lined a carrying basket with broad leaves and filled it with the threshed grain. She carried it down to the river and stood it in the shallow water near the bank. This is the ordinary method of starting germination in the grain, and baskets of millet may often be seen soaking in any small stream near to a village. It takes anything from 12 to 24 hours for the grain to begin to sprout, according to the heat of the weather. In this case the tiny shoots could be seen on each grain by midday on the following day, and the sprouted millet (known as *imimena*, from *ukumena*, to sprout) was then spread out flat on a sleeping mat (*ubutanda*) to dry in the sun. The drying must be complete and the beer may be spoilt if the weather is too damp at this stage.

The next stage consisted in the preparation of the yeast, the work of the third day. For this purpose a small portion of the *imimena* is ground into flour and placed at the bottom of a big water-pot. Boiling water is poured on top and the mixture is put aside to ferment. This is the process known as *ukushimpula*, and the thin sour gruel (*umusunga*) which results is left to stand until it begins to froth and bubble and finally to rise over the top of the pot. Temperature again affects the rate at which the

H

mixture will ferment, and in the present case it was two days before the process was complete owing to a sudden chill in the weather.

The yeast had now to be cooked (*ukuipiko musunga*). A great cooking-pot of boiling water was made ready on the fire and into this the bubbling *musunga* was emptied, the mixture being stirred off and on for about three hours and then left to cool. The remains of the *musunga* left behind in the vessel were heated up with more water next day and added to the main body of the ferment so that nothing should be lost. This is the process known as *kuipula* (to take the pot off the fire). The *musunga* was then left another two days to rise again.

In the meantime the rest of the *imimena* grain has been ground into flour and set aside in two or three flat winnowing baskets until the last process of brewing (*ukupoto bwalua*) was reached. This took place on the 28th, i.e. eight days after the setting of the grain to sprout. It is considered the climax of the whole operation, usually watched with excitement by near relatives of the brewer. The floor is freshly mudded over for the occasion and the winnowing baskets of ground *imimena* laid out on it. The brewer then dips a gourd into the *umusunga* now bubbling and frothing once more, and ladles the sour mixture on to the waiting baskets, stirring it thoroughly into the flour, until a thick brown sludge results. After standing for some hours this sludge is then transferred to calabashes and the brewing process is then complete. 'It is beer now' the family explained. After a delay of anything from 24 to 48 hours the *ubwalua* would be ready to drink, diluted as usual with hot water.[1]

This whole process took nine days, rather a lengthy brewing owing to a sudden change in the weather. Other brews I have timed have taken seven days, or even five in warmer weather. The length of time taken has important sociological bearings. It means that beer can never be made available suddenly, but can only be produced after a good deal of planning and work, and under

---

[1] Miss Hilda Shaw, Lecturer at the National Training College of Domestic Subjects, London, commented on this method of brewing: 'Whilst the sprout is developing the ferment diastase is forming and this converts some of the starch in the grain into sugar and boiling water which is then added will destroy all ferments and extract the sugar. On exposure to warm air, wild yeast will collect and multiply in this and form alcohol. The subsequent boiling will, of course, destroy most of the yeast.'

conditions which do not make it possible to be absolutely sure of success. It is also impossible to brew in secret. The whole village knows when the grain has sprouted, how long it has taken to dry, and whether the different processes, *ukushimpula* or *ukupota*, have taken place. Children discuss them eagerly. *Ubwalua* cannot therefore be concealed. 87407

CHAPTER VI

THE ROUTINE OF HOUSECRAFT

Housework.

COOKING is an occupation which has to be fitted into a seasonal as well as a daily routine. The Bemba housewife has to cleanse and tidy her hut and look after her children, as well as prepare the daily meals with all the accessory activities which this implies. Over and above, she is responsible, in this particular tribe, for more than half of the agricultural work of the year, and therefore the time she has free for cooking varies from month to month.

The actual housework of the Bemba woman does not fill so large a proportion of her time as that of a European woman. She has, to begin with, fewer material possessions and a smaller house.[1] Her hut is usually round without windows, and closed with a single door. On one side of the door is the fire-place with its three fire-stands and the drying rack above it. Opposite is the bed, a reed mat stretched across a tiny platform raised off the floor. Besides this, she has cooking vessels stacked round the wall, a blanket and one or two garments, and her husband's axe, spear, or bow. The hut itself is not 'lived in' in our sense of the word, except in wet weather. Natives sit and talk on their verandas or in the men's shelters and usually dance outside. The Bemba's house is therefore a kitchen and a bedroom only, and on special occasions a place where beer drinks are held. To tidy and clean an African hut is therefore a simple job compared with the work of a European woman in charge of a three- or four-roomed house, and living possibly in the smoky atmosphere of a town.

Nevertheless, some housework has to be done. The interior of a Bemba hut looks dirty at first glance. The smoke of the fire blackens the rafters of the roof. Dust and fragments accumulate on the floor, which has not the hard surface of the cow-dung cement used, for instance, in Nyasaland. There are no shelves or

---

[1] From measurements taken of 11 huts the average wall height was 6 ft. 1 in. and the diameter 14 ft. 2 in. The biggest hut measured, that of a chief, had a wall height of 8 ft. 4 in. and a diameter of 17 ft. The more modern type of hut built in this area is rectangular.

Winnowing the grain.
Pounding the millet.

recesses for storing objects, and dried foods lie in confusion on the rack above the fire, or are kept in pots or gourds standing round the wall. Clothes, if the owner happens to have a change, lie on or under the bed; weapons and bundles of bark are hung on pegs on the wall. Magic charms or medicines are concealed under the eaves. Nevertheless, in spite of this air of apparent disorder, the Bemba housewife has certain standards of cleanliness and 'turns out' her hut quite frequently.

The floor, used as kitchen table, chair, and cupboard, must be swept with a grass brush once or twice a day. Though it is not scrubbed, it is frequently mudded over afresh. This is done sometimes for ritual purposes before relighting a new fire ceremonially[1] and sometimes for reasons of cleanliness only. Small babies are allowed to urinate all over the floor, but adults, even in the last stages of illness, demand to be carried outside for this purpose however cold the night. Sleeping mats are washed frequently and blankets put out to air in the sun. The washing of eating vessels is simplified by the Bemba custom of sharing from one dish. Figures showing the employment of time by American farm workers show that these civilized housekeepers spend a quarter to half of the time devoted to domestic work in setting meals and washing up the dishes afterwards.[2] The Bemba housewife, on the contrary, has only two or three eating baskets to scrub and put to dry in the sun. Pottery cooking vessels or enamel saucepans are rubbed with ashes or gravel. Porridge spoons are stood in a special gourd of water and should not be allowed to touch the floor.

The washing of clothes has now become a very important activity to the native, and must be considered under the heading of housecraft. The bark-cloth wraps used before the coming of the white man could not be washed, but a primitive kind of soap made from the bark of a tree natives call *umupape* (*Seguridaca longipedunculata?*), was used to cleanse some of the imported Arab cloth. Nowadays, cotton goods are worn practically universally. Generally they are rubbed against stones in running streams, and in these circumstances it is not unnatural that the white cloth, so much liked by the Bemba, quickly becomes a dirty yellow. Those

---

[1] A frequent occurrence during the infancy of a small child.

[2] 'The Use of Time by S. Dakota Homemakers', Grace E. Wasson, *Homemakers*, Bulletin 247, S. Dakota State College of Agriculture and Mechanical Arts, March 1920, p. 16.

who can afford to use European soap[1] delight to do so, and laundry work, in particular ironing, is considered a fashionable employment and one that is a mark of wealth and status. As such, it is chiefly in the hands of the men, many of whom learn to iron in domestic service. The husbands as the wage-earners are in any case considered sole owners of both their own and their wives' clothes,[2] and when the young man can acquire a bit of soap he likes to wash and iron in public outside his hut, surrounded by an admiring crowd of small boys. Thus the washing of clothes is women's work in the old-fashioned villages, but a male occupation under more modern conditions.

Women care for their children devotedly, but rarely give up any time to them exclusively. Babies are washed with warm water and massaged each morning and fed with gruel twice a day (cf. p. 69), but otherwise they are slung on their mothers' backs wherever they go—to work or to a beer-drink—but are not definitely 'amused' for any period of time or taken for walks. Small sisters do most of the work of supervising the younger children, and thus relieve the mothers.

Preparation of Meals.

If the housework proper, as we have described it, is not a very heavy drain on a woman's time, the preparation of meals and all the associated activities are far longer and more complicated than in our society. Wood for the fire has to be collected daily, or every two days, and this is woman's work. A man fetches wood for his chief, or for a European when required to. For his wife he will only cut down a suitable tree stem on the way back from gardening, and leave it for her to pick up on her return. She usually carries a bundle of dried wood six to eight feet long on her head. When a village is newly built dry firewood is plentiful near home, but in two or three years' time the supply is almost exhausted and the phrase 'she has gone for firewood' (*Aya ku nkuni*) may mean an expedition of an hour or so. On the copper belt the problem has already become acute and well-paid Africans employ servants to gather their wood, or try to buy faggots in the native market —one of the causes of the great increase in the cost of living in urban areas.

---

[1] This practically only occurs in the neighbourhood of a white store.

[2] He wears her clothes whenever he likes, and I have seen men strip their wives as a dramatic gesture in a quarrel threatening to lead to divorce.

Water must also be fetched from the stream morning and evening (*ukutapa menshi*). A good housewife always has one or two *inongo* full of water standing to cool in her hut, and has warm water ready in the early morning for her husband to wash in, and for the baby's bath. No man ever draws for himself under village conditions, and the fetching of water is reckoned one of the essential duties of a wife.[1] The provision of drinking water for her husband is equally a woman's duty, and at a chief's court where old-fashioned ceremony is still observed, his wives kneel to offer him water in a gourd.

Besides collecting wood and water the woman has to provide relish, and this takes up much of her time at certain seasons of the year. During the rainy months regular expeditions are made daily to look for mushrooms. Women and girls go out with carrying baskets and line up across the bush, each picking what she finds. Such an expedition might take two or three hours. Wild spinaches have also to be looked for, and in the hot weather the girls are sent to gather *icikanda* orchids which grow in certain spots known to the natives, or the different wild fruits. Even when garden vegetables are available it may be necessary to walk two or three miles to a distant field to pick them. This is specially so when the gourds and pumpkins ripen, and it is reckoned that every other day the housewife must go out to her gardens to pick them (*ukusaba*) as they reach their prime. All these accessory activities have some-how to be fitted into the day besides the regular gardening and cooking.

The main processes of porridge making and cooking relish are themselves lengthy. The average time taken by seven women to thresh, winnow, and grind flour was 7·4 minutes a pound, and since about six pounds would be used daily by an ordinary family the time taken would be about three-quarters of an hour.[2] These women were, however, working uninterruptedly and knew they were being timed. An hour would be a more likely time under normal conditions. Different relishes take half to three-quarters

---

[1] A middle-aged widower and widow were discussing the possibility of marriage prosaically together. The would-be bridegroom said, 'Are you the kind of woman who always has hot water ready for her husband in the morning, and never grumbles when he asks for more?' The prospective bride answered, 'Yes, that is what I do. But are you the kind of man who gives his wife a new cloth occasionally and doesn't spend his money all on himself?'

[2] For note [2] see next page.

of an hour to prepare,[1] and if vegetables are cooked with ground-nut sauce another three-quarters of an hour must be added, since the process described on pp. 91–3 is a lengthy one.

In all, then, two and a half hours would not be too high an estimate for the preparation of the evening meal, making the total three hours to allow for fetching wood and water.

Thus cooking and all its accessory activities form much the heaviest part of the domestic routine. They add two or three hours on to the day's agricultural work. Even under the old economic conditions this must have led to difficulties at the seasons when the women's gardening activities are particularly heavy, for instance, at harvest time in May or June or during August and September when the cut branches have to be piled for firing and at the same time relish is short and wild plants have to be hunted for. At present with the proportion of men absent the housewife is of course responsible for even more agricultural work and does some of the hoeing, for instance, that her husband would have undertaken. In these circumstances she seems to be definitely overworked at some months of the year—or rather she has to scamp either her gardening or her cooking. For this reason families which have not got young girls to help scour the bush for relish go short of food when the agricultural day has been heavy. An unexpected job like defending the crops against locusts throws out the routine of the day, or if beer is being brewed, there is little time for other work.

Thus here, as in industrial communities, there is the problem of the housewife who is too tired to cook. From the records analysed in pp. 178–83 it will be seen that during the month of

[2] *Seven Women timed in Kampamba Village (time in minutes)*

	Flour in lb.	Threshing	Winnowing	Grinding	Total	Time per lb.
1	4¾	12	14	35	61	12·8
2	7¼	10	13	30	53	7·4
3	11¼	14	15	55	84	7·5
4	9¼	10	15	42	67	7·2
5	12	8	12	45	65	5·4
6	12¼	10	16	71	97	7·9
7	6	11	16	56	83	13·8

Average per lb.: 7·4 minutes

[1] Leaving out of account the dried legumes which have to be left to stew from four to six hours.

September (1933) two out of four women were too tired to cook properly on three days out of twenty and one on four days. Most of the housewives in the village failed to cook on one day. In this case there was the apparently extraordinary situation of women with granaries full of food failing to prepare their families a proper meal. In this particular case four housewives, all elderly women, whom I observed particularly, seemed to succumb, apparently quite unnecessarily, to a kind of lethargy. Whether this was from insufficient food, too hard work the day previous, or an absence of relish to cook with their porridge I do not know, but these women sat still most of the morning talking or doing odd jobs in a desultory kind of way. In the evening they still had not started to grind. I asked, 'Why aren't you cooking?' They said with a shrug, 'There is no relish.' 'Why didn't you go and fetch some?' 'Hunger, Madam! Our strength has given out.' (*Nsala, Mukwai! Maka yapwa!*) They were, in fact, sitting hungry with millet in their granaries and relish to be found in the bush. This is the kind of situation that puzzles the European, who feels certain that with a little more effort the native woman could use her resources to better effect. As a matter of fact, her catering usually becomes less intelligent when she is hungry or exhausted, rather than more so. Necessity, in fact, is not the mother of invention where a shortage of food is concerned, and I have several times seen Bemba react to similar domestic difficulties with the same kind of coma of resignation, when it seemed to me, at any rate, that a little extra push of energy would have solved the problem. The explanation of such incidents is probably partly physiological, and partly also the fact, already stressed, that a people accustomed from infancy to an irregular diet do not feel sufficiently indignant or surprised at missing a proper meal to resist such an event energetically.

Such a break-down of the working arrangements of a Bemba family are rare, but it is a fact that the combination of domestic work with gardening and looking for relish is difficult at certain seasons of the year, and that the food-supply of different households tends to vary with the amount of labour available.

Education in Housecraft.

I never heard a small girl given definite instruction in any branch of housecraft. Children sit endlessly watching the different technical activities of their elders, apparently without ever asking questions or passing comments. They are not strenuously encouraged, as are our children, to learn any particular process, whether cooking or gardening. Of a child who showed no particular inclination to take part in any activity, or refused to do a job asked of it, I have heard mothers remark tolerantly that the little girl had not yet got sense (*takwata mano*) and then give up the attempt. In any skilled process like pot-making, the girl who shows promise at the first try is encouraged to go on, but one less successful is not induced to make another effort. 'She hasn't got sense', would again be a typical comment. Thus learning is a very gradual process among the Bemba with little drive or competitive spirit.

Children practise housecraft among themselves. Little girls of 5 and 6 dig holes in the ground, and sit opposite each other with imitation pestles making believe to pound grain. They carry tiny bundles of firewood and pretend to cook. In fact these are among their few make-believe games. When slightly older they beg for scraps of food, and go to the outskirts of the village where they make small huts of grass and here 'play at houses', cooking on small fire-stands in old pots or cast-off tins. This is a more elaborate game in which small boys pair off with small girls as married pairs. Later, at about 10 or 11, the girls form a community of their own, a bigger girl 'marrying' a smaller one and keeping permanently with her.[1] At this time the girls often make fire-stands on their mothers' verandas and cook more seriously, serving up the meal to friends or even elders. But in every case it is not the parents who are instructing, but the older child the younger. This is also true of the process of learning the different kinds of edible mushrooms or the wild spinaches in the bush.

By 13 or 14 a girl can cook all the usual dishes. There may be a difference to the enthusiast between one lump of *bwali* and another, and Bemba husbands declare emphatically that this is so, but to make fine smooth porridge is a matter of care, not of learning a complicated technical process, nor can the cooking of relish be considered difficult. The brewing of beer is never attempted by younger girls.

Just before marriage, at 14 or 15, I noticed the elder girls become casual and disinclined to help either in the house or

[1] I have only notes on this point from one village.

Fetching water for the kitchen.

First steps in cooking.

Grinding the daily flour.

garden. It seemed as if they were no longer interested in the work carried out quite eagerly by the younger children, but were absorbed with the problem of their coming marriages and the beginning of housekeeping on their own. This fact adds significance to many aspects of the initiation rite (*icisungu*) which followed the attainment of puberty in the old days and still does in some villages. Many of its ceremonies give mimetic representations of cooking and housecraft, and some of the pottery images (*mbusa*) made for the occasions represent the housewife's duties symbolically. These parts of the ritual are all described as 'teaching the girl to cook'. As we have seen, she knows how to cook already, but this ceremony seems to have the function of impressing on the initiate the legal duties she is assuming at marriage. 'When she had not been initiated,' a woman explained to me, 'if she dawdled on the way to fetch water, or refused to grind for her mother, it did not matter. When she is married she must hurry if her husband calls.' This seems to show that the Bemba distinguish between the actual learning of a technical process and the impressing of a traditional attitude of mind towards a duty.

The real difficulty of housecraft is the organization of time and labour, the calculation of quantities by a system which depends entirely on empirical judgements, and, as we shall see, a knowledge of the rules of hospitality and the dues of different kinsmen. All these the girl learns to practise by working both before and after marriage, as a member of a large group directly under the orders of her mother; this cooking team will now be described.

PART III

DIET AND DOMESTIC ECONOMICS

CHAPTER VII

LOCAL AND KINSHIP GROUPINGS

The Problem of Distribution.

I HAVE described the nutritional habits of the Bemba and their methods of cooking and storing food. It now remains to consider their consumption of supplies. In any particular tribe the system of domestic economics determines the amount of food that is consumed. The traditional system of procuring and preparing the different meals fixes the quantities that can be eaten daily, in a community in which victuals cannot be purchased ready for use. The size of the group and the rules by which the food is allocated, regulate the intake of each individual. The type of nutritive inter-dependence between one consuming group and another ultimately affects the regularity and security of the people's supplies, especially in areas without any organized trade or exchange. For this reason, certain characteristic features of primitive dietaries, such as their irregularity from day to day or month to month, can only be explained by an analysis of the structure and functions of the different consuming groups in any tribe.

Among the Bemba it is rare for any individual to housekeep alone. Several households are grouped round one granary and even one kitchen, and are linked by close economic ties with a wider circle of relatives in the same village, with whom they constantly eat in common, and on occasion pool supplies. Hence, in order to understand the daily distribution, it will be necessary to study the composition of the Bemba family, the principles of kinship grouping, and the structure of the village itself.

Besides this regular unit of consumption each household is connected by bonds of sentiment and legal identification with relatives in other villages, 20, 50 or even as much as 100 miles away. In fact these kinship obligations result in quite a considerable distribution of food. If a man's crops are destroyed by some sudden calamity, or if he has planted insufficient for his needs, relatives in his own village may be able to help him by giving him baskets of grain or offering him a share in their meals. But if the whole community has been visited by the same affliction, such as a locust swarm or a raider elephant, the householder will move himself and his family to live with other kinsmen in an area where food is less scarce. The lack of permanence of Bemba dwellings and the ample supply of land makes such temporary shifts easy. In fact, with this particular economic system, it is simpler for the needy individuals to move to a district of plenty than for the food itself to be transferred to them. Hospitality of this sort is commonly practised in the hunger season, when families go all over the country 'looking for porridge' (*ukufwayo bwali*), or 'running from hunger' (*ukubutuka nsala*)—the rather dramatic Bemba phrase used to describe the custom of paying long visits to better-off relatives. Hence the legal obligations of kinship result in a particular type of food distribution, both within the village and the surrounding neighbourhood, which is not found in those modern native communities in which a more individual domestic economy is practised.

It must be remembered also, that food and beer are constantly used to fulfil all sorts of social obligations, to reward labour, or to honour men of position. Large quantities of victuals are actually distributed in this manner, and on this use of foodstuffs the political and economic life of the tribe depends. A study of Bemba catering must, therefore, include the division of the commoner's or the chief's supplies with these particular ends in view.

To conclude, we are dealing with a system of domestic economy in which the year's supplies of each householder are distributed between a group of relatives, either within the village or in neighbouring communities, who share the contents of a granary or an eating-pot, and a type of local and political association largely dependent on the provision of meals and beer. The amount of food available for each family, the regularity of the provision from day to day or season to season, and the variations from area to area are largely determined by these purely sociological factors.

The Bemba Village.

To describe the structure of a typical Bemba village is at first sight a difficult task, since one of its chief characteristics is its lack of permanence. The village buildings are moved, as we have seen, every few years, even though the new huts are usually built within a ten-mile radius, at the most, from the old. But it is not only the site of the settlement that is changed. The community itself alters both in size and composition. It consists in the first instance of a headman who has won permission from the chief to build a village by proving that a party of his near relatives is ready to live with him and to accept his authority.[1] Since polygamy is the exception rather than the rule among commoners, he cannot hope to find a sufficient following among his wives and their children as can the Southern Bantu patriarchs, but he must rely on the strength of a number of other kinship ties which are described in detail below. If he is successful, the village will grow. He and the elder men of the community will attract more and more of their relatives to live with them, while their own children are in the meantime growing up. Thus the composition of the village becomes more varied as the years go by. On the death of the headman, he is succeeded by his heir, his brother, his maternal nephew, or maternal grandson, and the latter in his turn may attract his own near relatives to join the village. The headman's title is passed on in succession just as long as a sufficient body of relatives are willing to acknowledge the new heir. Thus, of the 160 villages in Citimukulu's territory in 1933, 63 had been in existence during the headmanship of three holders of the title, 16 during two, 25 during one, and 46 were new villages just built. In 19 cases, old and new had been amalgamated.

On the other hand, the original headman may have been unsuccessful in holding his village together, and its component households will then have split off, so that the village gradually dwindles in size until it finally breaks up and disappears. This is the inevitable end of all Bemba villages, except in the case of the chief's or the hereditary councillors (*bakabilo*), whose ancestors have ruled over villages in the same locality for twenty or more generations apparently. The changes in the size and membership of a village may coincide with the death of the headman or the appointment of his sucessor but more often with the removal of the village to a new site.[2] The characteristic kinship and political system of the Bemba occasions such changes, and the practice of shifting

---

[1] The personal favour of the chief is also necessary.
[2] Cf. the example given on pp. 156–7.

cultivation provides the opportunity. One fact, however, remains clear. Whatever the changes in its composition, the village remains first and foremost a kinship unit, of which the majority of the inhabitants are directly connected with the headman himself. Even in the communities built in the Kasama area, where natives chiefly assemble for the purpose of looking for white employment, it is still considered unusual to join a community unless some kind of relationship with the headman or some other influential member of the village can be established,[1] although of course, in this case the kinship groups are breaking into smaller and smaller units and the structure of the community is much less closely knit.

The principles of local association among the Bemba are two in number—the rule of primary matrilocal marriage and that of matrilineal descent. The first is the predominant factor in fixing residence, and the nucleus of a Bemba village is a matrilocal extended family composed of the headman, his married daughters, their husbands, and the latter's children. But each man is legally identified with his mother's lineage group and belongs to her clan. He is heir to his maternal grandfather, or maternal uncle, and may therefore leave his wife's village to succeed to an office among his mother's people. In any case, he has the right to remove his family to his matrilineal lineage group after some years of married life. He is the legal guardian of his sister and her children, subject to the rights of his sister's husband,[2] and hence may have to support her if her husband dies or deserts her. If his rank is high, or he has achieved a headmanship, he will find that male and female members of his lineage group will want to come and live with him, wherever they may have contracted a marriage. So that there are many occasions when the matrilocal family grouping breaks down and residence

[1] One of the few regular prostitutes in the Kasama area, who wanted to build herself a hut in a village near the town to follow her profession there, felt it necessary to trace a relationship to the headman in order to establish her right to do so. The kinship was fictitious, but, as the natives said in explanation, 'She kept giving the headman presents and saying she was his sister's daughter until he said: "All right. Build a hut over there."' It was interesting that even an emancipated woman of this type apparently considered it essential to claim and occupy a recognized position in the local kinship group.

[2] There is a very even balance between the powers of the father and the maternal uncle nowadays—cf. my *Mother-right among the Central Bantu*. Essays presented to C. G. Seligman, 1934.

is determined by matrilineal descent, or even in some cases by patrilineal ties, as we shall see. So that we have to deal with a primary principle of local association—matrilocal marriage and a number of secondary ones.

The Primary Group—the Matrilocal Extended Family.[1]

Matrilocal marriage rule

By the rule of matrilocal marriage a man goes to live at his wife's village and works there for his father-in-law for a number of years. Thus, the aim of each man is to have as many daughters as possible since their marriage makes him head of a strong economic unit composed of his daughters, his sons-in-law, and their children. The more daughters a Bemba has the more fortunate he is considered to be. His sons leave him to go and live in their father-in-law's villages and become economically dependent on their wives' families. They move from home at betrothal (i.e. about 12 to 14 years) and remain in the village into which they have married until two or three children have been born. Even if they remove their families home later in married life it is more likely that they will go to their maternal grandfather or maternal uncle, than to their father. But a man's daughters, when they marry, build huts near his own, and if their husbands settle down happily in their wives' community, they remain there more or less permanently and form the backbone of their father-in-law's village, if he is a headman. Hence the Bemba proverb, 'A man is a granary on the veranda (i.e. a man acknowledging economic obligations but living far off) and a daughter is a granary by the door-way (i.e. a source of economic support near at hand).'[2]

Besides the advantage of the presence of his sons-in-law, a Bemba father looks forward to the arrival of grandchildren. With these he is on very intimate terms. As children they sleep in his hut and he and the grandmother play an important part in their education. In early married life the granddaughters will probably remain in his village if their parents are still resident there, and grandchildren of both sexes are welcome to return there later in life whenever they please. The children of a man's daughters are considered a very special asset, whereas the children of his sons, though treated with equal affection, usually live elsewhere. To

---

[1] Matrilocal marriage is still practised but its duration is gradually decreasing.

[2] *Mwaume butala pa lukungu: mwanakashi butala pa muinshi.*

have sons, he says is 'to throw away the seed' (*ukupose mbuto*), but to have daughters is to 'set up a local group' (*ukusange cifulo*).

In a new village there will probably be one matrilocal family group of the type described, i.e. a headman and his married daughters and their husbands and possibly one or two married granddaughters. But when the community has been in existence for a long time, or the headmanship has passed to one or two men in succession, there may be three or four of these matrilocal extended families composed of the daughters of contemporaries of the headman, either men who originally came from another village to marry one of his near relatives and have chosen to live with him all their married lives,[1] or contemporaries of the last headman who have preferred to remain living with his heir. These heads of matrilocal family groups are the most influential members of the community and are known as the 'great ones' of the village (*bakalamba*), and the household of a man who has several married daughters living under his care is known as a 'big house' (*iŋanda ikalamba*). Of the headman of one village who had seven married daughters and their husbands and children—some of the latter also married—living with him, natives exclaimed with rapture: 'Truly that is a big house! My word! That is luck indeed!'

Thus, the chief principle of local association in Bemba society is a man's legal right to the services of his son-in-law. The rule of residence results directly from the type of marriage contract. Among a number of other Bantu peoples, the transfer of material goods, such as cattle, is the essential element of the marriage transaction, and determines the relationship between the groups so united throughout the married life of the couple concerned. But among the Bemba, the marriage payment is insignificant, or was so until the present day. It consisted of a small betrothal present (*nsalamo*) such as a bracelet, a couple of bark-cloths given by the bridegroom to his father-in-law at the initiation of the girl (*fye cisungu*), and at the time of the marriage ceremony (*mpango*), these latter now being replaced by cloth, or a few

[1] This was apparently quite common in the old days, though rare now. In most villages one or two old men are described as having 'come here to marry' and in one village (Kacienja, near Shiwa Ďandu 1931 and 1934) a man had actually become headman of his wife's village, assuming authority over her relatives, although he was of course unable to officiate at ceremonies to the ancestral spirits of the community, which office he delegated to a member of his wife's lineage group. [2] *Iŋanda ikalamba iena! Mwandi! Te kushyuka!*

shillings in money. It was the labour of the son-in-law over a
certain period of years that was the essential tie uniting the families
bound in marriage. In the majority of cases this is still so at the
present day, though the changes produced by the absence of many
young sons-in-law at the mines will have to be described.

The Secondary Groupings—the Matrilineal Descent Group.

The matrilineal descent group can never be the chief principle
of local association in a society that practises matrilocal marriage,
permanent or temporary. Among the Bemba a man is legally
identified with his mother's lineage group. To this descent group
belong his mother (*nyina*, plur. *banyina*), her brothers (*nalume*,
plur. *banalume*) and sisters (*banyina*), and the latter's children
(*umunyina*, plur. *bamunyina*); his own brothers (*munyina*) and sisters
(*nkashi*), and the latter's children (*umwipwa*, plur. *bepwa*); and, two
generations below him, the children of his sisters' daughters
(*umweshikulu* plur. *beshikulu*), who also belong to his clan. In
this group the women members remain very closely associated throughout life. The girl lives with her mother and sisters
during girlhood and early married years. She may continue to
do so all her life. At any rate she constantly returns to visit her
mother even if she is officially settled in her husband's village
after some years of marriage. She summons her mother, and
probably her sisters, to spend long weeks with her, especially if
the birth of a child is expected. But the rule of matrilocal marriage
naturally divides the men of the matrilineal descent group from
the women, at any rate during their youth and early manhood.
A young man normally lives neither with his father's people nor
his mother's, but in the village of his bride. It is only if he has
contracted a marriage within the village in which he was brought up,
that he will remain associated with his sisters and parents. Neither
the girl nor the boy necessarily live in the village of their mother's
brother (*nalume*), who is their legal guardian, unless something
has happened to break up the matrilocal family group into which
they were born, or unless the boy has married his cross-cousin
(*umufyala*, plur. *bafyala*) and therefore the mother's brother becomes a father-in-law (*shifyala*, plur. *bashifyala*).[1]

Nevertheless, the ties uniting the matrilineal descent group
remain very strong and, as I stated, determine residence, in some

[1] Both types of cross-cousin marriage are practised.

instances. This is especially the case with the brother-sister relationship in which the emotional and legal bond is very close. A man calls his sister by a special term—*nkashi*—to distinguish her from his classificatory sister whom he calls *munyinane* (plur. *bamunyinane*). A woman calls her brother *ndume* as distinct from her classificatory brother, whom she refers to also as *munyinane*. Both usually speak of this relationship in what struck me as a specially sentimental tone of voice. Natives seem to take pleasure in describing the brother's duty to look after (*ukusunga*) his sister, and say as a reason for this obligation that 'the man and the woman were born together from the same womb'.[1] The relationship is the subject of many proverbs and folk-tales in which the brother and sister are represented as succouring each other. In daily life, the man is on easy terms with his sister, particularly in the case of the royal family, where the interests of the two are specially identical. In Bemba society where there is a very even balance between patrilineal and matrilineal kinship there are two possible legal guardians for a woman, her father, or her mother's brother. After her father's death her brother takes the latter's place if he is old enough. Otherwise the mother's brother will look after her. Either brother, or mother's brother, will protect her if her husband dies, and defend her interests, if necessary, during the latter's life.[2] In the old days it was apparently quite common for an elderly woman to return to her brother's village to settle there in her old age and this she was able to do even if her husband remained alive by providing one of the brother's daughters as a substitute wife—*mpokoleshi*—in her place. Nowadays, besides the older women, younger women, widowed, divorced or deserted by husbands away at the mines, put themselves similarly under the protection of their elder brothers, and the phrase *Aya kuli ndume*—'she has gone to her brother'—signifies the return of the woman to her own matrilineal descent group.

The brother and sister also exert reciprocal rights over each other's children. In the old days the *nalume* had supreme power over his sister's son, and could even offer him as a slave in compensation for some irreparable injury he had committed to a

---

[1] *Bafyelwe pamo mwuifumo limo.*

[2] If the brother is younger than the sister the position is reversed and I have found a young man with no obvious male guardian alive, living at the elder sister's village, having contracted a marriage there at her suggestion.

third party. He could send for him to accompany him to war or to make a long journey at the chief's bidding. Case histories of older Bemba show frequent instances of men having settled in villages far from their original birthplace because they had 'followed their *nalume*' on some distant expedition in warrior days and had remained there. Nowadays the *nalume* can only exert these powers if he is of superior status to the father, or if the latter is away, or dead. The *nalume* has also certain rights over his maternal niece—also called *umwipwa*. He is consulted about her marriage and usually given a share of her marriage payment (*mpango*), which is technically speaking 'eaten' by the father.[1]

Effect of money currency Direct European teaching and the introduction of a money currency have strengthened the father's authority over his children as against those of the mother's brother. The former pays tax for the household, buys the children's clothes, and pays the school fees. But, on the other hand, marriage is less stable under modern conditions, partly owing to the break-down of marriage morality and partly to the absence of so many men at the mines. In these circumstances, those few men who remain in the villages are bound to look after their sisters' children as well as their own in the last resort.

The paternal aunt, the *nyina senge*, also has rights over her brother's children and particularly his daughters. She is believed to have power to bless or curse her brother's daughter (*umwana senge*) with fertility or barrenness, and is much feared on that account.[2] In the old days she could demand her niece as a substitute wife for her husband—the *mpokoleshi* marriage described on p. 115, or as an additional one.[3] But the rights and duties of the *nyina senge* do not determine the residence of her *bepwa*, male and female, to any extent. However, it must be remembered that cross-cousin marriages unite the households of brother and sister even more intimately than before, and that where the boy marries his *nyina senge's* daughter, he will go to live in her village, just as he who contracts a union with his *nalume's* child, goes to live in the latter's community. The sample village analysed

---

[1] This custom, an act of grace to the *nalume*—not his right, has become more important nowadays since money from 2s. 6d. to £1 has been substituted for the two bark-cloths given as *mpango* in the old days.

[2] And also given a share of the *mpanga* if possible.

[3] Nowadays this right seems to be rarely exerted. I only met three cases of its occurrence.

in Chap. X shows a number of such cross-cousin marriages
uniting the children of brothers and sisters together and the
proportion of marriages of this type in Bemba society is 30 per
cent. according to my figures.

Hence in any Bemba village it is common to find the headman,
and the other elders of the community, responsible for the welfare of
the two types of group—a primary matrilocal extended family
composed of a man's wife, his daughters and their husbands, his
granddaughters and their husbands, and possibly his wife's mother,
and a secondary matrilineal descent group composed of a widowed
or deserted sister and her children married or unmarried, or her
grandchildren. In each case his duties may extend to relatives in
the classificatory degree if these are left destitute, or to kinsfolk of
the headman's predecessor in the same degree, i.e. mother, sister,
daughter. His relationship to the members of the two groups may
be represented thus and his pattern of behaviour to each entirely
different:

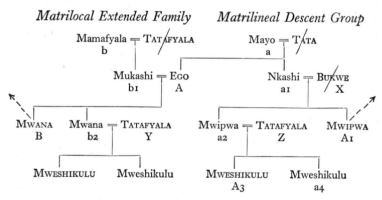

Matrilocal Extended Family   *Matrilineal Descent Group*

DIAGRAM: N.B. Men represented by capital letters; women by small type; a
line through a name represents death; an arrow means residence in another
community. A is here head of:

   (a) his own matrilocal extended family in which his daughter b2 marries
      and remains in his village and his son B marries elsewhere. He is also
      supporting his widowed mother-in-law (b);

   (b) the female relatives of his matrilineal descent group: his mother a, his
      sister a1, whose husband X is dead and whose daughter a2 is married in
      the village, while her son A1 has married outside. By cross-cousin
      marriages between A1 and b2 or B and a2 these two men would have
      remained in the village.

Mayo	= my mother	TATA	= my father
Mukashi	= my wife	Bukwe	= my brother-in-law or in-law generally

Nkashi   = my sister   Tatafyala = my son-in-law, father-in-law, ma-
Mweshikulu = my grandchild   ternal niece's husband
                    Mamafyala = my mother-in-law
                    Umwipwa = my maternal niece or nephew
                    Umwana   = my son or daughter

Additional Households.

Besides the relatives for whom he has the strongest responsibility, there are a number of other kinsfolk who may join a
headman and accept his authority. These are, roughly speaking,
of two types: (*a*) destitute persons, chiefly women, who want his
support, or (*b*) relatives of either sex who are not necessarily in
poor circumstances, but who may be attracted by an elder relative's personal popularity or rank to settle with him. These
latter may include young men whose normal male guardian is
dead, or middle-aged men who want to settle somewhere temporarily, until their own personal following has become big enough
for them to risk setting up a community of their own. These
additional households may include in the first category, widows
of the headman's *nalume*, whom he is bound to inherit or else
support; poor relations of his wife, or women who claim the term
of grandmother, mother, sister, cross-cousin, or granddaughter
but are only distantly related. The second group may consist of
male relatives of the matrilineal descent group—younger brothers,
maternal nephews, cross-cousins, or grandsons—who have chosen
to return to live with him after their period of matrilocal marriage
is at an end, or, if the headman is a man of high position, his own
sons—almost invariably the case at the court of a chief where the
'sons of the chief' (*bana bamfumu*) have a regularly established
position at the capital, bring their wives to live with them, and
rival the maternal nephews, the rightful heirs, for favours.
Nowadays, clerks earning good money in European employment
are similarly able to attract their sons to settle with them, and
the statement *aya kuli wishi* ('he has gone to his father') or even
atemwa kuli wishi ('he likes his father') may cause some comment,
but no surprise at the present day. Thus, the presence of the
father-son grouping in a Bemba village occurs, however infre-
quently, although such an association seems to run directly counter
to the rules of legal affiliation. Grandsons either through the
daughter or through the son also tend to join a grandfather of
rank or position.

Hence, though the Bemba village is a kinship unit, its composition is by no means rigidly fixed. There are certain main principles of local association, but the practice of temporary matrilocal marriage makes for a good deal of change from one community to another, and the even balance between the powers of the father and those of the maternal uncle allow a man a number of possible allegiances.[1] Admiration for rank, or for wealth under modern conditions, sometimes cut across the principles of kinship, so that men may be found living with more distant rather than nearer relatives. The former have a higher status. Added to all these factors the Bemba are great visitors and from childhood up spend months or even a year or two 'seeing' relatives (*ukumona bantu*) in different parts of the country, and this habit of movement seems definitely part of their social system.[2]

Modern Changes in Village Structure.

In spite of the possible variations in the composition of a Bemba village, it remains a closely knit unit. The pattern of behaviour between the different relatives and the legal obligations that bind them are traditionally fixed. If a man settles down in a community, and builds a hut there, he does so usually as a son-in-law of a man of that village, more rarely as a brother, a maternal nephew, or a maternal grandson, and very occasionally as a son. If a woman leaves her parent's village and joins another community she goes there either as the wife of a man returning to live with his people, or as a deserted or widowed woman taking refuge with the members of her own matrilineal descent group. In either case, the behaviour of each new arrival is fixed, and also their type of economic inter-dependence as will be described in the next chapter. In a modern village there are two marked changes. In the first place these settlements are no longer composed of close relatives of the headman, but consist of a series of small kinship groups —two or three households, a mother and two married daughters,

[1] Compare the much more fixed structure of the village in a matrilineal society where patrilocal marriage is practised, i.e. in Melanesian societies where the boy goes to live with his maternal uncle in adolescence and marries there, or in the composition of the kraal among the strongly patrilocal, patrilineal Bantu societies in South Africa.

[2] Missionaries claim that the building of permanent villages in this area would ease the problem of locating schools. This is true, but it would be unlikely to stop the children of the village being sent to 'see' their grandparents 30–50 miles away for six months at a time.

a man and his wife and his mother, &c. In these circumstances the unit of economic co-operation is smaller than formerly; the families detach themselves more easily and go to join other villages according to their fancy; and the authority of the headman is lessened, since his kinship with them is slighter than in the old-fashioned village.

A typical kinship unit of the old-fashioned type is described in greater detail in Chap. X. An analysis of the social structure of a number of such communities can be found in Appendix, Table E, for those who have a special interest in kinship problems. The economic system based on these types of local grouping must now be described.

The Village Scene.

The huts in a Bemba village fill a circular or oval space in the middle of a ring of garden-beds. Those on the outskirts are built side by side, anything from 3 to 20 ft. apart, each with its door facing to the centre. The huts in the centre are scattered without much determinate plan.[1] When building a village the older men take the good sites such as small eminences or ant-hills, and their huts tend to be larger and better built. Their sons-in-law either build close to them, or else, if there are sufficient young men to form a group of their own, these construct their huts round the open dancing space (*ulubansa*) at one side of the village. The granaries of house-holders living on the outskirts stand in a ring on the garden-beds, the others are placed near their owners' huts. The men's club-houses (*nsaka*) are nothing more than open shelters, roofs supported on uprights, and these are usually built at each end of the village.

Huts are circular or square in shape,[2] with broad verandas in the case of men of substance. A man and his wife sleep in each hut, but any child over two or three (the weaning age) is sent to sleep with its grandparents, and in an old couple's house it is common to find five or six small children stretched in a row on a mat in front of the fire. Young girls usually sleep in the hut of a young married woman whose husband is temporarily away, or with a widowed woman. They often change their sleeping-

---

[1] In the larger chiefs' villages the huts are divided into *icitente* (*ifitente*), separate areas under the control of a headman.

[2] The square huts are the more modern variety.

place each night. Boys build houses for themselves in twos or three.

Life is lived almost entirely in the open, on the verandas or on the ground in front of each house, and the doors are rarely closed by day. Each villager can see or hear most of what goes on next door in a community of an average size, i.e. of 30 to 50 huts. The Bemba even prepare their food as far as possible in the open—one of the most important sanctions for their particular system of distribution, as we shall see. Strolling through the village late in the afternoon the European will notice little groups of women and girls working together at different tasks. Two women may be grinding side by side at one grindstone, while others have carried their mortars to the door of the same hut and are pounding their grain in unison. On another veranda a group of young girls are shelling nuts, while the leaves for a vegetable stew are being cut and stalked by an older householder. Two grandmothers may be squatting by the fire stirring the porridge, while babies from various households are scrambling in and out of the hut on the lookout for tit-bits. Little girls between 8 and 12 belonging to different families come into the room to beg for something to cook on their own fires, and retire, laughing and talking, to miniature fire-places at the back of the veranda. Young matrons come in and out to borrow pots or a pinch of snuff—there is, in short a constant coming and going of women from hut to hut, while the boys and men of the different families are somewhere in the distance. Even the head of a household, returning from work, will not linger in his hut while cooking is in progress, but will stoop to enter the door, throw his spear silently on the bed and go off to wait elsewhere.

The division of the porridge each evening is an impressive sight in a big hut, and shows at a first glance that the catering far exceeds the limits of a single household. The housewife, probably an old woman, squats on the floor in front of the fire with four or five small eating-baskets beside her. From the great steaming pot on the hearth she takes lump after lump of porridge on the stirrer and slowly, appraisingly, scrapes off the right amount into each receptacle. A ring of younger women and children watch the spoon intently as it hovers a moment above each basket, and later descends to smooth each portion of *ubwali* into round balls. Next the relish is divided into a motley collection

of dishes and enamel basins, and each is covered with a basket.
Then the housewife hands them one by one to waiting children,
saying, 'For X', 'For Z', and the little boys and girls hurry off to
different huts or *nsaka* in the village carrying their loads on their
heads.

During meal-times a different form of grouping displays itself.
The unit of food preparation does not coincide exactly with the
unit of consumption, although both exceed the limits of the
individual family. The first division of the community at meal-
times is along the lines of sex. Men and women eat separately.
Even husband and wife never share a meal, except at night in
the privacy of their own hut. It is considered shameful for the
two sexes to eat together, and the Bemba women back from the
mines who occasionally copy the European custom of joint meals,
usually do so out of bravado, and are spoken of in bated breath.
To say, 'She eats with men' is almost equivalent to calling a
woman a prostitute in all but the urban areas, and the efforts of
some educationalists to introduce family meals as part of 'Christian
family life' have been hotly criticized by older natives.

This grouping of the sexes at meal-times is further subdivided on
the basis of age, kinship, and friendship. Nobody eats alone. Each
belongs to a set of his contemporaries who regularly share meals
together. The grouping by age is not absolute, but is customary
and follows the people's inclinations. In a small village it is usual
for all the *bakalamba*—'big men'—to eat together at their own *nsaka*
or to group together in turn on one of their respective verandas. In
a larger settlement there may be two or three such groups of old
men usually united by close ties of kinship. The young men eat at
the village shelter where their food is regularly brought them.
It may not be possible for all the young married men of a village
to eat round one dish, for the in-law avoidances, still punctili-
ously observed among the Bemba, prevent a husband from feeding
with any of his wife's relatives, real or classificatory. Hence it is
customary to find round the village *nsaka* at least two groups—
the young men born in the village and the outsiders who have
come into the community to marry their sisters or cross-cousins.
When the porridge arrives they form into two rings back to back
round their own dishes. In larger villages there is a greater choice
of possible associates, and personal friendship and geographical
propinquity help to fix the choice. Even where the *nsaka* system

has been almost abandoned, as it has in modern villages near Kasama,[1] the young men regularly eat in fours and fives, and any intelligent boy or girl in the village will tell you promptly with whom X or Y eats.[2] On a journey with a party of carriers, a European will notice that within a day or two his followers settle down to share their rations in messes of their own which they describe as a *conto*, which can be roughly translated as a place to warm oneself.

The women do not belong to fixed eating groups of this type. They share their food on the verandas of different huts, two or three nearly related households eating together with the children of each. Girls continue to eat with their mothers until they marry, and usually afterwards. Boys of 9 or 10 are considered too old to eat with the women and are expected to forage for themselves. They trap birds and moles, sit hungrily round the young men's *nsaka* waiting for remains, and only occasionally are lucky enough to get a special dish cooked for themselves.

It is clear then from the most superficial description of village life that food is prepared and consumed in a larger unit than the individual household; that the women of several huts join together to cook, and meals are shared by small groups based on sex, age, kinship, and marriage rules. The effect of such a system of catering on the dietary of the Bemba must now be described.

[1] The greater movement of natives in these suburban villages makes them unwilling to build shelters in order that 'others may sit in them'.

[2] It will be seen that these particular eating customs, common in Bantu Africa, make it exceedingly difficult to make quantitative records of the daily intake of each individual, as food weighed and cooked in one hut is eaten by a varying number of people in another—a difficulty that nutritional investigators will have to face.

CHAPTER VIII

THE DOMESTIC UNIT

Daughter Households.

IF the kinship of the women who regularly thresh and grind together be studied, it will be found that they mostly stand in the mother-daughter, grandmother-granddaughter or sister-sister relationship—that they are in fact the women of the matrilocal group. Among the Bemba, joint domestic activities are based on the kinship of the women householders, not that of the men as in patrilocal communities. These closely related women form a co-operating group—grandmother, mothers, and daughters with the grandfather at their head. The young man who marries into the group is in fact almost an outsider during his first few years of wedded life and only gradually acquires economic control over his household, let alone the right of choice of residence, or power to remove his children to his own village. The cattle handed over as *lobola* to the bride's father in South Africa are described as a permanent guarantee of the good behaviour of the married couple towards each other, but among the Bemba the bridegroom has to work for some years in a position of economic dependence in order to prove his worth as a husband or father at all, and during this time his wife can be removed if he fails to carry out his obligations. The bride and bridegroom at marriage have no food-supply of their own. On his bethrothal a youth goes to live in his bride's village.[1] He cuts gardens for his father-in-law, directly under the latter's orders, and does any other work, such as hoeing, that may be required of him.[2] He builds himself his own hut, which his future bride, possibly a young girl of 10 or 12, sweeps and tidies for him, and in which she is later allowed to go and sleep until signs of approaching puberty make her mother afraid she

---

[1] The following description applies to the system of marriage apparently practised before the coming of the white man, and still observed with certain modifications in the majority of cases. The changes caused by the introduction of money payments for service and by the absence of the young men at the mines will be discussed separately.

[2] Chiefly the tree-cutting preparatory to making millet gardens. A son-in-law always describes his own marriage as, 'I cut trees for him for so many years', and the money sent back to his father-in-law by a youth at the mines is called 'money for tree-cutting' (*ndalama shya kutema*)—now about 10s. a year.

may become pregnant before her initiation ceremony (*icisungu*) has been performed. After this rite the marriage ceremony itself takes place, and the bride returns to her husband's hut.

During this period of betrothal and early marriage the bridegroom is fed by his mother-in-law who sends him dishes of cooked food, which he shares with the other young men in the village. If he has married within the family or village, the bride's mother does not consider herself entirely responsible for his food, but still sends him dishes when convenient. The wife meanwhile continues to eat with the women of her own family. After a time a bridegroom may choose to make a separate millet patch of his own as well as clearing the bush and working in his father-in-law's garden, but in either case his nutritive dependence is unchanged. At harvest the grain is carried to the granary of his wife's family and for some years after marriage he is not allowed to build a store of his own. His wife in the meantime is equally dependent on her mother's household. She is not even allowed a fire-place of her own, and is considered unfit to cook or handle her supplies. A young girl's hut has a fire, but no cooking supports for her pots, and she does all her household work as one of her mother's working team. About a year after the marriage ceremony the girl is 'given a fire-place' (*ukumupela shiko*) by her mother, and is allowed to cook in her own hut the flour ground in her mothers'.[1] Hereafter the mother will occasionally give her daughter a basket of millet to grind and cook for herself instead of sharing in the family supplies. It depends how much food is available on any one day, for it is recognized that it is more economical for people to eat together from the same dish. But to be given grain to grind herself, whether for beer or porridge, is a privilege highly appreciated. It is the bride's initial step of independence, for it gives her the right for the first time to distribute food or drink to her own and her husband's friends. As a next step, the son-in-law builds his own granary, if his wife is considered fit to take charge of the grain-supply. The young couple continue to rely on the parent household for additional support, and the wife still cooks and eats her food with her mother and sisters. Later the young married people, themselves probably parents by this time, become completely responsible for their own commissariat, although the woman, if she continues to live in her own village, carries her basket of millet to her mother's

---

[1] I never saw this ceremony performed, and have no full account of it.

hut, and cooks and eats it there with her relatives and children. Delicacies such as meat, fish, or beer are divided between the houses. If the husband later removes his wife to his own village, the exchange of gifts and the visits of grandchildren still persist.

Thus in the old days the Bemba husband acquired sexual rights over his wife for five or six years before he could consider himself the economic head of his household, and even nowadays the period is normally two or three years. The power to allocate food and beer to his friends, the ambition of the young husband, is a privilege only gradually won.[1] Control over his children and the right to remove them and their mother to his own community, should he desire to do so, is achieved last of all. The bridegroom has in fact to change his position from being almost a stranger in his wife's village to one of considerable standing and even authority, when he comes to have married daughters and hence sons-in-law of his own. I have seen a young bridegroom stand sheepishly in the distance watching his wife laughing and talking with five of her female relatives on the veranda of her mother's hut. He was afraid to ask her to bring him water, scared by the sight of so many members of his wife's family all sitting together, and unable to join the group because of the in-law avoidance rules. Yet he would have been demeaned in Bemba eyes if he had gone to draw the water himself. Onlookers were much amused. 'Look he is afraid to call his wife,' they said, smiling, but made no offer to help. The position of a young son-in-law is in fact considered exceedingly funny, and Bemba delight to point out his embarrassing situation. Later in life, as the father of three or four married daughters with children, he has a very different status, and, if he choose to remain in his wife's village, he is accepted and honoured as one of the *bakalamba* of the community.

The husband's dependence on his wife's family is brought to an end by definite stages. These are ceremonially marked and the assumption of behaviour proper to each is traditionally defined. The relationships between a man and his affinal relations are not left to the hazards of an informal process of adjustment and individual reaction as in our own society. On his betrothal the son-in-law receives a series of ritual presentations of different foodstuffs from his mother-in-law (*ukushikula*) which make him

---

[1] Cf. Chapters XI and XII for discussion on distribution and conceptions of wealth.

free to eat the foods she has cooked for him.[1] After a period
varying anything from five to fifteen years he is ceremoniously
admitted to his wife's family (*ukumuingishya*) 'to make him enter
in', and after this feast and dance the keeping of the in-law taboos
is at an end. This rite takes place when the marriage appears
absolutely stable and two or more children have been born, and the
ceremony is no mere picturesque survival at the present day. The
early years of Bemba marriage are a genuine period of trial, and
fathers-in-law do not hesitate to refuse to admit their daughter's
husbands into their family if the latter have not won their full
approval. I heard of a case in which a man performed the *ukuingi-
shya* ceremony for his youngest son-in-law after a period of two
years, because he was a steady, likeable fellow, but postponed the
rite for ten in the case of his eldest daughter's husband who was less
dependable. It is only when husbands are scarce, under modern
conditions of absentee labour, that fathers are afraid to exert their
jurisdiction over their sons-in-law in the traditional way.

Effect of absentee labour

The Symbolism of Cooked Food.

The feeding of the *shifyala* is not only one of the economic
obligations of the marriage contract, but part of the complicated
pattern of etiquette prescribed between the bridegroom and his
wife's family. It is, in fact, one of those instances in which the
giving and receiving of cooked food has become symbolic of the
legal or economic relationship which entails it. It is particularly
important to notice that the preparation of porridge and relish is
the woman's most usual way of expressing the correct kinship
sentiment towards her different male relatives, for this actually
affects the distribution of food in the community. The case of the
son-in-law is characteristic.

The Bemba custom of sending food to the son-in-law, *ukutebeta
shifyala*, with all the ceremonial that surrounds it, is one of the
essential elements of the prescribed etiquette between the wife's
family and that of the husband. The young son-in-law may be
an outsider and a nobody in some respects, but he must be treated

---

[1] The full series of ceremonies are rarely performed nowadays, but the son-
in-law will probably be made ritually free of one or two of the chief foods.
Compare the observance of the *Hlonipa* customs of avoidance by the Zulu
bride, coming to live in her husband's village according to the principles of
patrilocal marriage, and the ceremonial by which she is gradually made free to
drink the milk in the kraal of her relatives by marriage.

with the right courtesies. He must have that due so precious to
the Bemba, and so constantly the subject of discussion—*mucinshi*
—which might be translated respect, courtesy, or recognition of
one's rightful status.

The first dish of porridge sent to the young bridegroom is
considered an interesting and exciting event even in present circumstances, when much of the ritual surrounding it has been
dropped. A little girl of 12, betrothed for the first time, explained
to me with shining eyes what would happen when her 16-year-old
bridegroom came to take up his residence in her village that night.
'We shall make him porridge,' she said in delighted tones, 'we shall
send it to him where he sits in the men's shelter. He has become our child, i.e. a member of our family, or a dependent of ours'
(*Asanguka mwana uesu*). Women like to speak of the food they cook
for their daughter's husbands. To provide big dishes of porridge
and occasional gourds of beer for her *shifyala* is a wealthy woman's
pride, and she will take great care to serve and cover the food
baskets in the correct way (*ukupikula*). In fact, the Bemba, who
delight in the ceremonious carrying-out of obligations, like to
make a parade of this custom of feeding the son-in-law, particularly to a stranger. A native sitting in my tent would often
turn and look through the open door and point out with a pleased
expression the small boys with baskets of porridge on their heads
who were walking off to the men's shelter, and exclaim with
satisfaction at the sight. A typical comment would be, 'Look!
They are carrying food to the sons-in-law! It is *mucinshi!* That
is our custom; and in the old days it was just the same.' It is not
uncommon for women to deny themselves food rather than let
their daughter's husband go short. In the hunger months I saw
a more or less starving old woman near Kasama prepare her last
dish of food for her son-in-law, who was himself a well-paid young
teacher at the Government school. She went without herself. 'It
is what is due to the son-in-law' (*ukucindika shifyala*), she said
shortly when I expressed surprise.

The young husbands themselves are, of course, equally insistent
that they should be treated with the right etiquette. If the wife's
family is short of food, or of labour to cook it, on any occasion,
there is no cause for complaint. But if it is once suspected that the
mother-in-law is merely being stingy, then the insult is felt to be
grave. It is a sufficient cause for the break-up of the marriage.

I met two attractive sisters left unmarried long after the usual time and asked the reason. I was told, 'Their husbands come and live here a short time, and then they go. They say, "The mother is mean. She stints us of porridge. She gives us no respect." ' In the same way I have heard young men discussing the pros and cons of cross-cousin marriage and concluding, 'Cross-cousin marriage is not so good. Our aunts (*banyina senge*) do not give us as much respect as other women would. They do not send us food every day or cover the dishes elegantly.'

The importance of the offering of food to the son-in-law continues long after the wife has become an independent householder, cooking on her own. His mother-in-law continues to send him dishes. In fact, the offering of food by the woman to the man is one of the essential obligations of kinship and other social ties. It is part of the legal duty of a wife to cook porridge for her husband and to allow him a predominant share of it, and hence it becomes a privilege and a matter of pride. I noticed that young girls, recently betrothed, would intimate this fact by saying shyly: 'I have begun to cook for him.' Older married women will beg, borrow, or work for food to supply their husbands if their own granary is empty. Each wife in a polygamous household will cook for her husband even if she has insufficient for herself, so that a husband may get two or three dishes of porridge while a wife and her children may go short. I saw a second wife, whose garden had been destroyed by locusts, live with her three children for two days entirely on mushrooms, while the last remnants of her millet were ground up daily to provide a diminutive dish of porridge for her husband, the latter amply supplied by his more fortunate head-wife, who had so much surplus millet that she sat at the other end of the village brewing beer with it. To my question as to why the second wife did not keep her grain for herself and her children and leave the first to supply the husband, the reply was immediate: 'Because she hates her fellow wife.' The rivalry natural between co-wives was expressed in the competition over the provision of food. The Bemba woman's prestige largely rests on her power to provide porridge and relish for her male relatives and to serve it nicely. These are the dues a man expects from his mother-in-law, his wife, and a number of other women in his kinship group.

It is the *umucinshi* that matters to both parties, as well as the filling of the belly. Hence the women in a village do not attempt

K

to organize the supply of eating-baskets sent to the young men's shelter. There may be two one day and twelve another.[1] It does not matter. Every mother-in-law sends just whenever she has time and supplies, so that the men of the village have a varying amount to eat from day to day. The regularity of the diet is thus directly affected by the symbolic use of offerings of cooked food.

The Cooking Team.

We have turned for a moment from our main subject, the joint preparation of food, but it will be seen that the system of inter-dependent matrilocal households provides two units of economic co-operation, the women's and the men's. The former look for relish, fetch firewood, pound, grind, and cook together, and usually do their gardening work in twos and threes. The latter clear the bush for gardens jointly and, more rarely, hoe in common. But it is important to remember that the ties of kinship between the women's group are stronger than those between men. The women who work together are usually the old grandmother, her married daughter, her unmarried girls and adolescent granddaughters, be-sides other female relatives temporarily with her. The team may not be as large, of course. Every household in the village does not belong to a 'big house'. There may be only two or three individual families linked together, especially in a new village. But the basis of co-operation is the same in each case—mother and daughter, grandmother and granddaughter, sister and sister,[2] &c., and it is the matrilocal family pattern which will be ultimately reproduced as a normal process of development. So much is this the case that the wives of a polygamist never cook together, but each works with her own mother, sister, or any other female relatives who may happen to be in the village.[3] It is the solidarity and common activities of groups of the mother-daughter type which form the basis of the Bemba village. A man's own female relatives, his mother and sister, may be dependent on him, but they do not form part of the cooking unit. In-law taboos prevent a woman from co-operating closely with her mother-in-law, and her relations with her sister-in-law are usually constrained, if not hostile.

[1] Cf. p. 183.   [2] Using these terms in the classificatory sense.
[3] The wives of a chief are often an exception in this respect. They seem to have accepted the status of polygamy more completely than the wives of com-moners, and the heavy work involved in cooking for tribute labour makes it almost necessary for them to co-operate.

A man helps his sister and her children by cutting them gardens or giving them uncooked food, but not by inviting them to share in the daily meals.

The men's group based on the matrilocal system is smaller and less closely knit. Between the sons-in-law attached to one household there is a feeling of close friendship and familiarity. These young men eat and work together, and the term *Ciufi munandi*, 'the man who married with me', or into the same family, is one of affection and good fellowship. There are no taboos between a man and his wife's sisters. He laughs and jokes with them because he may one day marry them, and he works in their gardens if they need help. But the young husbands often come from different villages and clans, and will want, as soon as they can, to have gardens of their own and perhaps to take their wives back to their villages. In the same way there may be co-operation from time to time between an old man and one of his own young kinsmen, such as his grandson or maternal nephew, but these also come and go, marry in other villages, and get work with Europeans. This group does not remain in close association throughout life as do the women of the matrilocal group, whether the latter remain in the same village or not.[1] This fact has important bearings at the present time. Though the unit of male labour is often nonexistent, with the absence of so many of the men at the mines, the domestic and gardening economy of the women remains for the most part intact, and there seems no doubt that women deserted for months or even years by their husbands are more happily placed in a matrilocal community than in a patrilocal one.[2]

The Value of the Cooking Team.

The practical results of this type of domestic economics should be considered, since it is apparently one that is likely to change

[1] One legal case concerned a young married woman, one of six sisters, real or classificatory, who had lived in the same village and worked so happily together that when her husband removed her to his own village after the necessary years of service, she could not bear to live away from her family. The contrast between the cheerful female group in her own village and her relative isolation in her husband's community was too great. She ran back home for the third time during my stay at the village (Pambalasa, 1930). Divorce was the final result. Such a case is an extreme instance of the female solidarity which is so marked in a matrilocal tribe of this kind.

[2] Dr. Margaret Read confirms this on the basis of a comparative study between the patrilocal Ngoni and the matrilocal Chewa of Nyasaland.

in the future. Is there any advantage, economic or otherwise, in this particular system of joint labour? To share food from the same dish is certainly more economical than preparing separate portions. There is always enough, the Bemba women say, if you eat out of one basket.[1] This is ensured by the custom of grouping of men and of women and children at meals.

Again, it must be recognized that joint housekeeping makes for greater security in a society with no system of exchange or purchase of food. To be attached to a 'big house' is to share its fortunes—to have the chance of delicacies like beer and meat as often as possible, and to be certain of support in case of a shortage. A comparison between conditions in a modern village where the kinship groups are smaller (p. 153) makes this clear. Where the unit of consumption is only one or two households the people may be better off at good seasons of the year but practically destitute in a bad one.

Joint cooking also eases the housewife's labour very largely. The younger women, in particular, like grinding and pounding together, and seem to work with greater enthusiasm in this way. The difficulties of combining lengthy cooking processes with gardening have already been described (Chap. VI and VIII). The woman with several young girls to help her may be able to work in her husband's fields and yet be able to provide relish for the evening meal. The isolated housewife may not, and the notes given on typical families (Chap. X) show this fact concretely.

Lastly, we saw that the Bemba system of education provides for no direct instruction in housecraft or a knowledge of the lore of the bush, but this information is acquired by a process of imitation through membership of a large group. Matrilocal marriage means that the girl is under the orders of her mother both before and after marriage for many years and thus learns the arts of organization, leadership, and the management of supplies by slow degrees. This seemed to me not the least important function of the matrilocal cooking team.

Domestic Economics in Modern Marriages.

The partial break-down of the matrilocal family system has had pronounced effects on the whole domestic economy of the Bemba.

---

[1] It will be seen (pp. 139, 41, 70) how housewives give their kinswomen grain to grind when food is plentiful, a small portion of flour when it is less so, and an invitation to share their dish when it is really scarce.

Nowadays the boy, on his betrothal, usually goes to work for Europeans, either in his own neighbourhood or on the copper belt. In the latter case he probably stays away a year or two and does not return to cut trees for his father-in-law. He sends back 10s. a year instead. Theoretically this money is intended to be used to pay a labourer to do the bridegroom's work, but this rarely happens. The father-in-law tends to spend this money immediately on some European object which he urgently needs and can get in no other way—a cloth, for instance, or a hoe. Thus a bridegroom may fulfil his contract most satisfactorily according to native standards, but yet the gardens he should have made may remain uncut.

After his return the young man marries his bride and probably lives in the village for a year or two. He usually works for his father-in-law during this time, but under modern conditions the old men are powerless to exact their full due of service, and I saw a good many cases in which young husbands idled in their wives' villages for a whole season, on the plea they had come back home to 'rest' (cf. p. 172). In any case, though they consider themselves entirely responsible for clothing their wives and children, they do not feel bound to feed them until later in life. The economic team of the father-in-law and his sons-in-law cannot exist under these conditions, with resultant effects not only on the food-supply of the family but on the agricultural education of the young men.

In other cases the young man gets permission to take his bride straight away with him to the mines after a few months of married life, or on his second visit there, which is the more common procedure. In this case it is the woman who forgoes the education in housecraft and manners she should have received in her mother's group. Girls of 16 or 17 transplanted from their villages in this way seem in a particularly defenceless position when living near their husbands' place of work, and it is probable that the matri-local system, while it makes for an easier adjustment for the women left behind in a 'manless country-side' under modern conditions, puts young wives at a particular disadvantage when they are taken from their homes and the support to which they have been accustomed. Whether it is housecraft, midwifery, or the weaning of children, they are divorced from the ordinary agencies of tribal education and that female solidarity to which they are used.

These are, as yet, isolated instances. As a whole, it can be said that the Bemba system of joint cookery and domestic co-operation continues to work in the old fashion, except in the few suburban villages in which the groups of households so united are much smaller, limited usually to two or three huts, and therefore the advantages of pooled resources are reduced. But the economic dependence of a young couple on the wife's parents which formerly acted as a test of the husband's suitability, a sanction for his good behaviour, and a means of education in technical activities, no longer functions in the same way. Where the husband is intermittently away at the mines, the father-in-law assumes a more complete responsibility for his married daughter and her children and for a longer period than before, but has to do without the advantage of his son-in-law's agricultural help, so that his obligations are often heavier than he can properly carry out.

CHAPTER IX

HOSPITALITY AND LABOUR PAYMENT

Types of Hospitality.

THIS description of the sharing of supplies between members of the individual family has already shown us the social and symbolic importance of offering and receiving food. Women, we saw, tended to cook dishes for their husbands and sons-in-law even if they went short themselves. They did so because they did not want to lose their self-respect. It is for this reason that the Bemba practice of hospitality affects so largely their consumption of supplies. Their rules in this respect are based on the conception, described in greater detail later, that the distribution of cooked food is an attribute of authority, and therefore prestige, and that its reception puts a man under an obligation to return to the giver respect, service, or reciprocal hospitality. As the Bemba say, 'You have eaten *namba* (the sticky gum from the *munamba* tree) and it sticks to your stomach' (*Ualye namba, yalambatila fye munda*), i.e. you have filled your stomach with food from some one and it puts you under a permanent obligation to him. Hence the act of distribution is valued in itself. The man who kills game at the nets or who brews beer for his friends probably does not eat or drink any more than they do, but he has the satisfaction of being able to act as host. As a corollary, it follows that the highest compliment he can give his guest is to provide him with cooked food or beer, which he in his turn can distribute again. Thus the most honourable form of hospitality is to send a man dishes of porridge and relish, a lump of meat, or a calabash of beer so that he can dispose of it as he pleases in his hut alone. The least honourable is to ask him to share in your dish, in what would seem to us a more friendly and convivial manner. It will be noted how far this people's idea of hospitality differs from our own. In this country, to prepare a meal for a respected relative and to ask him to eat it alone in his room would be a studied insult, much as the idea might appeal to some hostesses. But among the Bemba, hospitality is never an occasion for conversation or recreation, but a way of offering respect, or of providing food for those who cannot get it any other way. To give your elderly uncle a

basket of porridge to eat behind closed doors means that you consider him as a chief who can eat alone and distribute food as he
pleases. He is the owner (*mwine*) of the dish. To ask him to share
is to put him on a level with yourself or to treat him as a dependent.

Thus hospitality is perhaps a misleading word for the practices
described in this chapter, since it conveys the idea of entertainment and good cheer, whereas, except in the case of beer, the
Bemba provision for visitors consists in the division and subdivision of food into portions, to be eaten in a series of separate
groups. There is never a big party gathered to eat. The European
sometimes congratulates himself on the number of guests he has
been able to feed round one table, while the Bemba would be
more likely to brag of the number of separate dishes he had been
able to provide for his guests. This latter viewpoint makes the
exercise of hospitality quite a complex matter, and very much
increases the liabilities of the housewife.

As regards travellers, any Bemba who has not adopted European
values and standards of living provides food for all those who can
claim relationship, real or classificatory, to himself or his wife.[1]
Any young male visitor, such as a junior brother of host or hostess,
a classificatory brother (*umunyina*), or a cross-cousin (*umufyala*), is
usually asked to share in the dish that is sent to the host at the
men's *nsaka*. Such a guest would probably already be sitting
there with his contemporaries among the villagers, but if not he
might be found on the veranda of the hut allotted to him with the
air of deliberate detachment thought elegant on such occasions,
and would remain there until a child were sent to fetch him to the
meal. A more honoured form of hospitality is to send the guest
a dish of porridge and relish to the *nsaka* in his own right, so that
he is there able to distribute it among those present. A young
man who ranks as the child (*umwana*) of host or hostess, or a
maternal nephew (*umwipwa*) who is treated with a certain amount
of reserve by his *nalume*, a relative by marriage (*bukwe*) who should
not eat with the host, or a kinsman occupying a senior position
such as father or grandfather by virtue of inheritance would
receive hospitality of this sort.[2]

[1] Contact with European conditions of living affects the degree of nearness of
kinship recognized.
[2] By the system of inheriting a dead man's name and ancestral spirit (*ukupyanika*) quite a young man may be addressed as grandfather or *nalume*, and hence
may have to be treated with more respect than his age would warrant.

Elderly and eminent kinsmen, such as a father or grandfather of host or hostess, or the maternal uncle of either, have to be treated with even greater respect. They eat alone, as has been described. When such a person arrives for a few days' visit, a special hut is cleared for him[1] and dishes are sent him neatly covered, which he eats inside the house, calling a small child, usually a grandson, to finish the remains, since an empty platter is a sign of voracity, and is hence *mal-vue*. The manner of bringing the meal is considered specially important. The hostess usually stands at the door of her hut and yells across the village a high-pitched scream of instructions to the child who is carrying the dishes. He is to bring the guest water to wash, to kneel as he hands it, to utter a greeting at the door, and so forth, each sentence ending with that common Bemba phrase *Busaka! Busaka!*—'elegance' expressed in its duplicative form.

The feeding of female visitors is always a less formal affair, since the whole business of cooking and dispatching dishes (*ukutebeta*) is essentially the woman's way of paying compliments to her male relatives and not to her kinswomen. Most female relatives will be called to eat with the hostess and will even have helped with the preparation of the meal. An older woman must, however, be treated with ceremony. Sometimes she may get a separate basket of porridge, and sometimes the whole company moves to eat on her veranda as though the old lady were playing hostess herself. She then becomes the *mwine* of the dish. Members of the husband's family, as distinct from those of the wife, will usually eat alone. In any case, respected women visitors must always be invited to eat with courtesy by a child, who kneels and says, '*Mukwai*, they call you to eat.' Age distinctions are very important here. A young married girl told me she could never just shout to an older woman visitor with, 'Come over here, my friend. Hurry! Come quickly! Hunger is hurting! We are waiting to eat,' as she would to a contemporary. Even a 'modern girl' seems punctilious on such points. There are differences, too, in the rules of division of particular dishes. An eminent person might be asked to come to a young woman's hut if meat were being served, but not if in the case of ordinary food. In the hunger period an old

---

[1] Less distinguished visitors sleep with their relatives, the sleeping quarters allotted carefully in order to avoid breaking the comprehensive incest taboos and in-law avoidances.

lady of rank, whom I knew to have eaten little that day, refused an invitation to a meal. She asked me, with a sniff, who they took her for? Was she to cross the village 'just to sit down to a few mushrooms'?

The hospitality given to travelling chiefs must be reckoned in a different category. At the visit of the *mfumu*, each woman must contribute a little flour, and the headman produce chickens, the gift of honour, and, if possible, beer. But the presentation of the basket of flour and the live fowls is an act of homage, rather than mere provision for the traveller. It is brought by the headman and his elders and offered with the formal salutation of respect (*ukutota panshi*)—clapping and rolling on the back on the ground —and is reckoned as part of the chief's dues as the owner of the land (cf. Chap. XIII). But in any case it would be thought impossible to give a chief cooked food. He could not eat it because porridge cooked on 'impure' fire would endanger his life,[1] and it would be considered, I think, in the nature of an insult. Chiefs visiting each other will exchange uncooked food to be prepared by their respective staffs, but only a chief's head wife could send a royal visitor dishes of porridge and relish. All these distinctions show clearly the extent to which prestige is associated with the right to distribute food rather than its mere possession or consumption, and it is not surprising that the whole etiquette of feeding travellers is considered so important by a people constantly preoccupied with problems of status. Every traveller's departure is followed by lengthy discussions among the women as to what he received and what he ought to have received, and the Bemba proverb, 'Flour which is not yours is ash' (*Bunga ubushili bwenu, mito*), can be well understood.

Finally, there are strangers to be fed. This is an important matter at the present time since many natives, travelling four or five hundred miles up the motor road, are forced to stay *en route* at villages in which they have no close relatives. Hence it is important to discover what the old tradition of hospitality was and whether it is still observed. The correct procedure for a man entering a village is to ground his spear and sit down in silence in the veranda of the nearest hut. He should not speak until one

---

[1] The chief's wife has to make new fire either by friction or with matches and sometimes to mud the floor freshly before she can prepare his food when in a strange village.

of the inhabitants comes up and asks him his origin and works out in the interminable African fashion the line of his descent. Then it may become clear whose relative, if anybody's, he is, and therefore whose responsibility. This practice is usually followed still, but the old custom of making a ceremonial obeisance in front of the headman's hut, and thus claiming a meal from him, I only saw once observed. On the motor road hospitality rules are changing. Nearing Kasama I have heard natives coming up from the mines shouting, 'I am dying, I, a member of the such-and-such a clan,' and such an assertion of clan membership would have been enough to ensure a meal formerly. Nowadays this is emphatically not so. Villagers on the motor road would have been eaten out of house and home if they had stuck to the old rules of hospitality. A certain amount of food is actually sold along the route, usually at exorbitant rates, but there is no doubt that men and their families returning from the mines suffer real privation on the way.[1] The obligation to share food with nearer relatives is still observed even in urban districts, but not the wider ties of clan membership.

Permanent or Semi-permanent Visitors.

More permanent hospitality is offered to kinsmen who come to stay for six weeks to some months, either because they are short of supplies, have quarrelled with their relatives at home, are back on holiday from the mines, or because they want to amuse themselves by a change.[2] Women visitors who are near relatives of the wife, whether married or not, are easily incorporated into the women's domestic team. The matrilocal family group is merely extended to include additional real or classificatory mothers, daughters, cross-cousins, or grandchildren. For a short visit a hut will be cleared for them; for a longer stay a new house may be built. If the visitor is a person of status she will be given millet of her own to grind, if possible, since that is the highest compliment. If supplies are shorter, she will have a basket of flour divided out to her, or otherwise she will merely share in the family dish and her husband will eat at the *nsaka*. Usually the arrangement varies, according to conditions, from day to day.

[1] The Compound Manager at Luanshya estimated that a man returning from the mines on foot requires 10s. at least to spend on food *en route*.

[2] The former visits take place in the hunger months, January to March, and the latter in the hot season, August to November, when the garden work is done.

Grandchildren constantly arrive for long visits at the older couple's huts. Small children at weaning go to sleep with their maternal grandparents; when older they might travel a day or two's journey to stay with their father's people and may remain there for a month or more. Children with parents at the mines are also left very generally with their grandparents, usually maternal, and may live there until they are of marriageable age or after. They become the children of the household and the tie is probably more intimate with grandparents than it is with parents, and is certainly less subject to taboos. Children whose parents live in the village often eat with their grandmother for choice, just as they regularly sleep at her hut.

A housewife may also undertake to feed, temporarily or permanently, certain of her male kinsmen, if they are left widowers or are not yet married. This group includes her younger unmarried brothers and her sons. A son may always return to his mother's village if his wife dies or leaves him and he will be certain of a welcome. Men say that their wives often leave them at a time of famine and go home to their own people, but that a mother would never refuse to cook for her son. 'There is always food with the mother. Even if she has only a few ground-nuts left, she will fry them and give them to you,' a native put it to me. A woman has no legal obligation to feed her married son, since he belongs to his wife's local group, but the emotional attachment continues strong and a son will always be given preference if he returns to his mother's community.[1]

A woman will not regularly feed her father. There is a constrained and respectful attitude between them from the time of the girl's adolescence, but she will send him dishes 'for respect'. Her grandfather, on the other hand, whether paternal or maternal, she is especially bound to look after. A man has technically preemptive rights to marry his granddaughter and often jokingly addresses her as his 'wife' when she is a child, whether he intends to marry her or not, and it is therefore considered fitting that she should feed him in his old age if he is left alone.

[1] Many proverbs contrast the behaviour of the mother with that of other women, e.g. 'Rejoice that your mother is alive, the mother of your friend won't allow her food-rack to be touched.' *Sankata, noko acili po, noko ua mubio tekatilwa pa luino,* or 'In a village where you have no mother, your work is to beg,' *Mu mushi umushili noko, no kupula, milimo.* Cf. *Dictionnaire Français-Chibemba,* L. Guillerme, 1920.

A number of the husband's relatives also come on long visits. His male kinsmen, if unmarried or widowed, must be regularly fed by the housewife, who prepares them separate dishes if possible. If married and of junior status their wives will help with the cooking, since there is no strong avoidance between a woman and her husband's brother's wife, who may, in fact, become her co-wife if the former dies. But the female relatives of the husband, his mother and sisters, stand in a rather different category, as has been described, and a widowed or deserted wife who has 'gone to her brother' will work alone with her children and be given food of her own to cook.

In all these different forms of hospitality it will be seen how the giving and receiving of food has acquired symbolic value, and that the difference between cooked and uncooked food, special dishes, or the manner of serving them may indicate distinctions in rank, kinship, or age, and that much of the cooking done by the Bemba housewife is an expression of these various degrees of status.

Division of Meat.

Since meat is a perishable food that must be divided at once, it is natural that its distribution follows different rules. Every bit of the animal is known by name and graded according to its social value, but I did not find that the portions of game to be allotted to different kinsmen were so clearly defined as seems to be so in the case of cattle among a number of the pastoral Bantu. With a big animal the chief should be given tribute of a leg, while the headman of the village has some honoured portion according to convenience. The father-in-law of the hunter, his father, or *nalume*, have also their gift of respect, but the rest of the joints appear to be distributed according to the hunters' inclinations, and I have seen all sorts of portions—hind-leg, foreleg, or back given to these different relatives.

The cattle killed for sacrifice at the chief's court are, however, divided according to very definite rules—often according to the symbolic associations of each part, as for instance the gift of the heart to Citimululu at the slaying of an ox at the founding of his new village. I have taken notes at six such divisions of a beast, but the distribution cannot be understood without a knowledge of the functions of the different dignitaries of the court.

Labour and Cooked Food.

The use of food as a form of payment adds to the catering problem of any household. Porridge and relish are not only sent to a man as a form of compliment, but also given him as a reward for his work. The manner of serving or the type of food often makes the only distinction between the two acts. Within the limits of the Bemba economic system there is no other way of obtaining service for a man who is able to organize it, and support for the one who is not. All relationships between an inferior and his superior involve the former in giving some kind of labour, whether in the case of the son-in-law and the father-in-law already described in some detail; the young boy and his legal guardian of the moment, whether father, maternal uncle, or grandfather:[1] or the villager and his headman, and the subject and his chief. The women's duties of service to her kinsmen are less clearly specified, but they also do tribute labour for the chief as does a man. Besides these permanent relationships involving the exchange of labour for food there are a number of temporary forms of service recognized for specific purposes. Though it is impossible to make a clear distinction between the feeding of relatives and the feeding of labourers in a society in which kinship is the basis of economic co-operation, yet both types of distribution affect the dietary situation and hence must be described.

This exchange of cooked food and service is a very concrete conception to the Bemba mind. It is not one of the abstractions the anthropologist makes on the basis of observed behaviour. The difference between the work a man does for himself and that he does for another is recognized linguistically by the use of the special applicative form of the verb. To cut trees is *uku*tema, while to cut them for some one else, e.g. the chief, or the father-in-law, is *uku*temena; to hoe is *uku*lima, while to hoe for some one else is *uku*limina. The two are apparently such different activities in natives' eyes that they bother to stop and correct a stranger who makes a mistake in the linguistic forms. I have several times asked a man if he had been working at a task that morning, saying for

[1] In the old days a boy worked for his father before he married, but his maternal uncle had supreme rights over his labour. Case histories of older Bemba are full of incidents in which the *nalume*, if powerful, was able to send and demand the services of his maternal nephew and insist on his following him 200 or 300 miles from one end of the country to the other.

instance, 'Did you hoe over there this morning?' (*Bushye mwalima-po lucelo?*) only to be answered with an emphatic denial, 'No I was hoeing there for my chief' (*Nakarya! Naliminapo mfumu*).

The people seem perfectly conscious that legal obligations can be fulfilled by work and reckon up their services as concretely as we do debts in money, although of course with less exactitude. A man with a grievance against a relative was heard saying, 'He refused me porridge! I who bicycled three times to the river to sell his fish!' and such statements are quite common. In legal cases where there is a dispute, probably between the father and the maternal uncle over the guardianship of children, one or other of the disputants will nearly always mention at some time or other the number of times he has cut trees for the mother of the children, or hoed for her, and such service gives legal claims just as the payment of money or provision of food.

Naturally there is a distinction between near and distant relatives in this matter. Though all the members of a family who cook and eat together are supposed to do their share of the work, a close relation will be fed whether he pulls his weight or not. A young son-in-law may lose his bride if he is incorrigibly lazy, as we have seen, but within the lineage group a wastrel is accepted as one of the inevitable crosses of life and endured with more resignation than in our society:[1] but a more distant relative within the classificatory degree only could not be sure of such tolerance, and would have to claim his place in the group and his right to food by the work he did. In such cases the distinction between the co-operating kinsman and the temporary labourer is a fine one.[2] Even adolescent boys and girls recognize quite clearly those relatives who will feed them whatever they do, and those from whom they have to earn their keep. I have a number of cases illustrating this fact. For instance a girl of 14, found grinding alone late in the afternoon outside the house of a classificatory mother instead of her own grandmother with whom she usually lived, answered,

---

[1] 'Why do you make a garden for your sister when she has a husband sitting round doing nothing?' I asked a man once. 'Because that is his habit (*musango uakwe*) to go on sitting like that,' was the answer with a shrug. 'My sister likes that man. She refuses any other. First we scolded him and then we left it. We said, "Let it be! (*Cibe!*) That is his habit."'

[2] Urban natives who employ servants tend to engage their own kinsmen and to incorporate them in their household group, but a distant relative would have short shrift if he did not work, while a near one would probably still be supported.

when questioned, 'I am grinding here because I want to eat here. My heart is angry because my grandmother keeps scolding me.' A boy of 12 in another village seemed to be more assiduous than his fellows in fetching firewood. When I commented on his behaviour I was told, apparently as a quite sufficient explanation, that the child had left his own home in a neighbouring village because he did not like his mother's new husband. He had come to live with a more distant relation—a classificatory sister's husband—instead. With this more remote kinsman he evidently felt the need to ingratiate himself in order to establish his claim for support. The Bemba kinship system allows such great freedom of movement to young people that temporary changes of this kind from one eating group to another are quite frequent.[1] Thus the whole principle of the exchange of work for food is learnt as a practical expedient by children not yet in their teens, and it is on these reciprocal obligations to serve and to feed that the whole political and economic system of the tribe is based.

Organized Forms of Labour.

Outside the kinship group there are other recognized forms of labour. In the old days these included the institution of slavery by which a chief or notable acquired rights over the life and labour of men or women, and in return fed and protected them, and provided for their marriage and the upbringing of their children. Slaves, whether captives taken in battle (*ba mabuta*, i.e. of the bow), or Bemba deprived of liberty as a legal punishment, or given as compensation for some irreparable injury such as murder (*ba musoka*) or destruction of gardens,[2] lived as members of the owner's household group, sleeping in their own huts, but fed by him, and not possessing gardens or granaries of their own. No one would know the difference between a slave and a poor relative, I was told, except that the former worked harder and only ate the food left over by the household. Although slavery no longer exists, the

---

[1] The Bemba touchiness and readiness to detect criticism or slight is shown in childhood. Children who consider that they have been corrected over-harshly announce that they do not 'like' the offending relative any more, and it is not uncommon to say of a small boy of 10 or 12 that he does not like his father (*tatemwa kuli wishi*) and for him to move elsewhere for a time. His kinship system and type of housing makes it very possible for him to follow such inclinations.

[2] Or persons voluntarily enslaved *ua kuilila*, i.e. usually after having been irreparably insulted.

institution is worth mentioning as an example of a permanent relationship of exchange of food for labour, and as illustrating in an extreme case the Bemba concept that rights over labour include rights over movement, residence, and life and death.[1] The memory of this institution, still very much alive to-day, certainly affects the attitude of black to white and the ideas of service the older men at any rate are prepared to accept.

Another form of organized labour is the custom known as *ukupula* by which a man or a woman, but usually the latter, can offer service to a householder temporarily, most commonly at a busy time of the year such as harvest. In return he or she gets food, either in the form of a share of the family dish, or a basket of the grain that is being reaped. In such cases the employer is either a distant kinsman who would not be otherwise under any strong obligation to help, or he is no relative at all. The worker is considered to be in an inferior position and spoken of contemptuously or pityingly, as we might of a beggar.[2] Actually, the woman who goes *ukupula* may do exactly the same work as one of the near relatives of the family, and may be given much the same food, but she does not receive what she does by right of kinship, and the phrase *Alepula-pula-fye*, which might be translated, 'she lives by picking up casual jobs', is usually uttered with a rather scornful shrug of the shoulders. Only an absolutely destitute person or an imbecile would reckon to subsist in this way as a regular thing;[3] but as a temporary form of support, *ukupula* has become very common lately as one of the means by which the very large percentage of deserted wives can eke out an existence during the bad times of the year. Travellers returning from the mines, who can no longer reckon to be fed on the march as in the old days, also resort to the practice on occasion. I have seen them do an afternoon's hoeing on their arrival at one of the villages on the main road in order to secure an evening meal.

Another type of service rewarded by cooked food is the communal work done by a man in return for beer. Such working-bees,

[1] A chief could sell a slave to Arab traders, known as *ukuposa* 'to throw away'. A commoner could not do this, but a *nalume* could enslave his *mwipwa* in compensation for some legal fault of his own.

[2] *Ukupula* is often loosely applied to all forms of scrounging, but technically speaking means labour in return for food only. *Ukulomba* means to beg in the sense of asking a favour from a superior, such as a chief or an ancestral spirit, with no possibility of adequate return.

[3] The type of person who would have probably become voluntarily enslaved in the old days.

L

common in most primitive societies, are known as *ukutumya* among the Bemba. They consist of groups of men organized to do a day's tree-cutting or hoeing, or of women gathered to pile branches for burning or to reap. Most of the able-bodied men or women of a village would join such an outing, and *ukutumya* parties are usually reckoned as agreeable parties of friends and relatives, as well as a useful means of breaking the back of a big job such as clearing the bush or putting new grass-land under the hoe. The work rarely lasts more than four hours, and the toilers then return to the village, jubilant at the prospect of the beer ahead. However, in spite of the festive note of such *ukutumya* parties, there is a definite exchange of work and food involved. The hostess sends round a dipper of beer to the hut of the worker early in the morning (*ukulalike nkoko*), theoretically so that every one may taste the brew and be assured that the drink is worth working for.[1] The *ubwalua* itself is set aside for those who have been working during the day. I noticed on one occasion that the women returning from a hoeing party sharply rebuked one of the men of the village for coming to beg a drink from their calabash. They said he must wait until they had drunk their fill. He could have a pull later in the afternoon, when the beer was weak.

In any one year quite an appreciable amount of grain is actually used by the Bemba for *ukutumya* parties of this sort. I should assume that most householders brewed at least once during the season for this purpose, and the desire to have a surplus of grain is sometimes stated to be due to the wish to have 'plenty of beer to brew for my friends when they do my work'. The system is inefficient from the economic point of view perhaps, since the proportion of the day spent in beer-drinking is very large compared to that spent on actual work.[2] However, *ukupula* does give a man what he most wants at certain seasons, i.e. a supply of labour for the heaviest enterprises, such as tree-cutting and hoeing, and it has considerable importance at the present day, since deserted wives, without many relatives to help them, may be unable to get a house or a granary built in any other way. Old women congregated near the town of Kasama wander about from village to village collecting baskets of grain by *ukupula* labour, and

---

[1] Actually, any Bemba would rather drink sour beer than none at all.

[2] It is not uncommon to find the party returning at 11 or 12 a.m. in order to have time to enjoy the beer!

Women hoeing up an old millet garden before sowing. Mound cultivation. Men hoeing up new ground into mounds.

finally, after some weeks' work, brew beer, and invite men to a *kutumya* party so that they may get some necessary granary or house built.

Distribution at the Chief's Court.

The most considerable exchange of food for labour is that which takes place at the capital, whether in payment of tribute workers (*ba mulasa*), courtiers, executive officials, or visiting councillors on tribal business. This whole system of distribution illustrates clearly not only the political and economic ideas of the Bemba but the rules of hospitality already described. Each man or woman who works for the chief[1] should be given food. The men are provided with porridge and relish cooked by the chief's wives, and the women unthreshed millet to prepare for themselves. The workers eat together in one group. The boys and young men who act as personal servants to the chief are also fed separately with cooked food, being mostly unmarried men. Older courtiers, heads of sections of the village (*bafilolo*), or messengers (*bakapasso*) are treated in more honourable fashion. They are sent a share of meat sent in as tribute, or invited to share a pot of beer on the veranda of the chief's hut. At Citimukulu's court, tribal councillors (*bakabilo*), if present in twos or threes, are treated in the same way, but if the whole council is present on matters of state, they will probably stay for a week or ten days, and then they are regularly fed by the chief's wives. In this case the whole council—some forty strong—is divided into groups (*nsaka*) based on descent and historical association.[2] Each of these groups must be provided with a separate basket of porridge and a dish of relish, and sits eating back to back in the chief's enclosure. Honoured visitors, such as members of the royal family, are sent flour, chickens, or beer by the chief and cooked food by his head wife (*umukolo*).

The organization of these supplies is naturally a complicated business. At Citimukulu's court during nine months (April 1933 to January 1934) 561 men and 324 women came to do *umulasa* labour and were fed at least one day of their service. The *bakabilo* to the number of about forty met at least twice during the year, while it is impossible to estimate the number of other persons engaged on a big chief's business. The distribution is of such

---

[1] Cf. Chapter XIII. About three days a year at the present time.
[2] The *nsaka* of Katongo, of Citikafula, of Cikutwe, and of Citimukulu.

importance politically that it is supervised personally by the *mfumu* himself, who watches meat cut up in front of him and gives the orders for grain to be given out. A special steward is in charge of his big personal granary and hands out baskets of grain each morning to the senior wives in charge of the feeding of the *umulasa* labourers, or the brewing of beer for any special purposes. The wives themselves have their own small personal granaries and cook dishes for the chief which he divides as he pleases,[1] or make presents of beer as they choose. All the three or four senior wives distribute hospitality to honoured guests in their own rights, and the *umukolo*, in particular, is required to be very punctilious in sending dishes of honour to travelling notables.

All the *bamukolo* I met were women of a good deal of organizing ability, capable of supervising the younger wives, arranging for the endless grinding and brewing required in the capital,[2] and the stirring of the huge pots of porridge to be served in enormous eating-baskets about eight times the size of an ordinary *icipe*. Any one who sits in the inside of an *umukolo's* hut during the late afternoon will know at once by the bustle, the concentrated faces, and the ring of waiting food-baskets that important and responsible work is on hand.

The whole of this system of distributing food is of course necessary to the chief if he is to make gardens and conduct tribal business through his councillors. But it is more than this. The giving of food, as in most African tribes, is an absolutely essential attribute of chieftainship, just as it is of authority in the village or household, and the successful organization of supplies at the capital seems to be associated in the Bemba mind with the security and well-being of the whole tribe itself. This fact may be said to be symbolized by the institution of the sacred kitchen (*kamitembo*) at the courts of the big chiefs (Citimukulu, Mwamba, and Nkula). From the outside the *kamitembo* looks like an ordinary hut, although specially well built. It is one of the sacred houses built by the *bakabilo* with special rites at the founding of a chief's new village. In fact it is the first to be built on the site. At Citimukulu's founding ceremony a special hereditary official, the Mwana Bwalya,

---

[1] The cooking of the chief's own food is usually done by the *umukolo* herself, or by some old woman specially appointed to the task, since the taboos protecting his fire from sex impurity are very strict.

[2] Chiefs' wives do not have to pile branches in the fields, but do very heavy grinding-work for beer-making and feeding the workers.

crosses the Kalungu river near the capital at dead of night and has ritual intercourse with a woman given him for the purpose on the spot selected for the building of the *kamitembo*. Thus he 'warms the bush' (*ukukafye mpanga*) and leaves immediately afterwards secretly for his own village. On the place where his sleeping mat lay, one of the *bakabilo*, Cishika, the hereditary lighter of the chief's fire, must immediately make new fire by friction. This is the chief's sacred fire. The same patch of grass serves as site for the *kamitembo* house built a day or so after by all the *bakabilo* in concert after prayers by the Citimukulu and the burial of flour, salt, meat, and fish in the foundations. Once built the sacred hearth must be installed (*ukuteka ishiko*) and this is done as the climax of the long ceremonial founding of the village,[1] by killing a female sheep, and cooking it in the hut on the sacred fire with salt made from river grasses. This use of the traditional salt of the tribe is said to ensure that the land may be savoured (*calo cilowe*). Two big baskets are then cooked on the same hearth and carried to the chief, who tastes the porridge and meat and then hands it to all his *bakabilo* to eat. This is the way in which the 'spirits are put into the hut' (*ukubike mipashi mu ŋanda*), so that the life of the new village may begin.

After this the chief's fire burns perpetually in the *kamitembo* as also in two other sacred houses in the village and it remains under the special charge of the *umukolo*.[2] No person of sexual vigour may enter for fear of polluting the fire, and the chief's messages are carried there by small boys. Within the hut were piled in the old days the carrying poles on which tribute of beer and meat had been slung—signs of the chief's greatness —and the elephant tusks brought him. This is no longer done, but the beer required for big sacrifices to the land spirits is brewed in the *kamitembo*, and the chief and his head wife sleep here during this period, keeping sex taboos all the while. This is described as 'waiting for the yeast of the land' (*ukulindilo musunga ue calo*). Animals killed for sacrifices are also killed here, and the new crops cooked before being offered for the first-fruits are

[1] The ceremony of founding the last new village for the Citimukulu took from May to September 1933. I witnessed the first part of the ceremony but not the installation of the sacred hearth.

[2] The *umukolo* should only have ritual intercourse with the chief on ceremonial occasions and therefore as a person sexually pure remains a fit guardian of the tribal fire.

cooked on the same sacred hearth. It is in fact the sacred kitchen and storehouse of the tribe.

The whole institution of the *kamitembo* illustrates to my mind that close association between authority and the power to distribute provisions on which the tribal organization depends. The chief owns the food and receives tribute, and the chief provides for his subjects and distributes cooked food to them. Both these attributes are symbolized in the *kamitembo* house.

We started to discuss the use of food as a payment for labour as part of a study of domestic economics, but we have been inevitably led to consider the deep-rooted political and religious beliefs connected with this form of distribution. They are beliefs that are very much alive to-day and insensibly affect all attitudes between ruler and ruled whether white or black. The European generally gives his native employee food as well as money wages. He does so usually for the purely practical reason that he is afraid that otherwise his servants will starve and spend their money on clothes. But to the native the white man's provision of food puts him in a special relationship which is quite different from an ordinary business transaction. He becomes 'his man' in a special sort of way.

Tribal Distribution and the Individual Ration.

We have described the distribution of cooked food among the Bemba, and some of the social and economic uses to which foodstuffs are put. It remains to indicate the effect of these different cultural regulations on the daily intake of the individual members of the tribe. Briefly speaking, these are two in number. A fairly even distribution of supplies is produced in any one village on any particular day, but a great irregularity in the individual amounts eaten as from day to day or month to month.

The causes of these changes in the daily intake can be readily deduced from the foregoing chapters. The first is the varying numbers of helpers who join to form each elder woman's cooking team, giving to some ample labour for the lengthy processes of grinding and cooking, while others belong to so small a family group that they are unable to prepare a proper meal at the busy times of the year.[1]

[1] A point to be borne in mind when the advisability of establishing isolated homesteads for individual families is discussed.

The second cause is the varying number of eaters for whom the
Bemba housewife has to cater on any one day. It will be remembered that the head of a 'big house' is responsible for a permanent
group of eaters, i.e. her husband, the sons-in-law still dependent
on her, their wives and children, and her own unmarried children
of both sexes. Besides this there is an outer ring of eaters for
whom the housewife is ultimately responsible but does not always
have to provide, i.e. the older married daughters who have already
their own granaries, for whose families she will only cater in case
of sickness, heavy garden work or brewing, or absence on visits.
There are also married sons, or their near male relatives with
wives temporarily away, who may or may not have to be fed.
These near relatives form a constantly expanding and contracting
group, and their numbers are increased by travellers on long or
short visits and workers in the householder's garden. Besides
which the cooking of dishes as a form of compliment adds to the
catering difficulties. I have known the numbers fed by one woman
to vary from five to fifteen a day in the course of one week.

In a chief's village the head wife has an even more complex
task, as she may have to organize the feeding of bands of twenty
to forty *umulasa* labourers, several councillors on tribal business,
royal visitors, as well as on occasion the whole tribal council
numbering some forty men with their wives and retinues.

The chief's wife may know in advance the days on which she
has to feed workers or members of the council, but neither she
nor the commoner's wife usually knows until late in the day how
many extra kinsmen or visitors will have to be fed. For this reason
it may be impossible for her to do an extra hour or two's work to
grind additional flour. In such circumstances the same amount of
food has to be divided among a larger number of people, so that
each gets a smaller share, and much of the irregularity in the daily
intake is due to just this fact.

Even in those cases where it would have been possible for the
housewife to cook a larger dish, there may be a number of reasons
why she may be unwilling to do so. These are based on her
conception of her obligations towards her kinsmen in general, her
power of calculation, and her views as to the desirability of regular
meals. It is obvious that if the owner of a granary has to make
her supplies last from one harvest to another, while at the same
time carrying out her duty to feed a wider circle of relatives than

is customary with us, she is only likely to succeed if she cooks more or less the same amount of porridge each day, however large the number of eaters. In fact, this is what she does. Moreover the Bemba woman does not appear to calculate her supplies, consciously at any rate, on the basis of a fixed amount of food per person per day, nor has she ever fed people out of separate vessels, so that it is unlikely that she has a visual image of an average or suitable portion of food for each eater as has the English woman accustomed to taking a similar-sized helping on to her plate at each meal.

The Bemba usually take out of their granaries one of the ordinary eating-baskets of unthreshed millet (about 5 lb.) or for a big household a winnowing basket (about 10 lb.). In very exceptional circumstances they will take two. The Englishwoman rings up her husband to ask him anxiously if he is bringing home two extra guests to supper or three; the African woman will make the distinction more roughly between a 'great many' people or a 'few'. Unaccustomed from youth to expect regular and similar meals each day, she treats the appearance of visitors with less concern.

The effect of the Bemba methods of distribution on the tribal dietary have been shown to be pronounced. It may therefore be asked whether the introduction of a European system of housekeeping is likely to produce great changes in this respect. There is a widespread idea among white people that the adoption of the individual household would be a great forward step for the African. It is even considered to be a moral advantage to the native to be encouraged to acquire a feeling of sole responsibility for his wife and his own offspring. The European way of life seems to us to promise a race of thrifty, enterprising, hard-working natives, while their own condemns them to remain in their primitive state. From an ethical point of view there is in fact little to choose between the two economic systems. The older Bemba accepts far wider responsibilities for his kinsmen than his counterpart in this country, while the younger one undoubtedly does not. But in actual fact a number of Bemba near European towns are already living an individual family life, and therefore apart from the moral value of the one system as against the other, the changes in their whole nutritional situation are important to describe.

In such modern villages there are two factors to be considered. One of these factors is the isolation of native families and the other the gradual adoption of the use of money for the purchase of food. Both make for inequality in the standards of living as between household and household, which are not found in any rural village. Where a housewife lives alone with one or two married daughters instead of being a member of a closely-knit kinship group under one headman, she has less obligation to share. Where she buys her supplies with money, at any rate for part of the year, she considers herself free of all the tribal rules of division. Thus, in Kungu village near Kasama, I have seen a young couple eat meat alone while almost starving neighbours looked on. They shrugged their shoulders when questioned, and said, 'We bought this meat with money.' I have also seen beer drunk by men alone with no guests invited, even though the act was disapproved of. The effect of such new customs on the diets of different families is shown in the records I collected. Thus, in this area, one family spent 7s. 6d. a week on food, and their diet included 17½ lb. of meat, 2 lb. of tripe, and beer; another family spent 3s. 6d. a week on food, eating caterpillars, chicken, fish, and 4 lb. of meat; while a third household spent nothing on food and only managed to procure pumpkin, green leaf relish, and 1 lb. of meat during the week. In another village one woman had an average of 3 lb. of flour a day in the hunger season, and bought 2 lb. of butcher meat, while next door an old woman supporting a granddaughter lived for six days on gourds, some picked long before they had reached full size, while another ground up her seed millet into flour.

This inequality as between family and family much more nearly resembles conditions in our own society, and appears to be the necessary result of the adoption of a money economy. At present there is of course the added difficulty that individual housekeeping has begun to exist without any previous organization of trade, specialization of urban and agricultural workers, or regular possibilities of buying food. Thus the families in these communities are at present in an intermediate position—they do not have to share their supplies as do their fellows in the bush, yet they are much worse off during the hunger months, since they cannot rely on their kinsmen for support. Although it appears that most Africans must ultimately adopt the European system of economy, the encouragement of the single family household, before a system of trade has been established, might well lead to disaster.

CHAPTER X

DISTRIBUTION IN A TYPICAL VILLAGE

Character of the Village.

TO illustrate the distribution of food in an actual Bemba village I have chosen notes taken at Kasaka near Shiwa Ŋandu from 1 September to 7 October 1933. This was a settlement of twenty-nine huts, that is to say about the average size. The community was principally composed of four matrilocal family groups of which the male or female heads were near relatives of the headman. The members of the younger generation were closely knit by a number of cross-cousin marriages. Its structure was probably typical of the older Bemba village in which matrilocal marriage is still universally practised. Moreover, since the observations coincided with the recent copper slump, the proportion of adult men to women was unusually high in the village—i.e. nineteen men to twenty-three women—so that it was possible to see the traditional family units at their joint economic work. Kasaka stood at least 60 miles from the main motor road from Abercorn to Broken Hill and over 400 from the copper belt to the south, so that its direct contact with European civilization was slight, and native life had been little changed. On the other hand, the wage-earning possibilities were higher than in most parts of the country, since Kasaka stood seventeen miles from a European plantation (Shiwa Ŋandu) which afforded the younger men opportunities for work, and four out of the nineteen men were regularly employed there during the week, returning home at the week-ends. All but two of the fourteen younger men had visited the mines at least once, and one had been four times, but most of the women had never left their own country, or even this particular part of the territory. In this last respect the village was typical of conditions over most of the plateau. Certain environmental and seasonal difficulties as to the food-supply were of course limited to this particular area and these will be specified.

The financial position of the villagers can be gauged from the following figures: four out of the twenty adult males were too old to pay tax and therefore needed money only for occasional garments for themselves and their wives. Each had acquired one

cloth or blanket during the past year,[1] whether through a gift
from a son in work at the mines, the payment at a daughter's
marriage, or the sale of beer. One had been able to employ two
young boys to cut trees for him through the generosity of an
absent nephew. For the rest, these older men lived from harvest
to harvest without using money at all, and their position is typical
of their contemporaries all over the district. The four men
employed at Shiwa Dandu were regularly earning 10s. a month,
while most of the others had worked for two to three months at
a time locally to earn their tax and to make small extra sums for
clothes and other European goods. Three had used, or were
using, paid labour to make their gardens. One, an unusually
intelligent cultivator, had paid his tax by the sale of vegetables
to Europeans, and three had made a few extra shillings with
beer. It is doubtful whether on an average the men of this village
handled more than 25s. a head during the year, of which 10s.
went in tax.[2] In a community with fewer opportunities for work
locally, this sum would probably be smaller.

As regards its food-supply, the village was in a fairly satisfactory
position according to Bemba standards. Its gardens had not been
destroyed by locusts, and at the recent harvest the average figure
for the contents of its sixteen granaries was 2,804 lb. of millet. At
the time of observation, about three months after the reaping and
storing of the grain, the supply was still adequate and caused the
people no concern. Beer was brewed seven times during thirty-
two days and two gourds were brought into the village as presents.
These figures show that the millet-supply was quite sufficient, and
if the people went short of *ubwali* it was because the women could
not or would not cook it, and not because of its scarcity.

The relish situation was quite different, and it soon appeared
that the provision of *umunani* was the chief difficulty of the housewife at this particular season of the year. The garden vegetables
were over. The mushrooms would not appear for another two
months, and though there were stored legumes, &c., to fall back
on, there were such small quantities of these available that housewives were afraid to use them frequently for fear they would not
last till the end of the season. This left nothing for relish but
wild spinaches or *icikanda* orchids—food that had to be hunted

---

[1] At a cost of about 5s.
[2] The tax has since been reduced to 7s. 6d. per annum.

for in the bush some way off. The shortage of relish would have been more pronounced in the ordinary course of events than it actually was during my visit, for since the village stood in good game country, my party was able to provide three large buck for distribution among the inhabitants. The meat orgy described on pp. 158–9 occurred in this village.

The Composition of the Village.

Kasaka was a Bemba village built in what was originally a Bisa district. This part of the country[1] had been conquered by the Bemba under a former chief Mwamba shortly before the arrival of the Europeans, and he, according to the usual practice, had left a number of faithful captains and followers to hold the occupied territory for him, the forefathers of the present Kasaka being amongst them. The latter still spoke of himself as almost a stranger in a foreign land, and traced his origin from a district in the heart of the Bemba country about six days' journey away. Marriages between the Bemba and their conquered subjects had always been common, however, and a number of the inhabitants of the present village were plainly of Bisa stock,[2] and some even described themselves as Bisa.

The village itself was of fairly long standing as Bemba settlements go. The first Kasaka (Kasaka I on the accompanying chart) had been 'given a village' in 1914 by the then chief Mukuikile. He died in 1924 and was succeeded by the present Kasaka (Kasaka II), his younger brother, then a middle-aged man living at Mpika some sixty miles away, in European employment. The heir returned to his brother's village to mourn, to inherit the name, the spirit, and the hereditary bow of the dead man (*ukupyanika*), and finally, one of his widows. He had then to wait to see if his personality and prestige were sufficient to enable him to build up a village of his own. In all Bantu societies it is usual to find a delay of a year or so between the burial of a man and the final settlement of his succession and inheritance, but the Bemba kinship system allows such freedom of choice of residence to a dead man's relatives, that it remains for some time an open question as to whether his successor will be able to hold the remains

---

[1] The territory of Mukuikile, a sub-chief of Nkula.

[2] Slight differences in the religious and magic rites practised in this area seemed to be the only distinguishing marks.

of the village together or not. To the European it is extraordinary that twenty or thirty families can scatter here and there after a death and continue dispersed in this manner for two or three years, yet remain conscious of their unity and ready to join up again later, with losses and additions, to form a new community. But this is the case in Bemba society in which ties of kinship are eventually stronger than local association, and in the present instance Kasaka II returned to Mpika for a period of two years, taking with him the two most prominent women in the village, his two sisters, the latters' husbands and children. The majority of the other relatives, including the chief widow of Kasaka I, settled down temporarily in neighbouring villages where they had kinsmen.

The community reassembled in 1929, i.e. five years after the last headman's death, and had not moved its site before my visit in the autumn of 1933. Its composition showed clearly those two fundamental principles of local association already described—the matrilocal marriage rule and the strong identification of interest between the brother and the sister. There were four 'big houses' in the village, named for convenience A, B, C, and D on the chart. Kasaka's own family by previous wives had grown up and scattered and he was left living in his old age with NaMarya (A2), the widow of his dead brother, by whom he had two small children (A8 and A9). He was also responsible for four daughters of Kasaka I (A4, 5, 6, and 7), three of whom were married and one unmarried. Kasaka also fed Nakulu Marya (A3), the mother of his wife. This formed one matrilocal group in which the head of the family had succeeded to the care of his brother's widow and children.

The other two chief households in the village were those of Kasaka's two married sisters, NaMukonda (B2) and NaKabanda (C2). Here was a case in which matrilocal residence had persisted throughout the marriage, since these women's husbands, Malalo (B1) and Cabeluka (C1), had come from other villages in youth to marry and had remained in their wives' community all their lives. The groups of households attached to these two big houses have been named B and C respectively. To B belonged three married daughters (B3, 8, 9) and four married sons (B4, 5, 6, 7), and one young boy of 14 (B10). This was an unusual number of sons to remain living in their parents' village.[1] B5, 6, and 7 had all

---

[1] The opportunity of white employment locally probably accounted for it.

contracted intra-village marriages (to A5, D11, F2 respectively) and had therefore become attached as sons-in-law to groups A, D, and F, while Japesi, (B4), the eldest son of the family, had been deserted by his cross-cousin (A4) whom he had inherited as a widow, and had returned to live in his parents' village. To C belonged the households of two married daughters (C3 and 7) whose husbands (C4 and 8) had both come from other villages to marry them, and one son (C5) who had married a widow (C6) and had therefore been able to bring her to his village instead of going to live in hers. There was also a younger son of 15 (C9).

The fourth big house, D, was that of NaMulenga (D2), the sister of Cabeluka, the head of C group. This woman had accompanied her brother as a young married girl when he came from Citimukulu's territory, about five days' journey, to visit his mother's people not far from the present site of Kasaka. Here Cabeluka had found a wife, (Kasaka's sister, C2), and had therefore gone to live with Kasaka I, when the latter had been given a village. Cabeluka took his sister NaMulenga and her husband (D1 and D2) with him, showing how the brother-sister tie may result in a woman electing to stay under his care far away from her own country. Cabeluka and NaMulenga had remained together ever since. This grouping is interesting as showing how marriage and kinship ties may result in a man living all his life about 100 miles away from his place of birth and in a different chief's territory. To D belonged two married daughters' households— D3 married to Chambesi (D4), an 'outsider' by whom she had four children, the eldest daughter Mwika (D6) being recently married, making three generations of married couples in the matrilocal group. NaMulenga's younger daughter (D11) had also married her cross-cousin (B6) and had her first baby (D10) during my visit.

Thus the backbone of Kasaka village consisted of four matrilocal family groups (A, B, C, D), of which all except the headman himself had formed part of the original village of Kasaka I, and of which either the male or the female heads were united to each other by the brother-sister tie. In three cases (B, C, D) the husbands had joined their wives' community in youth and had never reverted to patrilocal residence, a practice which would be thought unusual nowadays.

Besides these four 'big houses' two or three other groups of families had joined Kasaka's community, though they were less closely related to him than the heads of the former. These groups have been named E and F. Nakulu Citembo (E1) was a classificatory sister of the grandfather of both Kasakas (ShiNkamba, cf. Chart A). She had remained behind in the village of Kasaka I and later joined that of Kasaka II with her daughter NaCitembo (E2), whose husband Macici (E3) was anxious to find work at the Shiwa Dandu estate. She was a youngish woman with one small girl and four boys (E6, 7, 8, 9,). Her younger brother, Dicksonee (E4), had married a girl in the same village, Jani (B9), 'because it is good to marry in a village where your older sister lives', while Macici's classificatory brother, ShiMutale Edward (E5), had contracted a similar marriage with NaMutale (B8.) These two young men were therefore sons-in-law attached to the big house B, and economically dependent on it, but they had their own relatives in Group E, who, as we shall see, supported them in time of trouble.

Group F was composed of the households of three sisters (F1, 2, 3). These were the daughters of Mwelua, now dead, but originally a member of Kasaka I's community and distantly related to him, who was sent to hold the country for the Bemba in early days.

NaMwice (F3) had rejoined the village of Kasaka II because her husband, Pensulo (F4), found it convenient to work near by, although he had no relatives of his own in the village. NaMwice had seven children (F5, 12, 13, 14, 15, 16, 17), one of them, F5, married to D10. The second sister, NaMulenga (F2), on the death of her first husband, had married one of the sons of group B, Wankie (B7), and being a widow, had to live in her husband's village rather than her own. Her new husband supported her two children (F10 and 11). These two sisters, F2 and F3, were subsequently joined by a recently widowed sister, NaCengo (F1), of whom they said, 'She has not yet found any one else to marry, and so she said, "Alas! Am I to live alone? Let me go and settle with my sister and wait".' She was supported by her two sisters' husbands and worked for them in return.

The process by which a Bemba village is built up around the central households of near kinsmen of the headman, afterwards augmented by other less closely connected relatives, is thus clearly illustrated by the structure of Kasaka. If a split were to occur in the future it would be likely to affect the more distant members of the family, i.e. Groups E and F, or the middle-aged householders, the fathers of growing families, such as Chambesi (D4), Nselela (C4), Mutaka (B16), or Pensulo (E4), who had come from outside to marry into the village, but who might now consider themselves of sufficient standing to be able to take their children elsewhere if they wished to do so. In fact, Chambesi asked permission to remove his wife and children to a new village set up by one of his relatives during my visit.

The growth and consolidation of a village group by means of intra-village marriages, whether between cross-cousins or not, is also illustrated on the chart. Among the fourteen young couples in Kasaka, there were eight cross-cousin marriages (A4–B4; A5–B5; B6–D11; D10–F5; A6–F6; B8–E5; B9–E4; C7–C8;), of which four took place within the village.

The Village Food-supply.

The daily food consumption in the village and its preparation and division will now be described and should serve to illustrate, by concrete example, the different methods of food distribution already enumerated.

In any such sketch of an actual community, the individual characters, with all their temperamental and physical peculiarities, and the dramatic incidents of everyday life, seem to stand out in bold relief, while the formal patterns of kinship, which we have just described, fade from view. We are watching a number of people who like or hate to share their food, or to prepare it in common, and not plotting a system of relationships on a kinship chart. But this is, of course, how the scene appears in the context of everyday life. The abstractions of the anthropologist are based on two types of material: viz. statements of natives as to what they believe they do, ought to do, or would like to do, and his own observations of a number of human beings of widely different personalities, reacting to a set of tribal rules in different ways—conforming to them or rebelling against them. A concrete account of the distribution of food in three family groups will not only enable the reader to visualize the whole process, but will give him an idea of the kind of observations upon which these generalizations have been based.

Calendar of Events.

The weather during the month of observation must first be *describe weather* described, since this naturally affected the food available and the energy of the villagers. It was typical of September in this part of the world, a month of change between the end of the cold season and the beginning of the hot season. In the first week driving winds blew and the sky was often cloudy and sometimes grey. On one day the men declared it too cold to go off to their tree-cutting, and on another the women waited to grind till late in the morning because, they said, their hands were cold and slipped on the stone. The dead leaves had already fallen, and the forest turned crimson with the new young growth. It became hotter and the people more languid. Children sat about in the shade at noon and seemed too tired to run or to play violent *Hot* games. There is a curious air of suspension about a native village *weather* in the hot weather. Women sit inside their hut doors and talk interminably in low murmurs, and the young girls lounge in groups of four and five in the shade and throw round polished seeds up in the air and catch them on the backs of their knuckles, a game which they play by fits and starts in a desultory way. One asked me to talk to her 'because of the boredom that is in a village when the weather is hot'.[1] By the 18th hot winds had begun to spring up, and on the 26th the first shower of thunder-rain fell. The wet weather set in in earnest in November. These notes on the climatic changes of this month should be considered in relation to the work done by the villagers during this time (cf. Chap. XVIII). I believe the slackening off of labour in this month is not only caused by uncertainty as to the coming of the rains, but also lack of energy due to the sultry heat.

Details of the activities of the people are set out below. This calendar is intended to give an impression of the work of the community as a whole, and any events such as a beer-drink or the killing of a buck, which affected the food-supply of the village.[2] Some of the notes, particularly those on the work done by the men, are unnecessarily full for a study of the food-supply proper, but they are included here in order to give some idea of the irregular

[1] *Citendwa ca muno mushi pa lusuba.*
[2] From 13 September to 1 October notes on the work of each member of the village were taken. Before this time, general observations only.

rhythm of work in a Bemba village, and to provide material for
the discussion on the people's use of time (vide Chap. XVIII).

September 1st, 1933. Two gourds of beer ready, one drunk by old
men, one by young men. A new baby born. Women gather
from other villages to congratulate, and spend two or three days
in the village. Women's garden work postponed during this
time.

2nd. Old men go out to clear the bush. Young men sit at home
finishing the sour dregs of the beer. More visits of neighbouring
women to see the new baby. Few women go out to do garden
work.

3rd (Sunday). Young men and women go to a church service conducted in a neighbouring village by a visiting Mission doctor
(Scotch Mission). No garden work.

4th. Visit of the Mission doctor to Kasaka. Protestants and Catholics
both attend the services. No garden work.

5th. Old men cut trees. Young men sit at home and shape axe-
handles. Some women working again.

6th. Old and young men working by 6.30 a.m. and hard at it till
2 p.m. Two gourds of beer divided between old and young in
the evening. Women working in their gardens normally.

7th. A buck shot by observer's party. Young men go out to fetch
the meat. Women grind extra flour to eat with it. Two gourds
of beer also made ready and drinking begins at 2 p.m. By 4
o'clock young men swaggering around the village, ready to
quarrel, which they finally do. Dancing at night. Old women
hilarious, and rebuked by their daughters for charging into a
rough dance on the village square. Not enough beer for the
younger women. They remain sober and express disapproval of
the rest. No garden work done, except by old men.

8th. Every one off to their gardens in high spirits at 8 a.m. Back at
12 a.m. Young men sit in shelter and drink beer dregs for two
hours, singing Scotch Mission hymns in sol-fa. Young girls go
out on a miniature fish-poisoning expedition, but catch nothing.

9th and 10th. Observers away. D10, son of D11 born. A crowd
of relatives from neighbouring villages come to congratulate.
No garden work said to have been done.

11th. The baby born on September 1st (daughter of a visiting
relative) dies. Mourners arrive from surrounding villages. Eight
young women (A6, B3, B8, B9, C3, C6, F1, F5) go to do their
tribute labour for chief. All garden work postponed.

12th. Mourning party leaves with bereaved mother, accompanied by
women of Kasaka wailing up the road. Young women still away

at capital. Little garden work done by women. Men tree-cutting half the day.

13th. Heads of A, B, C, D go visiting relatives twenty-two miles away, with their wives, to mourn. Clearing bush by two men (D1, E3). Garden work done by two women (D2, E2). Meat distributed.

14th. A1, B1, C1, D1 and wives still away. One man (E3) clears bush. Meat still available. Young women still away doing tribute labour.

15th. Three men begin digging dry-weather gardens by the river (A1, C1, C3). Little boys go bird-snaring. Young women still away at the capital. Nobody to get relish. No proper meal cooked.

16th. Eight men clear bush (A1, B1, B7, C1, C4, D1, E3, F6). One away hunting. Three young men home for week-end from work at Shiwa Dandu. Young women return from doing tribute labour in the evening, greeted by shouts from the whole community. Old women all remain in village.

17th (Sunday). Great heat. Young men sit about in shelter all day, comb each other's hair, shave, and delouse each other. No relish available. Women too tired to cook.

18th. Seven men work again clearing bush (B1, C1, C4, C8, D1, E3, F6). Five women piling branches (B2, B3, C2, C3, F2).

19th. Nine men clear bush (A1, B1, C1, C4, C8, D1, E3, E5, F6). One woman hoeing (C2). Three women piling branches (B2, C7, F2). Young women go fish-poisoning and catch one fish (about 2 lb.).

20th. Six men clear bush (A1, B1, C1, E3, E5, F6). One house-building (C4).

21st. Five men clear bush (A1, B1, C1, D8, E3). Five women pile branches (B2, B3, C2, C3, D2).

22nd. Three men clear bush (B1, B7, C1). One man hoes (H1). Four young men go fishing (C8, D10, E3, F6) with three of the wives (C7, E2, F5). Three piling branches.

23rd. Five men clear bush (A1, B1, B7, C1, D1). One goes on digging a dry-weather garden (E3). Five women pile branches (A6, B2, C3, C7, E2). One hoes (E2).

24th (Sunday). Four gourds of beer divided between whole village. Sufficient for women as well as men. Beer-drinking lasts two days off and on.

25th. Two old men only able to tree-cut (A1, D1). Young men afraid to climb trees because of 'beer before the eyes'. They sit in their shelter and make baskets. B4 hunts with his own gun.

One woman only does garden work (C3). Young boys snare
birds. Remains of beer drunk.

26th. Old men work (A1, C1, D1). Young men 'too cold'. B4 still
away hunting.

27th. Five men clear bush (A1, B1, C1, D1, E3, F6). One man and
four women carry meat sixteen miles to Shiwa (A6, B9, D4, E3,
F3). Meat orgy described on pp. 158–9.

28th. Every one (men and women) off at 6 a.m. Work till 2 p.m.,
declaring they are strong with meat. A little beer in the evening.

29th. Rain at night. First net-hunt possible. All men and children
join in. Nothing killed. Six women pile branches.

30th. More beer. Four men clear bush (A1, B1, C1, D1). E3 digs
dry-weather garden.

October 1st (Sunday). Young women whitewash houses (B9, D6, F5).

2nd. Headman provides beer for a working bee. All men join to
clear bush for him and drink afterwards.

This calendar makes no attempt to give a complete record of
the activities of the people, as unfortunately the data are not
sufficiently full. It brings out certain interesting points, however.
The first is the irregularity of the work done and the greater
industry of the old as compared with the young, especially among
the men.[1] By noting the chart letters of those who went to clear
the bush or to pile branches each day, it will be seen that the
only natives who went consecutively to work were the old men of
the village, those reckoned by the Government as too feeble to
pay tax. This is a point which will be referred to again (cf. Chap.
XIX). This was admittedly a slack time of the year, but it will
be noted that the arrival of visitors, such as relatives or the local
missionaries, births and deaths in the village or neighbourhood,
the absence of the young women doing tribute labour, or beer
parties, disrupted the work of the village or brought it to a standstill. On no single day did every man and woman go off to work.
On five days out of thirty-one beer was brewed, and on three of
these occasions most of the inhabitants were incapacitated for
work. I think this would be a typical situation in September,
which is one of the chief beer-drinking months. On two days
no porridge was cooked because of the shortage of relish and the

[1] Five old men worked 14 days out of 20; seven young men worked 7 days
out of 20. This will be discussed more fully later, but it is obvious that any
community in which the young and active males work exactly half as much as
the old must suffer as regards its food production.

fatigue of the old women left alone to housekeep with their daughters away. On nine days meat was eaten and a whole buck was divided on one occasion. The other fortunes and misfortunes of the kitchen affected individual households alone.

Three Families Housekeep.

To illustrate the preparation and distribution of food in detail, three matrilocal family groups have been selected for description out of the five observed. These are: A, B, and D, and the linking of the different households composing these units is indicated on the plan on p. 177 by dotted lines. The amount of food consumed by each unit is roughly shown on the tables on pp. 178–83 and it will be seen how, in each case, the size of the consuming group, the labour-supply, male and female, and differences in the social status and individual temperament of its members affect the daily intake of food.

Group A. Kasaka, the head of Group A and headman of the village, had three households under his care. He lived in his own hut with his wife NaMarya (A2). His three younger children, Kapea (A7), a girl of 14,[1] Marya (A8), aged 7, and Cileshye (A9) aged 5, came to eat, but not to sleep. Kasaka had his own dish of food, to which he called one or two of his old cronies, such as the heads of Groups B and C, joining them on their verandas in turn. His small son might have been invited to share the meal if his table manners had not disgusted his father, and so he remained eating with his mother and sisters instead. The second household of the group was that of Kampamba (A5), who was temporarily on a visit and whose husband was away at the mines. In the third house lived another daughter, Kampamba (A6), who had been married over a year. She had been given her own fire-place but not her own granary, so that her husband, Findee (F6), was still entirely dependent on his father-in-law for food. Usually a basket was sent to him at the men's shelter, but on five days out of nineteen his wife was given flour to cook for herself, or to carry out into the bush for his meal. In the fourth house lived Nakulu Marya (A3), the crippled old mother of

---

[1] Kapea engaged herself to be married to a young boy from a neighbouring village during my visit and demanded grain to grind for him, but the father refused, as the marriage had not received the formal consent of the bridegroom's parents. The boy was therefore merely allowed to share a dish with the other son-in-law and was not treated with the 'cooking of honour'.

NaMarya. The permanent group of eaters was thus composed of two men, four women, and three children, and provision for them depended on the amount of labour the group could supply and the energy and intelligence of its members.

Kasaka himself was a dignified old man, conscious of his royal connexions and a supporter of the traditional etiquette. He was a hard worker, who went out alone to garden on twelve days out of the twenty recorded, but as a character he had little force. His authority in the village was weakened by his fluctuating allegiance to the Roman Catholic Church, which prevented him from performing the customary rites to the village spirits in any whole-hearted way.[1] To help him, he had only his son-in-law Findee, who had cut trees for him for four years before marrying his daughter Kampamba, and who was making a garden of his own this season for the first time. Findee was a satisfactory son-in-law as young men go nowadays, but it will be seen that he only worked exactly half as many days as his father-in-law during the fortnight when notes were taken. Kasaka's other son-in-law sent financial support on occasion, as did his absent sons, but did no garden work. This is a typical situation in a modern matrilocal group, though it is probable that if Kasaka had had a stronger personality, a number of his dead brother's relatives, including his chief wife, would not have left him for the neighbouring village of Stefano, and he would have commanded at least a day's labour on his garden from his own villagers, according to tribal custom. As it was, he paid for their help with beer brewed for a working-party. It is common nowadays to find headmen trying to give the hospitality expected of their office without possessing larger supplies than commoners. At the time of observation Kasaka had two half granaries full of millet, i.e. about 4,808 lb., an empty ground-nut granary, a carrying-basket of maize cobs, and one of ground beans, with 4 or 5 lb. of beans, peas, dried leaves, and dried potatoes only. Thus he had a better supply of millet than most of the villagers, probably owing to the help of an active son-in-law, but very few relishes.

The fact that mainly determined the amount of food eaten during the period noted was the shortage of female labour. There

---

[1] Some of these rites were undertaken by his eldest sister NaMukonda (B2), but he disliked the fact that she officiated and occasionally resumed control.

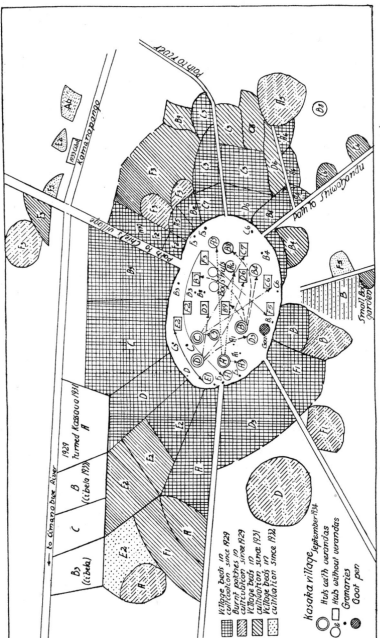

FIG. 3. Village plan of Kasaka. (Enlargement of centre section appears on p. 177.)

was only one young woman able and willing to search for relish
and to do much grinding. Nakulu Marya was crippled with age
and rheumatism, and a burden on the group rather than a help.
NaMarya herself was elderly, frail, querulous, and constantly
anxious. She was a poor organizer and lacked social support in
the village into which she had married as an inherited wife, and
she had no relatives of her own except her old mother. She was
criticized by the women of Kasaka's family, and as always happens
in such a situation, rumour had begun to saddle her with some
of the misfortunes which had recently fallen on the village.[1]
The difficult relationship between a man's wife and his sister,
inevitable in a matrilineal community, was intensified by the
clash of temperaments between NaMarya, who was weak and
timid in character, although technically the senior as the headman's wife, and NaMukonda (B2), domineering, efficient, and
sharp-tongued, with a large family of sons and daughters in
support. Jealousy, concealed beneath the surface, broke out
violently from time to time, culminating in a fight between the
two women at a beer-drink which sent NaMarya off for two days
to sleep in the grass shelter near her garden with her old mother
because she feared that 'her heart would get hot again' and she
might again abuse her husband's sister—a bad breach of Bemba
kinship sentiment.

Thus, both the temperamental peculiarities and the social position of NaMarya made catering a burdensome task for her at a
time when relish was hard to find, and as the wife of a headman
she had to dispense additional hospitality. The heads of the
other matrilocal groups, e.g. the sisters NaMukonda and NaKabanda (B2 and C2), would help each other when they were rushed
with work, but NaMarya could only rely on her daughter Ka-
mpambâ (A6), a quiet, steady girl who took her full share of the
work when present, but who gardened four days out of twenty
and went fishing, looking for relish, or carried meat to Shiwa
Dandu for a European employer on five days. Kapea, the
14-year-old girl, was intelligent and lively, but did not work.
NaMarya was afraid to scold her for a characteristic reason—she

[1] e.g. people said that the failure of the hunting ordeal at the founding of the
village had been due to NaMarya. She had not remained indoors all day as
behoved a headman's wife on such an occasion, but had gone abroad visiting.
They complained that she did not bother herself (*ukusakamanya*) about the village.
Charges of witchcraft frequently result from a situation of this kind.

feared her husband's sister would take the girl's side.[1] Thus the attitudes resulting from the tribal kinship pattern were emphasized by the contrasting personalities of the two women concerned. As a result of this domestic situation NaMarya devoted her time to making beer, which she declared was less trouble than fetching relish and a good substitute for food. She only went to garden four days out of twenty. On five days Kampamba cooked for her, but when the latter was away, the family did without.

The extent of a headman's hospitality can be seen from the chart on pp. 178–80. The total man-value of those fed by NaMarya varied from 3·6 to 10·8 and the number of eaters was constant on very few days. The seven mourners who came to wail the sudden death of a baby were the headman's responsibility. Honoured guests, 'sons of chiefs', and relatives of Kasaka who arrived on the 14th were given a hut specially cleared for them and a basket of food apart. A Mission teacher appeared on another day and also a stranger, who did formal obeisance in front of the headman's hut. In these circumstances it will be seen that the individual intake of flour varied greatly from day to day, i.e. from 6 lb. per head to 2 lb. The number of meals per day altered with the cooking strength of the group. On three days out of twenty no proper porridge meal was cooked because Kampamba was away doing tribute labour or working with her husband in the bush gardens; on one day Kasaka refused to take his share of the meal because there was not enough for the guests; on four days there was only one meal in the afternoon; on seven days, one meal plus an extra dish of potatoes in the morning, and on the remaining four days, two proper meals. Beer was drunk by the elders of the party on seven days, but not by the children. The figures for this family, therefore, illustrate the irregularity in daily intake due to the tribal system of hospitality and the variation in the number of meals caused by cooking difficulties, but the special problem of this group was its shortage of female labour and the inefficiency of the housewife in charge.

Group B, that of Malalo, provided a perfect example of the expanding ring of interdependent households which may form a matrilocal cooking unit. In the central hut Malalo lived with his wife NaMukonda (B2) and a varying number of his grandchildren, generally Sampa (B13), a boy of 9 and Ruti (B14) a girl, aged 8,

[1] A period of revolt and laziness seems typical of Bemba girls at this age.

the children of Mukonda (B3), the eldest married daughter.
Mukonda had her own granary and garden, but sent her younger
children to sleep with the grandparents after the Bemba custom,
and usually to eat with them. She was economically independent
of Malalo, but shared in the food of the parent household when
absence at Shiwa Ŋandu with her husband prevented her cooking,
or when she was tabooed from doing so. Malalo's second daughter,
NaMutale (B8) was still completely dependent on the central
household. She had been married over two years and had a small
son of fifteen months. She had been given her own fire-place,
and as will be seen, got grain to grind and cook for him separately
on several occasions during this month. She was once allowed
to take millet to brew beer in her own hut,[1] but she had no granary
of her own and her husband was a ne'er-do-well who seemed in
no hurry to make his own garden. Thus NaMutale cooked and
ate with her mother while her husband and baby were also fed from
the central household. Jani (B9), the youngest daughter, had only
just married and had not yet been given her own fire-place. Na-
Mukonda, a stern critic and disciplinarian, declared that she was 'not
old enough to take food from a granary' (cf. p. 125) and would only
waste the supplies and find herself 'hungry in the rainy season'.
Accordingly, Jani cooked and ate with her mother, and her
husband, Dickonsee (E4), was fed by his mother-in-law when he
came home for the week-ends from work. Thus in Group B we
see three married daughters representing the three stages by which
a Bemba girl attains independence from the parent household—
first a fire-place, then a granary, and lastly complete freedom of
ownership. Besides these households a number of other relatives
formed an outer ring and occasionally received food from Malalo.
These included his eldest son Japesi (B4), an unpopular, tedious
person, who had been deserted by his wife (A4) and had therefore
returned to his mother for support. She cooked for him throughout our visit and would no doubt have made use of his half-empty
granary if necessary. Two other sons of Malalo (B6 and 7) had
married in the village and were resident there, and though they
were fed by their respective mothers-in-law, NaMukonda occasionally sent them baskets of food or invited them to share beer. She
also sent flour to her sister NaKabanda (C2) when the latter
was too tired to grind. Her young son, Kampamba (B10), aged

---

[1] Giving one gourd to her mother and keeping one for herself.

15, slept in his own hut with friends and hung around the young men's *nsaka* for remains of food, but once or twice received a special dish of his own. Thus NaMukonda cooked for three men permanently, for two additional sons-in-law in emergencies, and sent presents of food to two sons when she felt inclined. Two women regularly ate with her, with an additional married daughter on occasion, and a varying number of grandchildren. It is improbable that she would have kept together so many of her children's households, including those of her three sons, as well as her daughters', if she had not had so pronounced a character. Malalo himself was a quiet little nonentity, who played second fiddle both in his house and out of it, but NaMukonda has already been described as an incisive personality. She was a good organizer, who met each domestic emergency with calm decision and who kept her large family in wholesome awe of her sharp tongue. Her withering comments on the follies of the present generation were a constant delight to me. They were uttered with a shrug, a lifted eye-brow, and a glance of understanding as though between two adults alone in a nursery of tiresome children. NaMukonda's social status in the village as a resident of old standing, the eldest sister of the headman, and the mother of a large family gave her added advantages, in addition to her strong character. It was significant that her house was always referred to as 'at NaMukonda's' (*kwa NaMukonda*) and not, as would have been more usual, 'at Malalo's'.

To feed this family, Malalo had one granary containing about 2,272 lb. of millet and only 2 or 3 lb. of dried peas, potatoes, and beans, but if in distress he had possibilities of help from his oldest son-in-law Mutaka (B16) and also rights over the granary of his son Japesi whom he was supporting. The latter, who possessed the only village gun, brought home any game he shot. Gideon (B6), the third son, was employed as an assistant to a white man's hunter and also gave occasional presents of meat to his father and mother, so that the dietetic situation of Group B was a good one. It will be seen how the addition of each extra supporting household strengthens the position of the whole family.

As regards the labour force available, Malalo himself was industrious, but without much physical strength. He worked in his garden on twelve days out of twenty during my visit. His oldest son-in-law Mutaka owed him no further service, but made his garden close to that of Malalo so that his wife might be happy working with her mother and sisters and might get additional help in this way. The youngest son-in-law, Dicksonee (E4), had done two years' work for his wife's family before marrying Jani, but was now working locally for a European and only returned from time to time to do gardening.

The last son-in-law, ShiMutale (E5), was an interesting character, as he represented a special type of graceless good-for-nothing found in the Bemba country to-day, a young man who gets all he can from his wife's people under the old system of kinship obligations, but gives little or nothing in return. ShiMutale was always elegantly dressed in a spotless white shirt, frequently washed and ironed in public. He was constantly parting and arranging his long hair in a small mirror according to the latest fashion, and spent most of his time lounging in the *nsaka*, playing with his baby son or twanging a Bemba lyre. His most active amusement was bicycling madly around the village swearing at the children in English, of which language he knew no other phrases. I watched him from my tent door during this month, and I must admit that I had not believed it possible that an active young man of about 25 could have done nothing so consistently for so many days on end without feeling the time drag. ShiMutale had at one time worked for Europeans and sometimes announced his intention of doing so again, but in the meantime he stayed where he was. He had paid no *mpanga* for his bride, claiming the cross-cousin relationship as an excuse for not doing so, and as will be seen from the table, worked exactly six days out of twenty as compared with his father-in-law's twelve.

This case is described in detail because it illustrates the way in which a certain number of young Bemba contrive to shirk their marriage obligations under modern conditions, and thus place a heavy strain on the economic resources of the matrilocal group. They do so usually on the plea that they are resting after their work at the mines, or are about to take other jobs 'soon', and they are able to flout their duties with impunity, since the shortage of men in the district makes parents willing to put up with sons-in-law whom they would never have tolerated under the old régime. A quarrel which broke out between ShiMutale and his wife during this month illustrates this fact, and also shows clearly how the period of matrilocal marriage acts to a certain extent as a time of trial for the young husband, even under the changed conditions of the present day.

On this occasion ShiMutale asked his wife, who seemed devoted to him in spite of his laziness and violence, to boil some sweet potatoes for him early in the morning so that he could entertain his friends. The potatoes were his own possession, since he had dug the beds on which they grew, although he had made no millet garden. NaMutale refused, because this would have made her too late to join her mother and sisters at work in the gardens. ShiMutale swore at her and pushed her roughly and she, after the manner of all Bemba women when insulted within earshot of their relatives, shot out a piercing yell. In a moment every one was at their door-way staring, and NaMukonda flung herself across the village in full torrent of abusive defence. This is a regular stage in every matrimonial quarrel among the Bemba— the arrival of the girl's mother, and, if possible, the man's too. People look at each other significantly and say, 'Look there! The mother has come.' They mean that the battle is set. On this occasion the villagers gathered together, and even the quiet Malalo followed in the wake of his more violent wife to support their insulted, but scarcely injured, child. The next stage in this typical quarrel came quickly. The angry women forced their way into the hut and threw out the cooking- and carrying-baskets, and removed the pots—all the women's possessions in fact. This is also the prescribed conduct in a serious matrimonial squabble.[1] The onlookers, like a chorus, commented: 'See, they have thrown out the pots.' Malalo finally led his sobbing daughter away, and the 'beaten' girl retired to her mother's hut with NaMukonda and her other daughter following, shouting obscene abuse.

The woman's family refused to cook for the husband, and though there was no chance of ShiMutale starving, more especially as he had a number of his own relatives in the village, yet the strike of the cooks had a special significance. It was a repudiation of the legal obligations of the marriage contract, just as the removal of NaMutale's cooking-pots in the first instance was a sign that a serious quarrel had begun. ShiMutale strolled about the village all day long, twanging the Bemba one-stringed lyre, with elaborate unconcern. His young friends idling in the men's shelter amused

[1] I have notes of eight matrimonial quarrels in which the procedure was just the same.

themselves by shouting to him slyly from time to time, 'Getting hungry, sir?' To which he replied on each occasion with would-be jauntiness, 'No sir! I am extremely full' (*Yo Mukwai! Naikuta sana*). He must have known, however, that he was not in a strong position as a son-in-law who had paid no *mpanga* and was known as a wastrel. Taunts to this effect had been freely shouted by NaMukonda in the heat of the quarrel, and the refusal of the in-laws to cook might have meant anything from a public protest to the beginning of a definite break, and in the latter case, ShiMutale as a father who had paid nothing at his marriage and had done no years of service, would have no legal rights to his small son.

The quarrel in this case ended quickly. NaMutale forgot her injuries and slipped back to her husband's hut after dark. NaMukonda, apparently rather worn after the morning's screaming, sat brooding on the veranda of her hut alone. Her comments on the affair were instructive. She had not liked the marriage, but the man was a cross-cousin. 'There are no husbands for the girls nowadays'—the Bemba mothers' inevitable refrain. If things went on like this the marriage would break up and the child would belong to 'us'. But then NaMutale was in the wrong in this quarrel! 'Really, the young people of to-day!' she said. 'The girls give their husbands no respect. A woman should always submit to her husband (*ukunakila ku mulume*) but now they just disobey. Then their husbands beat them and then', ruefully, in memory of the morning's agitation, 'it twists their mothers' hearts (*ukuongoloka mitima yabo*). And then what do you think? In the evening they say, "I like him again." They don't want to sleep alone on a bed all night, and so they go back to their husbands all the same. Really!' she repeated with a shrug, and eyes raised heavenwards in protest, 'The young people of to-day!' (*Aba uno mwaka.*)

Whether NaMukonda was right in attributing all matrimonial troubles to modern morals is impossible to judge. It seems to me probable that any system which involves a period of trial of the son-in-law in his wife's village must result in unstable equilibrium during the first years of married life, and that the elements of tension must have existed before, even if quarrels were less frequent and less open.[1] But this case illustrates clearly the strains

[1] A more serious quarrel occurred in the same month in the house of NaCi-

to which the matrilocal group is subject nowadays, the parents'
tolerance of unsatisfactory sons-in-law under protest, because
'there are no men in the country', the less strict tribal standards
of wifely conduct, and finally, the unstable character of marriages
in which no service has been done, or *mpanga* paid.

As regards its cooking team, Group B was well supplied with
labour, efficiently organized by NaMukonda, and it was possible
to see the matrilocal group functioning as it should as a means
of training the young housewife in her work of cooking and
distributing food. NaMukonda had two active young women to
help her (B8 and B9) and refused to cook for her grandchildren
on one occasion unless they also helped by digging up the potatoes
in time.[1] She herself, unlike most of her fellow villagers, had
finished piling the branches in her own garden, and though she
worked on eight days out of twenty helping her daughters in their
gardens, she never failed to cook because of her garden work.
The labour problem which was so acute in the case of Group A
was thus not a difficulty for Group B. Nor did NaMukonda seem
perturbed by the appearance of extra visitors. She entertained
travelling relatives, sent food to additional members of the family,
and her grandchildren, if not actually all fed by her, were running
in and out of her hut all day picking up food or digging up potatoes
from her beds—a situation which did not occur in Group A.
NaMukonda affected distress at the children's raids, but plainly
loved to have them with her. 'Little crocodile!' she would say
proudly of her favourite, the 8-year-old Ruti. 'She snaps at everything in the hut.'

The total man-power value of those she fed varied as much as
in the case of Group A, i.e. from 5·2 to 11·6, but the amount of
flour eaten per head showed a larger variation, i.e. from 0·4 to
1·3 lb. This family had a proper meal every day out of the twenty,

---

leshye (C8), who was beaten quite severely and without cause by her husband
Yolam (C9) when in his cups. On this occasion Group C refused to cook for
the son-in-law for three days, until NaKabanda (C2), realizing that Yolam was
a satisfactory son-in-law in other ways, said, 'Shall we refuse food to one of the
family because of a matter of beer? No! Let him share with us', and sent her
daughter back again. But Yolam was still uneasy, because he had no small coin
with which to compensate his wife and declared he was afraid of 'the things his
wife was thinking against him in her heart'. This means two bad quarrels between husband and wife in one month, and out of ten young couples.
[1] Her middle-aged son was also punished in the same way when he passed
what she considered captious criticisms on the cooking of the greens.

and ate one meal on five days, one meal and a snack on nine days and two meals on the remaining five.

It will be seen, therefore, that in the village of Kasaka which had a fairly plentiful food-supply, the daily consumption of millet did not fall much below the average for the district (cf. Chap. II), but there were great variations in the amount of food consumed daily, owing to such factors as the universal shortage of vegetable relish, the sudden appearance of meat, the amount of beer brewed, and the absence of the young women doing tribute work for the chief. There were also striking individual differences in the amounts consumed per head in the families observed. These variations can be accounted for by differences in the individual initiative and intelligence of the housekeeper, as in the case of Group A and Group B, in the amount of female labour available, or in the number of relatives or visitors entertained.

The distribution of food outside the permanent consuming group is shown in the case of hospitality given by all three groups to strangers, the anthropologist's servants, visiting teachers, &c., and the extra help constantly being given an outer ring of relatives in the case of Group B.

The record of the number of eating-baskets sent to the men's shelter daily shows in a striking fashion how the custom of the formal presentation of food to the sons-in-law affects the daily intake of each man. The village plan on p. 177 illustrates diagrammatically the dependence of the daughter household on the 'big houses': i.e. A3 and A6 are fed by or with the inmates of A; B3, 4, 7, 9 depend on B; C3, 5, 7 on C; D3, 6, 11 on D; while E2 feeds her mother E; and F1, F2 and F3, three sisters, regularly eat together. The heads of the big houses A, B, C, and D eat alone or together or on the verandas of their respective huts, but the young men eat in the *nsaka*. Of these there were 12, of whom 4 were generally away working during the week, leaving 9 regular eating mates B4, 6, and 7, C4 and 8, D10, and E3, 5 and F6, without counting the small boys who hung round the edge of the shelter waiting for bits. The women who supplied these men, in spite of being so closely related, seemed to make no effort to organize the daily supply of food to the *nsaka*. Each sent when she possibly could. Thus on some days two baskets reached the shelter, on others six, and the average daily consumption of each individual varied from 0·1 lb. of flour per day to 1·5 lb.

This rather detailed account of the distribution of food in a single Bemba village shows the extent to which sociological factors —the legal obligations of kinship and hospitality and the symbolism of giving and taking food-supplies—actually do affect the amount of food eaten by each individual in a community living as near the subsistence level as a number of African tribes do at the present day.

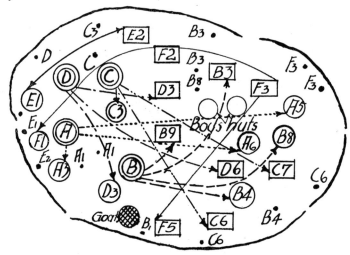

KASAKA VILLAGE

September 1934

◯	*Huts with verandas*
◯ & ▢	*Huts without verandas*
•	*Granaries*
⬤	*Goat pen*

Enlarged section of plan on page 167 showing huts composing different matrilocal groups.

Tables showing Number of Eaters and Individual Intake of Flour Per Day in Two Family Groups, A and B, Kasaka Village.

13 September to 2 October, 1934

Note 1. Man value obtained by allotting the figure 1·0 for each adult man, 0·8 for each woman or adolescent boy or girl, 0·6 for each child of either sex between 6 and 12, 0·4 for each child under 6 (called infant in this case).

Note 2. Abbreviations used: s.i.l. = son-in-law.
pot. = potatoes.
flr. = flour.
gr.-nuts = ground-nuts.

Note 3. The flour used is millet flour in every case.

FAMILY A. KASAKA

Permanent Group: 2 men, 2 women, 1 adolescent girl, 1 child, 1 infant. Total man value: 5·4

Date	Total man value	Remarks	Amount of food	Indiv. intake of flour	Meals	Remarks
Sept. 13	10·8	7 mourning relatives entertained.	10 lb. flr., 6 lb. meat, 2 lb. cow-pea leaves (fresh), ½ lb. gr.-nuts.	0·9 lb.	2 meals.	..
,, 14	10·0	Unexpected visiting relatives (3 men, 2 women, 1 child) and stranger claiming hospitality from headman. Host refuses to eat, as food is short.	10 lb. flr. Remains of yesterday's relish.	0·9 lb.	2 meals.	..

,, 15	3·6	Visitors gone. S.i.l. (F6) and wife away.	10 lb. pot.	··	1 meal.	No relish available in daughter's absence (A5). No porridge cooked.
,, 16	6·4	S.i.l.'s friend cooked for.	5 lb. flr., 2 lb. cow-pea leaves (fresh), 2 lb. pot.	0·6 lb.	1 meal, 1 pot. snack.	A5 given flr. to cook for husband.
,, 17	5·4	Headman told he cannot invite visitors, as too little relish.	5 lb. flr., ¾ lb. orchid roots, ¼ lb. gr.-nuts.	0·9 lb.	1 meal, 1 pot. snack.	A5 grinds by herself. Relish dug by children.
,, 18	3·6	Mother.	4 lb. flr., ¾ lb. orchid roots, ¼ lb. gr.-nuts.	1·1 lb.	1 meal.	A5 cooks for husband, sisters, and brother.
,, 19	6·4	Visiting school teacher fed.	4 lb. flr., 2 lb. cow-pea leaves (fr.), ½ lb. gr.-nuts.	0·6 lb.	1 meal, 1 pot. snack.	A5 cooks and finds relish.
,, 20	3·6	No visitors. S.i.l. and wife away.	5 lb. pot.	··	2 pot. snacks.	A5 away. NaMarya too tired to look for relish.
,, 21	6·6	2 friends of headman invited.	5 lb. flr., ½ lb. dried peas.	0·7 lb.	1 meal, 1 pot. snack.	··
,, 22	6·4	2 guests staying in village.	5 lb. flr., 2 lb. wild spinach (fresh), ½ lb. gr.-nuts.	0·8 lb.	1 meal.	··
,, 23	3·6	S.i.l. and wife away.	9 lb. flr., ½ lb. dried peas, 4 lb. pot.	2·0 lb.	1 meal, 1 pot. snack.	··
,, 24	3·6	Ditto.	6¼ lb. flr., ½ lb. cow-peas (dried), 3 lb. meat	1·7 lb.	2 meals.	Beer brewing all day.

Date	Total man value	Remarks	Amount of food	Indiv. intake of flour	Meals	Remarks
Sept. 25	3·6	S.i.l. and wife away.	12 lb. pot.	..	2 pot. snacks.	No porridge cooked—tired from brewing.
,, 26	5·6	2 men visitors.	5 lb. flr., 2 lb. cassava leaves (flr.), ½ lb. gr.-nuts.	0·9 lb.	..	..
,, 27	5·6	Ditto.	9½ lb. flr., 6 lb. meat.	1·7 lb.	..	..
,, 28	8·4	2 men visitors. Prospective s.i.l. fed.	6½ lb. flr., 10 lb. meat.	0·6 lb.	2 meals and 1 extra for visitors only.	..
,, 29	4·6	Housewife away.	4½ lb. flr., 2 lb. cow-pea leaves, ⅛ lb. gr.-nuts, meat left over.	0·9 lb.	1 meal, 1 snack of remains.	Housewife away. Daughter (A5) does cooking.
,, 30	5·4	Housewife back.	5½ lb. flr., 3 lb. pot. Meat left over.	1·0 lb.	1 meal, 1 pot. snack.	Beer ready for drinking.
Oct. 1	5·4	..	5 lb. flr., 2 lb. cassava leaves, ½ lb. gr.-nuts.	0·9 lb.	1 meal. Beer.	..

FAMILY B. MALALO

Permanent Group: 3 men, 3 women, 1 adolescent boy, 2 children. Total man value: 7·4

Date	Total man value	Remarks	Amount of food	Indiv. intake of flour	Meals	Remarks
Sept. 13	10·6	2 men visitors extra plus a s.i.l. whose wife was away, a daughter tabooed cooking and her four children.	6 lb. flr., 8 lb. meat, 10 lb. pot.	0·7 lb.	1 meal, 1 pot. snack.	..

,, 14	11·6	3 men visitors.	9 lb. flr., meat left over.	0·7 lb.	1 meal.	No pot. snack, since children refuse to dig pot.
,, 15	7·6	..	4 lb. flr., meat left over, 6 lb. porridge.	0·5 lb.	1 meal, 1 pot. snack.	Less cooked because young women away doing tribute labour.
,, 16	8·2	..	7 lb. flr., 2 lb. cow-pea leaves (fr.), ½ lb. gr.-nuts.	0·9 lb.	1 meal.	..
,, 17	5·2	2 men visitors arrive.	5½ lb. flr., 1 lb. cow-pea leaves, ¼ lb. gr.-nuts, 8 lb. pot.	0·9 lb.	1 meal, 1 pot. snack.	Daughter (B8) given flr. to cook for husband. Young girls fend for themselves, as they refused to grind. Housewife eats alone with husband.
,, 18	5·2	..	5 lb. flr., 2 lb. cow-pea leaves, ½ lb. gr.-nuts.	0·8 lb.	1 meal.	..
,, 19	7·2	S.i.l. home for night with friend and sent meal.	6 lb. flr., 3 lb. cassava leaves, ¾ lb. gr.-nuts.	0·6 lb.	1 meal.	..
,, 20	5·2	..	3½ lb. flr., 6 pot.	..	Pot. snack only. Flour saved.	..
,, 21	6·6	..	5 lb. flr., ¾ lb. beans, ½ lb. gr.-nuts.	1·3 lb.	2 meals.	2 meals, as flr. from yesterday eaten.
,, 22	6·6	..	4¾ lb. flr., 3 lb. cassava leaves, ½ lb. gr.-nuts, 4 lb. pot.	0·7 lb.	1 meal, 1 pot. snack.	..

Date	Total man value	Remarks	Amount of food	Indiv. intake of flour	Meals	Remarks
Sept. 23	11·0	..	5 lb. flr., 3 lb. cow-pea leaves, ¾ lb. gr.-nuts, 6 lb. pot.	0·4 lb.	1 meal, 1 pot. snack.	..
,, 24	9·4	..	5 lb. flr., 10 lb. meat, 4 lb. pot.	0·5 lb.	1 meal, 1 pot. snack.	Sufficient meat for 2 meals but game brought in too late.
,, 25	6·4	..	Flr. and meat left over. 4 lb. pot.	..	1 meal.	No grinding. Eat yesterday's supply.
,, 26	11·8	Sends dish to son, as extra meat available.	5¾ lb. flr., 2 lb. meat, 8 lb. pot.	0·4 lb.	1 meal, 1 pot. snack.	Gets small buck shot by son.
,, 27	6·6	..	6½ lb. flr., 12 lb. meat.	0·9 lb.	2 meals.	Anthropologists' meat divided.
,, 28	6·6	..	5 lb. flr., meat left over.	0·7 lb.	2 meals.	..
,, 29	6·6	..	5 lb. flr., meat left over.	0·7 lb.	2 meals.	..
,, 30	7·6	..	5¾ lb. flr., meat left over.	0·7 lb.	2 meals.	..
Oct. 1	6·6	..	4½ lb. flr., 2 lb. cassava leaves, ½ lb. gr.-nuts	0·6 lb.	1 meal. Beer	..
,, 2	9·4	Observer's 2 servants fed.	5 lb. flr., 2 lb. meat, 8 lb. pot.	0·5 lb.	1 meal, 1 pot. snack. Beer.	..
,, 3	9·0	Married daughter on visit.	1 lb. *cikanda* orchid, ½ lb. gr.-nuts.	..	1 small meal. Beer.	No flr. ground, as exhausted after beer.

Table showing Number of Baskets of Food divided between
Young Men (Kasaka, September 1937)

Date	No. of baskets of flour	No. of men	Amount of flour per head
Sept. 13	1	8	0·1
,, 14	2	6	0·3
,, 15	2	8	0·2
,, 16	3	6	0·5
,, 17	0	6	0·0
,, 18	2	6	0·3
,, 19	6	8	0·7
,, 20	4	8	0·5
,, 21	4	6	0·6
,, 22	4	7	0·5
,, 23	4	8	0·5
,, 24	Beer	..	..
,, 25	3	5	0·6
,, 26	5	9	0·5
,, 27	6	8	0·7
,, 28	6	8	0·7
,, 29	6	4	1·5
,, 30	6	4	1·5

PART IV

OWNERSHIP, BUDGETING, AND EXCHANGE

CHAPTER XI

OWNERSHIP RULES AND EDUCATION IN SHARING

SO far we have limited our discussion to the problem of day-to-day catering, and have studied the variations in individual dietaries produced by the system of preparing and consuming food. But one of the most important nutritional difficulties in this area is the regular annual shortage. We must therefore go beyond the question of the daily distribution of foodstuffs to consider the traditional methods of allocating the year's supplies. After harvesting one season's grain, the Bemba householder has little or no chance of procuring additional stores until the next year, and his wife, unlike most European women living under modern industrial conditions, has to budget for a year rather than a week. This is a task in which she regularly fails, according to our standards, and it is the reasons for her failure that we now have to seek.

The shortage may be due to a variety of causes—under-production with an insufficient margin of surplus, misuse of supplies by waste or by an excessive brewing of beer, or sheer inability to estimate future needs. Of these it is obvious that the first is the chief difficulty. From the figures given on p. 178–82 it will be seen that the Bemba produce on an average only enough grain to give them under 1 lb. of flour a day with no allowance for beer making; and that their supply of leguminous crops runs out in a few months. But the causes of under-production will be examined later, after the people's agricultural methods have been described.

This chapter will be limited to a discussion of the way in which the Bemba actually use the crops they customarily reap. What, for instance, are the tribal rules of ownership of food, that is to say, the householder's rights to consume or dispose of it in any way he pleases, and to protect it from other members of the community? To what extent is this people able to estimate quantities accurately and thus to calculate the amount of food they are likely to require over a given time interval? What is their whole cultural attitude towards the accumulation of foodstuffs, and the value they attach to stores of grain and vegetables as distinct from other forms of wealth. If we are anxious to study the yearly intake of the Bemba as distinct from their daily, and the seasonal variation in supplies instead of the day-to-day changes, all these different social and economic aspects must be discussed. The white man's despair at the African's apparent lack of foresight, whether in producing, eating, or selling his foodstuffs, makes it imperative to analyse just this type of fact.

Ownership of Garden Crops.

The food-supplies a Bemba owns consist of the crops standing in his garden and the millet or vegetables stored in his granary. Of these the crop of millet itself is individually owned. In fact, in the case of a new garden the natives seem to believe that there is some particularly close connexion, of an almost magical nature, between the owner and the patch of ground he has just cleared of bush. Although a man can lend his garden to another in the second or third year, or even sell the crops on it, he should do neither of these things in the case of the first-year patch (*citemene*), and I noticed that Bemba explaining this custom added in a particularly serious voice, 'because he is the owner' (*umwine*). The garden-beds round a village, on the other hand, are often considered the property of the wife, since she usually digs them, and either she or the husband has rights of disposal of the crops grown on them according to the labour each has spent on them.

Individual rights over particular crops depend on the nature of the plant and the time it ripens. A man's wife reaps the millet in his garden with any one whom she may invite to help her, but no other relatives of the family, however close, may start this work without her permission, and it involves a magic rite (*icibyalilo*)[1] which only she can perform. Crops of maize, Kaffir corn, or cucurbits grown on second- or third-year gardens are also individually owned. If a woman and a party of children went out to gather maize cobs I noticed that she and her own children entered the garden, while the others stayed outside. This is probably because this crop ripens in the hunger months, when it may be important to conceal from the village the number of cobs that are ready to pick. Close relatives of the family may step into a garden and help

[1] Cf. p. 299.

themselves if really hungry, provided they leave the cut stalks and
sheaves of the maize openly in the field so that the owner may see
that a kinsman has 'borrowed' food (*kuashima*), not a mere thief.
Gourds or pumpkins may only be picked with the owner's permission. Sweet potatoes and cassava roots, neither reckoned as a staple
food, nor regarded as essential substitutes during the hunger
season, seem to be dug up much more freely by a man's relatives.
Children, in particular, grub up roots from the garden of any
near relative on either side of the family, saying indignantly if
questioned, 'No, we are not stealing (*tatuleiba*). This is our place
here (*tuli kumiesu*).'

The theft of millet from gardens does not seem to be a common
offence. The grain has got to be pounded before it is eaten, and
this is inconvenient for a casual thief. He prefers to take maize
cobs, gourds, or pumpkins, which can be quickly cooked and eaten
as a snack, and which ripen in the season when food is short. The
penalties for theft vary with the season of the year. If a man steals
in the hunger months and comes and explains his predicament his
theft is apparently treated lightly, and he is merely asked by the
owner to return goods to the value of what he has eaten.[1] But
a thief caught red-handed trying to conceal his crime can expect
no mercy. In the old days, I was told, he was liable to be speared
on the spot, but that if this summary justice was not exacted, he
would in any case have to repay the owner far more than the worth
of the stolen food, 'perhaps four times as much, because he had
made the heart of the gardener hot'.[2] The same is true to-day.
In 1930, near Chinsali, a thief suspected of stealing maize cobs
over some weeks was finally caught in the act. He paid the owner
12s. damages for the theft of two maize cobs on the first occasion,
and 7s. 6d. for one on the second without the case ever coming
into court.[3] Another method of punishing a culprit, especially one
who has few material possessions with which to compensate for
his theft, is to lay a conditional curse on some property of his,
i.e. his own garden or granary. This is known as *ukusaka*. In this
case the injured party places branches across the entrance to the
thief's garden or granary and places a charm on them. He informs

---

[1] *Vide* rights of a hungry subject to take food from the chief's garden.
[2] Cf. the case of the owner who does not mind his relatives taking his mealies
if they do not insult him by concealing the theft.
[3] The maize cobs would be sold at about 3d. for a basket of 6 or 8.

the headman and chief what he has done, and will not consent to remove the curse until he has been fully compensated.[1]

During the harvest season rights of ownership are less strictly exacted, since food itself is plentiful. As one informant said, 'To steal heads of maize is theft because they ripen in the hunger months; to steal heads of Kaffir corn is not theft,' i.e. because there is food at that time.[2]

To protect their distant gardens from theft the Bemba resort to supernatural means only. Protective magic is used, but only to a small extent.[3] It is interesting to find that the Bisa, whose staple crop is cassava, which is readily stolen as it remains in the ground all the year round, regularly place in their gardens charms designed to afflict a possible thief with different types of illness. This custom, known as *ukuamba*, seemed to be universally practised on Cilubi Island. A man leaving home for a period would plant in a prominent place a stake with magic attached to it, and so strong was the belief in its powers that the owner himself was afraid to dig up the cassava on his return without first removing the charm. Among the Bemba, where the staple crop is less frequently stolen, such forms of protective magic seem to be, comparatively speaking, rare. Charms to be burned in a field to produce various diseases such as elephantiasis in garden thieves were described to me, but I never heard frequently of their use. In such cases I was told the culprit could only hope to recover if he confessed his guilt. A far more common practice is the use of a special form of curse, *ukula-pishya*, uttered after a theft has been committed, not before. This is done when gourds or pumpkins are disappearing from a garden and the thief is unknown. I have heard such curses uttered constantly during the hunger months, when the pilfering of vegetables is quite frequent, and a woman has no means of guarding them. The usual procedure followed was to announce in a loud shout in the quiet of an evening some such statement as, 'All you people, listen! One of my pumpkins went yesterday and another the day before. Now I am angry. I am really going to curse. To-morrow I am going to curse. Really and truly I am.' On several such

[1] I never came across an actual case in which this was done and think the practice is growing rarer. Cf. also the use of protective magic in gardens.

[2] *Kukontole mise ya nyanje bupupu pantu shilepya pa nsala: kukontole mise ya masaka te bupupu.*

[3] Cf. p. 356.

occasions whispered conversations followed and the theft, often the heedless act of a child, was confessed next day. Once the headman himself came to beg the angry woman not to proceed with her threat and himself brought compensation 'so that no one might die in the village'. Many such curses in fact remain as threats and form effective sanctions in that way. When actually uttered they are thought to invoke supernatural powers to punish the culprit. Bemba curse by the High God, Lesa, who is usually believed to strike guilty people with thunderbolts, or they curse by the dead chiefs of the land (*mfumu shye calo*).[1] Such a curse is thought to work automatically and can only be removed when the culprit has confessed and begged for mercy. The curser then gives beads to the spirits and prays, saying, 'You, my chiefs, we didn't understand everything. We beg mercy now. We cursed those children. We did not know. Now have mercy and do not kill them.'[2] The fear of the owner's curse appeared to me to act even at the present day as a very efficient means of preventing petty garden thefts during the hunger months.

Thus individual ownership of field crops is very clearly defined among the Bemba. It is interesting to note that bush foods are also subject to individual ownership rules whenever it is possible to exert them. Rights over meat and fish are described fully in Chap. XIII, but it is worth mentioning that natives mark as their own trees covered with caterpillar grubs so that they may come and gather them when they have grown sufficiently large and succulent for their taste. The man who first discovers a swarm of wild bees will also mark the tree in which they have settled for his own.

Rights over Granaries.

Control over the contents of the Bemba granary are governed by more complex rules. Roughly speaking, the labour given to the production of the crop gives a man the ultimate right of disposal, but this is subject to the superior claims of certain older relatives and ultimately to that of the chief himself. That is to say, the

---

[1] For instance, 'A man has stolen my food. I give him to the chief. I give him to Ba Matipa (the tutelary deity of the neighbourhood). Let him (Ba Matipa) come and eat that man' (*Umuntu ulengibila filyo. Nakupe mfumu. Nakupe Ba Matipa. Bese bakulye*). Kasakatula village, near Shiwa Ŋandu, 1931.

[2] (*Mwe shyamfumu shyonse. Tatuishibe fyonse. Twapâpâta nomba. Twalipishya bana balya. Tatuishibe. Nomba twapapata. Mwilabepaya.*)

owner may be the only person able to reap the grain and store it, but he may have to give portions of the crop to others on demand.

The granary itself is individually owned. In fact, it is considered unpardonable even to look into another man's *butala*, and children are taught not to play under the eaves of neighbours' granaries or to peer at the outside too closely. 'You children, you! You stare at the granary of another! That is bad what you do. (*Cabipa.*) Clear out now!' I heard an old grandmother shout on one such occasion.[1] There is no efficient way of closing the opening to a granary, and the stores are often left unguarded hours at a time while their owners are away in their gardens. But the tradition of respect of a neighbour's *butala* is so strong that thefts appear to be very uncommon, and these mud cylinders are the most private hiding-places a man or woman has. Treasured possessions, magic horns, money, or beer may all be concealed safely in a granary, and though the *ubutala* is apparently protected with special charms sometimes, I think these are designed to circumvent sorcerers, who are believed to steal crops by magic means (cf. p. 189), rather than ordinary thieves. The use of padlocks and keys, much affected by sophisticated people near white towns, is not likely to be as effective as the traditional tribal belief in the inviolability of the granary.

The right of disposal of the millet store is determined by a complicated adjustment of the claims of the man and his relatives and those of the woman. The millet garden is commonly spoken of as belonging to the man,[2] because it is he who originally cleared the ground for it. But a married man is described as making a garden for his wife. He may make a separate field of his own as does a chief,[3] but his wife's *citemene* is his first charge, and a polygamist must clear a millet patch for each wife and build each a granary. This duty is stressed at the wedding ceremony, when the

[1] When measuring the contents of granaries I found the owners sometimes reluctant to allow me inside. In any case other women always fell back and left me and the owner alone.

[2] Cullen Gouldsbury, 'Notes on the Customary Law of the Awemba', *Journal of the African Society*, vol. xv, Jan. 1916, p. 158, emphasizes the man's ownership of the food as against the woman's.

[3] Called an *umulasa* garden in imitation of the chief's garden made by tribute labour and belonging exclusively to him, as distinct from his wives. With the prevailing shortage of labour, husbands are rarely able to make two gardens, one for themselves and one for their wives. I only saw three described as *ayo umulasa* in 1933–4.

bridegroom is abjured by his father-in-law 'to cut trees' for his bride, and the work is so clearly part of the economic contract that a man telling his life history usually uses the phrase, 'Then I married and made my wife a garden.' I have even heard an elderly Bemba describe a widowed sister dependent on him as his wife, when giving answers for a Government census. Brother-and-sister incest is considered a horrible crime even within the classificatory degree, but the obligations to cut trees for a wife is so clearly recognized that the old man explained, 'She is my wife because I make her a garden.'

Hence the millet garden is the man's, although the use of the crop is given to the wife. But her rights are not absolute. They depend strictly on the continuance of the marriage, are forfeited by divorce or death, and are subject to the claims of the husband's relatives, who, since they live in another village, are constantly apprehensive lest they do not get their dues. If divorce takes place through the woman's fault, the husband's kinswomen can take the grain. Cases of this kind occur fairly frequently. At a village near Chinsali, a young woman refused to live with her husband because of his hot temper, and was unable to persuade her brother to give his 14-year-old daughter as a substitute, according to the old Bemba custom.[1] The injured husband retired to his own family's village to await events. After a few weeks a file of six women with empty baskets on their heads appeared from that direction. The wife's relatives stood aghast at the doors of their huts muttering, '*Yangwe!* They have come to take the grain.' They could only watch while the husband's kinswomen lifted the roof of the granary, emptied its contents, and left with their baskets full, after a brisk exchange of obscene abuse between both parties. A man's mother and sisters are his proper representatives on such an occasion and frequently intervene in this way.

On the other hand, if it is the husband who breaks up the marriage he will find it difficult to exercise his legal claims to the food remaining in the family granary. I was once present when a disreputable youth in a modern village decided to leave his wife and go off with another woman. Before doing so he placed a conditional curse on the cassava, sweet potatoes, and other remaining foodstuffs. The deserted wife retaliated by wailing in public on the village garden beds, with the support of her mother and sisters, for at least

[1] The *mpokoleshi* marriage previously described.

two and a half hours. Even if the husband had been in the right, it would have been hard to stand up against such a protest, but in this case the village was so strongly in support of the wife, that he removed the curse with the proper ceremony before nightfall. This was a particularly dramatic incident, but I heard of a number of cases in which deserted wives were left in complete possession of the family grain bin.

At death a man's ownership of the granary is also clearly recognized. All supplies of millet and food ripening on the garden-beds, theoretically speaking, go to his heir in the direct matrilineal line, but inheritance is often only fixed after some months' delay. Thus there is usually little food left in the granary to hand on to the heir selected. In any case it is considered hard-hearted for the latter to exercise his privileges if a widow and children suffer loss by that means.

Where neither divorce nor death takes place the balance of interest between the claims of the husband and wife, or rather between his relatives and hers, has to be gradually achieved by a process of mutual adjustment, often giving rise to a good deal of tension under the particular condition of matrilocal residence. Briefly speaking, the wife has, of course, full charge of the granary, and is entirely responsible for the care and allotment of the food. As in our society it is for her to decide for whom she cooks and how much. As she belongs to a cooking team of her own family relatives and shares with them, it is natural that her own kins-women in the matrilocal group are in a particularly strong position. On the other hand, the husband, ultimately the owner of the millet, has his own relatives to satisfy. For instance, we have seen that his sisters have very strong claims on his help. I have seen a chief's sister march into the royal enclosure, pull a cloth out of a trunk in her brother's inner room and take it away without permission, the owner merely laughing ruefully and saying, 'If I had been careful I should have hidden that cloth better.' These princesses also demand meat and beer from their brothers in an imperious manner quite at variance with the subservient behaviour of the chief's wives and courtiers. Among commoners the contrast is not so great, but the sisters are still in a privileged position. A man's mother will not have such freedom, since she is tabooed from coming into close contact with her daughter-in-law, but she also can exert her claims if in need. Women also take liberties with the

property of their maternal uncles, and I have seen a young woman
snatch fully half of a basket of wild spinach her *nalume* was carrying across the village. When questioned she shrugged her shoulders
and laughed, saying, 'Well, isn't he the *nalume*?' It must be
remembered, too, that elder brothers have rights to their juniors'
property quite irrespective of their needs. Nowadays men demand
small gifts of money as a share of their younger brothers' earnings,
and they also send for baskets of food on occasion, and often use
the word *kutula* which is that applied to the giving of tribute to
the chief. All these relatives of the husband take, or are presented
with, uncooked food, and are not incorporated in the wife's eating
group.

These different claims of each marriage partner are easily ad-
justed if the man has a separate granary of his own (*bwa mulasa*),
as used to be the custom. Where there is a single grain bin the
first years of marriage involve a good deal of mutual suspicion
between the husband's relatives and the wife's. The family, usually
living in another village, are always on the look-out to see that they
get their dues. I seen women arrive to look inside one of their
kinsmen's granaries to judge for themselves whether his bride was
being stingy or not. On one occasion in the hunger months a man's
mother arrived in quite a friendly spirit at her daughter-in-law's
hut, climbed inside the latter's granary and glanced at the contents
with an appraising eye. She came down saying, 'Let it be (*Cibe*),'
explaining to me, 'There are only three baskets there. I shall not
take them. I must leave it to my son's children.' Provided that
the husband's family are satisfied that the girl is not being mean,
they are quite content, but the danger is so clearly recognized that
at her initiation ceremony the girl sings a song carrying two clay
models of baskets, one on her head and the other in her hand.
She has to sing, 'She carries her marriage on her head, it is her
clan (i.e. her own people) which is dangling below' (i.e. the husband's relatives are in the superior place, on the head).[1] The right
to use all other foods, such as cassava, sweet potatoes, or legumes,
is not so frequently a matter of contention between husband and
wife, chiefly because these foods are not so highly valued and exist
in such small quantities. I did not hear of many quarrels in this
respect.

All these kinship dues are acquiring a good deal of importance

---

[1] *Cupo asenda pa mutwe uaseshya mukoa.*

Heads of cooking-teams. Four grandmothers ruling over 'big houses'.
Women and children eat together.

at the moment, since there is a chance of making money by the sale of millet or vegetables. Where a husband may not have exercised his claims to property in the form of food, and is anyhow obliged to put his wife in charge of it, he tends to consider that money from the sale of produce is his alone, and irresponsible characters sometimes dispose of food for low prices early in the year, leaving their families in want. I noticed also that the husband's relatives sometimes tried to make money in this way. In a modern village near Kasama I saw a man's sister claim all the money obtained by his wife from the sale of pumpkins at exorbitant prices to labourers in the district. She took 1s. 6d. from her sister-in-law and gave her back 3d., saying to me, 'Well, my brother cut her the garden, so the food is his.'

Prerogatives of Age.

Besides this balance of claims between the affinal relatives, the elder kinsmen in general have certain rights over the food in a young couple's granary. The woman's mother and elder sister can come and demand baskets of grain from her, while the man's elder brother also asks for food when he needs it. These dues are usually exacted as between elder sister and younger sister—usually own sisters—in each case the two refer to each other as 'My great one' (*umukalamba uandi*) or 'My little one' (*mwaice uandi*). The same holds true as between elder brother and younger brother and the same terms are used. An elder sister is very likely living in the same village as her junior, sharing supplies with her. In this case she merely exercises her rights over luxuries like beer or snuff, or perhaps commandeers some flour already ground. If, on the other hand, she has married into another village she occasionally comes and claims baskets of food if in need and has the right, denied to a more distant relative, to climb up the steps to her sister's granary and look at her store. Elder and younger brothers are usually living in different villages according to the rule of matrilocal marriage, but I have known a senior send to his young brother to claim a pot of beer. The father has no legal claims on his children, and I was told he would not send to ask his sons or daughters for food, but that they would give him presents 'out of respect' and he would come and stay with them. The mother, as we have seen, claims rights over the food of her son as well as her daughter. The *nalume* of the man can make

o

peremptory demands upon him, and I noticed that in old-fashioned villages this was often done, but the same would not be true of the wife's mother's brother. In the same way the father's sister, the *nyina senge* can ask a maternal niece for baskets of grain, although she would be unlikely to do so in the case of her maternal nephew.

The headman can ask his villagers to help him with food if he is in want, although this would be an unlikely occurrence, but the rights of a chief to send for supplies to help him in sudden difficulties, particularly over entertaining, are frequently exercised (cf. p. 253). In fact, so much is the idea of authority associated with the right to levy dues of this kind that natives use the word *ukutula* or 'to give tribute' of any demand made by an elder relative of a younger.

Modern Changes in Kinship Dues.

It is common knowledge that in many Bantu societies money is now being substituted for the older kinship dues levied on food or cattle. To what extent is this the case in the Bemba area? We have seen that the Bemba husband occasionally tries to sell the contents of his granary, whereas formerly, though he was actually the owner of the millet store, he allowed his wife the use of it. In the same way I have seen elder brothers make demands on their juniors for shillings or sixpences instead of asking for a portion of their grain or beer. But this seems only to occur in districts near white towns, and the practice was confined as far as I saw it to men of the clerk or domestic servant type. Big dues levied on young men's mine-earnings, such as are reported from so many parts of South Africa, and from the Ila district in Northern Rhodesia,[1] seemed very uncommon among the Bemba. I think this fact can probably be accounted for in two ways. First, in a society in which the power of the mother's family and that of the father's is very evenly divided, the elders are not in such a strong position to exact dues from their younger relatives as they are in a markedly patriarchal or matriarchal society. Among the Bemba it may be the father, the maternal uncle, or the maternal grandfather who is the boy's male guardian, and it will depend on personality and general circumstances which finally maintains his authority, but in a typical patrilineal society such as those of the

[1] Smith and Dale, op. cit., vol. i, p. 385.

Southern or Eastern Bantu there is no doubt that the father, and after him the elder brother, has the predominant rights over the property of the young. Secondly, and this is a point which we have to recur to frequently, the fact that the Bemba never kept cattle or any form of wealth that could be measured or counted naturally affects their attitude to money. To change from the 'cattle standard' to money currency appears to be an easy transition in some ways, and all over Africa natives are earning money and turning it into cattle or, conversely, giving cattle to relatives who sell the beasts and so get money. But where kinship prerogatives consist of undefined rights to exact service and to demand food when in need the substitution of money seems a less obvious equivalent. Where it occurs, and it is beginning to occur, it creates an entirely new relationship between elder and younger, son-in-law and father-in-law, rather than a modification of the old. Nor have the elders the same bargaining power with the young as in some Bantu tribes at the present day. We are told from such widely distant areas as South Africa and Uganda that boys who earn money away from this tribal area return to give a share to their fathers or brothers for fear the latter will not provide them with cattle or goats for their marriage payments.[1] The Bemba boy on the other hand gave service for his bride and was therefore not beholden to his elders to any large extent, and is not so to-day. He gives money to his father-in-law for his bride, and he distributes presents among his relatives as he pleases, but this is considered an act of grace, I think, and not a due. It is not true to say that the young Bemba of to-day are hampered in their progress by the exorbitant demands of the old.

Education in Distribution.

To conclude, the Bemba system of food consumption is determined by rules of individual ownership subject to the claims of elder relatives. How is this set of economic values impressed on each new generation? What sanctions exist to enforce the various rules involved?

Among the Bemba it is clear that there are certain well-marked attitudes towards the use of food which the child learns to adopt almost from babyhood. In the infant's life edible objects are things which his mother and near relatives never refuse to give him on

<hr />

[1] K. Oberg, 'Banyankole Kinship Organization', *Africa*, vol. xi, April 1938, pp. 153, 158.

demand, and conversely, his circle of close kinsfolk are those who never deny his requests for food. The Bemba mother suckles her baby whenever he crys, and as he grows older she never says 'No' as long as there is anything in the house which he can eat. To refuse to feed a child who is hungry is one of the worst possible crimes and the words 'To refuse porridge' (*ukutano bwali*) are usually uttered with a special note of disapproval in the voice. Folk-tales describe with moral indignation the behaviour of the woman who denies a hungry child, and the infant is early aware of his rights with respect to food. Even babies are touchy in this matter and always on the look-out for offence. I have heard children of 8 or 10 burst out on to the veranda of a mother's or a grandmother's hut sobbing in a most heartfelt way: 'They have refused me porridge' (*bantano bwali*). Examination might prove that the child had merely had a slightly smaller portion of porridge than its fellow, but it felt the insult deeply apparently. I have seen an older girl flounce out of the house of an aunt using the same words, 'They have refused me porridge', when she had merely not been invited sufficiently heartily to join the evening meal. In the hunger season this phrase *bantano bwali* is constantly on fretful children's lips.

But this expectation of food is limited to a definite circle of relatives. Those households which the child describes as 'at our place' (*kumiesu*), i.e. chiefly those of his mother, her sisters, and his grandmother, are early distinguished, and I have often watched toddlers, starting on a slow and arduous progress from hut to hut, wherever they might expect to find dainties and knew they could take them without rebuke. Within this circle of relatives the child early realizes that he is only getting what is his due. The European child brought up in the individual family expects to be fed by one or two people only, and knows that the others who entertain him are doing so by way of exception out of kindness. He is constantly taught to express gratitude to such individuals and this training begins so early that in most European languages there is some monosyllable such as 'ta' which the baby is taught to use when it cannot pronounce the more formal 'thank you' properly. The Bemba child on the other hand is at home in a far bigger circle of relatives and takes their help for granted. From any member of this wider ring of kinsmen he can count on support as his due. One native explained when I asked why a certain young man had

received a present from his relatives without saying thank you: 'He doesn't thank because they are his own people. If it had been an outsider, he would have said: "Thank you, Sir", because it would have been from pity they gave to him. To one's own people one does not thank, not at all! You say that is good. That is all.'[1]
Hence perhaps the widespread complaint of the European that the Bemba is ungrateful and that there is no proper term for 'Thank you' in his language. Also perhaps the frequent disappointment of the white man who has given some unusually valuable Christmas present to his servant only to find that the gift is often taken for granted as part of 'the latter's regular perquisites'.

From these facts it will be easy to see how the association between authority and the power to give, on which the political life of the tribe depends, is impressed in concrete fashion on the mind of the smallest child. But food is also something that has to be shared, and in this attitude the Bemba baby is definitely trained even in the first year. Children share from one dish and the mother or elder sister tears off for each a lump of porridge with a little drop of relish rolled inside. An unexpected present or find must be divided with any other babies sitting near. Any European food, such as an orange or a bit of bread, that I might happen to give away was torn into the tiniest fragments, and mothers who are such lax disciplinarians in other respects, speak quite sharply to their children on this one issue. I have seen a woman seize a lump of pumpkin out of a baby's hand and say in most vehement protest: 'You give some to your friend you child, you! You sit and eat alone! That is bad what you do.'

As the Bemba child grows older there is a third attitude he has to acquire, i.e. that food is something over which his older brothers and sisters have definite rights—not elders generally, but the seniors of his own family group. He is taught that they may pounce on any delicacy he may be eating. This I first noticed among groups of children in one village, mostly parties of brothers, sisters, and cross-cousins. An older boy would take without comment any orange or biscuit I might have given to a younger child. All boys between 10 and 15 regularly wait for the leavings of the young men's meals, and have no other portion allotted to them. I have

[1] *Tatota pantu ni mwana uabo. Nga ni umbi, aleti 'Ea Mukwai' pantu ni ku luse bamupela. Ku bantu babo teti atote nakarya! Ukuti asose 'Cawama', epela!*

even seen a grown-up man seize a piece of fish from a small sister of 8, who expressed absolutely no surprise. An older girl will catch the wrist of a younger sister who has been given some snuff and scrape the precious powder out of the young girl's hand, leaving her only a little pinch for herself. The younger sister may make a face, but will not protest. In the same way I have seen a young husband call to his wife to throw him a lemon she had been given. She exclaimed: 'You crocodile you!' but threw him the fruit quite good-naturedly. Hence the rights of the elder or the headman or the Chief described in Chap. XIII, are based on beliefs very early inculcated, of what are a relative's dues. Here again the different attitude of European mothers is noticeable. In a society in which individual initiative is on the whole encouraged, and age has no particular prerogatives, we tend to see that the youngest child gets his fair share at the dinner table or in the nursery and often teach the elder children to 'Give it to Baby first'. The Bemba mother on the contrary always says: 'Let your elder brother (*umukalamba uobe*) have it! Give it to him first', and on this recognition of precedence the whole organization of daily life as well as the political system finally depends. Bemba children in fact do not seem to resent the rights of their elders, and I noticed that both little girls and boys often repeated the words *umukalamba uandi* ('my elder') in tones of great affection and pride. The constant competition between the older and younger members of the family that is so pronounced in our society does not seem to exist.[1] We encourage our children to take a pride in their personal possessions, to handle them carefully, look after them, 'put them away'. Bemba children have no material possessions beyond the twig bow or the maize cob doll, but all the objects they use they are taught to yield up on demand from an elder. In adult life the man who gives presents to his elder brother, and still more the woman who honours her elder sister, is praised with particular enthusiasm.[2]

[1] Bemba brothers are not in competition with each other for the family inheritance as among the patrilineal cattle-owning people of South Africa. There is little material property to inherit, and in any case the boys marry early in life and hence join different economic and local groups.

[2] When I travelled with my older sister for some weeks in this area I noticed that whenever I carried something for her or gave her precedence, a delighted murmur went up from the watching women: 'She honours her *umukalamba*. Look, she is carrying it for the big one.' It meant conformance to their own code.

Sharing and Supernatural Sanctions.

This definite training in a particular method of distributing food is still further enforced by supernatural sanctions. The Bemba are deeply convinced that relatives who die with a sense of injury have the power to return and afflict the living with misfortune, illness, and even a lingering death from a wasting disease. To injure a man or a woman in this way, and in particular to deny them food when hungry, ill, or cold, is to refuse them their kinship dues. In fact, the definition usually given of such a haunting spirit (*iciwa*) is that it is 'someone who died with grief catching him at the throat' because when he was old his children would not give him food. Of such a calamity the Bemba are genuinely afraid. Even sophisticated young men of the present time speak nervously of the possibility of certain near relatives, particularly the mother, or the mother's brother, dying aggrieved, and there is no doubt that the fear of supernatural punishment is still a very strong sanction enforcing the sharing of food and the provision for dependents.

Besides these positive inducements to share, it must be remembered that the Bemba system of distribution is closely correlated with their type of housing and particular methods of preparing food. We have described the housewife threshing and grinding out of doors, with her store cupboard at some distance from her hut. It is impossible, in a Bemba village, to conceal the fact that extra flour has been prepared, that beer is ready for drinking, or that there is an unexpected supply of meat. The complete publicity of primitive housekeeping is one of the most effective sanctions for the system of distribution of food which they commonly practise. It is important here to notice that Bemba housing is changing under the influence of the white man. The native is taught to build huts with more rooms and even to store his food in his own enclosure. It remains to be seen whether the Bantu will continue to be so generous, according to our standards, when they can conceal their supplies as effectively as we do ourselves.

It can be said therefore that if the Bemba people share their meals and extend hospitality to a wider circle of relatives than we do, it is because from their earliest years they have never been able to consider food as something which could be procured, owned, and consumed by one individual alone. In childhood, or in subsequent dependent positions, it must be supplied by elders; throughout life it must be shared with contemporaries, and special delicacies such as meat and beer must be subject to older kinsmen's rights. Food is something over which relatives have rights, and conversely relatives are people who provide or take toll of one's food. The purely possessive attitude to property with all its concomitant virtues, such as thrift, foresight, or self-reliance, are not inculcated in the Bemba child and would probably unfit him for life in his society. The so-called communism of the Bantu—like any other form of distribution of material goods, is deeply rooted in a system of ideas, a common acceptance of particular laws of ownership and obligations to share and to give, and the habits necessitated by the material equipment used and possessed by the tribe. It remains to ask how the individual Bemba housekeepers budget for their needs within this framework of ideas and customs. What mathematical concepts guide them in their calculation of their needs? What general economic values impel them to measure, store, or 'squander', according to our lights, their food.

CHAPTER XII

BUDGETING, WEALTH, AND EXCHANGE

Budgeting.

THE housewife's fundamental difficulties in budgeting will have been obvious from the previous account. In the first place she has to cater for an unknown number of eaters and, secondly, she may have to give some of her year's supply of grain to her elder relatives on demand. In these circumstances it is hard to understand how a woman manages to have any supplies left at all by the end of the season, and to anyone who listens to Bemba talking among themselves the problem seems even more insoluble. On the one hand the niggardly woman is constantly abused. As we saw, marriages are broken up if the mother-in-law does not provide generously for her son-in-law, and in a number of other relationships stinginess over food is equally fatal. On the other hand the housewife is criticized if she runs short of food at the end of the season. There is a special phrase—*cipumba ca muno mainsa* (a fool in the rainy season)—applied to an inefficient housekeeper of this type. A man is considered unfortunate if he is married to such a person, and women shrug their shoulders contemptuously when speaking of her. As we saw, the handling of the grain stores (*ukubansa*) is considered such a difficult art that a young girl is not allowed to undertake it until several years after marriage. Hence, however impossible it may be for the Bemba housewife to calculate her supplies exactly, there are evidently degrees of failure which the society does not tolerate.

There are a number of factors which have to be considered under this general heading of budgeting, and all are relevant to a study of general economic incentives in this particular group. To begin with the Bemba woman cannot keep her granary store for the use of her own family as is the case in our society. The economic conditions under which she lives necessitate reciprocal sharing of foodstuffs, rather than their accumulation, and extend the individual's responsibility outside her own household. Plainly, therefore, it does not pay a Bemba woman to have very much more grain than her fellows. She would merely have to distribute it, and during the recent locust scourge the villagers whose gardens escaped destruction complained that they were not really better off than their fellows for 'our people come and live with us or beg us for baskets of millet'. But within small limits there is a difference between one housewife and another in her successful management of her grain bin. For one thing, as has been described, she generally cooks roughly the same amount of food however many visitors arrive. The careful housewife also restricts her brewing of beer to necessary occasions, i.e. for a ceremony or a working party, unless she has plenty of millet. Further, there are certain traditionally accepted ways by which she can avoid her tribal obligations. Within limits she can conceal her supplies. The young girls at their initiation ceremonies are in fact taught to hide a little food for their husbands at night, 'to give him the thing which is put by in the dark at night', and I have often seen women take a pot of beer and conceal it in a friend's granary on the reported arrival of some elderly relative. To refuse hospitality with a pot of beer sitting on the hearth would be an impossible insult, but a bland assertion that 'Alas, Sir, we poor wretches (*ifwe balanda*)! We have not a thing to eat here' is sometimes necessary. This would not be done in the case of a near relative, but only with a more distant kinsman of a classificatory type, or one of the well-known 'cadgers' of the family.

Bemba etiquette is also on the side of the housewife, since children are taught from their earliest years never to ask for food except in a near relative's hut, and not to look around a hut or into a granary. In fact, one definition of a witch or a wizard (*umuloshi*) is a person who comes and sits in your house and says, 'I expect you are going to cook soon. What a fine lot of meat you have to-day', or 'I expect the beer will be ready this afternoon', or some such remark. The girl at an initiation ceremony I witnessed was taught to sing a gesture song about a tortoise:

> *Fulwe pa fyakwe*
> *Aingishyo mukoshi*
> *Mu ci fwambaka;*

i.e. 'The tortoise in his own house puts in his neck under his shell' of which the moral is said to be: 'Don't be like the tortoise which shrinks its head into its shell when it is at home, but when it is abroad, (i.e. in somebody else's house) puts its head out and asks for things or peers around.'

Thus though the demands of near relatives are imperative, part of the art of good housekeeping consists in knowing where to draw the line without giving offence, and in successfully appraising the respective claims of different kinsmen, and it is this art which Bemba girls only acquire slowly by dint of joint co-operation in their mother's team.

Methods of Measurement.

Besides the means by which she satisfies her kinship obligations it is important to consider the actual methods by which quantities are measured in this community and hence how the needs of the year are estimated. The householder's powers of calculating her assets depend on the system of numeration used in this particular culture, the material apparatus for measuring, and last but not least, the incentives the people have to estimate the quantities of their supplies. In short, can the Bemba count, and do they consider it necessary to do so? The difference is of considerable importance practically. European systems of commensuration are so exact that a woman could reckon the daily intake of each member of her family with the accuracy of a laboratory feeding experiment, if she wanted to do so. But we know that in fact the planning of weekly food-supplies varies according to class and locality in every possible way, from the family with a large regular income that can buy large quantities of stores at a time and reckons to use similar amounts of different commodities each week, to those living under more precarious conditions that customarily drink beer on a Saturday evening, eat a large meat meal on Sunday, and exist for the rest of the week as best they can, running out for extra groceries as long as the money lasts. Among the Bemba the power of calculating quantities is far less exact, and the incentive to estimate nutritional needs precisely is even less than in our own community.

The Bemba system of numerals is very similar to that employed by the other Bantu peoples—that is to say numbers up to ten are expressed by words and the use of the fingers arranged in a series of different positions, increase in quantity being emphasized by a rising tone of the voice. The four fingers are used in counting with the thumb folded in to the centre of the hand. Thus the index finger raised alone on the right hand means one, the index and second fingers joined means two, the third finger raised with a gap between it and the first two fingers stands for three, and the two pairs of fingers with a gap in between for four, while the closed fist represents five. The other numbers are indicated on the right hand, while figures above ten are represented by giving the ten sign with two closed fists and then starting to indicate the units again.

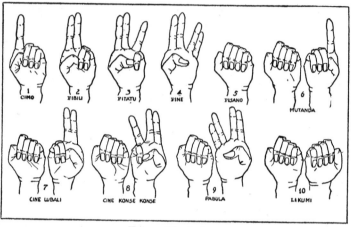

FIG. 4. Hand-signs.

The method of representing high numbers is thus exceedingly clumsy and any Bemba who have come in contact with Europeans have quickly adopted our system of counting.

In point of fact high numbers are not needed in ordinary Bemba life since the objects to be counted rarely exceed 20 in number, in distinction from the cattle-owning Bantu who reckon herds by the hundred and thousand. In fact the Bemba seem quite uninterested in big numbers as such. Their folk-tales, unlike those of a number of primitive peoples, do not dwell on the hundreds of cattle, horses, wives, spears, &c., that the hero possesses, but merely on the difference between 'many' and 'big' and 'very many' or 'very big' expressed with great emphasis of the voice and a rising tone.

There are no definite units of length, weight, or capacity in this community. Though the Bemba are perfectly capable of measuring length accurately in such operations as house-building or furniture-making in which it is necessary to do so, they work by comparing the sizes of different objects such as two poles with a strip of bark-fibre, and not by the use of mathematical units. They do not attempt to measure the length of garden, merely distinguishing between a big garden and a small one. Their estimation of walking distances is notoriously misleading, since here subjective factors intervene, and they not only give the answers calculated to cheer or depress the European with them, but also themselves count a difficult journey, or one usually undertaken by loaded men, as actually longer than an easy one.

No attempt is made to measure weight, although the Bemba have a shrewd sense of the carrying power of the different members of their family. They estimate capacity by means of the different receptacles commonly used in the household. These vary in accuracy. The carrying-baskets (*umuseke*, plur. *imiseke*) containing about 50lb. of grain, probably vary from 10 to 15lb., while the eating-baskets (*icipe*, plur. *ifipe*) containing about 6lb. are probably more uniform in size. Granaries differ markedly in capacity, and the measurement of the contents of these grain bins has been shown to be exceedingly difficult, both because of the opacity of the walls and the unequal lengths between the binding withes.[1]

Nevertheless these difficulties of estimating weight and capacity could probably be overcome if there was sufficient need to do so. In fact, however, the owner of a granary usually considers it quite unnecessary to assess its contents. The people do not count the number of baskets which they put into the *ubutala*, and in a village where I asked each man how many baskets he had reaped, the estimates given me varied from one extreme to another, and were completely inaccurate in the only cases where they were tested. I only met one native who had attempted to measure the contents of his grain bin. He was an exceedingly intelligent, enterprising man who had worked on a farm in Southern Rhodesia, owned a motor-bicycle and the first plough seen in the area, and was, besides, a very good tailor. He had started to reckon the number of baskets put in an unusually large granary with a tally of beans on the ground, but even he gave up the attempt after the slightest

---

[1] Cf. Chap. V. The type of foodstuff here makes a difference, e.g. among the Yakoë of Cross River, S. Nigeria, a man stacks his yams tied to poles in vertical rows and is able to assess his wealth quickly in terms of the number of his yam-sticks. Daryll Ford, 'Land and Labour in a Cross River Village, S. Nigeria', *The Geographical Journal*, vol. xc, no. 1, July 1937, p. 34.

Among the S. Bantu a man counts his cattle and thereby assesses his wealth, and in Melanesia he counts his heaps of yam and taro.

discouragement, i.e. when some fowls began to eat the beans. Repeated questioning failed to produce a gardener who was prepared to estimate the size of his garden or of the crop, though many would say 'I shall want a big granary for that millet' or 'It will fill half a granary'. But a comparison in any one year of size of crop to size of granary and to number of eaters, I never heard made.

It must be realized too that the incentive to measure food-supplies depends largely on whether it is intended that they should be exchanged, or used as a means of assessing wealth, status, or some other attribute valued in the particular society. For instance in some parts of both West and East Africa marketing, either by direct barter or with the use of a money currency, is highly developed; and here, as we should expect, the weights and quantities of different foodstuffs are most accurately measured. Again, in parts of Melanesia, where kudos is associated with the reciprocal exchange of valuables and baskets of food, the computation of these objects is naturally made with a great deal of emotional intensity. The same can be said of the Indians of North-Western America, who reckon status by the credit a man obtains by offering or destroying in public quantities of blankets and copper plates in the elaborate system Potlache exchange. Among the Bemba, however, there is no such reason why the exact size of a man's harvest should be ascertained, and no fixed values even in money by which a man's income can be assessed.

Magic and Food Calculations.

Apart from this lack of desire to measure their assets it is important to notice that the Bemba, probably as a reflection of the general uncertainty of their budgeting system, are definitely convinced that identical quantities of food do not always last the same length of time or satisfy the same number of eaters. On the contrary they believe that its power both to last till the end of the season, and to satisfy the hunger of the eater, depend upon special magic properties which can be given to it by human beings, if they perform the necessary rites. Even quite educated natives support this view. How is it, they say, that one woman fills her granary at harvest and finds that it is empty long before the year is done, while another reaps the same amount but the food lasts in her *ubutala* until the new grain is ripe? Why does one woman serve out porridge so that every one gets up quickly feeling satisfied, while the guests of another eat and still feel empty? The answer is magic (*ubwanga*). Food, and millet in particular, is specially subject to witchcraft (*ubuloshi*). Wizards stick horns in their granaries to attract the grain of other men. They also send out mysterious black birds (*mawa*) at night to steal the food of neighbours and convey it to their own granaries. How does this happen? The Bemba answers that he does not know, but that it is a well-known fact that wizards have more food than other men. A more subtle form of sorcery takes the goodness out of the millet while it is still growing in the gardens, so that when it is reaped and eaten it has no power to satisfy a hungry man. To protect himself against these dangers counter-magic is the gardener's only hope, and even without definitely suspecting witchcraft, all the Bemba I questioned told me that food could not be expected to last unless some magic of durability had been performed—a magic rite that would keep the granary full (*ukuisula pe na pe*) and would act upon the food so that one little eating pot would satisfy a family instead of two, and 'the little bit of porridge give strength to the heart' (*akabwali kalekosho mutima*).

All these results are produced by the Bemba charm *icibyalilo*, still almost universally used to-day. The form of the charm varies from family to family although there are certain common elements, such as the doctoring of the grain with medicine smoked through it (*ukufutikila*) or by sprinkling (*ukusansa*), the mixing of the old harvest with the new to maintain continuity, and some rite of sympathetic magic by which people are made to feel full with the new grain in order that this property of satisfaction may be conferred on the rest of the crop. All sorts of intermediate forms exist, and the fact that Christian women sometimes sign themselves with the cross before reaping to make the food last shows how strong is this belief that nothing but supernatural aid can carry a woman safely through the hazards of Bemba catering.

The full *icibyalilo* rites are complex and take place in three stages. At sowing, the medicinal herb (*umuti*), sometimes mixed with an activating principle like scrap iron or a piece of rubber, is mixed with the seeds that are sown and sometimes a small portion is buried in the centre of the field or little fire-stands built there for the cooking of the new grain at the approaching harvest. At reaping, a little knot of millet is usually tied in the centre of the garden and a small fire lit underneath upon which a potsherd full of water is set to heat. Medicine is thrown on top when the steam begins to rise. It is believed that this medicated steam travels right through the field (*ukufutikila*). After this a little paste made of the old year's flour is dabbed here and there on the new heads of grain (*ukusansa*). In some families the first grain is carried back to the village in a special basket and the empty granary must be smoked with the same medicine before it is filled. It is common, too, for a little porridge made with old and new flour mixed to be given to two small boys to eat ('Because the stomachs of small children get quickly filled'). The remains of the porridge added to a basket of new grain is then tipped into the granary by one of the little boys who shouts, 'You granary fill up now!' (*We butala uisule!*).

In conclusion, the Bemba consider it more or less normal for food to be scarce, and both their agricultural system and methods of distribution make it impossible entirely to prevent such a happening. Traditional magic belief teaches that only by supernatural means can the dangers of a shortage be avoided. This firm conviction combined with the temperamental optimism of the Bemba and their lack of interest in hard agricultural work makes them believe that somehow something will happen. *Butala mumina ua lusato.* 'A granary is like the oesophagus of the python', i.e. you think it looks very small, but really it can enlarge to hold a great deal.

The people's system of measurement and their material equipment makes it difficult for them to estimate their supplies exactly, and in any case it does not pay them to have much more food than their relatives stored in their granaries. All these reasons account for their failure to achieve that attitude of mind which the European describes as 'foresight' or 'thrift'.

Material Possessions of the Bemba.

The problem of the annual shortage of the Bemba must now be considered from the general economic point of view as distinct from that of the individual housekeeper. What incentives have the Bemba as a whole to accumulate sufficient surplus to provide them with a margin of safety in case of calamity? It is clear that there is not sufficient food grown in the country, but is it certain that if production were higher and if, for example, the soil were better and the labour supply more ample, that the people would fill bigger granaries and secure a better diet? This question must be answered in the light of the dominant economic interests of this particular tribe and their conceptions of wealth. We know that many primitive people accumulate large stores of food from motives entirely different from our own. The Trobriand Islanders make stacks of yams far beyond their ordinary daily needs in order to fill the yam stores of their sisters' husbands, and to acquire kudos by this fulfilment of their kinship dues. They delight in producing surplus food in order to display it and offer it in public exchange. Other Melanesian and Polynesian peoples work as seems to us unnecessarily hard in order to pile up supplies for periodic feasts. But W. E. Armstrong and F. E. Williams have shown how such feasts in south-eastern New Guinea gave a great stimulus to social and economic life and have argued against their suppression even on economic grounds.[1] Similar examples of the social importance of accumulating animal or vegetable food, as apart from its use as a food-supply, could be given from all over the world. We have to ask ourselves, therefore, whether the Bemba reckon wealth in terms of surplus food and whether prestige is attached to its possession. Since the economic values of a primitive people are inevitably affected profoundly by contact with Europeanism, it will be necessary to answer these questions to make a comparison between conditions as they probably existed at the end of the nineteenth century and are still operative in the more remote parts of the country, and those newer ideas of wealth which are found among natives in closer contact with white civilization.

To begin with, it can be said quite categorically that neither in pre-European days, nor at the present, were or are a man's possessions in food or other objects used as a measure of his social status. The material possessions of the Bemba are too limited and of too impermanent a character. A glance inside a Bemba hut will show how few objects it actually contains even at the present day. The poverty of the people, judged by our standards, is striking, and it is remarkable even compared with the neighbouring tribes. One axe, one spear, one hoe, a bed-mat, four or five cooking

[1] F. E. Williams, 'Depopulation of the Suan District', *Anthrop. Report, Papua*, No. 13, 50–6.

pots, and the same number of baskets and a couple of blankets would be the usual equipment. Few men own more than one cloth, or an outfit of European clothes such as shorts and a shirt, or the tattered remnants of these. Women rarely have more than one frock or cloth. Besides these, the people treasure certain hereditary objects of no economic value such as the bow of the man, the bead girdle (*umushingo*) of the woman, and certain beads, ivory bracelets, or anklets. A few Bemba own goats and sheep, and many keep chickens and pigeons. All these possessions are individually owned and bequeathed to descendants according to rule, i.e. the heirlooms described above descend to the legal heirs, the maternal nephews or grandsons. Any personal property made by a man, or acquired by his efforts, may go to his own sons, his wife, or his sister, as the case may be. His clothes or money, or his hut, for the year or two it remains habitable, go to his wife or his children, and the working pots and baskets to the wife or the sister.

If the material possessions of the Bemba are few in number, they are also impermanent. Few objects can be reckoned as lasting more than four or five years. It is impossible to protect the wood of houses and furniture from the ravages of white ants, and the same applies to baskets, mats, and most of the other contents of an ordinary hut. Even sacred relics guarded with the utmost care seem to have been frequently destroyed in the past by insects or fire, and most of the surviving heirlooms are those of iron or copper, ivory, or a few beads. This in itself affects the people's attitude to property, and the social values associated with its accumulation.

To turn to present-day conditions, it must be realized that a money income is not yet a universal measure of wealth in this community. The amount of money the individual Bemba handles each year is very small. I put it at 15s. to £1 on an average (cf. Chap. X). Money can only be obtained by work for Europeans or occasionally for fellow Africans. The average unskilled wage was 7s. 6d. a month during my stay, and the opportunities for regular employment in the country were very few.[1] Practically only the domestic servants and clerks could be considered as regular wage earners, and these were naturally a very small proportion of the community. A certain amount of money is said to

---

[1] Cf. the figures for absentee labour given in Chapter I. It was reckoned in 1934 that in the Kasama area only 30 per cent. could have earned their tax of 10s. locally.

be brought or sent back from the mines, but it is difficult to reckon how much.[1] From superficial observations it seemed that most natives returning from the mines brought clothes and other European goods with them, not money, and that the circulation of cash from this source had very much decreased since the cessation of recruiting with its associated system of deferred pay in 1931. Grain is bought by the Government and mission schools in the area, and a few objects like baskets or mats are sold by craftsmen, but the total sources of money revenue are still exceedingly limited, and anything like a persistent accumulation of money does not exist, and could not exist whatever the people's economic ambitions.

Conceptions of Wealth.

If, then, in the old days a man's material possessions were no measure of his wealth, on what did his economic privileges or status in society depend, and what were the chief ambitions he pursued? Roughly speaking, the aim of every Bemba was to secure rights over the service of others, whether slaves, relatives, fellow villagers, or subjects. This would enable him to make slightly larger gardens than his fellows, or in the case of a chief, to form a band of retainers and counsellors and an army. With the economic privileges he gained through their labour were correlated political position and status. In fact the latter were considered the more important assets. The employer, if he may so be called, gained not only labour for his garden, and warriors for his army, but the prestige of a large following. 'How did you recognize a man of rank or wealth [umukankala] in the old days?' I once asked an old courtier of Citimukulu. 'By his clothes?' 'No! not by his clothes. He only got cloth if the chief gave it to him from time to time. Otherwise he wore bark-cloth like every one else. You would know him by his little band of followers [kalibumba kakwe], his kinsmen, or the slaves he had.' And this is a statement that can be made with equal truth of a chief to-day, of a European, or indeed any one in authority. 'He came with a lot of people' is a comment which is always received with respect, and I believe the fact that so many natives employed at the mines pay quite a high proportion of their wages on hiring servants is

[1] The Merle Davis Commission estimates that one-fifth of the total earnings of urban natives returned to the rural areas in N. Rhodesia. *Modern Industry and the African*, 1933, p. 184.

a reflection of this desire to build up a following.[1] 'Why do you pay 5s. a month to three boys to work for you when you only earn 60s. yourself?' I once asked a mine clerk. He answered simply: 'Because I am a clerk. I am not an ordinary man.'

Bemba ambitions are shaped accordingly. In the old days a young man could only hope to rise by attaching himself by marriage to an *umukankala*, by joining the village of a rich relative, a grandfather, a maternal uncle, or more certainly still by currying favour with a chief. This latter he could do by putting himself under the protection of a kinsman who lived at the capital, and joining the ranks of the *bakalume ba mfumu* (boys or pages of the chief) and doing odd services for the *mfumu*. Thus he obtained food, personal favours, and finally advancement, and possibly a wife. Hence the wide use of charms to secure the goodwill of the *mfumu* and to make oneself appear agreeable to him.[2] This is still true to a large extent to-day.

As distinct from the youth, the aim of a middle-aged man, who had already married and risen in the social scale, was to attract as large a following as possible of his kinsmen, and ultimately to found a village himself. His married daughters and their husbands were more or less bound to live with him in any case, but more distant relatives were only attracted to do so if they liked or respected him or felt it to be to their economic advantage.

Besides this, a prospective headman had to have the support of his chief, whether he desired to form a new village or merely to inherit the position held by one of his kinsmen. Appointment to offices such as headmanships was limited to men of senior age and descent of a lineage group or even a local branch of a clan; but of those eligible, only men who had won the favours of the chief could expect to succeed. To achieve the position of headman a man had to wait in patience, plot, plan, and try to ingratiate himself with the hospitality he offered and to impress his fellows with his *mano* (good sense). This aim holds good to this day, and to this purpose the ambitious man gives himself entirely, some-

---

[1] The need for firewood fetched at some distance from the compound is of course another factor.

[2] *Umuti ua cisense.* Cf. L. P. Mair's account of the social ambitions of the Ganda: 'To the Muganda the political system of his tribe was not only the machine which dispensed justice and organised the execution of the king's command, but a social ladder which every man of ambition might hope to climb.' *An African People in the Twentieth Century,* 1934, p. 173.

times testing his power by settling in temporary grass huts (*imitanda*) with his closest relatives to see whether more distant kinsmen will be attracted to live with him, or going about the country assiduously visiting kinsmen. I met an old native of high family on the copper belt who had lived in the urban area ten years saving up money to buy muzzle-loading guns and attracting the nucleus of a small village group by dispensing hospitality at the mines. 'They will go back with me,' he said, 'when they see I am a great man, and that they will have meat at my village.' Once a village has been founded, the headman's efforts cannot be relaxed, for with the Bemba practice of shifting villages, a kinship system which allows of many types of local grouping, and the Government regulations that any man with a following of nine other taxpayers can split off to form a new community, it is naturally difficult for a man to keep together a large enough following. He must still dispense food, avoid dissensions, and use magic. Otherwise at each shifting of the village people may leave him.

The aim of chiefs, or indeed of any member of the Royal clan, is very similar although their objectives are on a larger scale. The possible heirs of a chief, his brothers, maternal nephews or grandsons, try to win favour with the ruling chief and to prove that they know how to exert authority and govern a village (*ukuteko mushi*), and hence they tend to congregate at the Chief's Court to carry out responsible tasks for him, and in some cases are given headmanships on trial.[1] Once a young *mwinaŋandu* has attained to a sub-chieftainship he hopes to rise to superior positions. These are chiefly given according to seniority, but, where a man has proved himself unworthy, a different choice would be made. Any holder of the title of chief has, further, to keep men living in his village, and to attract visitors to it. The greatness of the dead Citimukulus is always described by accounts of the immense size of their villages, the number of their courtiers, and the great crowd of visitors and eminent people who sat at their feet all day long. Even to-day capitals are much larger than commoners' villages, and the status of chiefs is still reckoned very largely by the number of huts built round them. A man whose subjects tend to leave his

---

[1] The present Mukuikile was given a headmanship to one of the Chambesi villages as a young man, but was proved irresponsible and only attained his present position as chief on his return from long years spent as a cook at Livingstone.

territory, as well as his village, has a bad reputation, and this often happens at the present day, although formerly a commoner had little power to leave his chief's country.

This desire to attain authority, whether over slaves, kinsmen, villagers, courtiers, or the inhabitants of a district is, therefore, the dominant factor we have to consider. The accumulation of food is entirely secondary to it, and only exists in so far as it permits the necessary concentration of service, as for instance, in the chief's capital. Meat and beer are needed, as we saw, to feed labourers, relatives, and courtiers, and are essential to the working of the tribal machine. To give with a flourish was the glory of chieftainship, as Livingstone found when the Citimukulu of his day (Citapankwa) sent after him the ivory tusk he had sat on because he had touched it.[1] Actual possession of great quantities of foodstuffs does not seem to have been a particularly cherished ambition of the Bemba. They valued a reputation for giving, not for having, and the distribution of food brought by villagers as tribute or levied as toll on the conquered peoples was a measure of wealth. Old men boast to-day about the amount the former chiefs used to take from the Bisa or surrounding peoples, and they respected a man who was able to exact the biggest levy of such tribute. I never heard a chief boast to another about the size of his granaries, but often about the amount of food brought to him and distributed by him.

In fact chiefs particularly valued the fact that some of their food was brought to them and not grown in their gardens, for it gave them some kind of resource to fall back upon. The Bemba say: 'We will shake the tree until it gives up its fruit', that is to say we will nag the big man until he divides his supplies. If a chief attempted to dry meat and keep it for subsequent division his followers would sit and stare at it and talk about it until he was forced to give them some, but supplies brought irregularly from other villages provided constant fresh resources.[2]

Therefore the chief seems to have aimed at having just sufficient crops to put him in a position of security, but not at increasing

[1] Gouldsbury and Sheane, *The Great Plateau of Northern Rhodesia*, 1911, p. 17.

[2] An interesting illustration of this fact is that the paramount chief often asked me to keep his quarterly salary from the Government because 'Otherwise my children and grandchildren will keep on coming and will do obeisance and ask for cloths'.

his supplies indefinitely. To-day the big chiefs make proper gardens every two years (*ukutema pakalamba*), and fill enormous granaries which they reckon to last for two seasons or more. They definitely do not try to produce the maximum amount of food possible each year as the following table shows. It appears that

Annual Cultivation by Four Chiefs

1 = Full cultivation. $\frac{1}{2}$ = Small gardens.
o = No cultivation.   .. = No records obtained.

	1926	1927	1928	1929	1930	1931	1932	1933
Citimukulu .	..	..	..	..	..	1	$\frac{1}{2}$	1
Nkula . .	1	o	1	$\frac{1}{2}$	$\frac{1}{2}$	1	o	$\frac{1}{2}$
Mwamba .	..	1	o	Village moved	o	1	$\frac{1}{2}$	$\frac{1}{2}$
Nkolemfumu .	..	..	..	..	..	1	o	o

this was always the custom even when labour was easier to get. Thus the *mfumu* had about four times as much food accumulated as a commoner, but there was not a much greater difference than this between them. In any case the difference in wealth was a difference in power to distribute, not in the amount possessed.

The position of the commoner is different. Not only has he no reason to accumulate beyond a certain point, sufficient to give him enough to eat and to distribute in a small way, but he is also afraid to do so. To be much better off than his fellows would be dangerous. A man who is full when others are hungry is hardly considered to have achieved the good fortune by natural means. An occasional stroke of good luck is not resented, but to be permanently much more prosperous than the rest of the village would almost certainly lead to accusations of sorcery.[1] It might also be thought presumptuous (*icilumba*), an aping of the chief, and it would certainly cause a number of elderly female relatives to come and claim support from the lucky man. For these reasons the Bemba not only aims at a very modest competence, but he usually denies that he is as well off as he is. Unlike the Trobriand Islanders who boast about the fullness of their yam stores, the Bemba invariably denies that he has any food at all: 'We've simply swept the granary clean' (*twapyangafye!*) is his usual comment.[2]

---

[1] One of the reasons witchcraft is so much more common in urban areas where inequality in wealth is so much more striking. } N.B.

[2] Compare the structure of the Trobriand granary designed to reveal the

We can see in fact that as far as the production of a large surplus of millet is concerned there were no strong motives in this society to do so, either to attain kudos, to fulfil marriage contracts, to increase material prosperity, or to leave wealth to the next generation.

New Economic Ambitions.

This general attitude to accumulation exists to a large extent to-day, and among the older men the same political ambitions remain operative. The desire to build up a village is still very pronounced, and I have known cases where members of the royal clan, earning good wages at the mines, threw up their jobs if offered a headmanship at home. In the same way, I found that young men who had succeeded to some headmanship or small office, such as a hereditary priesthood, early in life, preferred to hold this position rather than leaving to work for Europeans.

But for the rest of the community the introduction of British rule, money, and European goods has cut completely across old economic objectives with marked effects on the food-supply. In particular, the strength of the Bemba craving for clothes is almost impossible to explain to a reader without African experience. To understand it, it would be necessary to listen to the constant talk of natives about clothes and prices anywhere near a white town, to watch the men and women crowding round the European stores in a place like Kasama—where the tailors sit and machine their customers' frocks in the street—or to see the swagger of the booted and trousered young man in front of the women of his village. This would give some idea of the passionate desire of these people to possess, by some means or other, European clothes. It must be remembered that cloth was always thought valuable in this area since its first appearance in the hands of Arab traders in the middle of the nineteenth century. Bales of cloth were exchanged for slaves and remained the chiefs' monopoly, so that to wear cotton cloth, as distinct from the local bark-cloth, was a sign of royal favour. In any case the Bemba, like the Luba-speaking peoples of the Congo, have been described as fully clothed up to their armpits by the earliest

contents and that of the Bemba in which even the householder is not quite aware of the amount of food she possesses. B. Malinowski, *Coral Gardens and their Magic*, 1935, vol. i, pp. 242–3, 245–55, 257.

travellers in those regions.[1] So the desire for garments of some
sort is not a new one, but it is the first time in history that it
has been open to commoners, as distinct from chiefs and notables,
to raise their status in this way. Clothes are a source of excitement and delight at this stage of transition, and a sign of distinction
between the civilized man and the bush native.[2]

I have described this craving for European goods because it
directly affects the production and storage of food. Conditions
in this area are such that money cannot be regularly earned or
accumulated, or used to produce an all-round improvement in the
standard of living. But the desire for clothes is at present one of
the chief incentives which drives men to leave the territory to look
for work, and a man gone to the mines is said to be away 'clothing
his wife'. Further, as regards the stay-at-home native, it can be
said at once that where millet can be sold for money, either to
Europeans or to urban natives, the natives always succumb to the
temptation. It is unfortunate that in this area the chief saleable
crop is a staple food, for it means that the people sell their supplies
often at the lowest prices without thought of the hunger they must
presently suffer. Dealers in grain will tell you that in times of
famine millet is often produced somehow and from somewhere, if
only it can be sold for money. I have myself seen women near the
motor road sell their last basket of grain for a cheap cotton vest
torn in a week with the hard garden work. The old realistic attitude towards the value of food described in Chapter III seems
completely abandoned in these circumstances. Old men sometimes say: 'You can't fill your belly with shillings', but the younger
men and women would rather go without food than clothing, and
wherever money has been substituted for tribal obligations formerly paid in work or foodstuffs, these sums are never spent on
food, but always on European goods. The cases of the payments
to the father-in-law have already been described, but it is equally
true that money paid to the chief in lieu of his garden labour would

[1] As compared with the Ila on the Kafue River who have remained naked
until very recently.

[2] A missionary, clad himself in an open shirt, shorts, and sandals, once asked
one of his teachers why he went about on a sweltering day in a thick suit with
long woollen stockings and two shirts. The teacher replied: 'You could go naked
but people would still know you had clothes in your cupboard, but if I didn't
wear my clothes people would say I was an uneducated fellow with nothing
more than a pair of shorts.'

probably not be used for this purpose but for acquiring European objects of different kinds.

To conclude, we are dealing with an economic system in which the accumulation of large quantities of any type of material goods was neither very possible nor considered desirable. The accumulation of food was not an end in itself for the chief or notable, but rather a means to enable him to build up a large following of people which was to him the highest aim in life. His economic assets consisted in rights over food produced by others as well as in the cultivation of millet himself. For the commoner, the possession of excessive food supplies was definitely considered unsuitable, and people were afraid to admit they had such a store. In short the surplus crop was not a Bemba ideal. Under modern conditions the desire for European goods, and in particular clothes, leads the people to squander even their available food supplies on objects which have become more important to them.

The Use of Money.

Money has been used in this territory for about thirty years. The first white administrators in the district were told to encourage its circulation as 'a civilizing influence' and, as soon as possible, wages were paid and taxes levied in currency and not in kind. European stores were opened shortly after, and very few of these shops will now accept payment in kind instead of money. It is, therefore, worth considering this specific question: Has the introduction of a money currency facilitated the distribution of food?

In the first place, the use of coins in everyday life is still very limited. This is chiefly due to the shortage of money in the area as a whole. No native could hope to substitute cash payments for all his present kinship obligations or other needs of life because he would rarely be in a position to do so. But it is also a fact that the Bemba still use money in a completely different fashion from our own. They regard it as a medium to be used in specific transactions only. These are, naturally, the purchase of European goods and the payment of tax, and, less obviously, marriage payments, sums paid for native crafts, the fulfilment of ceremonial obligations, and debts of honour. The Bemba buy European goods with money because they can get them in no other way. They pay taxes in money for the same reason. The substitution of small sums for the marriage payment has been an easy transition from

the old custom of giving the father of the girl two or more bark-
cloths. In 144 marriage contracts I recorded small sums of money
were paid in 86 cases, i.e. 59 per cent., and in six villages where
I made marriage censuses an average of 6s. 6d. was paid for the
mpango of the girl. The old bark-cloths were replaced by calico
cloths, and many *mpango* are still paid in this fashion, and later by
the money to buy the cloth. The 10s. given the father-in-law as the
'money to cut the trees' is merely the wage for a month's work at
European rates.

Baskets, pots, axes, and other objects made by the Bemba craftsmen were always paid for by goods in kind or by service, and for
these dues money has been nearly everywhere substituted. Even
then, the purchase is not subject to the ordinary laws of demand
and supply, since once the regulation sum for a basket or a pot has
been fixed at 3d. or 6d. there it will remain, however scarce the
materials of which it is made.

The use of money in Bemba ritual life is largely due to its rarity
value. It has the prestige of an object that comes from a foreign
country and which is possessed by few members of the community.
Before the arrival of the white man it is clear that articles that came
from far off, brought by Arabs, or sent as presents to the chiefs, had
a particular value, and were kept as presents of honour or marks of
status. Hence they were considered particularly suitable as offerings to the ancestral spirits. The use of bark-cloth for this purpose
was common here as in other parts of Bantu Africa, but it was not
the local bark-cloth that was hung on the shrine of the ancestor,
but the valuable calico brought by Arab traders. In the same way
I have seen barrels of guns stuck in the ground over the grave of
a chief (Cilubi Island on Lake Bangweolu) and have been asked
by the Paramount for china plates for the same purpose. He told
me that plates or tea-pots had been offered to the spirits in this way
in the old days because they were 'valuables' (*ifyuma*) and because
'we had not seen any before'. Cattle taken in war were also considered necessary for some ancestral sacrifices, although the Bemba
are not a pastoral people. Money has apparently acquired a similar
rarity value which it has not yet lost. A present of a coin is appreciated not only on its own account but because of the kudos it
gives. Most Europeans hesitate to give money as a present to an
equal or to a superior because it is a currency used for the ordinary
run of economic transactions, and therefore seems to give a

commensurable value to the incommensurable gratitude, friendship, or respect which he wants to express. He prefers to exchange his coins for some other object, possibly of far less practical value to the recipient. The African chief, on the contrary, is more flattered on receiving a coin, however small, than anything else, because, as he says: 'money is respect (*umucinshi*)'. Small coins are constantly used as presents of honour to relatives, and it is quite common for a servant who wants to make an elegant gift to his white master to do so by presenting him with a threepenny or a sixpenny bit. Sums of money are used as compensation in cases of injury or insult.

In particular ceremonies money again performs special functions. At a marriage or an initiation rite coins are used instead of the old bark-cloth, and also as a payment for ritual services or as a means of removing taboos. Sixpence or a shilling may be offered to the woman who lights a girl's fire on the morning after her marriage, to those who whitewash the hut after a funeral ceremony, or to remove a taboo on eating. At the ceremonial founding of the chief's new village there is now a fixed tariff ranging from 1s. to 10s. for the hereditary priests who are in charge of the rites, such as the lighter of the sacred fire, the opener of the sacred relic huts, or those who purify the chief, wake him ceremonially in the morning, or beat his hereditary drum. In all these cases the coins are used as valuables much as the ivory tusks, cloth, or bracelets of old days were employed, and their rarity makes them the most suitable objects available at the present day.

With this special attitude to money, it is not surprising that the Bemba still consider it waste to use coins for the purchase of food. money is too rare and too hardly come by to be thrown away on a commodity that can be got in some other way. Only a few years before my visit an old woman was discovered dying of starvation in a disused hut on the motor road with a 2s. piece tied in a fold of her cloth. It had apparently never occurred to her to use the money to buy supplies on her journey to the mines to look for her son. Younger people have naturally changed in this respect, but it is still true to say that money is never 'wasted' (*ukuposa*) on food unless it is absolutely necessary, as it is near the white towns. Even then the transition to a sale from a gift from a kinsman or a subject is a very gradual one. People buying from relatives pay less than the normal rate, and usually add some service to the transaction. Chiefs buying from subjects, as we shall see, pay nominal

sums for a particular object against the background of the complicated interchange of services in which the relationship of chief
and commoner consists. They pass from one economic system to
the other in the course of a day or a week, and they still consider such
transactions irregular or out of the usual. They are not calculating
to save money, nor do they rely on it in the ordinary course of events.

The Bemba wants money occasionally, and then in relatively
speaking large sums—10s. for his tax or 5s. for a cloth. These
sums he usually wants urgently, and is prepared to make unusual
efforts to earn the money or to sell any property he has to get it. Less
than a given amount apparently seems to him almost useless. In
fact, when opportunities of earning money are so scarce the gap
between 1s. and 10s. may well seem unbridgeable, and hence there
is no attempt to save in order to reach the higher sum. I noticed
that in the outlying districts natives who brought goods for sale
asked for the specific sum they wanted almost irrespective of the
amount of food they were selling. If I refused, I was often told:
'Well, 5s. is what I want, if you won't give me 5s., please take it as
a present.' In the latter case the native returned to the old system
of exchange by which presents offered put the recipient under an
obligation to return and, if possible, to return more than he had
been given. In the same way, carriers called out for labour will
go on long journeys but do not like to sign up for short ones.
The idea of regularly accumulating small sums of money in order
to acquire greater ones only exists among natives who have a
regular earning capacity, and it is natural that it should be so.
The old attitude of the Bemba towards the amassing of food and
goods, combined with their present limited opportunities for
acquiring money, absolutely prevents the regular saving of money
to be used to purchase better food.

The introduction of money has encouraged natives to sell more
millet than they should, but its circulation is not sufficient to
make it useful as a general means of exchange, and the people's
attitude to its use still prohibits them working for a regular
sale and exchange of food, such as will be necessary if the kinship
system of the people still further breaks down.

Types of Exchange.

In this connexion it will be useful to summarize the traditional
attitude of the Bemba towards trade or barter itself, and to describe

any type of exchange of goods that actually existed in pre-European days, as apart from the joint consumption and pooling of food within the different kinship units. Formerly it seems clear that, except for food brought to the capital, the only goods which circulated about the country were articles such as ironwork—chiefly hoes—brought from the surrounding tribes, salt carried from the local salt-pans near Mpika, and the various objects such as guns and cloth traded by caravans of Arabs. In most of these cases the goods were brought to the chiefs—whether given as tribute by conquered peoples or fetched by parties of his men. Commoners occasionally went to the Lunda area to fetch hoes, or to the salt-pans to bring back balls of salt.[1] Fish was carried as tribute from the bigger rivers or fishing pools, but probably not traded to commoners to any extent.

The environmental conditions of the Bemba account to some extent for their poor development of trade, since conditions are, generally speaking, so uniform in this area that there is little reason for one district to exchange goods with another. In the neighbouring swamp area, on the other hand, the Bisa, Ushi, Unga, and other tribelets have control of great supplies of fish, not possessed by the other plateau natives, and they live on small islands each of which seems to lack one essential commodity—whether it is firewood, clay for pots, tall trees for canoe-building, soil for millet for brewing, &c.; and here the people, unlike the Bemba, live by trade with each other and with the European. But besides their environment the history of the Bemba probably limits their trading interests. A dominant tribe can get what it wants from subject peoples and an autocratic chief can monopolize such commodities as ivory, salt, or Arab goods so that the commoner does not reckon to trade with them at all. The Bemba concepts of wealth just described also affect their desire to barter or sell, and make it difficult for them to do so.

But, whatever the reason, the Bemba of to-day have no tradition of commerce, no habit of exchange, and as yet no abilities in this direction. They barter very little and have taken poor advantage of the Government's recent efforts to introduce markets at Kasama, Mpika, and Chinsali.[2] Without roads suitable for motor transport

[1] I am not clear what these parties took as goods to trade with, but heard of particular cases where men worked for the hoes they needed.

[2] The Pim Report [Report of the Commission appointed to inquire into the

such markets could hardly develop to a large extent, since the
villages are widely dispersed, and a woman bringing in food to sell
is limited by the weight she can carry on her head, i.e. about 50 lb.[1]
But nevertheless it seems clear that the Bemba differ strikingly
from other tribes in their ability to take advantage of modern
methods of trade. For instance, no hawkers licences were issued in
the Kasama district in 1937, whereas fifty-five were issued among
the cattle-owning Mambwe round Abercorn.[2]

The types of trade that I observed among the Bemba in 1934
were as follows: (a) The occasional hawking of such objects as
snuff, baskets, mats, or fish by members of surrounding tribes,
e.g. the Nsenga from the Loangwa valley, who are great traders;
(b) occasional expeditions made by the Bemba to other districts
to fetch supplies of something they need, e.g. fish from the
swamps; (c) sporadic exchanges of food for money or goods between local natives during the hunger season; (d) barter or sale of
food to natives permanently living in white employment and therefore often without their own gardens; (e) the barter or sale of craft
goods such as axes, baskets, mats, &c.; (f) the sale of grain to
Europeans. Except in the case of the sales to town natives or to
Europeans, none of these forms of exchange is organized or even
continuous. The traffic appears to consist of a series of isolated acts
which have little reference to previous transactions of the kind, and
are not governed by any recognized system of comparative values.

Thus in the remoter villages the people will tell you, 'A man
came through the village yesterday and sold us snuff—a lump like
this (shown by a gesture)—for an eating basket of grain', and it is
clear that this was a single instance and that nothing like a regular
schedule of prices or rates of exchange governed the transaction.
The hawker may not appear again for a year or two. The expeditions made by the Bemba themselves to surrounding territories
have something entirely casual about them. I have seen parties of
young men leaving a Bemba village to 'buy fish' among the Bisa
of the swamps. Such groups would go off in holiday spirits,

Financial and Economic Position of N. Rhodesia. Colonial 145], 1938, p. 28,
comments on the poor success of these markets; and cf. also the figures as to
the number of native-owned stores in the district as 6 only in 1935, p. 53.
Native Affairs Report of the N. R. Government, 1935.

[1] The lack of a smaller coin than the 3d. bits formerly prevented native trade
developing, but the Government has introduced cupro-nickel 1½d. bits since 1934.

[2] Ibid., 1937, p. 53.

combining the excursion with a series of visits to relatives on the way. They usually seemed to have kinsmen in the villages to which they were going from whom they hoped to get extra presents of fish, to buy more cheaply than usual or, at any rate, to live for a week or so on fish! They were prepared to walk three or four days to their destination and the same distance back, and to return with two or three baskets of fish to last them during the ensuing months. The whole affair struck one as more like a picnic expedition undertaken, Bemba-fashion, on a sudden impulse, than as part of an organized economic undertaking, and it seems that such journeys to other districts to fetch particular local commodities are similar to those made in the old days at the command of a chief. But it must be emphasized that this form of barter was an occasional event rather a habit of life, and it still is so to-day.

It is only in the case of the fish trade from the Bangweolu swamps that a regular price is charged per basket. During the hunger season the food situation could be greatly eased by regular barter, since there is often considerable inequality between different villages as to their supplies, but not only is there no regular marketing place in the villages, but all such acts of exchange are completed by natives who are in too great a hurry, too hungry, or too much at the mercy of the whim of the moment to strike what to us would be a sound economic bargain. At this season the people seem to plunge into a series of exchanges of one food for another on which the outsider is inclined to think that they lose each time. A few examples will make this clear. Thus, in January 1934, I saw three women with empty granaries go a journey of twenty-five miles to buy millet with some tobacco one of them had been presented with. They returned with three carrying-baskets of grain (i.e. less than the value of the tobacco), which they started to use. One immediately began to trade some of her millet for beans, another brewed some beer with a large part of the grain in order, she said, to make a shilling to buy more millet again. This was obviously not an economic proposition, since her shilling would have bought her very little new grain at the end of another twenty-five-mile walk, but with the fatalistic attitude produced by some weeks of food shortage, and lack of the habit of regular trading, she probably preferred the exhilaration of a beer drink to a careful hoarding and measuring of her supplies. In the same village a woman had returned from the mines two years ago with five cotton

frocks. Two had worn out and two were in use, but the fifth remained. Driven to desperation by the food shortage, she walked
to the Chambesi river and exchanged her 5s. frock for a 2s. basket
of fish. On her return thirty miles to her home, she immediately
sold some of the fish for a small quantity of millet (again at less
than its current price) and with the millet made two gourds of beer.
One she sold for a shilling and the other she and her relatives
drank. In all such cases the Bemba in the hunger season seem to
walk huge distances, make bad bargains on sudden impulses, and
then squander the products of the expedition.

Near Kasama, where there are natives living in the white township or its neighbourhood, the Bemba lack of trading ability is
shown even more strikingly. Here there are a number of men
employed by Europeans, unable to make gardens either because
they have been too short a time in the district, because they have
left their wives behind, or because cultivated land is short. They
have to buy food from the surrounding villages with money or with
goods.[1] They prefer the latter because it is more economical:
'Salt is better because you can give a little at a time. Besides,
women often want salt in a hurry and they agree to sell you what
you want.' But here again, in 1934 at any rate, the buyers had to
spend money on snuff, cloth, or salt without knowing which the
sellers would happen to want that day, and there was no fixed
rendezvous at which purchaser and seller could be certain of
meeting. The wives of the domestic servants in one compound
I knew used to get up at five in the morning and go along the
different country roads hoping to waylay the incoming villagers
before they reached the town. Quite frequently they came back
empty-handed after waiting some hours because the sellers had
gone the other way! Want of leadership and a rapidly changing
situation may explain this lack of organization, but surely no tribe
with the slightest tradition of trading would have failed to make
some arrangement by which the sellers and purchasers of goods
could be certain of meeting.

Bemba, who are recognized as being more skilled than their
fellows at crafts—pot-making, basket- or mat-weaving, or the

[1] A clerk of a steady economical type estimated that he spent 6s. 2d. a month
for himself and his family out of a 16s. wage, while two Government messengers'
budgets came to 5s. and 7s. 6d. respectively. A cook, known to be a prodigal
spender, as he called it, 'wasted' £1 a month on food and beer for himself and
his two wives.

forging of iron axe-blades or spear-heads—exchange their articles for goods, service, or money. But I never met a man who traded regularly in this fashion, who lived on the proceeds of his industry, or who travelled about the country selling his wares. In fact, the greatest initiative I ever noted was shown by one of Citimukulu's old hereditary priests, who sold baskets to villagers for chickens, and then sold the latter, ten or twelve at a time, to Europeans.

Trade with Europeans consists for the main part of sales of grain to the Government stations or missions. In 1934 the price varied from $\frac{1}{2}d$. a lb. during harvest months to $1\frac{1}{4}d$. during the rainy season in the Chinsali area. The Government station at Mpika also bought £140 of salt at $1d$. a lb. But it is difficult to estimate the total amount of food sold over the whole area.

To conclude, it can be said that the Bemba, owing to their particular environment and social organization, reckon to live by means of mutual support within their kinship groups, and only resort to the barter or sale of the goods they need sporadically, or on occasions of necessity. Then either temperament or their patterns of economic thought make them extraordinarily inept, according to European standards. Marketing, like any other form of economic activity, is evidently based on a system of values developed in earliest youth, and the trading instinct seems to be difficult to acquire by a people who have not been through such a training. The contrast between Bemba children and those of the Bisa of the fishing villages in the Bangweolu swamps is striking. There the children are accustomed from earliest infancy to hear the sales of fish and other commodities discussed, and I found that they themselves continually talked of the values of different objects, and even of their own services. When I asked them to do something for me they replied automatically, 'How much will you give me? Yes, but what kind of beads and how many?' Having struck their bargain, they kept to it. The Bemba children, on the other hand, accepted such requests for help by politely clapping their hands, as to a chief. They never bargained or refused, but on the other hand they considered their services made me liable to help them and feed them, and they were constantly on the look-out for their dues. They left the work if they became convinced, for some reason or other, that I did not 'like' them. In Bemba society economic transactions are based on a system of personal relationships—ties of kinship or political status—and in the Bisa country on an organized system of commercial exchange superimposed on these social ties. These and many other incidents made me think that the introduction of marketing in the Bemba area would be a slow process liable to many set-backs, however essential it be to their progress at the present time.

PART V

THE PRODUCTION OF FOOD

CHAPTER XIII

LAND, AND LAND TENURE

Introduction.

THE food-supply of any territory must depend on two sets of factors—the physical properties of the environment itself, and the customs and traditional lore of the people who are trying to exploit it. It is as necessary to know the methods by which the people of a particular district produce their food, their economic motives, and the rules that govern the use of the land's resources, as it is to know the nature of the soil, its vegetation and fauna, or its general climatic conditions; and it is the former aspect which the anthropologist contributes to the study of native agriculture. I shall describe, therefore, the general attitude of the Bemba to their environment, their system of land tenure and land selection, their agricultural, hunting, and fishing activities, their seasonal calendar, their type of economic co-operation, and the religious and magic beliefs that affect their production of food.

As an anthropologist, I was of course anxious from the start to see as much as I could of the food-producing activities of the people, since for the majority of the Bemba, even at the present day, these fill the bulk of their time. Living consecutively in different types of village, I was able to watch a variety of agricultural processes. These I have tried to describe as far as possible in the natives' own terms rather than in those of modern agricultural science, since my aim was to study the Bemba's own rudimentary principles of cultivation, as these determined their food-production. With regard to the land, I was unable to classify the different types of soil, since no survey had as yet been made in the area,[1] but I considered it my function to collect the terms usually used by natives to describe the soils they cultivated, and to note their customary method of assessing the fertility of any

---

[1] The ecological survey now being made in N. E. Rhodesia had not then been undertaken.

piece of ground or its fitness for special purposes. I studied in as many cases as possible the reasons that led them to select ground, either for village sites or for gardens, the whole complex of religious, magic, and political ideas associated with the land, and finally its system of tenure. These are the type of facts that give us the actual as distinct from the potential resources of the land.

The different agricultural methods of the Bemba are described largely in terms of native comments. The success or failure of these I did not try to assess, except through the natives' own eyes, or my own untrained observations. The average yield of different crops has been calculated, in the case of the cultivation of the neighbouring Mambwe, on experimental plots at the agricultural station at Abercorn.[1] Similar experiments are being made in Bemba country at Shiwa Ŋandu. I had neither the time nor the specialist comparative knowledge to touch this aspect of the question at all. On the other hand, I considered it important to study the Bemba's own system of estimating the productivity of his gardens, whether expressed in numerical terms or not. Was he able himself to assess the yield in any particular year and to plan out his needs for a future season? To what did he attribute his failures or achievements—to errors of judgement or to the hostility of supernatural powers? In brief, I wanted to study the people's traditional objective in gardening, the methods by which they thought they could attain it, actual or ritual, the way in which they calculated their achievements, and the motives which made them work more or less hard.

It was of equal sociological interest to estimate the extent of individual variation in the ordinary agricultural practices, and to account for it, if possible, in terms of personality differences, the influence of white contact, or inequalities in general economic conditions. The primitive cultivator is often said to follow tribal tradition blindly, without choice or reason, but in actual fact when seen in his own garden he appears as a man struggling in a hard environment with a bewildering number of alternative courses of action, and there are as many grades between the fool and the wise man as in any community of our own. The conservatism of the tribal African has, I think, been exaggerated. In reality, most of the Bantu have been changing their agricultural practices in contact with the surrounding peoples for generations,

[1] Cf. W. Moffat, op. cit.

and a good many experiments are actually made in the course of an individual's life. Where soil selection depends on accumulated experience, as it must do among shifting cultivators, this is especially the case, and a man could make many agricultural blunders between youth and manhood if he were acting alone. His type of education and system of co-operation in gardening prevent him from doing so to a certain extent. And it is for this reason that individual differences in agricultural skill, leadership, and the way in which economic knowledge is handed on to the next generation are facts of importance from an agricultural point of view.

The basis of the Bemba system of domestic co-operation has already been described (Chap. VIII), but it will be necessary to study the village and kinship groups as agricultural units and to estimate as far as possible the labour force required for each particular process and its relation to the cycle of other activities—political, religious, domestic, or recreational—which go to make up the daily or seasonal routine. The problem of diet in relation to the labour supply is obviously of particular importance in an area with such a large proportion of adult males away.

General Attitude to Land.

A group of Bemba walking from place to place through their tribal territory view surroundings from an entirely different standpoint from our own. Different objects excite their interest and admiration, and they comment on the scenes they pass through in different terms. This general attitude of the people towards their environment is important to describe. It expresses the line of their economic interests, and ultimately determines the legal rules by which their land is used.

Now the main aim of the Bemba cultivator is to grow as much millet as possible in any one year, and millet gardens are made by cutting off tree-tops and burning their branches. For this reason, when walking through the bush the Bemba are constantly on the watch for many and high trees. To these natives the whole stretch of land is in a sense one unit. It is all 'bush' (*mpanga*), and all potentially cultivateable. The differences between productive and unproductive soil, in their eyes, is the presence or absence of trees. What the European regards as yet another stretch of monotonous bush is to the Bemba a possible garden site. Trees are the ultimate source of his food-supply. More than this, they are the means by which all the material equipment of his life is secured. Huts, granaries, fences, beds, stools, drums, canoes—in fact, all the furniture of domestic and village existence—are made of wood. Bark forms the rope (*umwando*) used for nets and snares, or the rough strands (*lushishi*) with which poles are lashed together in building.

The skill and the speed with which the Bemba handle wood is amazing. A new-comer to the country is surprised to hear a fellow European arriving at his camp shout casually, 'Make me a table and a couple of chairs just there,' and to see the furniture grow out of the ground in the space of about half an hour. But this expertize, very widespread among the forest peoples of Africa, is ultimately dependent on the natives' knowledge of the properties of the different woods in their environment and on their perpetual watchful attention of the bush around them. Near their homes they must know where to find straight poles for uprights, pliable branches for roof frames, and hard wood for the handles of spears and other implements, and for five or ten miles round a village there are everywhere signs that an axe has been at work—a trunk newly barked for fibre, a raw stump showing where a tree has been felled, or a pile of new wood shavings marking where poles have been cut and trimmed before being carried back to the settlement. It is no wonder that the people seem to have a passionate interest in trees as such. Torday classifies many of these Central African peoples as 'forest-dwelling Bantu',[1] and it is an apt term.

All Bemba children of the age of 10, or even under, can point out the different species of trees quickly, even though they do not know their full uses until later. A European with no botanical inclinations finds it hard to distinguish between so many similar-looking trees, but the Bemba can name fifty or sixty species without hesitation. This interest is mostly utilitarian. The flowers which star the bush with such brilliant colours after the rains do not seem to attract the people, unless they can be used as medicines. Many flowers have no names. Most natives are merely irritated when a white man asks questions about the more striking flowers on the path. They answer, 'That is a flower [*ni maluba*]. Yes, and that is a flower also! They are all just flowers [*malubafye!*].' On the subject of trees, however, their faces light up and they are endlessly willing to talk.

This vivid interest in the forest is reflected in magic belief. It

[1] *African Races*, E. Torday, 1930.

is well known that in most Bantu languages the word for tree (*umuti*, or its equivalent form) is used for medicine or charm. It is not only that Africans have a wide knowledge of the curative properties of the roots, leaves and bark of different trees, but that they believe them to possess magical properties against ill health, witchcraft, or evil spirits. I know no Bemba charm which does not contain the roots, bark, or leaves of at least two different trees.

To his knowledge of the species of trees and plants in the neighbourhood, the native allies a keen interest in their whereabouts. As he walks through the bush he registers almost unconsciously the presence or absence of certain trees in a way that constantly surprises the European. Such memories seem indelibly impressed on the Bemba because of their practical importance. Driving 400 miles from Broken Hill to Kasama, the centre of the district, there is nothing to be seen all day but a flat expanse of trees, mostly deciduous, with hard shiny leaves, and dusty shrubs and grasses block the view from the road. Europeans tend to find this bush country unbearably monotonous, but the African apparently sees quite a different scene. To him such a route would be described in terms of trees. Every turn in a fifteen-mile walk would be defined in such phrases as, 'Where that big *mupundu* grew', or 'Where that *umusuku* stood with the broken branch', and so forth, the whole punctuated with cries of enthusiasm: 'That was a fine tree!' These people's thoughts and interests are in fact entirely concentrated on objects that the average white man simply does not see.

Besides their need for wood the Bemba rely on the bush for the animals and birds, caterpillars, insects, and the plants which are indispensable for their diet, and they are constantly on the look-out for such objects as they walk. Both men and women have the power of continuing an animated conversation without ever missing a single honey-bee nest or a distant mushroom, and remembering how to locate such a find a second time. I once stumbled on a bush path, turning suddenly to look at a strip of sunset against a black cloud. The native who helped me up said sympathetically, looking at the bough which he believed had riveted my attention, 'Yes, I saw that swarm of caterpillars too, but the grubs are not big enough to eat yet. I shall tell my wife to fetch them later on. I shall say, "Look for the *umutondo* tree to the east of where the path forks".' His observations had been made in a flash during our talk, but he had registered the memory for future use. He had, in fact, a vivid, if entirely selective, interest in the vegetation around him.

The natives' passionate enthusiasm for hunting adds another interest to their travel through the bush. To them the country-side can be roughly classified according to the type of game that is found there, and in ordinary speech the people describe an area by saying, for instance, that it is a land of elephants or hippos, or that it is a lechwe or reed-buck district. But apart from an interest based very largely on their craving for meat, the Bemba seem fascinated, like other African peoples, by the charac-teristic appearance and habits of the animals themselves—the fantastic size of the elephant, the laugh of the hyena, the ferocity of the lion or the crocodile. The hunter tracking his quarry through the bush is plainly keyed to a pitch of concentration watching for every sign of its tracks, but men and women simply travelling from one village to another will also seek for traces of game of any sort, just from their interest in the habits of the animals them-selves. The different species of fish have not the same fascination for the majority of the Bemba, although they form quite an impor-tant source of food. But they seem deeply interested in the rivers of their country. They compare the value of different chieftain-ships, not only in terms of the game in each particular district, but also of its supplies of fish. Rivers are among the most striking landmarks in this country and form the natural boundaries of chiefs' territories. Each tributary stream, however small, has its name which is used to define the position of different villages in the neighbourhood, while the bigger rivers seem to be a source of aesthetic delight, though perhaps merely as the potential source of so much food. I noticed on different trips that carriers spoke with real enthusiasm of the size of any large river that we were about to reach, and I have heard the natives from one district compare their rivers braggingly with those of other areas. A knowledge of the exact course of different rivers is only gradually acquired by a travelled man and is much admired. I once heard a group of children under 12 arguing hotly as to the order in which different local streams flowed into the Manshya river near-by. The discussion became so heated that a series of bets were arranged as to the results. It was characteristic of a tribe with few material possessions that the wager should consist of a stated number of slaps, to be given by the winner and accepted by the loser!

This question of the general economic and aesthetic interests of the native in his environment needs to be discussed at the outset. It lies at the root of the fundamental difference in outlook between the European and the Bantu with regard to land. The Bemba does not measure land, assess its value in size or productive capacity, or conceive of this value as a figure to be permanently maintained at a given figure by the expenditure of effort and capital. He views the country round him as all one unit, all accessible to him, and all ready to supply his needs—trees to be used for wood, ash for his gardens, building material or medicines, and wild plants, game and fish for food. Whether or not he succeeds in wresting a living from the *mpanga* depends on his constant and intent observation of his surroundings, his traditional knowledge, and, the next important factor to be considered, the help of supernatural powers.

Land and Supernatural Blessings.

The Bemba believe that the *mpanga* is under the influence of supernatural beings, the spirits (*imipashi*) of dead chiefs who reigned over the country, or of the ancestors of the headmen in charge of individual villages. They conceive of the bush as a whole, yielding or withholding its produce according to the good or ill will of supernatural powers. The garden of an individual Bemba may fail owing to his own folly, or the hostile magic used against him, but it is a calamity more to be feared that the *mpanga* itself may refuse its spoils. It is obvious that where a people's livelihood depends to any extent on uncultivated plants, fish, or game, the element of uncertainty must actually be pronounced, and the Bemba believe that this 'luck of the bush' is in the hands of ancestral spirits to grant or withhold at will. When a native uses the word *ukushyuka*, 'to be lucky', or its opposite *ukushyama*, he may do so casually in general conversation, just as we sometimes speak laughingly of fortune having been for us or against us on any special occasion. More often, however, he uses the words in a more serious sense, which may cause him to lower his tone or look around to see if he is being overheard. Spoken in this manner, *ukushyama*, 'to be unlucky', means to be an individual who has, either by breaking a tribal code, or failing in some ceremonial observance, or in carrying out his obligations to his chief, roused the anger of the *imipashi* on whose beneficence he depends. In the same way the Paramount chief who is remiss in his duty, whether ritual or otherwise, risks the displeasure of the tutelary spirits of the whole land, and may plunge the entire tribe into a state of imminent ill luck. The results of such a withdrawal of supernatural blessings cannot be clearly prophesied, but they are expected to include deaths in the royal clan, general epidemics, or locust swarms, failure of the women to bear children, the sudden appearance of man-eating lions, drought, and blighted harvests, as well as the failure of the whole *mpanga* to yield its food-supplies. At such times, the natives say, men go out to hunt, but the game stays hidden in the bush; they set fish-traps and catch nothing; they look for mushrooms and find none.

For this reason a chief, when he prays to the spirits, asks for every type of blessing on the land and not for the success of cultivated crops alone. For instance, Mulewa Cimfwembe, one of the hereditary councillors of Citimukulu, described to me an occasion in the past when the Paramount had prayed for rain, saying, 'You, the owner of my land, look now! We have not yet seen any porridge, fish, meat, and all sorts of food,'[1] i.e. the withholding of rain was a symptom of a displeasure that might be expected to result also in a shortage of fish and game as well as the millet harvest. Rain fell as the result of this prayer and then, the narrator continued, 'We saw food in great plenty, and meat, and fish, every sort of food! Every one walked in peace. The lions did not spring on the people, no! And they (i.e. the people) killed many elephants.'[2]

The *imipashi*, that is to say when they had relented sufficiently to send rain, also withheld the ferocity of the lions, and stilled the quarrels of human beings. Their blessings are conceived as being given on a sort of 'all or none' principle in fact. Such beliefs hardly seem to have been shaken by white contact. Most Bemba explained the recent locust scourge as a sign of the spirits' displeasure, and even sophisticated natives pointed out that the coming of the pest had coincided with an unusual shortage of game and the fall in the price of copper that was producing unemployment at the mines.

[1] *Mwe mwine mpanga yandi, moneni! Tatumona bwali, sabi, nama, fyakulya fyonse . . . &c.*

[2] *Twamone fyakulya fingi sana, ne nama, ne sabi, fyakulya fyonse! Bonse baleendo mutende. Nkalamo Tashîkata bantu, yo! Ne nsofu shingi balêpaya.*

It is difficult to discuss a primitive people's sense of the supernatural without drawing on metaphors familiar to our own religion or introducing a type of mysticism which may be quite alien to the culture concerned. We can only let the Bemba speak in his own words, and the traditional phrases in which he describes the luck or ill luck on his land do, I think, reflect this very deep belief that the fertility of the forest as a whole depends on supernatural forces who can will that it should release its treasures, or else deny them completely to mankind. When describing the misfortunes of the territory at any time in the past or the present, a Bemba uses such phrases as *calo nacikama*, 'The land is dried up', or *calo nacikosa*, 'The land has become hard, or difficult to deal with', or *cintu cakana mu calo*, 'Something has refused in this land'. When the late chief Nkula sent a message to the Citimukulu, asking him to offer prayers to his dead ancestors to avert the locust swarms, which were then causing widespread havoc, his emissary used the words *cintu cabushye mpanga*, 'Something has caused penury all over the land', and later, in the same speech, *cintu cawishye mpanga*, 'Something has overthrown (causative form of *ku-wa*, to fall) the bush'.[1] The word used to describe the misfortunes which are expected to follow the death of a big chief, is *calo cawa*, 'The land has fallen down'. When a traveller falls ill on visiting the *calo* of another chief for the first time, Bemba say, half laughingly, that he is paying tribute to the dead chiefs of the district, *ukutule mipashi*. I myself was struck with a branch of the protecting *Mwenge* tree when entering the country of Shimwalule, the hereditary burier of the chief, for the first time, to prevent me succumbing to this illness.

When fortune is good, and the country is in a condition to yield its prosperity, other metaphors are used. The land is said *ukusumina*, 'to consent or agree', or *ukubuta*, 'to be light or white', a verbal image depending on the natives' association of good fortune with bright shining things, objects coloured white like beads, white clay, and white animals and birds like the egret, which are always considered particularly beautiful and lucky. *Ukubuta*, when used of the forest, means to be clear and open, e.g. of a part of the bush cleared of brambles where it is easy to walk. This idea is often expressed in prayers used by hunters going out to set up their nets for a drive. 'Now lead on ahead of us!' said a headman of

[1] Heard at Citimukulu's village, 5.i.34.

Kasakatula village before a drive. 'You child (i.e. member of our family) pierce the way through.'[1] At Kasaka village the headman who struck the nets for a blessing said, after calling the spirits by name, 'Light up the bush in front of us with a torch! Make it completely light. Let us kill meat.'[2] Such a series of quotations give some indication of the kind of attitude I have been trying to describe.

Locality and Residence.

Peoples who practise shifting cultivation are generally assumed to have no particular attachment to one stretch of land rather than another. We have already described the periodic movements of the Bemba village in relation to their agricultural system, and the individual's fairly frequent changes from community to community associated with his kinship principles and rules of residence at marriage. In such circumstances it would be surprising to find among these Central African people the same passionate devotion to a village site, or set of fields or gardens, which is reported from some of the over-populated Melanesian islands or those West African villages where fixed cultivation is practised. The permanent associations of the Bemba are a series of human relationships within his lineage group, and a reliance on certain tutelary deities associated with the soil, rather than attachments to a strip of land itself. It is not true, however, that the Bemba are without a sentimental fondness for different parts of their country. The majority of village communities tend only to move from site to site within quite a small radius—about five miles square—and are more closely connected with other communities in the same chief's territory than anywhere else. Also the people seem to cherish the warmest feelings for the deserted sites of the villages they have left (*icibolya*, plur. *ifibolya*) and even for those of other people. For the first few years after building a new settlement, villagers constantly go back to their derelict gardens to gather self-sown cucumbers and marrows, or to pick bananas on their old village sites. This connexion with the old site may last for some three or four years. But when the *icibolya* is overgrown with weeds, and small shrubs have sprung up on it, it is still spoken

---

[1] *Nomba tangileni pantanshi. We mwana, tungulule!*
[2] *Muno mpanga musanike umwenge! Mubute tutu! Tuipaye nama!*

of with affection and a sort of pride. 'Come and see our *icibolya*', children used to say to me, sometimes taking me a three-mile walk to see a mere clearing in the bush where the undergrowth was still low, and only faint traces of garden mounds could still be seen. Here they would stand and gaze, sometimes in an almost reverent silence, sometimes trying to reconstruct the past life by suggesting what had happened here and there, and sometimes looking for overgrown fruit-trees. I noticed that carriers going through a new district would always stop at a deserted site, comment on its size, and speculate with eager curiosity as to whom it had belonged.

This attachment to deserted sites is due, I believe, to something more than mere human interest. For the stability of the village group it is important to preserve a sense of continuity between the community which built its huts on one spot and then moved to another. For one thing the name of the village is unchanged unless the whole group splits up, since it is customary to refer to such a settlement by the name of its headman, as for instance *Kwa Kapongolo*, 'at Kapongolo's', and in case of inheritance the heir assumes the dead man's title. Among the various rituals for founding a new village (*ukusokolo mushi*), it is common to find that some symbolic object from the old village—a rafter from the roof of the headman's hut, or a stick from his ancestral shrine—must be carried to the new. The new village must also, in the native phrase, be made 'warm'. It must be turned from uninhabited bush into a human community. It would be dangerous to sleep in a new settlement unless the headman had preceded with his wife (*ukutangila*) and had performed an act of ritual intercourse and lit a new fire 'to warm the village' (*ukukafyo mushi*). Later, divination is carried out by a ritual hunt (*ukusoa libanda*) to find out whether the *imipashi* are favourable. Bemba huts themselves may be built in a day or two, but the founding of a successful village community cannot be achieved by a single act. It requires the slow forging of human ties, and the gradual establishment of common interests and a sense of security among the inhabitants—a process which may take a year or more to complete. The chief Mwamba told me, in explanation of the fact that a year-old village had not yet performed the annual first-fruit rites, *Tabalaikala bwino*, 'They haven't properly settled down yet'; and it is the rule rather than the exception for chiefs to wait to carry out the elaborate ceremonies of offering to the ancestral spirits known as *ukupepa* until they have established their rule for a number of years.[1] The term 'shifting cultivator' carries some suggestion of feckless, impulsive conduct. It ill describes the Bemba's anxious consideration of new sites, the ritual precautions they observe for so long when moving their settlements, their efforts to keep perpetual continuity between successive villages, the long probationary period before they are ready to consider themselves established, and their affection for the *icibolya* left behind.

Village Sites of Chiefs.

The *icibolya* of a chief is a place of particular interest. I have been led miles out of my route to look at what was said to be an old village site of one of the Citimukulus, but was now quite indistinguishable from the rest of the bush. Such spots would be shown me with the same kind of reverence and possessive pride with which we might display a ruined castle to a foreign sightseer! Even when the exact geographical position of such sites has been forgotten, their names are often remembered to the present day. Chiefs, as distinct from commoners, give new names to each fresh village they build, and the life of a capital lasts longer than that of the ordinary *umushi*. This name, which is always bestowed by the ruler himself, is supposed to make allusive reference to some decision he has recently taken, or to a topical event. For instance, the late Nkula called the new village he founded in 1934 *Mano yacepa*, 'Common sense is short', because his people refused at first to follow him to a new village site and then hurried after him when they found what good land he had chosen. Even some temporary grass huts the Citimukulu had been living in for the previous two years had a name alluding to the fact that the people had refused to co-operate in building the new *umusumba*. Many such village names survive from the past. Any old man who tells the well-known tale of the migration of the Bemba from Lubaland to their present territory, gives a list of the names of successive villages built by the immigrant chiefs *en route*, while in narratives of more recent years dates are placed with a reasonable degree of accuracy by describing events as having occurred when a particular Citimukulu was still living on such-and-such a site. Some chiefs are nicknamed by the title of a village or its neighbouring river,

[1] Cf. Chap. XVII.

e.g. *Mwamba wa pa Milenge*, 'The Mwamba who built on the Milenge River'.

This strong feeling for the preservation of the sites of old capitals is expressed ritually in a number of ways. After the burial of a chief the dead man's hut must be ceremonially destroyed, *ukutoba itembwe*, and a sacrifice of an ox offered. After the rubble on the house site has rotted away, a spirit shrine (*ulufuba*) is built on the spot, and prayers offered there subsequently. Many such shrines are still honoured. The ritual performed there ultimately depends on the Bemba belief, which natives readily express, that the *imipashi*, besides going up and down the land, being present in the huts of their descendants at dusk or dawn, or lingering on burial groves, may be expected to frequent the village site which they inhabited in life, and on which they died, and that they may readily be invoked there.[1]

The intense interest of the Bemba in these historical sites in their neighbourhood has a considerable sociological importance. Malinowski has given us information from a Melanesian Island to show how clan myths associated with certain geographical spots in the territory, constantly repeated by its members, and said to be owned by them, form what he calls a 'mythical charter' for the right to use the land.[2] Among the Bemba there is no developed mythology of the doings of miraculous beings associated with different localities, but many historical traditions of the actions of former chiefs, and of the whereabouts of their villages. One can only imagine that the performance of rites at these deserted sites, or even the constant narration of different happenings associated with these ancient *ifibolya*, gives the natives a valuable assurance that such powerful chiefs actually did live in the particular area and may be called upon to protect it, and that the present holder of the title, as the direct descendant of men who built capitals all over the district, has the requisite power to approach them.

Burial-places, as distinct from deserted village sites, are forgotten quickly. The mortuary ritual of a commoner is hurried and unimpressive, and the burial-ground of a village is a place avoided by natives, and on which no rites are carried out. Chiefs are buried in clumps of evergreen swamp forests. The Citimukulu, Mwamba, Nkula, Cewe, and Nkweto at the big thicket known

[1] Chap. XVII.
[2] Malinowski, *Coral Gardens and their Magic*, 1934, vol. i, pp. 341–58.

as Shimwalule in the Chinsali district, the most secret and carefully guarded shrine in the territory. The bodies of lesser chiefs
and royal princesses are buried in another grove about four miles
from Citimukulu's village.[1]

Other sacred spots in Bemba territory are certain rocks, waterfalls, caves, or other unusual geographical features, named after
legendary beings, who are described either as having lived at the
spot in question, as having been found there by the immigrant
Bemba, or as having performed some dramatic action there—jump-
ing into a waterfall or drowning in a lake. It must be remembered
that on this flat plateau, roughly 700 miles across, the sight of a
mountain or rocky crag is rare and waterfalls of impressive size are
few. Natives tend to speak of even low hills with interest, and
most rocky summits or big caves are associated with the names of
supernatural beings, who may be invoked there by the hereditary
priest in charge (*shimiapepo*) at the order of the territorial chief.
These sacred spots are not believed to have been sites of human
habitation, nor by their very nature could most of them have been
inhabited. The spirits associated with them are emphatically stated
never to have been chiefs. They are *ngulu*—the name also used for
a man or woman who believes himself or herself to be possessed by
ancestral spirits. Were they people at all? 'Yes, but not people
who go about like we do' (*Te muntu ua kuendaendafye*). That is
to say they are legendary figures quite outside the tribal hierarchy
of spirits, of whom little is remembered. Some natives say they
were the first inhabitants of the country, but others deny that they
were ever human beings at all. Pythons are said to inhabit some
of these sites and to be worshipped there.

There are thus two types of spirit centre in the country—those
of famous chiefs of the past, whose lineage can still be traced and
whose descendants rule over the present territory. These cleared
the bush here and there, built villages, and made the *mpanga*
'warm', ruled successfully over communities, died, and became
protective influences over the inhabited district. The other spirits,
ngulu, are also believed to hold power over a definite locality,
but they never belonged to the lineage group of the Bemba and
their names are not associated with habitable village sites but
only with remarkable features of the landscape which in themselves arouse awe.

[1] The site of the village of the first ancestress of the Bemba, Bwalya Cabala.

R

To conclude then, we are dealing with a tribe in which residence is never fixed in one exact locality, whether for the community or for the individual, but in which we find, almost paradoxically, a deep sentimental attachment to different parts of the country—either because they are being used, or have been used, as human habitations, because of their historical significance, or else their association with supernatural beliefs. We are describing a people living in a sparsely populated country, in which there would seem to be no sound economic reason why a community should settle in one spot rather than another. But the choice is not in fact unlimited. It depends on directly sociological factors such as membership of a kinship group and acceptance of a political allegiance, a belief as to the sphere of influence of certain supernatural beings, and lastly the factors, which we must now consider, the tribal rights as to the use of land.

Divisions of Land.

Europeans living in Northern Rhodesia often declare that the Bemba have no system of land tenure, and at first sight there is a good deal to be said for this point of view. A new-comer to the country notices at once the lack of boundaries between the garden beds round a village. As he travels through the bush he cannot avoid being struck by the apparently haphazard way in which natives sometimes start to make gardens, cut a few trees, and then abandon the site, and by the fact that they do not even mark out the limits of the space they mean to clear in any one year. The observer will also notice that in the course of ordinary conversation no Bemba lists among his assets his possession or occupation of a given tract of land. Few disputes as to the ownership of land or its rights of use appear before the courts, and the question does not usually figure in contested inheritances.

But because the land problem is not so acute in this area, as it is in many parts of present-day Africa, we cannot conclude that there are no tribal rights as to its use, and in fact from some points of view it is even more important to discover the exact relation of man to land among a population of shifting cultivators, than it is in a tribe where the rules of ownership are more formalized.

To begin with, how is the land initially subdivided?

Icalo. The biggest division recognized is the *i-calo* (plur.

i-fyalo). This is a term applied to the whole of the Bemba territory, but also used to describe the district under the rule of a particular chief. The Paramount and the territorial chiefs under him, such as Mwamba, Nkula, Nkolemfumu, Mpepo, Cikwanda, &c., each rule over a tract of country with more or less definite boundaries, which has its own name dating back to the very early days of the Bemba occupation.[1] Each of these districts is known as the *icalo* of such-and-such a chief. Some are sub-divided into smaller districts under the rule of a sub-chief. Thus the *icalo* may be defined as a political division, and its inhabitants have a certain economic unity since they all pay tribute to the one chief and expect to receive help, supernatural or material, from him.

Mpanga, the word used for 'bush', is also sometimes applied in a more restricted sense to mean the area immediately surrounding a headman's village, that is to say the few miles between one small stream and the next. The *bakabilo* or hereditary councillors of the Paramount, claim to be owners of their *mpanga* by right of descent from the first holders of their titles, who were appointed to the district by the first Citimukulu. Therefore they may not move their village beyond the distance between one river and the next. They claim supernatural powers over the area, and in some cases may prevent the chief from being carried through it.[2] But in the case of an ordinary headman the term *mpanga yandi* hardly means more than 'the neighbourhood of my village'.

Mpanga may also mean the strip of bush between one open marshy place and the next. This country is so well watered that a traveller along an inter-village path passes one tiny stream after another at intervals of four to five miles, and the Bemba make a rough calculation of distance by this means. 'We shall pass three *mpanga* and camp at a village in the fourth', they say, and the term gives some idea of the probable length of the journey.[3]

Cultivated land is divided into (a) *mputa*, or village mounds, a circular band about 300 yards across round the village, (b) *ifitemene* (sing. *icitemene*), the millet gardens which are cut in the bush each year, at first near the village and then farther and farther out until

[1] e.g. Ituna is the *icalo* of Mwamba, Icinga that of Nkula, &c.
[2] The Cimba, Munuca, Citikafula, Katenda, Cikutwe, all have this right since the sacred relics they possess are so powerful that they might harm the Paramount himself.
[3] C. Doke records the same method of measuring the journey's length among the Lamba, *The Lambas*, 1931, p. 18.

they lie sometimes eight or ten miles away. The word *icitemene* is derived from *kutema* (to cut down trees) and it is applied to a new millet garden in the course of being cleared and prepared for sowing. Hence Government reports now refer to the '*citemene* system' to describe the characteristic Bemba method of clearing the bush. However the garden, after it has been sown, is known as an *ubukula* (plur. *amakula*), and in its second and subsequent years of life, when it is planted with other crops, it is called an *icifwani* (plur. *ififwani*) and continues under this name until the cultivated land reverts to bush. The average size of an *ubukula* has been calculated to be about one acre, for which a strip of bush about eight acres is usually cleared of trees, but the gardens, though roughly circular, have no fixed size or shape. A smaller *ubukula* usually less than a quarter of an acre in size, such as those planted with fast-growing millet (*mwangwe*), is known as an *akakumba* (*plur. ukukumba*).

It will be seen, therefore, that the descriptive terms applied to land never refer to fixed units of measurement, but either to the political district in which a man lives, to a natural vegetation division in which his successive villages are usually built (*mpanga*), or to the temporary use to which the land is being put (*mputa*, *icitemene*, *icifwani*, &c.).

The Chief as Land-owner.

A Bemba's right to the use of any part of the bush depends upon his political allegiances, first to a headman and then to a chief. He cannot cultivate as an isolated individual, even though he has uncontested rights of ownership of any land he may have cleared. Every Bemba reckons himself the subject of a territorial chief. He calls himself the '*umwina*' (subject, connexion of, member of) such-and-such a ruler, e.g. *umwina* Citimukulu, the subject of Citimukulu or by the historic name of the *icalo* itself, *umwina* Lubemba, an inhabitant of Lubemba.[1] In the first place, then, how does his status as a subject actually determine his use of land? What right has he to select in the *icalo* of his chief a strip of bush for a village site, or for agricultural purposes?

[1] The word '*umwina*' is difficult to translate. Besides the meanings given above, husband and wife refer to each other as *umwina uandi*, 'the person connected with me, or with whom I am tied', and a football team on the copper-belt uses the word for a member of the team. It must be distinguished from *umwine*, the owner of a thing or leader of an affair.

In answer to a direct question as to the ownership of his *icalo* any chief will reply quite simply that the whole territory belongs to him, together with the food that is produced in it, its game and fish, and the labour of its people. 'It is my land, all of it! Every bit of the bush (*Calo candi conse! Mpangafye yonse!*)', said Citi- mukulu to me when describing his territorial rights. But it is important to know what such a grandiose statement actually means in terms of concrete fact. How and when does the Bemba chief exert his triple claim to own the land, the food, and the labour of his *icalo*?

Most Bantu chiefs claim to be regarded as the supreme landlord of their territories, and, in many cases, particularly in South Africa, they do actually determine the use to which it is put. Among the Southern Bantu, for instance, it is usual for the chief to allot land for cultivation to his *nduna* or headmen, who in turn distribute it to the people. He also reserves prior rights to particular grazing grounds or other soil of value. The land shortage resulting from European settlement all over Africa has given great importance to this prerogative. In East Africa the Ganda king appoints his nominees to rule over different districts as chiefs, moving them at will from place to place. To these territorial heads the peasant must apply for a strip of land to cultivate. He may be given a plot anywhere in the district, whether near his own kinsmen's village or not, and he pays dues to the chiefs at whose pleasure he holds the ground. This right of allotting land has had important prac- tical consequences, since it formed the basis of the system of rent payments to landlords instituted by the Uganda Agreement of 1900.[1]

Bemba chiefs, though they claim just as complete an overlord- ship over their land, do not actually allot ground for cultivation. Their own wealth they reckon in terms of the numbers of their subjects, not by the amount of land in their possession. The only district map that would be of use to them would be one showing the density distribution of the population. The Paramount Chief had the right to 'give' a district to one of his relatives in the old days, and he still appoints the successors to the territorial chieftainships. He may also give a village to one of his near relatives—usually a son, a daughter, or a maternal nephew—and he does so frequently even at the present day, placing his own

[1] L. P. Mair, *An African People in the Twentieth Century*, 1934, Chap. VI.

nominee in a position of authority over the local group. By so
doing he gives his relatives the right to command the service of
their villagers however difficult it may be to exact such labour
nowadays. But these royal headmen have no more power to
determine the use of land than has a commoner, and probably
they do not cultivate much more. To a commoner the chief
merely grants permission to settle in his *icalo* as a member of a
village community under the rule of a particular headman, and
here he may choose what land he pleases. The supply is so
plentiful that the question of exact distribution is not a matter
of great importance. It is the political affiliation that counts.
The chief looks upon a man as a subject and not as a tenant,
although the status of subject does actually confer the right to
use land.[1]

The statement that 'all the land is mine' does not then mean that
the ruler has the right to take any piece of ground he chooses for
his own use. His own gardens are made in the neighbourhood of
the capital, and in any one year it is expected that commoners will
wait to cut trees for their *ifitemene* until the chief has chosen the
site he wants. But after that the people are free to clear the bush
where they please. The same is true of the choice of land to be
used for the village beds. At the founding of Citimukulu's new
village in 1934 I found that the chief had already marked out his
mputa and had sown them with Kaffir corn before any commoners
had started to dig their beds, or to build their houses. In the
succeeding April the chief went out to choose a site for his big
millet gardens, and after this the villagers began to select their own
sites.

I never heard of a case where a chief took land that had already
been occupied by a commoner. It would not have paid him to do
so. In the old days he would have been expected to feed any
inhabitant of the capital who was hungry, and nowadays, when

---

[1] Very little has so far been published as to the position of the chief among
other N. Rhodesian tribes. Among the Bisa of the Bangweolu swamps and the
contiguous Baushi and Baunga, the chief seems to have no rights of allocating
land, confirmed J. Coxhead: 'The Native Tribes of N.E. Rhodesia', *J.R.A.I.*,
Occasional papers No. 5; but among the cattle-owning tribes of the Nyasaland
border (Ngoni and Cewa) and along the Kafue river (Ila)—both areas where
southern influence is prominent—the chiefs claim the right to allot land
for cultivation or for grazing, either directly or through the local headmen.
Cf. J. Coxhead, op. cit., p. 24. Smith and Dale, 1920, op. cit., vol. i, p. 307. The
same is also true of the Lamba. C. Doke, op. cit., p. 89.

natives are much more free to move about the country than formerly, he would be afraid his subjects would leave him. I have, however, seen a case of a chief borrowing land temporarily. In November 1931 Nkula asked one of the villagers for the use of his garden mounds so that he might sow them with ground-nuts for one season. The word used was *ukuashima*, or 'to borrow', and in this case the original owner of the beds had apparently the right to ask the chief for ground-nuts for the use of his family at any time he pleased. I saw the chief hand him over a large sack on his request. Otherwise the commoner's rights to land he has occupied seem to be respected, and according to native informants the same held good even of the autocratic rulers of pre-European days.

On the other hand it is impossible for a Bemba to cultivate in a chief's territory without the latter's permission. In the old days if one chief trespassed, even unwittingly, on the ground of another, the former had to give a substantial present such as an elephant tusk or a cow to the latter. Nowadays Citimukulu told me he would expect a gift of beer, even if it were a close relative who had made a garden within the boundary of his *icalo*. It is apparently a usual way of picking a quarrel to start cutting trees over another chief's borders, ill-defined though the latter often are. The late Nkula, giving evidence before a white magistrate during a case of disputed succession, said, 'I knew he wanted to claim the stool (i.e. office of chieftainship) because he sent men to cut trees on my land.'

A commoner, as distinct from a fellow chief, has to come and make obeisance to the *mfumu* and ask permission to settle. He usually brings a present to court, and is welcomed as adding to the economic assets of the district. Near Kasama in 1934 I once met Citimukulu touring his villages. Two elderly men from the territory of Makassa, near Abercorn, about 100 miles away, arrived with their younger relatives carrying a gourd of beer. They rolled on the ground and clapped (the usual formal salute) and said they wanted to settle at a certain village, but that the inhabitants were hostile to the suggestion. The Paramount received them with enthusiasm, always keen to add to the number of his subjects. He told them to settle where they wanted to cultivate, and to bring him tribute of what they grew. In the old days failure to get formal permission to cut trees in any *icalo* would have been punished by seizure of half the crop, or the burning of the cut branches before they had been properly piled.[1] I was told that nowadays a chief would not take such a drastic step, but that he would certainly send for the intruder and demand tribute. The shifting cultivator is not free to build a hut where he pleases, although in this empty country he is not limited as to the amount of bush he clears.

The Chief's Supernatural Powers.

It must be remembered too that a Bemba wants not only the right to make a garden, but also an assurance that the bush he cultivates will give him food. Now the productive capacity of the *mpanga* depends, he believes, entirely on the beneficence of the tutelary deities associated with it, and the goodwill of these supernatural beings can only be secured by the prayers of the chief and his observance of a particular way of life. When the Bemba chief is installed (*ukupyanika*) he acquires, as guardian spirits, the *imipashi* of the dead rulers of the land, of whom he is of course the lineal descendant in the matrilineal line. Thereafter he is believed in his own person to affect the fortunes of his land. He is 'to spread his spittle in blessing on the land' (*ukufunga mate mu calo*); he is to rectify it (*ukulungame calo*); he is to work it (*ukubombele calo*). In fact the Paramount should not leave his territory for fear that its fertility should suffer, and in March 1934, when the Citimukulu was summoned to Lusaka to meet Prince George, he was obliged to offer special prayers and cloth to his *imipashi*, explaining the compulsion put upon him. He told the spirits that the Europeans to whom they had given the land must be obeyed. 'We have got to go on a journey. Those who installed us in this land, your people, have called us to see the son of the King. Now we cannot refuse. No, not to those who gave us many possessions and money and many cloths. You Kampampa Mutanshi (the first ancestor) here is your cloth! You the Great one, who gave the land to Pokili (the next ancestor) so that he might stay in the capital. Let Lubemba prosper. For we are going to strange lands. Farewell.'[2]

[1] Cullen Gouldsbury denies this and says that a pot of beer only need be given to the chief by a tribesman while a member of another tribe would have to accept the rule of the chief and then give half the product of his gardens as tribute. Cullen Gouldsbury, 'Notes on the Customary Law of the Awemba', *Journ. of the African Society*, vol. xiv, no. lvi, 1915, p. 375.

[2] *Tuli no bulendo. Abatuteka mu calo, bantu benu, na batuita kukuya mona*

The illness of the chief is liable to bring misfortune, or rather to be associated with a general condition of ill luck, and is even now a source of fear, as I observed myself on several occasions. At his death the prosperity of the land is brought to an end just as the political organization is temporarily at a standstill. No crops are planted by the chief's family and no first-fruit rites are done. *Icalo cawa.* (The land has fallen down, i.e. the state has collapsed.) The sex life of the chief has also a mysterious effect on the welfare of all his people. His sexual power gives vigour and 'warmth' to the land. Hence the phrase *ukukafye calo* (to warm the land), and the rule that a territorial chief should never sleep with a woman when travelling outside his territory.[1] By a sexual act the *mfumu* can bless seeds or other objects required for the use of the tribe. But this power is alike the cause of danger. By breaking a sex taboo—such as approaching the spirits without the right ceremony of purification, the ruler can bring incalculable harm on the community. Of such a man I heard the comment, 'Why does he like women? Does not that imperil the land? That is not a chief. No!'[2]

Besides this powerful and mysterious influence over the land and its people, the chief is also able to influence their destinies by his power of access to the tribal spirits. This right is based on his possession of the *benye* or sacred relics by which the most powerful ancestral spirits of the Bemba can be invoked, and also by his supreme control over the spirit-centres of his whole *icalo*. The economic rites he performs at these different shrines will be described in detail later. Suffice it now to say that this supreme control over the supernatural resources of the *icalo* gives the territorial chief what Edwin Smith has called the 'spiritual ownership'[3]

---

mwana Cingi. Nomba teti tukane yo. E batupela fyuma fingi, ne ndalama, ne nsalu shingi. Mwe Kampampa Mutanshi imyala yobe! Ni mwe mukalamba, mwapela Pokili ukuti ekale pa musumba. Nomba lubuke lubemba. Ifwe twalaya mu fyalo. Shyalempo!

[1] The Paramount in any case should not leave his district.

[2] *Cinshi baletemwa ku banakashi. Te kucile calo? Te mfumu iyi! Yo!*

[3] Cf. E. W. Smith and A. Dale, op. cit., vol. i, p. 388. It is important to realize that in many parts of Africa the spiritual owner of the land is not identical with the political owner. A warrior people extends its boundaries and occupies land under the guardianship of the tutelary spirits of other tribes. In this area it is common to find that in territory seized by the Bemba from the neighbouring Bisa or Lala during the last century, the conquering people are offering prayers to the dead chiefs of the conquered, and are dependent for this purpose on the services of a Bisa or Lala priest. The chief Nkula sends cloth to Mungulube, the

of the land, and the Paramount chief who has to initiate all the economic rites of the *icalo*, has thus the supernatural overlordship of the whole Bemba territory.

But the question that concerns us immediately here, is whether this spiritual ownership of the *icalo* by the territorial chief actually affects its productive use, in other words, the rights of each individual to cultivate the land. If we are to consider as the study of land tenure 'the relationship of man to soil in its widest sense', as Malinowski suggests, then the position of the chief as a combined ruler, landlord, and priest is obviously a relevant factor.[1] The people's belief that the productive capacity of the land depends ultimately on the prayers of a ruler descended from the original occupants of the land, is the basis of their system of local grouping into villages under a headman who performs subsidiary rites to local deities, and a chief who is responsible for the communal rites and for the welfare of each *icalo*. It is also the sanction for the chief's political authority and economic prerogatives, and however much these religious beliefs have weakened at the present day, they are still the dominant force behind the politico-economic machine.

Thus for the chief's claim that 'all the land is mine', we might substitute the explanation that the chief is the spiritual overlord of his *icalo*, and that on this fact depends his power to organize economic units for its exploitation and to receive dues: that he reserves the privilege to select garden sites for himself near his own village, but that he never claims the right to seize land occupied by others, or to allocate ground for cultivation to his subjects as is the custom in many other Bantu tribes. Any individual Bemba can cultivate as much ground as he pleases in the *icalo*, if he is a member of a village community, accepts the status of a subject and fulfils the resultant obligations to his chief. Otherwise he cannot settle in the district at all. This discussion of the

descendant of one of the dispossessed Bisa chiefs near his capital and asks him to pray to the 'owners of the land' (*bene*). At Kasaka, near Shiwa Ŋandu, the Bemba headman descendant of a family sent from Lubemba to occupy Bisa country, has put up seven shrines to Bisa spirits, known or unknown, whom he believes to be associated with his village site. He is still anxious lest he should have forgotten some. In other cases one branch of a clan has become localized in an outlying district of Bemba country and claims control of the local shrines, and the head of the family demands dues of fish or game in consequence.

[1] Cf. Malinowski's definition of land tenure, *Coral Gardens and their Magic*, vol. i, p. 319.

relation between the political and religious functions of the chief and his rights as a landlord has certain practical implications. At a time when money payments are being substituted for old tribal dues in many parts of Africa, it is important to be clear what the Bemba chief originally claimed, and still claims, and it can be stated definitely that however peremptory his demands on his people's labour and garden produce, he seems to have left them complete security as to their use of land and to have allowed them the right to select particular plots—a freedom probably associated with the ample supply of land in this area.

Tribute on Land.

We must now turn to the second claim of the Bemba chief, viz. that he owns not only his land, but also the food that is produced in it. 'Everything is theirs!' (i.e. the chiefs') as Candamale, formerly the hereditary burier of the royal family, expressed it, 'The meat, the fish, all the trees, all the land, and the honey'[1]—which is equivalent to saying that the Bemba chief gives his subjects permission to settle in his territory, but that all the crops they grow belong by right to him. Our problem is to discover the forms in which these dues are exacted.

This is a difficult aspect of land tenure to analyse. The economic privileges and duties of African kings have suffered inevitable changes with the institution of European government and the introduction of a money currency. Bemba chiefs and elders speak with enthusiasm of the 'good old days' when subjects brought constant gifts of food to the capital. 'All day long they carried tribute (*batula*). They brought millet and beer and meat. They were always bringing tribute. There was always food at the *umusumba*!' is a typical account of the state of affairs as they delight to describe it.

From these day-dreams of a glorious past it is difficult to extract a case of concrete fact. The most extreme instance of the exercise of the chief's rights of ownership over food seemed to me to be contained in an old councillor's memory of an actual incident which took place before the coming of the white man. He told me that in the reign of Cikwanda, a former Paramount, a rich commoner had fled the territory of his chief to take refuge elsewhere. The Paramount immediately sent a messenger to the headman of the fugitive's village saying to him, 'Take possession of X's food,

[1] *Shyonse shyabo! Inama, lisabi, imiti yonse, ne calo conse, no buci!*

and look after it for the chief'.[1] The relatives of the exile had apparently no rights at all to his property. When I commented to the present Citimukulu on the apparent injustice of this action he said, in defence of his ancestors, 'Well, but all the food and all the gardens belonged to the *mfumu* in any case', thus expressing the rights of ownership in the most absolute form. But it is clear that in the ordinary course of events the chief limited himself to certain dues, such as demands for food for himself and for his followers in any emergency, hospitality when travelling through his domains, and a regular tribute of certain crops, game, and fish. All these claims are exercised at the present day, to however limited an extent.

All Bemba chiefs get food brought them whenever they travel, as do also royal princesses holding titles, and sometimes the sons, nephews, and grandsons of the royal family. Two headmen of villages on the roadside told me they were excused paying annual tribute because they had regularly to entertain their chiefs when travelling to and from the Government office at Kasama. Another headman who had given up carrying annual tribute to the capital, owing to the distance, still claimed that he would bring flour, chickens, and beer to the *mfumu* if he heard the latter was travelling through the district. Young men at work with Europeans bring the chief no tribute in kind, but near Kasama sometimes carry him sums of money varying from 1s. to 3s. when he visits the Boma there. I saw the employees on the estate of Shiwa Dandu give the late Nkula 1s. or 2s. each when he came on tour.

The people readily admit also their duty to give the chief food when he sends for it, and indeed with primitive methods of storage it would be almost impossible otherwise for him to accumulate enough food at the capital to suffice for sudden emergencies, such as the arrival of honoured visitors, or the presence of councillors on tribal business. The process of brewing which demands anything from four to seven days for completion also makes it difficult for the wives of a chief to keep sufficient beer for all occasions. During 1933–4, a year of shortage owing to locust raids, I saw Citimukulu send out constantly for millet, fish, and beer to feed

---

[1] *Ulebakile mfumu fyakulya fya kampanda.* Cf. also Cullen Gouldsbury's statement that the chief would put a taboo on the gardens of a man who left him without permission. 'Notes on the Customary Law of the Awemba', *Journ. of the African Society*, vol. xv, no. lix, 1916, p. 175.

his councillors during a long series of meetings held to discuss the deposition of one of the hereditary officials, the appointment of the chief's new head wife, and the building of his new capital. He also sent out for food and beer for himself and his wives. I also saw many instances at the courts of Citimukulu, Nkula, and Mwamba of the chief's practice of sending a messenger round neighbouring villages to ask for beer on the sudden arrival of visiting chiefs or Government officials. In November 1931 the chief Lucembe received a messenger at 8 a.m. to announce the arrival of a neighbouring Bisa chief, Cunda Ponde, to ask for his daughter's hand in marriage. Lucembe carried on a ten minutes' conversation with the messenger, during which time he was evidently thinking hard. The moment he was alone he dispatched followers in four different directions to fetch beer, mentioning certain villages by name. It arrived slung on poles, and carried at a jog trot, at about noon, for it is the business of a chief to know exactly which of his villages has supplies of any particular food at any given time. In fact one of the important functions of the administrative officials and messengers who go between one *umusumba* and another is to report on the state of the millet harvest, the ground-nuts, and legumes of the villages through which they pass and the game killed there, and the chief's need of supplies at the capital is one of his greatest incentives to encourage agricultural production.

A regular annual tribute in certain foods (*ukutula*) is a due considered apart from these unexpected levies on supplies. The payment of such tribute is almost universal among Bantu peoples. Here it consists of an offering made on each year's harvest (millet in particular), beer and also, under certain conditions, a tribute on game, fish, or honey found in the bush. It is difficult to be clear how big this tribute was in the old days. At present the people tend to exaggerate its size—the chief because he is anxious to show how powerful he is, and the commoners because they like to complain of their sufferings. Both the chiefs Nkula and Lucembe told me on the first day of my visits to them that their subjects brought them 'one or two' baskets of millet every harvest as well as beer, but afterwards started to grumble as to the difficulties of getting their dues enforced, and I saw myself that the supplies brought in were actually small.

Thus of fourteen villages in which I collected figures in 1933–4 three had sent no tribute, one having special exemption on ritual grounds; one fishing village had sent three carrying baskets of fish, one voluntarily and two sent for; five had sent two gourds of beer each voluntarily; two had sent one gourd of beer and one carrying basket of millet; and two were waiting to send gifts until the chief asked for them. These figures show that the due is not fixed at the present time, but that an offering of some kind or other is usually made during the year. It is important to note that the contribution is made from the village as a whole. It is as a member of a village that a man gets permission to cultivate land, and it is the community as a whole under the leadership of the appointed head-man which makes the offering. To collect it the headman puts an empty basket outside his hut and calls on each housewife to make her contribution. The levy on each person would thus be little more than 2 or 3 lb. per head, or about 3*d.* worth at current rates.

The tribute of game and fish comes under a different heading. In all Bantu societies so far described the chief gets a portion of an animal killed, or found dead in the bush, with special rights to some animals such as the elephant or hippo, and to leopard skins. To the Bemba the finding of game in the bush is essentially a matter of luck—the good fortune which only the *imipashi* can bring if approached by the ruling chiefs in the right way. Hence it used to be considered particularly important to carry a portion of the meat as a present to the capital as well as to the headman's hut.[1] In the old days, the meat of all big animals such as elephants or hippopotami belonged to the chief, and such game was in fact hunted only at his orders. A part of any buck killed in nets or pits would also be carried to the capital. The chief's portion does not seem to have been specified very clearly, and was variously des-cribed to me as either a front leg and breast or a hind leg. Nowa-days game is scarce, and the powers of the chief greatly diminished, but it is still true that the inhabitants of a capital probably bring the whole of the buck to the chief for distribution; those in the neighbourhood bring a portion of the animal, while in distant villages tribute is brought in the case of unusual good luck or an unexpected find of a dead animal in the bush—treasure trove to which a chief has particular rights.

In the case of fish, the supply is too irregular to make possible an annual tribute, except from villages lying in the big rivers, such

---

[1] Though the chief must have been powerful to enforce these rights and people admit that game was sometimes 'hidden in the bush' (*ukufisa mu mpanga*).

as the Chambesi. The supply of dried fish from these areas was formerly an important asset of the chief of the district, and even nowadays Citimukulu and Nkula appear to get one or more big carrying-baskets of fish from these fishing communities each year, and more if the supply is plentiful.

In conclusion, therefore, it is clear that the *mfumu's* claim to own the food of his *icalo* is limited to his demand for supplies in times of emergency, to hospitality when travelling, and to tribute of millet, beer, meat, and fish, and that the latter offerings are made by the headman of each village and not by an individual alone. It is impossible to compare the amounts of food received by the modern chief with those given to his predecessors, since we have no concrete facts to go upon. But it is evident that the people still acknowledge the claims of the modern ruler to some tribute, however small, and even in cases where the *mfumu* is forced to pay money for food, as happens occasionally, he is yet expected to give less than the current prices for the goods. In April 1934 I saw Citimukulu pay money for beer during a time of great shortage, but he got two gourds of beer for one shilling instead of one, and Nkula, during the previous November, bought millet with salt, but again gave less than the usual rates of exchange.[1] The old *ukutula* dues have neither completely lapsed, nor have they been superseded by money payments. Hence, their economic and political importance lasts to the present day.

The substitution of money for tribute in kind has only taken place to a very small extent in this area. Many South African chiefs are able to levy substantial dues on the earnings of their own men at the mines. Schapera states that it is common for a tribute of one pound to be demanded by a chief from all those who have been away at work. He gives an example of a Tschwana chief, who, as early as 1882, sent an age-grade to Kimberley to earn £8 apiece to buy guns and ammunition, and recently (1932) of another who made a levy of £5 for a National school.[2] In

---

[1] In somewhat the same way most Bemba women are willing to sell grain to the Government at less than they can get from their fellows. In spite of the patient effort of officials to explain to them that they are perfectly free agents in the matter many are themselves convinced that they are under compulsion to bring what the Government send for, and to accept any price offered, and that they win the favour of the authorities by so doing.

[2] *Western Civilization and the Natives of South Africa*, ed. I. Schapera, 1934, p. 46; also I. Schapera, 'Economic Conditions in a Bechuanaland Native Reserve', *S. African Journal of Science*, vol. xxx, 1933, p. 645.

the absence of tribal treasuries in all the Native territories of South Africa, levies have been make in cash for building schools, making roads, boring for water, &c. In the Bemba area the amount of money in circulation is very limited and the recent institution of tribal treasuries will make it possible for various social services to be provided from this source. There is also the historical fact that the chiefs of the Southern Bantu had formerly the right to 'eat up' the cattle of their subjects and hence it is but a small extension of this right to 'eat up' cash earnings. In the Bemba country, on the other hand, there was very little property in the possession of a commoner that his chief could seize.

Tribute Labour.

It only remains to discuss the third claim of the Bemba chief, viz. that all the labour of his people is his by right. All Bantu chiefs of whom we have any information have claims to the labour of their subjects. The tribe itself is in essence a chiefdom, a body of men who are loyal to one ruler. From the historical material we have available, it is clear that such units were built up first on a kinship basis. To the body of men who acknowledged kinship, real or fictitious, to one chief were added other elements, until the group grew to a large size. It was allegiance to the one chief which kept these people together through their long period of migrations and constant wars. The subjects of a chief were his men in a particular sense, even though the position of the freeman was distinguished from that of the slave in areas where subject peoples were incorporated as servants, or the institution of slavery existed.

The service a man owed his chief was either economic or military, that is to say, he might be employed in the cultivation of the royal gardens, clearing the roads, or building the chief's huts, or, in the old days, he might serve as a warrior. In some cases, the service a subject owed was specified and the army or labour force was organized. In other cases, the chief had a general right to call for assistance when in need. Thus, among the Nguni group of South Africa, and in particular among the Zulu and Swazi, the tribal organization on an age-grade basis was adapted to further military ambitions, and the subjects' service to their chief resembled a form of conscription, in which every young man of the tribe was drafted into a 'regiment' held in readiness to work for the king in

Tribute labour. Carrying in the Paramount Chief's crop of ground-nuts, 1933.

Tribute. Fishing villages send four baskets of fish as their dues to the Paramount Chief, who is sitting with his beer-pot on top of the mound, 1933.

Tribute labour. Carrying blessed seed to sow Chief Nkula's millet garden, 1933.

his gardens, cattle kraals, village, or on the battle-field. Such
an organized labour force still exists to-day in Swaziland in the
amabutho or regiments of the Swazi chief.[1]

Among the Central Bantu, the chiefs had despotic powers over
their subjects—in fact the right of life or death.[2] They had also
general claims to the service of their people in whatever way it was
needed. The Bemba king was the ruler of a military tribe as was
the Zulu chief, but his army was evidently less highly organized
than in the case of the Southern Bantu, and it was the village that
provided the military contingent, not the age-grade. Over and
above this, each chief was able to exact special dues of service to
be used for agricultural purposes, known by the term *umulasa*. Our
problem, therefore, is to discover the form in which these specific
dues of tribute labour are exacted and how they affect the people's
right to use the land. Is the service given in return for permission
to cultivate, as the squatter on a European farm works so many
months of the year in lieu of rent; or is the *umulasa* work given as
part of a series of political dues by which a man's allegiance to his
chief is expressed?

At present, the tribute service is a specified one and not a very
extensive obligation. The exaggerated demands made by some of
the South African chiefs on their subjects are not found in this
area. The people rarely work more than two or three days a year
and are very seldom called up more than once.

The amount of tribute labour demanded formerly is difficult to
estimate. Here again survivors from the past delight to exaggerate
the splendour of their rulers. They tell of the numbers of commoners who used to pour into the capital to serve the Citimukulu
and they describe their work. It consisted for the men of tree-
cutting, hut-building, hoeing, fencing, sowing, and in some cases
of the traditional female occupations such as piling branches and
reaping; while the women piled branches, reaped, carried in millet
or ground-nuts from distant granaries, cleared paths or pulled up
ground-nuts. These are still the tasks for which *umulasa* labour is
used. The tribute service was and still is an act of recognition of

[1] H. Beamer, 'The Development of Military Organization in Swaziland',
Africa, vol. x, 1937.
[2] If a family took summary revenge for a murder they had, according to
Gouldsbury, to pay the chief a slave, as they had killed one of his people without
permission. Cullen Gouldsbury, 'Notes on the Customary Law of the Awemba',
Journ. of the African Society, vol. xiv, no. liii, 1914, p. 381.

the chief's authority as well as an economic task carried out for him. Nowadays labourers who arrive at the capital must do formal obeisance to the chief by rolling on the ground in front of him and clapping (*ukutota*), and when they leave they repeat the process with full ceremony. Chiefs seemed to me to speak of this act of homage with pleasure. One described the *umulasa* system in words like this. 'They come: they work for three days: I make them porridge and then they come and make obeisance and go.' It is interesting to watch the men and women returned from the fields gathering on the outskirts of the village so that they may all walk in to the chief's enclosure together, and make their salute formally.

The *umulasa* system itself has been very strongly affected by European contact. In the early days of British administration it was discouraged, though never actually forbidden. Now many officials seem conscious of the value of the system as maintaining the chief's authority, but the latter's rights to *umulasa* cannot be enforced in a white court since they are held to be contrary to the Geneva Conventions on 'Forced Labour'. This lack of Government support has lead to the refusal of many natives to do their service. The introduction of paid labour has also struck at the roots of the system. 'The white man came to teach us not to work except for money', one old Bemba said, when bewailing the uncompromising attitude of the modern youth.[1] The exact amount of labour now done for the chief is difficult to assess. It is clearly very much less than before. Of twelve villages I visited during 1931 and 1933 five had sent no labour during the year (three of these owing to ritual privilege) and the others had sent contingents varying from two men and women to ten and twelve women respectively. The service is limited now by common consent to the inside of a week or even three days. From figures taken at Citimukulu's village during a nine-month period from April to December 1933, I estimate that 561 men were called up to work and 329 women, and that these worked on an average 3·89 days in

---

[1] The common association in the native mind between Christianity and European economic values is clear from the statement of a young Bemba asked to help some one in a difficulty, 'I am a Christian. I don't do things for nothing.'

[2] The figures of men-days worked were as follows:

MEN. Tree-cutting 855; piling branches 143; sowing millet 89; reaping sorghum 68; fetching food from different villages 14.

WOMEN. Piling branches 446; carrying grain from temporary granaries 146;

the case of the men and 3·5 days for the women.[2] These labourers were drawn from 81 villages out of 160 showing that it is very far from true that every Bemba works for his chief at the present time. Added to this the number of adult males at work outside the territory means that the supply of available labour is almost halved. Two small chieftainesses, Canda we Eiya and Mulenga, complained that they could get no gardens made for them without the support of their territorial chiefs, and in May 1933 Mwamba, one of the biggest of the latter, had chosen the site for his capital, but could not get sufficient labour to build it until the copper slump sent men home to their villages. Citimukulu himself constantly grumbled that he could not get his gardens made, and even his band of personal followers and singers was very much reduced.

It is nevertheless a fact that the chief's rights are still recognized, even if he cannot always enforce them. Where money payments are substituted for tribute labour—and this only takes place very occasionally—it is an accepted principle that the *mfumu* should pay below the current rate. Thus in March 1934 Citimukulu summoned two bricklayers to work *umulasa* for him, offering them 2s. 6d. a week instead of 7s. 6d., the current wage, and this sum was considered generous. Chiefs also pay the tax of some of their followers, in return for work done, and in this case the latter usually get food and other court perquisites, and do an indefinite amount of labour. I saw Nkula pay a 4s. court fine for two subjects who were unable to find the money, but he ordered them to build him a house in return, for which the current pay was 10s. The legitimate claims of the chief to service are still perfectly well recognized in compromise arrangements of this kind.

It is also obvious that no system has yet been devised as a substitute for *umulasa* labour. To pay even the small force of labour Citimukulu employed during the period in which I took notes, he would have required nearly £56 at the current rate of wages out of a total annual salary of £60 for all personal and tribal expenses. So that it must be acknowledged that even if the *umulasa* system

---

hoeing village beds 126; fetching fish and other foods 76; cleaning paths 96; digging up ground-nuts or Livingstone potato beds 68; reaping 12. TOTAL 970 men-days.

For the building of the chief's new huts in a new village 807, including 421 spent making a brick court-house, as against 386 to build 10 huts of the ordinary type. 174 men-days were spent by the women in white-washing or making cement floors of the same houses.

is functioning inefficiently at the present time (cf. p. 264) it is the only means by which the political machinery of the tribe continues to exist.

Tribute as Rent.

It will be asked at once how far this tribute in labour and kind can be classed as rent? If by this term we mean a fixed amount of work or goods given in return for the right to use a fixed amount of land, then obviously the dues of the Bemba chief cannot be so described. They are part of a series of mutual obligations observed between subject and chief, of which the right to land is one of the gains to the commoner, and the right to service just one of a series of chiefly prerogatives. To make the situation clearer we should list the advantages both parties gained by the arrangement. Why did the commoner work for the chief? Partly because he was afraid of his power and partly because there were positive inducements to do so. We saw that a commoner who made a garden in the chief's *icalo* without permission was liable to have his crops seized in the old days. Some natives now say that refusal to work *umulasa* or *ukutula* would have meant mutilation in pre-European times: others argue, 'No. Since it would be stupid to cut off the hand of a man who would then be unable to work *umulasa* for his chief again.' One man told me that with the first default a man would have been scolded, and at the second his chickens and granary would have been seized. But in actual fact no old man I talked to could remember an actual instance of a man refusing to pay his dues, and I think such occasions were probably limited to open acts of defiance on the part of powerful young members of the royal clan trying to set up power on their own. Of commoners I constantly got the answer, *Ukuti bakana shyani?*, 'And why should they refuse?', with genuine surprise in the tone. The fact that the Bemba believed that their gardens were unlikely to yield without the chief's blessing has been stressed again and again in these pages. While some natives deny that the *imipashi* would refuse their beneficence to men who refused to work for their chief or give tribute, others assert equally emphatically that this is so, and all are convinced that it is definitely unlucky to offend him. To say of a chief, a white man, or any one in high authority that he is angry (*ukufulwa*) is a serious thing, even at the present day. Small lapses are not expected to be followed automatically by supernatural punishment, but a series of broken obligations such as really to offend a chief are viewed with apprehension by young men as well as old.

Besides this it was the positive aim of every Bemba to win the good will of his chief as we have seen, and the headman who willingly brought workers for the *mfumu* was sure of favours sooner or later. It is possible to watch a headman courting the chief in this way even to-day, and he himself uses any privileges he has had confirmed under the Native Courts Ordinance, such as the right to give a man permission to build a village, to reward any subject who tries to please him.

The tribute labourers got food and beer during the visit and they worked under pleasant conditions in large gangs of friends. Even during my visit I never heard complaints of *umulasa* where the chiefs had means of feeding their workers, and the visit to the capital is considered an opportunity to meet relatives and celebrities, to put grievances before the chief, or to transact any other business. The people still definitely prefer their ruler to have a big granary. It gives them, I think, a sense of security—a feeling of certainty that there will be food at the capital and a knowledge that they are working for a powerful and successful man (cf. p. 214). Besides this, a hungry man has technically the right to call upon his chief for help. I did not hear of this claim being made very often, but still, in a sense, the *umulasa* garden and *umulasa* granary are recognized as belonging to the people. A man can steal from the tribute garden of a chief, but not from those of his wives, and I have sometimes heard old natives speak with pride of 'our' granary, adding, 'It was we who filled it to overflowing'. Thus the commoner got by his labour the sense of supernatural support, a personal approach to his chief, food in return for his work, support in time of starvation, and, as we shall see, leadership in economic pursuits. The chief in return got extra supplies of food to distribute, the means of supporting his tribal council, the necessary labour for tribal undertakings such as road-building, and last, but not least, prestige (cf. Chap. XII).

In brief the extravagant claims of the Bemba king to own all his land and everything that grows or lives in it, only gave him the right to exact small regular dues on the labour and produce of his people, and to call on them for further help in times of emergency. These levies exist, but are very much reduced to-day. They formed only one element in the relationship of mutual interdependence between subject and chief by which the commoner, in return for accepting the political authority of his ruler, gained complete security as to his rights of occupying any amount of land he could use. He still has this security to-day, and can still be certain of the right to use his land in any way he pleases, except of course by selling it.

Land Tenure and Political Organization.

The political organization of the Bemba is based very directly upon this system of land tenure as is the case in most Bantu societies. The *umulasa* system makes for tribal cohesion in a sparsely populated district, because it emphasizes the unity of the village community and brings the people in direct personal contact with their chief—possibly their only opportunity of meeting him during the year. For the young at any rate, the week spent at the capital is an education in the political machinery of the tribe, and a means by which the authority of the chief and his council is displayed. The bringing of tribute to the *umusumba* could not be defended on the grounds of economic efficiency alone. It is a common sight to see, for instance, meat brought a two days' journey from one part of an *icalo* and distributed in a rather high condition, to *umulasa* labourers from another, and the inhabitants of a village who brought a basket of millet as tribute to the chief, at one time of the year, might consume an almost identical amount of grain in the form of porridge when next arriving at the capital to do their *umulasa* labour. But where the economic life of the people is so clearly dominated by the political, the exaction of these dues on land has an important secondary function in maintaining authority in the tribe.

It is also obvious that it is the chief's right to tribute and labour that gives him sufficient surplus food to feed his servants, his executive officials, his panel of legal advisers, and his tribal council. Some of these live at the capital but do not willingly give their days to hearing cases unless the chief gives them beer or food.[1] Others come from long distances, and will only spend the necessary fortnight or three weeks at the *umusumba* if they are fed. Without a full granary the chief is apt to find his whole civil service, if we may

[1] Since my visit a payment of £1 a year to twenty-five of the *bakabilo* has been instituted. 'Pim Report,' p. 188.

so call it, melt away. Besides this, his prestige will gradually go when he is no longer able to carry out his obligations on the same scale as before. The situation has in fact reached a kind of impasse at the moment. Because the *mfumu* gets less labour, he makes smaller gardens and has less food to feed his workers, so that they in their turn are less willing to serve him another year. From figures I collected during my visit it was clear that in some capitals the labourers were getting no food at all in return for their work. The late Nkula employed a hunter, and had a reputation for giving his people meat. Consequently he always seemed able to get work done for him. Sub-chief Lucembe was a hunter himself and lived in good game country. He was therefore in a fortunate position. But Citimukulu sometimes sent men away without food, or gave them one meal in two days, while the women were supposed to bring their own supplies and cook for themselves. Mukuikile, a sub-chief in the Mpika district, fed the men, but not the women. It is clear from these instances that the modern chief is no longer able to carry out his obligations to his people. Those who grumble at the chief's lack of hospitality have reason on their side, but to refuse to do their service as a protest increases the difficulty.

As a second result, many chiefs now fail to keep their panel of advisers and councillors at court to transact the necessary tribal business. I have seen the Citimukulu hear cases alone with his clerk, and during 1934 the *bakabilo* summoned by him on important matters of business invariably melted away before the end of the meeting because they had not enough food. It took a period of three months of alternately summoning the council and then dismissing it because of shortage, before the work could be carried through.

Chiefs are also beginning perforce to refuse food to the hungry, and even to their poor relations. In January 1934 Citimukulu gave up the distinction between his *umulasa* granary and his personal one, and fed his wife and family on anything he could lay hands on. The right to take food from the royal mounds (*mputa*) already limited to near relatives, was still further curtailed. In July 1933 I heard the guardian of the Paramount's granary walk round the village at night shouting, 'Listen everyone! Hunger has fallen! No one is to dig up cassava from the chief's *mputa*. If he is hungry let him come to the chief and make obeisance and he will be given something.' It is true that this failure of commissariat occurred during a year when the locusts had done their maximum damage and in the case of a chief who was plainly a poor organizer, but the art of chieftainship is difficult to practise even in the most advantageous conditions at the present time. A servant of the late Nkula, who was a chief of far greater ability than the Paramount, told me rue-fully that his master no longer fed all the inhabitants of the capital as he used to. 'He just sends me round the village to sit with the elders of each division (*icitente*). If I hear so much grumbling that I am afraid they will begin to leave the capital, I tell the chief and he sends them what food he has.'

Such failures of the chief to provide for his subjects, little though he may be accountable for them, insensibly weaken his prestige at a time when the Government is most anxious to build on that attribute. The tradition of the generous king survives as a stan-dard against which the modern ruler is constantly measured, and measured to his disadvantage. Despite all evidence to the contrary, the Bemba commoners continue to believe that their chiefs could give them more if they only tried. They make such remarks as, 'These are not chiefs at all! Look how much Citimukulu Ponde or Citapankwa gave our forefathers', and these memories actually determine the prestige given to a chief at the present day.

If it be asked whether the Bemba chiefs could not substitute money payments for *umulasa* dues, the answer is simply that their salaries are not large enough. The Paramount gets £60 a year, of which in 1934 he spent £22. 12s. on clothing his wives and family, £15. 10s. on paying and clothing his messengers, personal servants, and band, and £2. 10s. on cloth for the ancestral shrines, thus leaving for personal needs, demands from relatives, ammunition, &c. the sum of £18. 10s. 6d. or only 30s. a month.[1]

The other big chiefs have even smaller salaries, e.g. Mwamba has £50, Nkula £40, and some of the sub-chiefs as little as £10 a year. Added to this fundamental difficulty, the Bemba chiefs do not consider their salaries as funds to be used for the benefit of the tribe. They are something new, a sort of unexpected windfall given as a sign of the Government's favour. They are not yet part of the warp and woof of tribal organization. The food he gets, the chief distributes, the money he does not.[2] Nor does it seem that the newly instituted tribal treasuries perform any of the functions

[1] Cf. my 'Tribal Government in transition', *Journal of the African Society*, vol. xxxiv, no. cxxxvii, 1935, for a discussion on this whole question.

[2] To a body of discontented councillors Citimukulu explained, 'If I had any elephant tusks, you know I should give them to you.'

of the old dues on land, since they are to be used for new developments such as road-building, schools, clinics, &c., and not to institute paid service for unpaid labour dues.[1]

Here, as in many cases of adjustment between black and white, there appear to be two difficulties—the European's failure to understand the tribal machine, and a fundamental difference in point of view. 'Forced Labour' has an ugly sound to our ears. The claim of the African chief to be landlord of his whole territory is apt to strike the European as almost fantastic, and the administrator often feels it his duty to protect the natives of any particular district against any exorbitant demands their rulers may base upon it. To the white philanthropist it appears fundamentally unjust that a man should have to work without pay, at the arbitrary command of another, and that his right to live and cultivate in an area should depend on his willingness to work for the political head of that district. It is taken for granted that the *umulasa* system should be abandoned as soon as possible, as suiting ill with European conceptions of justice and the individual method of land-holding which it is hoped the Bemba will finally adopt when they have been taught fixed methods of cultivation.[2]

At the same time, the discouragement of the *umulasa* system,

[1] The annual revenue of the Bemba from the new treasury scheme has been reckoned at £1,303, of which £995 goes in salaries to chiefs, &c. The recent Pim report recommends that 20 per cent. of the native tax should be remitted to the native treasury instead of 10 per cent. as at present. Op. cit., pp. 184, 190.

[2] As far as abstract justice is concerned, there would seem to be little to choose between black and white conceptions. The European attitude to unpaid service prevents the Government from approving of the *umulasa* system, and also made it impossible in 1933 for the administration to accept service in lieu of money during an economic slump, in spite of the frequent requests of Bemba chiefs that their people should be allowed to work off their tax in this way. This seemed incredible to the native. His traditional obligations to his chief were, after all, paid in commodities which were easily available—food and labour—whereas the Government demands for a money tax made it necessary for him to leave his territory in most instances to look for work. Otherwise, he suffered imprisonment, in which he did a month's unpaid labour for the Government, and was released, still owing arrears of tax! (By the tax-relief scheme of 1935, tax defaulters were allowed to work off their tax at slightly below the current wages, on public works.)

European concern at an institution which binds natives to work for their chief in return for the right of cultivation seems also inconsistent, since the squatter system of land-tenure is the only means by which a large portion of the native inhabitants of South Africa claim any right to land to cultivate at all, and, in the latter case, the natives work a legal minimum, varying from ninety days to six months a year in return for the right to settle. Added to which, the Bemba is free to go where he pleases without reference to his chief, whereas the South

without adequate provision for the running of the political machine, naturally reduces the efficiency of the chief and his council to a dangerous extent, and even with such a provision, the abolition of all voluntary service for the tribe brings one of the most educational influences to which Bemba youth is subject, to an end.

To conclude, Bemba rights to the use of land are part of a reciprocal series of obligations between subject and chief. The former accepts the political status of subject and membership of a village group. He gives respect, labour, and tribute to his chief, and in return he is able to cultivate as much land as he pleases and to occupy it for as long as he needs. The latter prays to the tribal spirits in order to make the land productive, initiates economic effort, feeds the hungry, and maintains his court and tribal councillors—all that the Bemba mean by saying that he is 'working' his land. The political machinery founded on this system of land-tenure is breaking down with changing religious beliefs and the chief's diminishing power to exact his legal dues. But from the agricultural point of view the position of the commoner remains secure, and no Bemba chief has yet profited from changing conditions to limit his subjects' right of cultivation or has tried to exact a profit from his theoretical ownership of land.

Rights of Selection and Occupation.

I have discussed rather fully the rights of the Bemba to occupy land as these are traditionally defined between subject and chief. What is the situation as between one commoner and another? As far as the chief is concerned a man may clear the bush anywhere in the *icalo*, if he accepts the status of a subject and membership of a village community. This fact was made clear to me when listening to a case brought before Citimukulu's court. On this occasion the headman of village A on one side of a river complained that villagers from B on the opposite bank had crossed the stream and cut gardens in the bush immediately near his village instead of cultivating on the other side. Citimukulu heard the case at some length, but gave his decision without hesitation. He declared that no action lay, and dismissed all the litigants. He said to the assembled court, 'They are all my people. It is my *icalo* and

African squatter native cannot leave a farm without permission from his owner, and in some districts the native who breaks his contract with his landlord is convicted under a penal code.

not the *icalo* of others! No. Let them cut trees wherever they like! (*kutematemafye*, i.e. the duplicated stem with the addition of the particle *fye*—which gives an idea of haphazard or unsystematic action.) It is I who am the owner of the *mpanga*. It is not your river! No. Let them work to find food, and then let them bring tribute here, millet and Kaffir corn and beans. Let them bring tribute of all. Are they not all my people?'[1] The statement that it was every one's duty to produce as much food as possible, and to give tribute of it to the chief, was clapped by all the councillors present, and the hereditary priest, Cimba, the oldest man present, when specially consulted on the subject, said, 'Yes, that is just how it was in the old days. It was always the same. The people made gardens wherever they liked, and brought food to the chief.'

But are we then to conclude that any individual Bemba has the right to make a garden wherever he pleases, however inconvenient to his neighbours? In the eyes of the chief this may be so, but as between headman and headman the rights of cultivation are limited by a number of factors, economic and sociological. To begin with, when choosing the site for his millet garden there are a number of positive inducements for a man to choose ground near his own village rather than in the territory of another. He wants the shortest walk possible between his hut and his garden. He is cultivating as a member of a kinship group, and therefore wants to cut his trees for his garden in the same neighbourhood as those of his father-in-law, and the husbands of his wife's sisters (cf. Chap. XVIII). This is all the more important since when the grain is ripening the whole group want to build grass huts (*imitanda*) near their gardens to watch the crops against birds, and they thus set up a little settlement together.

Besides the obvious advantages of making gardens near the village, the whole question of the people's rights of cultivation depends on the system of human relationships within their local groups. The variable composition of the village and the ease with which families split off and disappear, make the Bemba very apprehensive of actions likely to disrupt the group. Any European who listens much to the ordinary conversation of these natives will be

---

[1] *Bali bonse bantu bandi. Ni calo candi. Te calo ca kwa bambi, yo! Batematemafye! Ni ine mwine mpanga. Te umumana wobe! Babombe ukusange cakulya. Kabili batule kuno, male, na masaka, ne lilanda, batule. Bali bonse bantu bandi?* 17. V. 31.

impressed by their constant emphasis on the value of peaceful relationships, whether within the village, or the kinship group. They are afraid of the man or woman whose quick temper or sharp tongue makes them liable to take offence or give it. I have heard several men seeking wives in a strange village ask anxiously of their acquaintances there, 'Does she come of a quarrelsome family? Do they make offensive remarks?' (*Ikusose fibi*.) Neighbours with good reputations are those whose 'hearts do not get hot quick', and who tend to ignore insults—*ukusula*—a traditional cultural attitude by which a man can acquire kudos by voluntarily giving up his rights so as to avoid friction. This pattern of toleration is impressed on the Bemba from their earliest years. Parents who rebuke their children for little else are yet quite firm on this one point: no quarrels must be allowed. A sobbing child of six, about to punch a smaller boy who had knocked over his mud-pudding, was picked up sharply and told to repeat, 'The chief of another tribe may stay where he pleases' (*Mfumu shya bene baikalapo*), i.e. every one has a right to do as he pleases. Such incidents are quite common, and similar behaviour is noticeable as between children and adults. An elderly relative often shrugs his shoulders at a child's decision to do or not do something it is asked, and says (*Ni mwine*) 'He is the owner of the affair', i.e. the child must decide. The legal relations between one man and another are discussed with the same conscious effort at toleration. Certain obligations are fixed and definite, and acknowledged by the whole community, but there are a number of issues in which the rights of two individuals are not so clear, and a clash of personal interests seems to be threatened. In such cases the man of sense and good breeding does not try to define his claim. He avoids putting the matter to the test in the interests of peace.[1]

It is this anxiety to avoid friction which influences the people in their choice of land for cultivation. A chief may not care whether the villagers of one community cut gardens in the land bordering the huts of another, but the villagers themselves will be afraid to do so. They do not want to risk the anger of the neigh-

---

[1] There is also a supernatural sanction behind this pattern of human behaviour. The man who dies feeling injured, or with a sense that he has been denied his rightful dues, becomes a *iciwa*, or haunting spirit, avenging the wrongs he has suffered on the living. Hence the uneasy feeling of the Bemba when any one publically announces a grievance, or is known to have been wronged. Thus religious belief, norms of conduct, and the type of agricultural system practised, all combine to determine the legal rules for the use of land.

bouring headman, and they will be afraid that their gardens will
not prosper if he withholds his blessing from their enterprise. In
the case brought before the Paramount Chief (p. 266) the inhabitants of village B had not wantonly cut gardens in the ground of A,
but the son of headman B had married the daughter of headman
A, had gone to live at A according to the rule of matrilocal marriage, and had then deserted his wife and returned to B to marry
another woman there. Instead of relinquishing his garden near A
he continued to clear new bush there. Under ordinary circumstances it is extremely rare for a case of this kind to be brought
before the court. If there had been no contributory cause of dispute, it would have been much more usual for the villagers of B
to stay on the poorer soil their own side of the river, rather than
risk a quarrel with the inhabitants of A.

Again, as between the members of one village, though natives
tend to inform the European that they may cut trees wherever
they like, and that they need not ask the permission of the headman before choosing a site, yet in fact they are not so free as their
statements indicate.[1] Young people are afraid to take ground they
believe to have been chosen by elder members of the community.
If two interests clash a man would rather abandon a site on which
a week's work has been done than risk a dispute. At the beginning
of the tree-cutting season it is usual for the men of a village to
gather together in the *nsaka* of an evening and to make informal
announcements as to the ground they mean to clear. The elders
take the lead in such discussions. Next morning each individual
starts out for the bush, probably with two or three friends, and
each blazes trees (*ukukome nkwa*) to mark the strip he intends to
use. It is rare for a man to mark out the limits of the area he means
to cultivate, nor in fact does he usually decide there and then how
far his garden will reach (*icikongwana*, plur. *ifikongwana*). It is only
occasionally that one tree is cut at each corner to mark the boundaries, and there seems to be a feeling that it is presumptuous to
do so. It is considered as an almost arrogant statement of claim.[2]

---

[1] Cullen Gouldsbury states that formerly the headmen allotted ground for
millet gardens, but I heard this denied. 'Notes on the Customary Law of the
Awemba', *Journ. of the African Society*, vol. xiv, no. lvi, 1915, p. 377.

[2] It was interesting to see that in the villages where natives had begun to
employ paid labour they were obliged to mark out the limits to be cut by the
labourers in self-defence. It seemed to be an imitation of the European method
of giving piece-work.

Once a tree in the bush has been blazed, a man has absolutely secure possession over the strip of ground marked. He will arrange the branches he cuts on the ground with their stems all pointing in one direction. The owner of the next *icitemene* will lay his branches in the opposite direction, so that there can be no chance of dispute as to the ownership of the wood cut. Even if he has to leave the territory before completing his *icitemene*, the half-cleared site remains his property to leave or dispose of to his relatives as he pleases. When he has reaped the first year's millet and the garden becomes a *icifwani* ('old garden') the same rights hold good. A man may leave his *icifwani* fallow for two or three years without any one disputing his claim to its use, and even if he is absent some years in the mines, there is no question of any outsider trying to dig up the garden and sow it as long as any of his relatives remain in the district and show any inclination to use it. I think land would have to be exceedingly short before a Bemba would risk a quarrel on this account, so deep is this belief in the rights of occupation conferred by clearing the bush.

The rules governing the ownership of the village gardens are more precise, and it is interesting to find that the Bemba conceptions of land tenure are sufficiently elastic to allow the development of a perfectly definite system of undivided rights of use when there is any shortage of ground.[1] Every one wants some *mputa* near the village so that he can grow beans and maize near to his hut,

---

[1] Mrs. Gore-Browne collected material in 1933 to show that the Bisa inhabiting Cilubi Island in L. Bangweolu have adapted their system of tenure to conditions of land shortage. At Matipa, the village of the Paramount Chief, the most fertile ground for cultivation was that of deserted village sites, the huts of the new village being built 500 yards or so from the old. The chief had full rights over these old sites (*ifibolya*) and could cultivate them or allocate them to his followers, but once allotted he could never take a garden back while living relatives of the owner wished to use it. Thus the cultivated ground round Matipa's village contained (*a*) gardens of the present chief made on his own *icibolya* and to be left to his heirs, (*b*) gardens allotted by him to his councillors, (*c*) gardens allotted by the previous *Matipa* and inherited by their heirs.

At Nsamba's village, a neighbouring Unga chief, the *mfumu* also allocated village land and similarly at the capital of Kasomo, an Ushi chief. Forest gardens were inherited in the matrilineal line (i.e. by a man's maternal nephew) and have been in use for some twenty or thirty years in this way. They only revert to the chief when no member of the original family claims them. This is an interesting example of a combination of individual, inherited rights over land with a recognition of the chief's powers to allocate. It is not, I think, a system specially characteristic of the Bisa, as distinct from the Bemba, but an adaptation to unusual environmental conditions.

and in the case of a big village the circular strip of land surrounding the houses is only barely adequate to give each his due. The same desire to avoid quarrelling over land is still apparent, but fixed rules govern its selection. The site of a man's *mputa* is determined by the position of his hut. When a village is being built the old men have the first right to choose where they will build their huts. After that the young men group themselves—usually together at one end of the village. The strip of ground behind each hut on the outside ring is the property of the owner of the house. Those who have built in the centre of the village must cultivate beyond. The owners of the outside houses are allowed to cultivate as far as the nearest natural boundary, such as a river or path, if they desire to do so, otherwise they must announce where they intend to stop so that others can cultivate beyond them.

The village plan on p. 177 shows how owners A, A5, B, B4, B9, C, C7, D, D3, D6, F, F2 cultivate ground immediately behind their huts while the others have strips farther out into the bush.

At first sight it is difficult to understand how the conflicting aims and ambitions of each individual can be satisfied in practice. But it must be remembered that a Bemba, cultivating alone, cannot hope to dig up more than a certain amount of land, and he estimates his capabilities in the coming year with fair precision, as do also his neighbours. But his own conception of good form seems to weigh with him more than such purely economic considerations. He does not want to appear presumptuous, or to make claims beyond his status. It is bad for a young man to demand as much ground as an old, even if he occupies an outside hut, or for a single woman to fix wide boundaries to her patch. Fear of the accusation of pride (*icilumba*) or that reputation for personal ambition, which is so often associated with charges of witchcraft in this society, are important factors in fixing the limits of village beds, and the whole division seems to be arranged without much formal allocation. A man estimates his neighbour's intentions and gauges public opinion as to his own status, and acts accordingly. He does not even put boundaries (*mpaka*) between his beds and those of another for fear of accusations of sorcery, and if there is a doubtful issue it can be taken for granted that personal relations and questions of relative status are always put before agricultural considerations. I have seen at least two cases where a man considered that his privilege had been infringed upon, but decided to ignore the injury rather than to risk disturbing the personal relations in the village.[1] In the case of new-comers arriving at a village and wanting ground for *mputa*, they may either cultivate beyond the gardens of the older inhabitants, or in some cases a man may subdivide his own beds among his younger relatives. At Kasakatula three heads of families had divided up ground in this way to their sons-in-law.

The following text written for me by an educated native clearly describes the attitude to land appropriation, whether for millet gardens or village mounds.

'In the month of April, and also the month of May, that is when people mark the trees to cut their *icitemene*. It goes on through the cold weather, and one or two here and there go on until September. Now it doesn't do to cut trees unless everyone agrees to cut. And to mark the trees, the people in the village one by one, they choose sites and arrange their boundaries where each is to reach to. When one man has built himself a grass hut on the spot, another must not come and cut near it or it will be a serious cause of grievance. People who quarrel about trees, their fellows call them fools, people of no sense. They say, "You are not the child of an animal (i.e. human being). No! You are the child of a sorcerer. You cut trees like a sorcerer does" (*Tauli mwana ua nama. Yo! Uli mwana wa muloshi. Uletema buloshibuloshi*). Because they say, "The trees are the plumes on the head of God. They are not to be fought over" (*Imiti ingala shya kwa Lesa. Tashikomenwa*). It is the right thing to arrange boundaries in a peaceful way. No one fights about trees unless it is an unnatural child, a sorcerer! Any person of good repute when he sees one of his friends has marked a site for cutting, clears out, and if he has sense goes and discusses the matter with him. One man, if he has begun to cut trees where another has marked the site, let him clear out of it and leave the branches he has cut and go and cut trees somewhere else, and don't let him start right near the boundary either. And when people go to dig up village beds, no one else can take the ground where they have begun. When people quarrel with each other about hoeing, or fight with each other, their friends will say, "They have no sense", or else, "Those are people with a bad name". Because people ought not to fight with each other over land. And more than this, people who pick quarrels over a matter of land, they are likely to be sorcerers. There aren't many ordinary people

---

[1] e.g. in Sept. 1933 the headman of Kasaka village (cf. Chap. X) made a dry weather garden in ground which his son-in-law, Pensulo, had decided to cultivate. For several days the friends of Pensulo knew that he was angry, but after an interval word was passed round the village that he had decided to ignore the whole affair—i.e. *ukusula*. He had a smaller garden, but acquired personal prestige.

who would do a thing like that. No! People who quarrel over land or fight over it, they will find themselves unlucky, even nowadays. A decent man, if one of his neighbours starts to abuse him or to accuse him falsely over land, he will just clear out and go and hoe somewhere else, or else they take the matter to someone else to decide. And another thing, nobody ought to make a boundary to show where his ground ends and another begins. If he did a thing like that his neighbours would say he was a sorcerer because he had set up a boundary. His neighbours would not hoe right up to his boundary. When a person has done an unlucky thing like that his people begin to count who quarrelled with him, and who called him a sorcerer, and that is why people of good reputation do not like to set up boundaries to divide off their ground from that of their neighbours, but just to divide up the land amicably.'[1]

Another type of cultivateable soil over which there are well-defined rights are the house-sites (*ifitantala*, sing. *icitantala*) of a deserted village recently abandoned by its inhabitants. These sites are considered very desirable ground, as will be seen, and it is interesting to find that where land acquires value in this area, the tribal conceptions of land tenure are easily adapted to regulate its use. According to two or three statements made to me, a chief could take the whole of an *icibolya* and cultivate on this rich soil for one year before passing it on to the commoners. But I never saw this done myself. The usual practice is for each owner to claim absolute rights to cultivate on the site of his old hut and its immediate environs, or to allot it to one of his own relatives if he is away. Individual ownership is strictly respected in this case, and these rights of cultivation become important when villages begin to move round a very small area as they do near Kasama.

As in the case of millet gardens, the occupier of village beds has absolute rights over his *mputa* while they are in use, and for so many years afterwards that it is clear that he never intends to return. Even where the soil of the village beds was valuable, as at Kacienja, I saw a strip of ground left fallow for four years because the owner was away. Near Kasama also, where good garden ground is extremely scarce, I saw at Mubanga village a large piece of ground left deserted near a densely populated village. People wanted the land but were afraid the absentee owner would be angry if he heard it had been taken. At Kasama village itself there were further examples of the same type.

[1] Statement made by Paul Mushindo.

T

In the land-tenure map in the Appendix it will be seen that 32 owners continue to cultivate their old *ifitantala* or house-sites after moving to a new site adjoining the abandoned one.

As land can never be permanently owned by one individual the laws of inheritance only apply in a restricted sense. If a man dies his near relatives can reap his crop and continue to use the garden site as long as they please. After that it reverts to bush. I know no case of land having been sold even in the areas near white settlement. A man can sell the whole of the crops of his garden, and even the branches piled before burning, but never the ground. The sale of crops is becoming fairly common near Kasama where there is a good deal of movement from one village to another. A garden of cut trees might fetch £1 to £2 and the beans off a big patch about 10s.

Conclusion.

In conclusion it can be said that each individual Bemba has freedom to select ground for cultivation as against the rights of his chief and his fellow commoners. While no individual ownership of land is recognized in our sense of the word, yet each individual has security of tenure in so far as he requires it in regard to a kinship system which permits of frequent moving from village to village, and methods of agriculture which only allow him to cultivate a garden for four or five years.

The question of the future of the traditional system of land tenure raises a number of practical points. It is possible that fixed methods of cultivation will be adopted before long by the Bemba, and it is often argued that the native will not improve his cultivation while he has no fixed rights of ownership over his land. But the foregoing pages should show that it is not insecurity of tenure which is keeping the Bemba from further agricultural development. In fact the introduction of individual tenure and the sale or lease of land would only be of value to the Bemba, as to other Bantu peoples, as a measure of protection against land-hungry Europeans should these become a danger. As elsewhere, the concept of land as a saleable commodity will revolutionize native society. In the case of the chief, land ownership will be severed from political responsibility,[1] and the commoner will acquire the right to exploit

[1] Cf. L. P. Mair's account of the state of affairs among the Ganda where the Uganda agreement of 1900 resulted in 'the almost complete dissociation of

land to his individual advantage, and such phenomena as absentee
landlordism, mortgaging, and excessive fractionation, that have
been so pronounced among the Indian peasantry, may appear. At
the present, rent-paying only exists in a few areas, particularly on
the copper-belt, where the Government allocated a number of
eight-acre plots to be let to natives living round Ndola, Luanshya,
and Nkana at rentals of about £2. 10s. a year. This step, taken in
order to give the urban native a feeling of security and individual
possession, was eagerly welcomed by men of initiative as a means
by which they could build their own houses and provide accom-
modation for their dependent relatives, whom it was then practically impossible to house in the Government locations or mine
compounds. But, paradoxically enough, the introduction of rent
seemed to me to have produced the feeling of uncertainty as to the
use of land for the first time. This was partly because the rent was
a new imposition in native eyes,[1] and partly because the dues of
the chief were and are enacted in commodities the people possess
—labour and food—instead of money, which they sometimes cannot obtain. Also the produce taken to a chief varies according to
the state of the harvest, and only sufficient for the ruler's own
needs is demanded when times are hard. But rent is a fixed sum
whether the money is available or not. The only natives I ever
met who were definitely anxious about their possession of land
were those on the three-acre Government plots outside Luanshya,
who were caught by the slump in 1933 and were threatened with
eviction if they did not find rent. They seemed quite content that
the Government, like the chief, should levy toll on their earnings
when they had any, but thought it unjust that they should be asked
to pay money if they had no means of getting any paid work.
I heard for the first time the statement that it was no use developing the ground, since one might not have the money to pay the
rent next year.

As a matter of fact, there does not seem any reason why the
Bemba should not adopt a fixed method of cultivation in the rural
districts and adapt their traditional form of occupier tenancy to

rights over land from governmental functions'. *An African People in the Twentieth Century*, 1934, p. 166.
[1] Near Kasama I was visited by four men returned from the mines who asked
indignantly why the missionaries taught that the land belonged to the High God
(*Lesa*) if the people had to pay rent to the Government for it?

this end. It has been shown in many parts of Africa that the Bantu system based on the practice of shifting cultivation is quite easily adapted, without any need of Government interference, to situations in which bush land becomes limited or acquires additional value for any other reason. The Bemba rules of ownership of village gardens or deserted house sites, or the more complex regulations of land tenure found among the Bisa on the Bangweolu islands, show that even in this area individual rights over land can become very clearly defined when ground for cultivation is scarce, but that the introduction of a rent-paying system and the right to sell or lease land is quite unnecessary to secure this end.

CHAPTER XIV

SOIL SELECTION

ONE of the chief agricultural problems of the shifting cultivator is obviously the selection of the land on which he is to
plant each year. The European or Chinese peasant, who is born
and reared on one patch of soil, knows every yard of the ground
from which he has to wrest his living. Each fertile strip, each
stony outcrop or water-logged meadow, is a known quantity—an
advantage to be exploited or a difficulty to be circumvented. But
the African moving from patch to patch across the bush requires
quite a different type of knowledge. He has usually more than
enough land on which to grow his crops, but he has to choose, in
the empty acres surrounding him, the best strip to clear, and if
he chooses wrong, his garden may fail or give a poor yield. Our
first problem is therefore to discover whether some traditional body
of knowledge guides the Bemba in their choice, and if so, what
measure of success or failure their method of land selection gives.

Alternatively there may be a number of social and economic
reasons which govern the people's choice of a village site or of
garden lands, and these may seem to them more important than
the production of the maximum food.

Choice of Village Sites.

For instance, the Bemba choose a suitable site for their villages
before they mark out their garden plots. They pick ground for
villages as near as possible to a good supply of trees to cut for
their millet gardens, but a convenient water-supply is also of
great importance to them, and there are a number of sociological
factors which weigh with them. Some headmen, for instance,
must continue to build more or less in the same spot even after its
soil is nearly exhausted and all the high trees in the neighbourhood
cut down. They do so for political and religious motives. Most
chiefs are bound by tradition to keep their villages in a certain area,
whatever its economic defects. Any visitor to the capital of the
Paramount Chief will hear complaints as to the scarcity of trees
for cutting, and will notice that the inhabitants have to make
their gardens as much as a day's walk away from the village. Even

the chief and his followers have to move into temporary grass
shelters (*imitanda*) during the tree-cutting and harvest seasons, and
commoners will camp near their gardens for as many as four
months of the year. The *bakabilo*, or hereditary councillors of the
Paramount Chief, are also prevented for politico-religious reasons
from moving far afield. Of Citimukulu's 160 villages, 52 were
under the rule of hereditary councillors or priests in 1934, and of
this latter group I should judge that at least 30 were bound for
traditional reasons to remain fixed to one locality. For commoners
the choice is much freer, although they have a strong tendency to
build within a five-mile radius of their relatives. But I have known
them make a village on poor soil because they wanted to live on
the motor road, or near to a white man's farm. The people also
cultivate exhausted soil in areas near a white settlement like
Kasama, where the villages move from site to site, sometimes at
a distance of a quarter of a mile or so, in order to be near the town.
The fishing villages on the banks of the Chambesi are similarly fixed
without special reference to the soil possibilities since in this case
the value of the fishing is greater than that of the agricultural
produce. At Molema, near some valuable fishing pools in the
Chambesi, the ground has been under continuous cultivation,
chiefly with cassava, for four generations.[1] Apart from these
special cases, it can be said that the majority of headmen build
villages in the best soil they can find within an area of five or ten
square miles of their last site.

Choice of Garden Sites.

Having founded his village, the next step for the Bemba is to
choose his garden plots. In this case he is looking first and foremost for suitable ground for millet cultivation. He has no other
object in mind. To select the most suitable spot for his garden he
is guided first by certain general factors such as the presence or
absence of plenty of high trees and grasses. He divides the *mpanga*
into two main categories—the ordinary woodland (*umutengo*) in
which gardens are made, and the tall grass-bush country (*icipya*,
plur. *ifipya*) which passes locally into thickets (*amateshi*). The
ifipya are not cultivated though they may be fertile. They are the
haunts of buffalo and elephant and are commonly avoided by
native paths. The hunter goes there but it is difficult to find a way

[1] Cf. Chap. XVI, p. 341.

through the high grass, and the native's attitude to such stretches of country-side can be gauged by the fact that they call a large expanse of grass-bush land 'a bad *icipya*'. In the familiar wood-land of his villages and gardens he looks for trees that 'crowd close together' (*ukutitikana*), arguing that soil which yields good trees will give good food.[1] He also realizes that if the trees stand close together their branches will be easier to cut and pile. Some Bemba told me, in answer to questions, that certain trees and grasses in-dicated suitable soil for the making of gardens, and I collected from different, mostly elderly informants, a list of ten such trees and four grasses. But these natives, though they repeated to me the names of the different trees they looked for, did not, except in one case, attempt to describe the type of soil they expected to find associated with these special trees. They gave me the impression that they judged a stretch of bush as a whole—the trees and grasses and the general 'look' of the land, rather than by any systematic use of indicators, and their answers were by no means unanimous.[2] It appears, in fact, that the Bemba, in common with other ash-cultivators like the Kaionde, are far inferior to many other tribes in this territory in their power of land selection by means of tree-indicators, and that it is possible that the heavy dressing of ash they employ is sufficient to make soil differences of less impor-tance to them as far as their millet gardens go.[3] Fundamentally, the Bemba is looking for plenty of branches and brushwood to make ash. After this, since he clears four to ten acres of bush in order to make a garden of an acre, besides choosing a thickly wooded strip of country to provide him with timber for burning, he has also to select the exact spot (*icitendekelo*) on which he wants to prepare his seed-beds. This he considers a very important point.

[1] Cf. Smith and Dale, op. cit., vol. i, p. 136, mentions that the same argument is used by the Ila.

[2] e.g. one informant said he looked for *umutondo* and *umuombo* trees; a second for *umuputu* and *umusompa*; a third for *mpundo*, *ngalati*, and *umusoso*; and a fourth for *icitando*, *umulambo*, and *icipolo*. As a negative indicator the Bemba speak of the presence of the *umufungo* tree (*Anisophyllea pomifera*), of which the bark is used to make a caustic alkaline salt to give bite to snuff. They maintain that this bitter substance destroys the millet seeds, but it is interesting that the tree is also believed to have a special magic influence over the soil and that a sapling must be ritually cut at the annual tree-cutting ceremonies of the chief. Its roots are used widely in curative medicine also. It is, therefore, difficult to know whether the tree is avoided on account of its physical or magical properties.

[3] Personal communication from Mr. C. G. Trapnell whose ecological report on this area is not yet published.

He will even make two small gardens (*tukumbi*, *sing.* *kakumbi*) instead of one larger one, rather than sow on a patch which has been barren of trees (*kaseswebebe*).

Soil Types Recognized.

Besides his use of trees and grasses as indicators, the Bemba classifies different soils according to their colour, texture, and the type of country in which they are found. Thus they speak of—

(1) *Sand soils*—*Umushili ua nsenga* or *ua buta* (white)—a general term used to describe the white sandy soil which is common on the plateau. This soil they divide up into two types, *ulusenga lukalamba* (strong sand), i.e. the best type of sandy soil, and the *ulusenga lunono* ('weak sand') on which they realize that very little will grow. Sandy soils are also described with reference to their dryness or dampness. Thus *umushili ua nyika* refers to the damper soil of one of the marshy plains or open valleys referred to as a *nyika*, and *umushili ua lupili* (hill soil) is supposed to hold the moisture, according to the native account, 'because the hill puts a shadow over it', while the loose soil at the bottom of a hill, *umushili ua cisonso*, is dry and poor.

On these sandy soils the Bemba grow millet, Kaffir corn, legumes, ground-nuts, cassava, and sweet potatoes, but they do not hope to get two crops of millet from the poorer type of sand, and say they prefer to plant Kaffir corn on the redder, more loamy, soils. Legumes bear more heavily, they say, in the richer sandy soils, and cassava grows 'as thick as a man's arm' when it is in 'the great sand' or in soil by the river banks.

(2) *Red soil*—*Umushili ua kashika* or *umushili ua nkanka*—is a rich red clay loam which is said to stick together in lumps 'like porridge'. This type of soil fills the Bemba with enthusiasm. 'That is the soil for food', they cry. Any crop will grow on it they think, but it is the soil specially selected for Kaffir corn. They point out that Kaffir corn grown on sand will bear stunted plants after the first year, but when sown on red soil produces fine heads for three or four years. Only ground-nuts are sometimes described as growing better on sandy than on red soils.

(3) *Black soil*—*Umushili ua fita*. This term covers various types of soil, described as being 'strong' (*uakosa*), as sticky to the touch (*uatelela*), or as not running through the fingers easily (*ushyafutuka*). Sometimes it contains clay (*ue lamba*), especially the very black soil

by the banks of a river (*ua matipa*), which is so stiff that the Bemba
tell of a typical nightmare in which the dreamer is trying frantically
to run, but each time his foot gets caught and held in the *matipa*
mud. In fact, *umushili ua fita* is a colour description rather than a
classification and covers various dark soils—peats, &c. of different
characteristics. But Bemba say black earth is good for cultivation
and is not easily exhausted. Maize grows well on it, but it is considered bad for cassava and sweet potatoes, and not the best for
ground-nuts.

Ant-hills (*ifyulu*) are believed to be composed of special soil, and
on the flat plain of the Chambesi bed, near Molema, the people,
who have no trees to cut for gardens, cultivate almost entirely on
the slopes of these small hillocks. Millet is said not to flourish on
them, but Kaffir corn and maize grow to a good height.

(4) *Refuse soil—Umufundo.* In selecting ground for their mound
cultivation (*mputa*) the Bemba value very highly the sites of
deserted villages, which they believe to be particularly fertile. Of
any soil which has been enriched either through its own vegetation
or by previous cultivation, the turning in of grasses to rot, or the
remains of human habitation, they use the word *umufundo*, which
seems to describe a particular quality of ripeness or maturity.[1] Of
this type of soil the native speaks with a conviction and enthusiasm
which contrasts sharply with the hesitating way in which he casts
his vote for other types of ground. Contemplating the soil of an
icibolya, or the high grasses on an ant-hill, he will cry with ardour,
'*E mufundo!*' his voice rising high in tone—the usual sign of
delighted conviction. He will be endlessly ready to talk about
umufundo, and to account for its properties. The deserted *mputa*
of a previous village are fertile, he says, because of the decaying
vegetation on them, and the rich crop of grass which grows in the
cleared space now unimpeded by bushes. The natives say that
the amount of refuse thrown out daily on the *mputa* makes them
fertile, and it must be remembered that the chaff of millet is thrown
out every day after the threshing from every house in the village,
during a period of three or four years. At Kacienja village I found
the headman looking round for some deserted *mputa* on which
to make his new village; and around Kasama, where the country
is covered with old village sites, the natives anxiously search
for signs of the undulations left by disused mounds of earlier

---

[1] It is also applied to any crop which is beginning to swell and ripen.

cultivators. The site of the village itself is also believed to provide a very rich soil, because 'many things have lain and rotted there' and because of 'the many footsteps of people passing'.

Most natives will add that human excrement makes soil rich. A specially fine crop of cassava has been explained to me as due to the excrement of children. But here there is a certain amount of contradiction. No Bemba will admit that an adult could ever defaecate on a village bed. This would be strictly counter to etiquette, among a people who have a horror of touching night-soil. Only small children would commit such a breach of good manners, it is maintained, in spite of ocular evidence that the rule is sometimes broken. Hence a native will admit that the fertility of an old village site is partly due to human manure which gives it *umufundo*, but will scold children for using the *mputa* for such purposes. At Canda we Eiya an enraged woman even threatened to call down a curse (*ukulapishya*) on the children who had evidently defaecated on her garden beds. She screamed out, 'You children, you! You go on defaecating on my cassava, you! You make us eat excrement. That is not a good thing, no! I am really going to put a curse on you this time.' It is not surprising, therefore, that in the few places where cattle are kept, the natives object strongly to the idea of using kraal manure.

House sites themselves (*ifitantala*) become a heap of rubble and decaying sticks after the hut walls have been demolished, and a season's rain has fallen on the ruins. After a year, or perhaps two, the raised mound on which the house stood formerly is soft enough to plant. The Bemba sow maize on it or tobacco plants. Whether the surface soil has a high percentage of lime from the plaster walls, or is merely rich in nitrogenous matter from the hut refuse, it is clear to the naked eye that maize flourishes on these *ifitantala*. At Kungu village in April 1934, the plants grown on the deserted house sites were 3 feet higher than those planted elsewhere. This frequent use of the soil of village sites is an important point. Most Europeans in the district look forward to the day when the Bemba will build permanent houses and adopt fixed cultivation. There would be obvious advantages in such a course from many points of view, but on this poor soil, in the absence of cattle manure, the practice of shifting huts, while continuing to use the deserted site, gives the Bemba the richest soil they have for certain crops, such as maize and the various cucurbits.

Successes and Failures in Soil Selection.

In spite of their rudimentary classification of different types of forest and soil, the Bemba method of land selection seems to provide a fairly wide margin of possible failure, and regular testing of soil by trial and error is part of their traditional routine. Their ritual of founding a village seems to indicate that they themselves consider the choice of a new site an important and even a dangerous decision. Without supernatural aid the headman believes he cannot hope to keep his followers together, but he is also afraid he may have to move his village for economic reasons, i.e. because he has made the wrong selection of site. I have seen communities move their huts for ritual reasons—the death of an important person or the apparent hostility of the spirits; because of some unforeseen disaster such as elephant raids or damage by pigs or monkeys; and because of a wrong choice of soil.[1] There is actually some element of risk in the selection of a site, and it is not surprising that the Bemba follow the village founding ceremony— usually the planting of the first stake (*ukushimpa*) in the headman's new hut—by a hunting ritual (*ukusoa libanda*) to discover from the sex of the first animal killed whether the spirits (*imipashi*) are going to bless the gardens during the year. In many districts, too, a series of subsequent divination tests are carried out with the object of confirming the confidence of the people in their new choice of site. At Kacienja, near Shiwa Dandu, a ritual hunt took place after the building of the first spirit hut of the new village to see if the *imipashi* were satisfied with the choice of the site, and intended to bless the people with food there. The building of a second hut to other *imipashi* was followed by another ritual hunt. Although these rites are not carried out all over the country nowadays, they may be considered as an indication of the native's evident anxiety as to the successful building up of his new community, and his apprehension as to the possibilities of the site he has chosen.

As regards the selection of their gardens the Bemba are also not infallible, in spite of a certain empirical knowledge of the properties of the soil. I noticed that the failure of crops planted in the village mounds was not uncommon, in the first-year beds especially, and secondly, that the natives seemed to expect to proceed along

[1] e.g. April 1933 Canda we Eiya moved on account of raids by wild pigs, and two villages in Nkolemfumu's district (July 1933) because of elephants. Cf. also the case of Munuka village described on p. 284.

trial and error lines as regards the cultivation of these mounds. In April 1933 at Munuka, near Citimukulu, the headman had about 300 beds of cassava which looked stunted. The villagers had moved out into *imitanda* in the bush to look for new soil. At Shikafyola, near Nkula, I saw, in November 1933, soil turned up by the river and then abandoned. It was found to have lumps of clay inside and said to be too hard to work.[1]

At Kacienja, near Shiwa Dandu, I saw the headman planting some of his mounds with cassava in 1930, and trying each strip in turn apparently, until I visited him again in 1933 and found him still unsuccessful. These are admittedly only isolated observations made during years when the Government was making the planting of cassava compulsory, and when the natives were given no special instructions as to the handling of what was still, to them, a somewhat unfamiliar crop. But there is additional evidence to show that failure is not unexpected when mounds are planted. Natives use a special word, *ukupansa*, which means to 'try the soil'. It is common when building a new village to dig up one hillock or two in the surrounding land and to plant it with different crops. If they bear well, the soil is regularly hoed next year. In November 1933 Chief Nkula told me he had a few *mputa* round the village, and was starting to try the soil by the river for cassava. 'We shall keep on looking for soil on which to plant,' he said.[2] At Kungu village, near Kasama, an enterprising old lady, who was employing two male labourers on the proceeds of the sale of milk, had the whole slope of a hill dug with mounds on which she was putting ground-nuts, beans, maize, and cassava. She called this 'to try at random' (*ukueshya pambilibili*) and told me that as a result of her experiment she was convinced that nothing but sweet potatoes would succeed on that ground. Bemba also frequently plant maize on new mounds where it cannot succeed and hence they are bound to fail in the first year.

As regards the millet gardens failure is rarer, and a man's choice of soil much freer, but I have seen half-cleared gardens abandoned because 'the trees did not seem thick enough where I began to cut', and in March 1934 I noted that two out of the twelve gardens made by the Citimukulu failed completely. Some natives said that it was because the owner of the garden, one of the chief's wives, had committed adultery, and others that the millet must have been

[1] *Bumba mukati. Kwalikosanganshi.*   [2] *Twakulaeshya uko tukalima.*

sown on top of a site long abandoned. Apparently they knew some one had once grown a garden here, but they did not know whether the soil would be exhausted. They said, 'We thought we would try.'[1]

I do not know whether such conscious experimentation in soil selection is common among Bantu cultivators. Trial and error methods seem in keeping with many of the temperamental characteristics of the Bemba, as these are expressed in a number of different activities. They appear to the European to act on sudden impulses in many spheres of life.[2] It is not thought at all unusual for a man to dig three or four garden mounds in the bush and then desist, and I have seen four maize plants growing in a clump on the edge of a path with no better explanation than, 'The owner was walking along with seeds in his hand and he said, "Let's plant some here!" and he found they came up well', or, on another occasion, 'I do not know why he hoed there. I expect it came into his heart!' Some of the apparent testing of ground can probably be accounted for by sudden whims of this sort on the part of the cultivator.

But there is no doubt also that lack of precision in the methods of soil selection has also to be reckoned with. A native who can choose quite successfully the patch of bush which is likely to grow most millet, finds it more difficult to plant the five or six necessary crops he has to grow in the limited space he has available on the village beds, more especially as this ground has usually been allotted to him on more or less sociological grounds—his position in a family group, or the site of his hut, for instance. For this reason a certain amount of trial and error is probably a definite characteristic of the agricultural system of the tribe.

Incidence of Knowledge of Soil Selection.

This short description of Bemba methods of land selection shows us that there is a certain body of knowledge on the subject actually existent in the community, in spite of the regular acceptance of trial and error methods, and the fact that these people seem behind other tribes in the territory in this respect. Compare the information given in a primer of tropical agriculture with that extracted, with infinite patience, from an old Bemba in the course of many

---

[1] *Twati 'katueshye'.*
[2] Cf. The temperamental characteristics of the Bemba described in Chap. I.

visits to his gardens, and you will find there is a rough correspondence between the two. But the question is whether these rudimentary principles be described as a traditional system of land selection passed on to each successive generation? To answer this question the incidence of this type of knowledge within the community must be described.

I have notes of fifteen soil indicators, trees, and grasses given me at one time or another by members of this tribe; but it must not be thought for a moment that every native could have given me these. The majority told me that plenty of trees in the bush meant plenty of food from the garden cut there, but very few young men, at any rate, gave me more specific information than this. Some of the older men would give me two or three of these indicators, but usually with some hesitation, as though unused to generalizing in this way in answer to a question. On the other hand, some intelligent chiefs, accustomed to organizing agricultural work and issuing instructions, were more definite on the subject. For instance, the late chief Nkula, a capable organizer and the most intelligent Bemba I ever spoke to, laughed at my suggestion that garden sites were chosen at random—*pambilibili*. With characteristic energy he led me at once to his own *icitemene*, striding ahead at a great pace and discussing the properties of different trees as he went. White people, he kept on saying, knew nothing about the *mpanga*, even the *Bwanas* at the mission who taught the boys how to grow food. 'They do not look at the bush to see the trees,' he said. On arriving at his garden he pointed out not only the thickness of the bush but this tree and that, and showed me the various grasses which had been cleared away, speaking with great decision and confidence, although he could give no reason why such-and-such a tree should indicate a particular soil. Other elder natives, probably just as capable of land selection through the instinctive judgement they had acquired, became confused when asked to describe their system of choice. Several middle-aged men denied that you could know what a soil would grow from its appearance and said you would just have to try it. Many of the younger people plainly had not acquired any principles of selection at all. Nor in some cases did they attempt to exercise their judgement on this point. An intelligent boy in European service smiled at my questions and said, 'The old men pick up a handful of earth and let it run through their fingers and say, "It is of this

kind or that", but *I* don't know.' Two young married women, asked
the same queries, tossed their heads and said, laughing, 'Do you
think we are old women that we can understand the things of the
soil?'

My evidence, admittedly inadequate on this point, would be
that most Bemba, young or old, can select forest that will produce
sufficient ash for a millet garden, but that soil selection in a rudimentary form is only practised by some of the older and more
efficient cultivators, whose knowledge is acquired through experience. Several informants described this process to me as learning
how to understand the things of the soil or the trees of the bush.

In the old days the young man acquired this knowledge gradually by working under the orders of his father-in-law, who always
selected the garden sites. He did not start to cultivate on his own
for some years (cf. Chap. VIII) and evidently never received formal
instruction on the subject. Under modern conditions the boys of
the tribe are away at the mines and do not acquire this instinctive
power of judgement of the soil possibilities through long experience. Elders lament this fact openly, and it seems probable that
the little actual soil selection that was formerly practised, will be
diminished in the coming years.

CHAPTER XV

METHODS OF CULTIVATION

AFTER selecting the garden site as carefully as possible, the Bemba are limited to three main methods of cultivation.

(a) *The burning of brushwood and branches* on the garden site by which the weeds are destroyed and a finely powdered seed-bed is prepared for the staple millet (the *icitemene* method);

(b) *The alternation of different crops* which allows for the use of the former millet garden for four or five years (the *icifwani* method); and

(c) The digging up of soil into mounds (*mputa*) to be used for sowing legumes, maize, and Kaffir corn, and for planting cassava and sweet potatoes—either old soil, or new ground made into mounds by piling up green sods and covering them with earth.

I shall describe these processes in turn and the attitude of the people towards them.

(a) *Millet Cultivation* (the *icitemene* method).

Cutting the trees (*ukutema*). All forest-dwelling peoples in tropical zones must evolve some method of clearing bush or jungle land for purposes of cultivation. The trees must be either stumped or cut down, and the thick undergrowth which springs up with each rainy season has to be cut, and this may form one of the hardest of the gardener's tasks. But to the Bemba this process of tree-cutting is more than a method of clearing the bush. It is an essential part of the cultivation of the millet on which the people entirely depend. They cut the bush to get sufficient branches to pile high on top of their gardens, so that when the stacks are fired a thick layer of ash is deposited and the soil underneath is burnt completely. They even cut trees over an area about six times as big as their future garden, in order to get sufficient fuel to burn. It is for this reason that their method of clearing the bush is important.

The Bemba most commonly pollard trees (*ukusaila*), as distinct from stumping or from cutting the trunks down waist-high (*ukubungula*) which is more characteristic of the Bisa and Lala. Thus their millet gardens never look like a flat, cleared field.

The crop springs up round the base of the lopped trunks, which remain standing till they begin to sprout again.

Methods of shifting cultivators often cause the administrator anxiety as they appear to be a wasteful method of using land, and it is true that the *icitemene* system, which has been particularly severely criticized, involves the pollarding of many trees. In the Abercorn district, it was estimated that 21 square miles of wood were cut in order to make 1,346 gardens, or $6\frac{1}{2}$ acres of forest to make $1\frac{1}{4}$ acres of millet garden.[1] The trees grow again in a period variously estimated as 20 to 30 years, but the *icitemene* method certainly necessitates the making of fresh gardens each year in order to produce the essential millet.

However, the European, after 30 or 40 years occupation of the country, has not discovered any better method of producing millet in this particular environment up to the present, or even anything as good.[2] The burning of the ground destroys the weeds and produces a fine friable soil as a seed-bed. It also increases the phosphates and potash in the soil, and turns it slightly alkaline from being slightly acid and makes it more highly saturated with calcium.[3]

It is difficult to find out how long the Bemba have followed their *icitemene* custom, and why they differ from kindred peoples in this respect. Some natives say that 'We learnt *ukutema* here. The Bemba hoed like other people when they were still in Lubaland,' but there is no clear information available as to the tree-cutting methods of the Congo peoples at the present time. Suffice it to say that, however they acquired it, the Bemba consider their own system of clearing the bush as characteristic, and therefore superior to that of other tribes. The method of shearing the trees of their branches is exceedingly skilled. It is the man's task *par excellence* in the whole economic routine. The Bemba are daring climbers. They swarm up each trunk grasping with both hands and pressing with their naked feet, and once up to the branch level, swing themselves up among the boughs, springing or gliding with amazing agility. No tree is considered too high or too dangerous to climb.

[1] *Native Agriculture in the Abercorn District*, U. J. Moffat, 2nd Annual Bulletin of the Dept. of Agriculture, 1932.

[2] Moffat calculates that the average size of a household's garden in the Abercorn district is 3–4 acres and the production of grain per household is 3,200 lbs. Report to the Diet Committee of the N. R. Govt., 1937.

[3] Mr. H. B. Stent's Analysis of the soil of a newly burnt garden. Annual Bulletin of the Dept. of Agriculture, 1933 (p. 48), also U. J. Moffat op. cit.

If a trunk is too wide to be swarmed, a narrow pole is cut from the surrounding bush and slanted up against it, or the climber may choose to swing by his arms like a monkey from a convenient bough in a neighbouring tree.

All Bemba are exceedingly neat and deft with an axe (*isembe*).[1] Each axe-head is fixed at an angle of about 45° through a slit drilled with red-hot iron in a knobbed holder (*umupini*) about 2 feet long. A man never parts with his axe. He carries it everywhere with him swung over his shoulder as he walks.[2] At the beginning of each tree-cutting season the axe-blades are reforged by native smiths, who heat the iron white-hot in a charcoal fire blown with skin bellows, and hammer it out to a new fine cutting edge. During a morning's work the axes are constantly rubbed on stones, often between the cutting of each tree. The blade is thus kept very sharp, and when the shaft is held at the right angle, it will sever a branch from the trunk with two or three deft slashes from alternate sides. I have seen a man clear a good-sized tree of branches in ten minutes in this way, and at the tree-cutting season the bush resounds with the blows of axes and the splintering of wood. Heavy boughs crash as they fall through the undergrowth beneath. At the top of the tree the work becomes more and more dangerous. A man may be left standing on a fork at the summit with one of the vertical stems as yet uncut. He has to clasp it with one hand to steady himself, while with the other he slashes at the trunk he is clinging to. He swings his axe till he hears the warning crack and feels the branch sway. Then he slides his body quick as a flash down the mutilated stump of the tree, yelling in triumph as he hears the bough fall.

Every year two or three deaths occur during the tree-cutting. Other men are disabled through falls. The Bemba recognize the work as dangerous, and we have seen that they delay the clearing of the bush until their strength is at its maximum (p. 50); until they have recovered from the effects of a beer-drink (p. 18); or until the weather is warm so that their hands do not slip on the axe-handle.

---

[1] Axe-heads appear to have been among the few implements which the Bemba smiths knew how to forge. Most axes are still made by native smiths, although more often than not, with European iron, stolen or bought. Only a few are bought at the stores.

[2] As a proverb illustrating parental affection the Bemba say, 'A child is like a little axe. If it hurts you, you just throw it over your shoulder.' *Mwana, kasembe. Nelyo kakukoma, nakakobeka na pa kubea.*

The burnt garden. A circular patch of ashes round the blackened trunks
of the mutilated trees.

Tree cutting. At the top of the tree the work becomes more and more
dangerous.

Sons and nephews of chiefs are not allowed to tree-cut because of the danger, and hence sometimes find themselves almost destitute in old age under modern conditions. Tree-climbing is not an art which can be acquired in later years. Bemba ritual reflects their apprehension over tree-cutting. It will be seen that the prayers said at the beginning of the *ukutema* season, make constant demands for the safety of the men who climb the trees (pp. 366–72).

Nevertheless, the Bemba particularly pride themselves on this *icitemene* system. They constantly brag of their climbing feats as they talk together round the fire, the morning's trees growing taller and taller in retrospect. 'Look at that man! He is an absolute monkey!'[1] is a high compliment to pay to a cultivator. Young men try to go out together to cut trees (*ukuteme cima*), and when the chief's gardens are being cleared as many as thirty or forty boys sometimes work together on the first day.

The young men seize their axes, and rush whooping up the trees, squabbling as to who should take the highest trunk. They dare each other to incredible feats and fling each other taunts as they climb. Each falling branch is greeted with a special triumph cry. I collected about forty different *ukutema* cries at the cutting of Citimu-kulu's and Mwamba's gardens in 1933–4. These are formalized boastings like the praise-songs commonly shouted before a Bantu chief. The cutter likens himself to an animal who climbs high, or to a fierce chief who mutilates his subjects, cutting off their limbs like the branches of this tree. A squirrel might be afraid of such a tree, he says, but not he! 'The wind failed to bring down this trunk! But look at me!' Each shout is followed by a prolonged whoop of E-e-eh![2] The noise is deafening for the first half-hour,

---

[1] *Moneni uyu! Ni kolwe uine uine!*

[2] The cries I collected at Mwamba's village (13.v.33) and near Shiwa Dandu (18.vii. 33) show (*a*) six comparisons between the climbing man and different animals, e.g.

Fulwe tanina—lelo anina ku mukolobondo.—The tortoise does not climb—but to-day he climbs the *mukolobondo* tree. Native comment: This means that a man is afraid to climb, but then he is jealous of his friends who climb so well, and so he begins to learn, and now he can climb, i.e., even the tortoise who cannot climb at all is spurred to efforts against his usual customs.

Kabundi kamunina mfwa. Bacunga balanina no kubwelele.—The lemur climbs to his death, but the night ape climbs and comes back. Native comment: 'See how people who climb take the habits of animals. The *kabundi* is an animal who climbs to the top of a tree even if it falls and is killed, but the *bacunga* runs up a little way and comes back. The man who wants to climb a high tree is not

as the great boughs rain down from above. The old men stand beneath and watch indulgently. 'Why does he hang by one hand like that?' I asked of a particularly foolhardy act. 'It is the pride of his youth,' was the answer (*icilumba ca bulumendo*)—a quality which is described with disapproval, but also a kind of wistful admiration by the old. Is it a wonder that a Bemba boy, asked to adopt a less 'wasteful' method of cultivation, replies, 'Yes, but to lop the branches is a kind of play'! (*Ukusaila ni kuangala!*)

In a commoner's garden there is, of course, less excitement over the tree-cutting, but the same emotional attitude is shown. No single bough of a tree, however inaccessible, is ever left uncut. Why? 'Because the women would laugh at us when we come back to the village in the evening. Besides, isn't it the custom of the Bemba?', and the speaker then usually starts to laugh at the methods of other tribes, people who stand level on the earth to clear the bush (*ukubungula*) or who cultivate on the ground (*ukulima panshi*). I was once asked anxiously whether Englishmen practised the *icitemene* system in their own country. I gave a long and conscientious description of the merits of English agriculture, but as I spoke I heard one of the young men behind me observe to his friend with a snort of derision 'Hm! Afraid to climb, I suppose!'

Piling the branches (*ukukule fibula*, or *ukuanse fibula*). As he lops the trees on his *icitemene* the gardener should trim the boughs with their withering leaves, cracking the projecting twigs if necessary, so that each branch will lie flat and make an even pile for the

afraid to fall. No! He says if I fall and die, it is no matter, to me! He is the *kabundi*. But other men want to climb a little way and then hurry to the ground again.'

(*b*) Four cries compared the tree-cutter to some legendary chief: e.g. *Tombo Tombolya! Muuma ngoma kumakunkutu!*—'*Tombo Tombolya!* (man's name). You beat the drums with the stumps of your arms!' Native comment: 'They shout thus because they take the arms off the tree and the leaves; that is the same as to mutilate a man. Tombo Tombolya was a man. They cut off his arms. He has to beat the drum with his stumps,' i.e. the trees are to be mutilated by the climber as the chiefs used to mutilate men.

Five cries referred to the food that was to result from the tree-cutting, e.g. *Cinkoyombe! Naleka! Naleka! Naleka!*—The porridge left over! I have left it! I have left it! I have left it! Native comment: 'A man, when he has a big lump of porridge and very little relish, he eats, he eats, and he ends up with a lump of porridge left over without relish to go with it. That is a *cinkoyombe*. They shout like that because it is all a matter of food. They have gone out to cut porridge (*ukutemo bwali*). Where they cut, there they will sow millet—the seed will turn into millet again. That is why they shout like that. Just because it is an affair of food.'

burning (*ukusankula*). He must lay them on the ground in some semblance of a row with all the stems pointing in one direction (*ukuloshye mikongole mukati*). This will distinguish his branches from those of his neighbours, who make it their business to point their boughs in the other direction. It also eases the work of the women who have later to lift the heavy branches and stack them. A careful man helps his wife in this way—an old man, as an informant usually adds in explanation, taking it for granted that the two terms are synonymous. 'Young men leave the branches as they fall, "*pambilibili*", to use an expressive native term, which we should translate by "all anyhow".'

Next comes the business of stacking the branches. Here the rationale of the *icitemene* system becomes evident. The aim of the native is plainly not to clear the bush of obstructions, but to collect the maximum amount of brushwood to burn. It is the ash which he considers valuable, and the burning of the soil. The woman who piles the branches carries them as high as possible from the ground, so that twigs and leaves should not snap off in transit, and thus waste valuable fuel.

Piling the branches is the hardest work a Bemba woman does, and I have heard the wives of urban natives say that they were afraid to go back to the villages 'where we have to pile branches'. The women lift boughs, often fifteen or twenty feet long, stagger as they balance the length on their heads, adjust themselves to the weight, and start off with the load. All morning they come and go in this way. There is a good deal of skill required in the stacking of branches. They must be laid with their stems to the centre, so that they radiate out in a roughly circular or oval pile. The branches must be piled evenly one on top of the other until they reach a height of about two feet. If any portion of the garden is only lightly covered with boughs, the soil beneath it will be only partly burnt. Natives point to barren patches in a millet field and say the branches were not properly piled on that spot. As the end of the work approaches the woman makes a circular edge to the stack (*umukubililo*) by arranging small branches round in a ring. This is to prevent the fire from spreading too far into the bush, and to provide an extra thick pile of ashes for planting cucumbers and gourds round the edge of the garden.

The work of *ukutema* begins with the cold weather in April or May, and it may last right through till August or September.

Sometimes a woman works side by side with her husband, piling up branches as he cuts them from the tree. Both may move out into temporary shelters (*imitanda*) built near their gardens, and live there for some weeks together. But the branches are harder to carry when they are heavy with leaves and green sap, and the Bemba reckon that any but a woman who 'loves her husband',[1] i.e. a specially devoted or newly married wife, would prefer to wait till the boughs have dried! The important thing is to finish the work before the end of the hot weather, when the parched bush often bursts into flame, and fires sweep across the gardens before the *ifibula* have been properly stacked. If the work has been delayed into September the man hurries to help his wife, and both carry in the last branches, stacking together in haste. Laggards are sometimes reduced to making several small gardens (*akakumba*, plur. *utukumba*), instead of one or more large ones, piling the boughs where they have fallen from the trees. With the last branch stacked, the family rest. The women begin to enjoy themselves, and go on a round of visits to friends. The country is covered with circular heaps of dried wood waiting through long sultry days for the firing of the bush.

Firing the gardens (*ukuoce fibula*). The firing of the *icitemene* is an exciting and important event in the agricultural year. No one may set light to his branches until a special signal has been given by the chief, otherwise one blazing garden might set the whole bush alight and possibly destroy in a day the unstacked branches of countless gardeners. Heavy damages are claimed by a man whose *ifibula* have been burnt before they were ready. In the old days a native who set fire to the bush, whether accidentally or on purpose, had to give up his own *icitemene* in compensation, and if he had destroyed too much property to be able to make the damage good, he became the chief's slave. If the chief's own gardens were burnt, some say the culprit would have been mutilated or beaten; others that he would have been made to work for the chief. Nowadays financial compensation is asked for, and I have records of cases in which sums from 10s. to £3. 10s. were demanded as a return for what is, after all, the loss of the whole prospect of harvest for the year.

The chief must give the signal for the firing of the branches as late as possible in the dry season to give the people time to finish the work, but he must not wait till the rains have fallen

[1] *Aletemwa kuli wiba.*

and damped the dry wood. Territorial chiefs try to synchronize
the burning in one neighbourhood, and I have seen a messenger
go from Citimukulu's court to Nkula's village, four days' walk
away, announcing the date when the Paramount's garden would
be fired. Besides the performance of common ritual, this is the
only occasion when the whole Bemba territory is organized as one
economic unit.

The signal for the firing is the lighting of the chief's own pile
with the correct rites.[1] A bush fire burning fiercely gives a red
glow to the sky at night, and I have seen natives living near
Nkula's capital stand on their village beds at dusk, watching the
colour deepen over the horizon. They talked in excited tones,
and shouted to each other in triumph, 'Look over there! He has
fired his gardens now! See how red it is now! The gardens of the
chief are burning now!' And so the news travels from village to
village through the district. In each separate community it is the
headman who first sets light to his *ifibula*. At Pambalasa, shortly
after my arrival in Bemba country, I saw the sons of the headman
and his married daughters file silently into his hut one evening at
sun-down. After ten minutes or so they emerged, and the men of
the party swung off into the bush single file, head averted, very
anxious not to be noticed. The other villagers explained, with the
lowered tone and glance with which they usually describe a ritual
act, 'They have gone to kindle the branches at the headman's
place.' I found that the family had been calling for the blessing
of the ancestral spirits inside the hut, and hence had been concerned lest I should see what they were doing. Next day,
however, I saw a commoner set fire to his piled-up branches.
'New fire' is needed to set light to the gardens, i.e. fire made with
fire-sticks or matches bought at a store. Arrived at his garden,
the owner watched the way the wind was blowing, and stood so
that it blew away from him. He made a rough torch of bundled
up grasses and spat into the air calling on his *imipashi* for
blessing. Then he set fire to the torch with a match, and ran
round the edge of the wood pile lighting the twigs here and there
as he ran. The piled-up branches, dry and brittle from three or
four months' exposure to sun, crackled and flamed in a moment,
and the children ran wildly round and round, shouting with

---

[1] Cf. pp. 372–3. Signals for firing the bush are among the orders a chief
is specially empowered to give under the 'Native Authorities Ordinance' of 1929.

excitement like creatures possessed. The older people stood watching, quietly satisfied. Next morning nothing was left but a circular bed of ashes around the blackened trunks of the mutilated trees. The heavy work of the year was done. The *icitemene* (a thing cut) had become an *ubukula*, a garden, now.

Sowing the millet (ukutanda male). After the burning of the gardens nothing remains except to wait for the rains. The main millet crop (*amale yakalamba*) needs to be sown when the ground is soft from the heavy rains in December or January, but the quick-growing millet (*mwangwe*) is planted in the small garden patches earlier, usually in November, while millet sown in a third-year garden (*icifwani*) is known as *nkungwila*, and is scattered over the dry soil before the coming of the first rains. This process is called *ukupamina*.[1]

Either a man or a woman may sow millet, but the owner himself will do so if he is at home. The job is a skilled one, and a man with a high reputation as a sower is often asked to plant the garden of a younger man. An educated native told me that seed sown by a good sower would produce ten baskets of millet as against five from a garden badly sown, but I never tested this statement.

Seeds are carried in a gourd or basket, and the sower first marks out the garden with a stick into strips about a yard wide. This is to ensure that each part of the ground is covered. The sower walks up and down each strip casting the seed broadcast with a flick of the wrist that sends the tiny seeds flying in a fine spray (*ukuposa male*). The woman walks backward behind him throwing up earth over the seed with a forked stick (*ulukoba*) in the case of hot-weather sowing, or scattering it wide with a hoe (*ukutanda*) if the newly burnt garden is being sown. This is a difficult art. A clod is swung sideways shoulder high on the hoe, and then tossed over with a light movement that scatters the earth evenly over the ground, so that the millet seeds lie with a surface covering of soil. After this a careful cultivator will dig a small trench about ten inches deep round the edge of the field to draw off the heavy rain. Some other crops are sown with the millet or before it. Gourd and pumpkin seeds, etc., are planted one by one round the edge of the garden at the beginning of the rains or before them. The perennial Kaffir corn (*sonkwe*) is often sown broadcast over the

---

[1] This millet is also known as *icikuku*, probably from the wind of that name that blows before the rains.

garden directly before the millet, a handful or two being scattered widely so that the *sonkwe* heads shoot up here and there among the *amale* about six feet apart. Cassava cuttings are sometimes struck here and there before the millet is sown. The millet seedlings themselves germinate in about six or eight days, and the crop ripens on an average in four to five months.

It will be seen that sowing is quite a skilled process among the Bemba, but it is a quick, light task, for a whole *ubukula* can be sown in about an hour.

Fencing the garden. The advantage of the *icitemene* system is that after sowing there is no more work to be done till harvest. The burning so effectually destroys the weeds that the hoeing and re-hoeing, which is the constant burden of many other Bantu women, is quite unnecessary. Nor do the Bemba spend much time watching their millet against birds, although this is very necessary in the case of Kaffir corn. They merely have to guard their gardens against thieving baboons, as the millet ripens, against elephants, or in certain parts of the country, to fence it against wild pigs or various buck. There is no effective protection against raiding elephants, but in parts of the Chinsali and Mpika districts the natives build watching platforms about ten feet high known as *amapungu*, (sing. *ulupungu*) and sit there all night with muzzle-loading guns. Scarecrows of flapping leaves are sometimes hung up to protect gardens against birds or monkeys, and old men still use their bows and arrows on baboons, although with little effect. 'Monkeys are clever like men', the natives say, but luckily they eat maize rather than the staple millet. Traps made with rope nooses concealed in the ground are sometimes set for haartebeest and other big buck.

In the game or pig districts, fences are built (*kupindilo lubao*). Bemba do not fence for aesthetic reasons, and indeed male labour is usually too scarce to allow them to do so for purely economic purposes. In many areas the garden runs right into the bush, the trailing vines of pumpkins straggling into the *mpanga* with that feckless, 'untidy' look which is characteristic of this type of millet cultivation. But most of the chiefs' gardens are fenced for greater safety, and those of commoners in areas where pig and buck are plentiful. The work is delayed till the last possible moment before the millet is ripening, i.e. in February or March.

To cut a fence for an average-sized *ubukula* is about a month's

work for a man, and it is extremely hard labour. Stout poles of
about five feet high and five inches in diameter are trimmed to
a point and sunk in the earth about six feet apart. The inter-
vening spaces are filled with horizontal logs, threaded between
the uprights, supported on forks, or tied with bark. The result
is a fairly impenetrable wall which can only be entered through
a rough gate. But even at this cost of labour a fence is not
reckoned to last more than two years. The timber rots with
rain and is eaten by white ants. Another difficulty is the fact
that only a man can make an *ulubao*. Deserted wives try nowadays to set up a makeshift fence, with one cross-bar between
flimsy uprights and leafy branches laid aslant it, but it is inefficient
and will only last a month. It is one of the grievances of women
whose menfolk are absent that they can rarely find a male relative
to build them a fence, even if they have been successful in per-
suading one to cut them a garden. It is a trouble which is, of
course, limited to areas where game is plentiful, but in these the
women are sometimes reduced to desperation by constant raids on
their millet harvest. Near Kasama I watched from a distance a
woman running down a hill-side and up the slope opposite to her
village, wailing in short staccato cries as she ran. It was like the
lamentation at a funeral ceremony, and people stood aside to watch
her as she passed. They explained as an apology for such an unusual
display of emotion: 'That is a single woman (*umushimbe*). She is
alone. The pigs came to her garden last week, and then the other
night, and now to-day. And so her heart has become heavy. She has
no more food.' Such conduct contrasts sharply with the usual native
stoicism in the face of disaster, but it gives some idea of the pitch
of despair to which widowed or deserted women are sometimes
brought at the present time, for want of male help in economic tasks.

In other parts of the country the people dig pits with mounds
between them round the edge of their *ubukula* instead of making a
fence. They laugh and say the pits will not keep the pigs off
always, but that they are quick to make. They say the animals
are puzzled by the holes and begin to run to and fro and to say,
'*Yangwe!* I can't get out!' and so they get discouraged and go away.
The Lala system of enclosing a number of small gardens within
one fence to save labour (*ukuanse lala*) I only heard of once in the
Bemba country at Mungalaba, near Mpika.[1]

[1] Information sent me by Mrs. Gore-Browne.

Harvest. Women reaping the chief's field, Citimukulu, 1934.

A garden fenced against wild animals.

Harvesting the millet. The millet begins to ripen during April, first the quick-growing *mwangwe* or that sown in dry weather (*icikuku*), the self-sown millet known as (*icimbuka*), and then the main crop (*amale yakalamba*) in May or even June. All these cold weather months the people mostly live in grass shelters near their gardens, the women reaping, the men cutting trees for next year's *icitemene*. In a new village there is plenty of timber to cut near by and the move to the *imitanda* seems unnecessary, although the Bemba appear to enjoy it as a kind of holiday. They like, too, to break off from the main community in small family groups. Often a man of standing will use the opportunity to see if he can collect unofficially a large enough following to enable him to set up a village of his own. People worsted in a quarrel, angry, insulted, accused of witchcraft, or in arrears with their tax, retire to *imitanda*, always sure of a plausible explanation of their conduct. In a village which has been built three or four years the gardens may lie far out into the bush at a distance of eight or ten miles, and in this case it is really necessary for the people to camp near them. Otherwise traditional agricultural practice seems to be made an excuse for temporarily leaving the village when desired.

Women alone do the reaping. They use small knives about four inches long, petal-shaped, and fixed into tiny handles about two inches long. These they grasp in the palm of the hand, and cut off each millet head with the blade, dropping it into a small basket. To choose the right moment to harvest is important. Unripe grain is wasteful; over-ripe blows too much dust into the eyes; damp heads hang down and are hard to cut. An educated native told me that a field sufficient to fill three-quarters of a granary would only provide enough to fill one half if the millet were reaped at the wrong time, but this statement I never tested.

The reaper must stand with the wind behind her, or she will be blinded by dust. She usually walks to the centre of her garden, clears a small space, does magic to give the new food lasting power (*icibyalilo*),[1] and then reaps one basket and puts it out to dry. Later she is usually joined by others and the women work in rows across the field. In a chief's garden as many as twenty women may be working together in this way. Sometimes

[1] Cf. pp. 206–8.

crops of different kinds are sown together and the reaper must distinguish each apart and return to the field as each ripens.[1]

Millet is sometimes stored in temporary granaries (*nkoloso*) out in the fields, and then the grain must be brought home basket by basket to the permanent store in the village—sometimes as much as a week's work. To fill the granary the roof is raised, and the millet tipped in from baskets and then trodden down, and this process brings the cycle of millet cultivation to a close.

It will be seen that in this form of cultivation the people's emotions seem entirely centred round one process—a particular method of tree-cutting which is their pride and delight, and closely associated with an elaborate form of ritual to be described later (cf. pp. 367–72). It is this activity which the Government has constantly tried to discourage. Since the early days of the B.S.A. Company, white officials have argued with Bemba chiefs on the subject and the district notebooks at Kasama give reports of visits to the district by governors and other officers, who evidently instructed gatherings of chiefs to forbid the cutting of trees. The answer of the Bemba was, in effect, 'If we don't cut trees, we shan't have any food.' Finally, in 1907, a definite order prohibiting tree-cutting was promulgated, with the inevitable result that the people grew practically no millet, and in at least one district they had to be fed by the Government for fear they should starve. The effort was then abandoned. It is true that these orders were issued to the natives without any suggestion, apparently, as to an alternative method of cultivation. The research at present undertaken may result in the necessary discovery.[2] But it is doubtful whether any system of 'cultivating on the ground' (*ukulima panshi*) will have—at any rate for some years—the glamour of the old, and it seems likely, ironically enough, that those very factors which were formerly important incentives to production—the cultural emphasis on the value of tree-cutting and the religious rites associated with it (cf. Chap. XVII) —will act at the present day as barriers in the way of change.

---

[1] At Citimukulu's, in an old garden, I saw a woman reap once early in the year to get self-sown millet (*icimbuka*), next to harvest the *mwangwe*, and lastly the *amale yakalamba* itself.

[2] e.g. Mr. Moffat's suggestion as to the possible adaptation of the Mambwe system of throwing grassland into mounds in the cold weather, leaving them fallow during the dry season, and breaking up the hillocks during the rains and scattering the millet seed broadcast over the flattened surface in January and February. op. cit.

(b) The Cultivation of Subsidiary Crops.

The subsidiary crops of the Bemba are planted either (a) with the staple crop, e.g. cucurbits planted round the edge of an *icitemene* garden, or perennial Kaffir corn sown broadcast with it sometimes; (b) on an old burnt garden (*icifwani*) after the millet has been reaped off it; (c) on the beds round the village (*mputa*).

Ground-nuts (*mbalala*). Ground-nuts, the crop that comes next in importance to millet, are usually sown in an old burnt garden, after the straw of the millet of the previous year has been burnt (*ukuoce mpimbili*) in the dry weather, October or November. The soil is then hoed up very roughly. The seeds are sown in the early rains (November–December), and can be planted if necessary up till the mid-rains (January). To plant them the sower makes a series of dents in the soil with a hoe (about 18 inches apart) while another follows and drops the seeds in one at a time to a depth of 3–5 inches. The earth is then trodden in with the feet. A man and his wife often hoe in this way, side by side, while a child follows and drops in the seed, or at a chief's court a party of *umulasa* workers go out together planting the field in groups of ten to twenty. I have also seen a woman make holes all over the field, then drop in the seed, but there is no attempt to sow the seed in straight lines. Occasionally ground-nuts are sown in the village beds after scattering the mounds dug there for previous crops (*ukupasa*), but the yield is not reckoned so good by this method.

If the field is overgrown with weeds it will be cleared in February. Otherwise there is no work till the harvest in May. Then the women go out to pull up the ground-nuts (*ukufuke mbalala*). They work in threes and fours, each catching hold of a plant with her left hand and hoeing up the roots with her right. Then they sit down in front of a pile of plants and shake the roots free of earth and remove the nuts. The digging and carrying of the ground-nuts is quite a serious task and may take the women a week or two. Temporary granaries are sometimes made in the fields to store the nuts until they can be removed to the village. Nuts overlooked at harvest spring up the next season, and these self-sown nuts (*shya makoka*) are considered quite an important source of food. Ground-nuts are an old crop, and there are innumerable medicines mixed with the seeds at sowing (*icibyalilo*). No first-fruit rites are performed in this case, but a queer usage survives by which a man can ask his friend for a handful from a new basket of nuts without possibility of refusal. This is known as *ukushiliko mutwe* (to take the taboo off the head). I cannot explain the custom.

Other crops—Mound-cultivation. Most other crops the Bemba plants on mounds (*mputa*) raised above the ground. These he makes either in the old burnt gardens, after three years use usually, or else in the beds round the village. The mounds are irregularly spaced all over a garden.[1] Of 10 measured *mputa* the average height when new was 2 feet, the diameter across the base 6½ feet. Those intended for cassava are usually built about 3 feet high because of the length of the root of the crop. When the Bemba use the word *ukulima* (to hoe) it is usually mound-making they mean. On mounds the Bemba plants roots such as cassava and sweet potatoes; legumes, i.e. beans, peas, cow-peas; cucurbits; and grains, i.e. maize and Kaffir corn. He thinks legumes and root crops are better suited to mound-cultivation because of their habit of growth. He says the trailing vines of the legumes spread over the surface of the *mputa*, and the cassava roots strike down into the newly dug soil. He explains, too, that *mputa* are raised out of the damp in the wet weather and that the roots of the plants are thus kept from rotting. But he also uses the method as a means of renewing the soil, and it does, in fact, expose a new surface of earth to the air. When the soil is old, he says, you must dig it up into *mputa*, and it is part of the regular cycle of cultivation in the old burnt gardens to dig up mounds in the third or fourth year.

Bemba make *mputa* of two types, from turf and from old soil. Round a new village they cut clods of turf with the hoe (*ukusapika*) and pile up the tussocks of grass in heaps. Earth is then flung on top to a depth of a few inches (*ukushikila*). This is heavy work and should be done by men. New *mputa* of this type are known as *mputa shya nsokwela* (mounds of the foundation, i.e. of a village). They may be made in the dry weather (May–September) and allowed to stand while the vegetation rots inside. The value of decaying vegetation is apparently recognized by some gardeners. One explained to me that richness (*umufundo*) was obtained in this way because 'things have rotted inside' (*ifintu fyabola mukati*).

---

[1] Daryll Forde states that among the Yaköe, a Semi-Bantu people on the Cross River, S. Nigeria, these mounds are so evenly spaced by the natives by eye that he was able to estimate the size of a field by counting them. op. cit., p. 31. This is not so among the Bemba.

On the other hand, most Bemba leave the making of their new *mputa*, in characteristic fashion, to the last moment, and dig up the mounds in December, January, or February, when the ground is soft and easy to work. In this case they plant beans or cassava on the surface soil of the turf heap next day. In fact some young men seemed quite unaware that the soil became richer by being left to stand, and merely said they piled up the turf into mounds because they did not know what else to do with it.

Any legume or root crop can be planted on these grass mounds. I never saw maize, Kaffir corn, or cucurbits sown in this way and informants told me that the soil was not 'rich' enough for them.[1]

The second type of *mputa* is made on the old soil, either of burnt gardens or village beds, which the natives believe they can renew by deep digging. In fact after the first year or two of cultivation their only means of maintaining the fertility of *ififwani* or village *mputa* is to make and remake the mounds, and this they will do for several years. The soil may be re-dug with varying degrees of thoroughness—expressed by the Bemba with their rich vocabulary of reversive and intensive verbs by such terms as *ukufukula*, to toss up the earth; *ukufukulula*, a more complete process, to remake the mound entirely; *ukupilibula*, to turn the soil upside down; *ukupilibwila*, to turn it completely upside down. The most thorough and efficient re-digging of the village beds is to remake the *mputa* entirely (*ukutukulula* or *ukufukulula*), some time in the middle of the rains, so that a hump appears where a hollow had been before. This is hard work delayed as long as possible— usually three or four years after the founding of the village—and properly requiring male labour.[2]

A less drastic method, usually followed during the second year of cultivation, or where the owner is a widow or a deserted wife, is to halve the *mputa* and make a series of smaller mounds about $1\frac{1}{2}$ feet high between the old. This process, known as *ukupetula*, allows the native to sow crops for another year with a chance of success, although he will admit that it is not so good as the complete remaking of the mound. He may also take advantage of his

[1] Mr. C. G. Trapnell tells me he has seen Bemba 'try' new mounds with maize, Kaffir corn and cucurbits in other parts of the country.

[2] In five villages I visited (Molema, Citikafula, Kasaka, Mubanga, Kacienja) this complete process had been undertaken after three years' cultivation: in one village which had good soil (Kampamba) after four years, and in another with unusually good red loam soil (Nkula) after five years.

favourite device of burning the ground, especially where Kaffir corn or maize have been grown the previous year. In this case he strips off the straw left standing on the *mputa* during the hot season (September), piles it in the hollows between the mounds, sets fire to it, and leaves the ashes for the first rains to fall. Then he covers the spot with a small heap of earth and thus makes tiny *mputa* between the old ones. A clever cultivator was enthusiastic about this method and said, 'If you burn the soil and make small *mputa* on top and the rain has fallen on the ashes, that gives *umufundo*. You can plant anything on top then, maize or sorghum or beans, everything!' Thus starting from a general idea that subsidiary crops are better planted on mounds, and that old soil can be renewed by exposing a new surface to the air, there is every variety of mound-making practised by the Bemba, from the thorough redigging every two or three years to the semi-renewal of the mounds done annually.

Hoeing is considered hard and unromantic work by the Bemba, quite unlike millet cultivation. Both sexes hoe, and the people go out in two's or three's to dig mounds; a husband and wife together or two or three related women. Occasionally a man will get up a working party to be rewarded with beer, and will thus put a big stretch of ground under cultivation. But I never heard the slightest interest expressed in mound-making, and older men take it for granted that the young people will not bother with it. '*Tumputa twa balumendo*' ('The little mounds of young men'), they comment in passing small and hurriedly made *mputa*. This attitude to mound-cultivation has important results on the food produced. To dig new mounds for village beds at the foundation of a settlement is necessary, and it is an almost invariable practice to dig up an old burnt garden into *mputa* after the last crop of millet has been got from it. But, in the succeeding years, the digging and redigging of the beds, to get the best results from the soil, depends on the individual's energy and determination, and, as the main hoeing season falls during the rainy months, i.e. the time when food is shortest, the work is often carelessly done or left till another year. '*Ubunaŋani bwaisa*' ('Laziness fell on us') was a comment made.

Planting. Women usually keep the seeds for their subsidiary crops mixed in one gourd in what seemed to me a rather haphazard manner, and many natives denied that they selected seeds with any care to secure good strains. However, after questioning a number of cultivators, I came to the conclusion that all natives distinguish the slow- from the quick-growing millet (*mwangwe*), the perennial Kaffir corn (*sonkwe*) from the more common annual (*amasaka*), and the quick-growing maize (*kaliminwa*) from the slow-growing (*punga*). These strains they keep apart and sow separately. The long-vined cow-pea (*ililanda lya nkula*) is also distinguished from the shorter (*ililanda lya nceshya*) or another variety with small pods (*ililanda lya busulala*). Pumpkin and gourd seeds are actually selected from plants that bore well the previous year, especially in the case of the gourds used to hollow out for beer-gourds, dippers, or oil flasks. But, for the rest, though older natives distinguish about twenty different kinds of millet, according to the colour or size of the seed, and many varieties of maize, Kaffir corn, and legumes, they do not seem to select one type of seed rather than another when planting their gardens.

Women generally plant the subsidiary crops, especially those on the *mputa*. This is not a long operation, since the aim of the gardener is to sow a succession of vegetables, and therefore she plants her mounds from week to week throughout the sowing season.

The art of sowing consists in the careful planting of seeds on the mounds to suit their habit of growth and time of ripening. The Bemba reckon to grow at least two different vegetables on each *mputa*. Thus, pumpkins are often planted round the base of a mound on the top of which maize or Kaffir corn has been sown. Their long vines trail between the *mputa* while the grain crop shoots up on top. Sweet potatoes are also paired with Kaffir corn, since the former are dug up in October and the mounds can then be left to 'get rich' (*ukufunda*) till the latter is sown in December. cassava and sweet potatoes make another pair, and these are planted together. The cuttings of cassava are stuck vertically on top, and the sweet potatoes at an angle on the sides. Beans and peas are also commonly grown with Kaffir corn or maize. The long-vined cow-pea (*ililanda lya nkula*) is very carefully placed on the top of a mound because of its growth.[1]

Natives are convinced of the value of this system of mixed planting. Near Kasama, a man who had filled his *mputa* with cassava only was criticized as being lazy, although the mounds

[1] It may even be scattered broadcast on a *icifwani* garden with small mounds dug in between or mixed with Kaffir corn and sown in the same fashion.

were pretty well covered with cuttings after the fashion of the Bisa, some of whom grow cassava as their staple crop and in Cilubi island seemed to produce much finer plants by growing it alone. Several natives have complained to me that sweet potatoes injure other crops by their spreading habit. 'They creep about and steal the food of the beans, and the peas and the Kaffir corn', but they nevertheless continue to plant them with other seeds, 'because we want to have a lot of food'. Mixed cropping, as practised by the African cultivator, is believed to have many advantages under primitive conditions, on the grounds that it prevents the complete exhaustion of the soil by one crop, guards against erosion, and often provides a low-growing crop with shade from a higher one. But among the Bemba the fear of being without a necessary food sometimes leads unskilful cultivators to stuff their *mputa* so full of different seeds that the plants jostle each other for room (cf. p. 324).

In any case, the placing of seeds is obviously important with such a system, and the women plant one or, at the most, two at a time, making a cleft of about four inches deep in the soil with a hoe and dropping in the seed. This process is known as *ukubyala*, as distinct from the broadcast sowing of millet (*ukutanda*). I have seen Kaffir-corn seeds that came up too thickly transplanted (*ukunukula*), in one village, but many natives are loath to thin out seedlings either of Kaffir corn or pumpkins. A gardener gazing at a mound crowded with seedlings said, 'Yes, those plants are pressing against each other. Each will steal the food of the other. But are we to throw them away? Would not that be a slight to the spirits (*ukutuke mipashi*)? Is it not they who gave us the food? And are we to throw it away? That is what they do at the mission school. They plant beans and then dig them into the soil. That is bad what they do there.' Here religious belief definitely affects agricultural practice.

The sowing season lasts, in effect, from September, or even earlier, to February. Some crops can be sown in the dry weather in the months just preceding the rains (*ukupamina*). Others are planted in the early rains—November or early December—the time known by the natives as *ukupokwa kwa mfula*. The heavier rain falls in the mid-season—December and early January—and the last sowings are made at the end of the rains—February and March—the two months known as *ukulekeleshya kwa mfula*. Dry-weather sowing is only practised in old gardens when the soil has been softened by pulling up some previous crop.[1]   Natives say that the seeds get warm in the earth, while it is still 'hot', and these sowings ripen the earliest.   Cucurbits, maize, and legumes, except peas, may be planted in this way.   All crops can be sown in the early rains, except the main millet supply (*amale yakalamba*), and in the mid-rains everything except maize, which is said to be injured by the heavy fall then.   Only legumes can be sown advantageously at the end of the rains, and then they are planted for leaf-relish only, since the pods, ripening late in the year, are considered to be too small and hard to be of much use.   Double crops are only obtained in the case of the cow-peas.

Cassava and sweet potatoes are propagated from cuttings at any time during the rains.   Technically speaking, the men plant the cassava and women the sweet potatoes, although this division of work is not very strictly kept.   The cassava cuttings are taken carefully, the cut being made just below a nodule of the stalk. Cassava, which has seen two or three years' rains, is sufficiently mature for this purpose, and occasionally bundles of stalks are roughly put into the ground in October or November, to be used later for cuttings when required.   Sweet potatoes seem to be shoved in anyhow, leaves, root, or stalk—'Sweet potatoes? They just like to grow!   You can stick in any part—it is their habit to grow (*umusango uabo*).'   Sweet potatoes are ready for eating after the wet weather is over, but cassava is at its best after the second or third season's rain.

Thus it will be clear that the planning of successive sowings is a matter of some importance, and the Bemba sometimes use considerable ingenuity in arranging early and late planting and the use of quick- and slow-maturing varieties of seed.   At one village,[2] which had at the time plenty of male and female labour, I saw the village beds laid out in an orderly series, with beans and peas at every different stage: just germinated; two inches above the ground; eight inches above it; beginning to clamber and beginning to ripen; but very often the work was not so successfully organized, and the different owners' gardens looked as though each woman had sown when and what she could, according to whether her

---

[1] e.g. the millet sown as a third-year crop after the ground-nuts of the previous year have been rooted up. Cf. p. 317.

[2] Mucaka, near Citimukulu. April 1933.

husband had been able to dig for her, whether she had been given sufficient seed, and whether she had thought ahead.[1]

The following table shows the succession of the different crops:

	Sown	Reaped
Millet (main crop, *amale ya-kalamba*)	Mid-rains (Dec.–Jan.)	May–July
(quick-growing, *mwangwe*)	Early rains (Nov.)	April
(old burnt garden crop, '*nkungwila*')	Pre-rains (Sept.)	April
Kaffir corn (main gardens)	Mid-rains (Dec.–Jan.)	July and Aug.
(village beds)	Early rains (Nov.)	July
Maize (main gardens)	Pre-rains (Sept.–Oct.)	Feb.
(village beds)	Early rains (Nov.)	March
Ground-nuts (main gardens)	Early rains (Nov.–Dec.)	May
	Late rains (Jan.)	June
Ground-beans (main gardens)	Early rains (Nov.–Dec.)	March–April
Cucurbits (main gardens)	Pre-rains (Sept.–Oct.)	Jan.
(village beds)	Mid-rains (Dec.)	Feb.
Beans (main gardens and *Cow-peas* village beds)	Pre-rains (Sept.–Oct.)	Feb.
	Early rains (Nov.)	March
	Mid-rains (Dec.–Jan.)	April
	Late rains (Feb.–March)	May–June

Weeding. The Bemba only weed or hoe from sheer necessity and not for appearance sake. On the *ifitimene* neither is necessary during the first year of cultivation because the burning has destroyed the weeds. In the next year ground-nuts should be hoed if overgrown, and cassava beds should, if possible, be dug over in March or April. This is rarely done, except in chiefs' gardens. It seems likely that the Bemba never hoed their gardens constantly as some Bantu peoples do, but the number of *ififwani* that now seem quite overgrown with weeds is probably due to the shortage of male labour. *Mputa* should, technically speaking, be weeded. All over the second- and third-year mounds high grasses spring up during

[1] Another example of intelligent planning was seen in a new village of keen cultivators (Cikwe) in May 1933. Here one owner had seventy-five *mputa* of cassava and potatoes, planted in the early rains and now ripe for use, and three hundred and forty being planted for future use. He also had a hundred and forty-five *mputa* of cow-peas ripe then, thirty-seven of Kaffir corn, and forty-six of ground-nuts. Another owner had a hundred and twelve *mputa* of cassava and potatoes from the beginning of the rains, a hundred and seventy-four recently planted, and eighty-six dug up to be left for cultivation with the succeeding rains, forty-eight *mputa* of cow-peas ripe at the moment, and ten recently sown for leaf-relish later on, and a hundred and one *mputa* of Kaffir corn, while the three other important householders had about the same proportion.

the rains. In any case, these mounds could never attain the demure appearance of an English vegetable bed sown with a single crop planted in fixed lines, but in the wet weather they become a riot of vegetation of every sort. Grasses, cassava, and maize shoot up together, and pumpkin vines trail across the paths. The Bemba view the sight with calm, and even appreciation. 'Look at the weeds', I exclaimed in involuntary criticism on one occasion. 'Yes,' said my informant, 'that is fine soil! Look at the Kaffir corn coming up too.' The people argue that it is no use attempting to weed during the rains, since more weeds will only spring up.

I do not know how far the yield of the village beds would be improved by weeding. Some youths were quite ready to point out the greater height of the cassava in a neighbour's bed as due to his assiduity in weeding. Others distinguish between different kinds of grass, some harmful and some not, or between different crops, some of which, e.g. cassava, with its two or three years' growth, need hoeing, and others, such as maize, which they maintain do not. At chiefs' villages where labour is more plentiful, Kaffir corn is hoed once, in March or April, and is sometimes given an extra hoeing in January. Then the straw is pulled up and burnt (*ukuoce mpimbili*) in October and November. Cassava beds are dug over in March or April. But commoners do not reach such a high standard at the present day, and the young men tend to do the minimum of hoeing, at the last moment, when the ground has grown hard. In fact, some men, particularly those newly returned from the mines, or working in Kasama, declared to me confidently that the whole tiresome business was superfluous—a statement that I took as a sign of the times, since their elders shrugged their shoulders and commented, 'The laziness of youth.'

Harvest. Except in the case of Kaffir corn (*amasaka*) and groundnuts there is no regular harvest season for the subsidiary crops. At a chief's village, where much of the former is grown, tribute labourers go out to reap the corn in June or July. They cut the stalks down (*ukuteta*) and then cut off the clusters of grain about six inches below the head (*ukukobola*) and carry these back in baskets. But in many areas the ordinary householder grows so little Kaffir corn now that she picks two or three heads at a time as they ripen, dries them on the roof of a hut, and grinds them at once into flour, usually mixed with millet. The perennial variety (*sonkwe*) is usually so treated.

The other crops of maize, gourds, and legumes are gathered as they ripen. There is no general harvest of the crops and the process is known as *ukusaba* (to gather) rather than *ukusepa*, reserved for the reaping of the millet proper. In fact, all these subsidiary crops are known as *ifyasabasaba*, i.e. things to be gathered, not reaped. Each pumpkin or cucumber, whether grown in the millet gardens or on the village beds, is watched with loving care as it ripens, and its shape and size is constantly described and discussed. Women visit their distant gardens every other day to pick each vegetable as it reaches perfection, and this coming and going between village and garden makes quite heavy work at the end of the rains. Maize is also picked cob by cob, as it ripens, since the Bemba do not store this food, but eat it fresh. They do not even enjoy eating it half a day old. There is a curious belief that the cobs should not be stripped off the stalk inside a *icifwani* garden, but the whole stem itself cut down and carried out—'It is a custom of respect to the maize' (*umusango ua mucinshi*). Legume pods are gathered as they are needed, as an English woman picks peas from her vegetable garden, except for the pods or leaves which require to be stored (cf. Chap. V). Root crops are dug up as required.

Additional Methods of Cultivation. Besides their new and old burnt gardens and their village beds, the Bemba know several subsidiary methods of cultivation which they practise at certain times and in particular localities. These include (i) Livingstone potato gardens (*ifibundu*), (ii) river-side gardens for dry-weather cultivation (*icibela*).

(i) *Ifibundu.* The Livingstone potato is only grown in certain areas, in spite of being one of the oldest crops. I found it planted most extensively near Citimukulu's village, whether because the soil was considered specially suitable, or because old customs linger in this area, I do not know. The *ifibundu* beds are prepared in a more elaborate manner than any other Bemba garden-bed. Long grasses are first pulled up (*ukuseba*), and then the grass tussocks are broken up with a hoe (*ukukontaula*). After this comes the characteristic *ifibundu* process known as *ukushima*, which means ordinary hoeing followed by prodding the ground with the apex of the hoe to break it up, and scattering it until it forms a fine soil. Such beds are prepared in May or June, after the rains are over, but before the ground has become too hard. An improvident gardener may wait till later, but he will give himself harder work. The *mumbu* are propagated by two methods—sowing the potato itself and striking cuttings from the plant. The seed potatoes are planted half at a time, and begin to sprout when the weather gets warm. They are not ripe for eating till the following rains, when the gardeners dig them up from time to time to test them.

The potatoes grown from cuttings are planted in September. About that time the natives cut off the leaves and stalks of the *mumbu* level with the ground, for fear that the potatoes already formed in the soil should begin to sprout again with the rains. But the shoots should not be thrown away. 'They will swell into roots like a pumpkin does, and will begin to run out into the ground.' The rest of the *ifibundu* bed, left vacant for the purpose, is therefore re-planted with cuttings and the potatoes are ready to be dug in the subsequent May.

Natives seem to consider that there is something romantic about the cultivation of *mumbu* and that it is 'distinguished' to have an *ifibundu* bed. Besides this, the potatoes ripen at the end of the rains, i.e. the time when supplies are shortest.

(ii) *Icibela*. These are dry-weather gardens made near river beds. I saw them made among the mixed Bemba-Bisa peoples near Shiwa Ŋandu, but not elsewhere. The cultivator digs up the turf into mounds and then leaves these upturned sods to dry. Then he sets fire to this dried grass and covers each mound with earth. These gardens may be planted as early as August or September, as the soil is sufficiently damp, and by this means different subsidiary crops are secured very early in the year.

Attitude to different crops. When the Bemba grow millet they are not only producing their favourite food and working at their favourite task, but they are engaged on a whole series of activities which have rich traditional and emotional associations for them. None of the subsidiary crops arouse such interest, but each has its own value to the native, based on its historical associations, its importance as food, its magic properties, or the time and care it takes to grow. All these attitudes affect Bemba food production.

For instance, ground-nuts are a favourite food and grown on a sufficient scale to make the cycle of planting and harvest part of the regular routine of the year. The people seemed to take pleasure in talking of ground-nut cultivation and of the state of the crop. They use 'medicine' to grow it, as has been stated, but otherwise little ritual surrounds its use. Kaffir corn, on the other hand, is very much liked as a food, but it does not grow well on all soils, and needs a good deal of labour to protect it from birds. Therefore it is less and less planted. Nevertheless, it is still the crop which has the greatest ritual importance, and there is something almost romantic in the natives' attitude to it. People stop at a field where it is grown and smile and say, 'How lucky the owner is to have such good soil.' They describe *amasaka* districts with appreciation. It is associated with chieftainship, since Kaffir corn is necessary for much of the tribal ritual, and the greater supply of labour at the capital makes it easier to grow it. The perennial Kaffir corn (*sonkwe*) is easier to grow since it is not attacked by birds, but many Bemba do not rate its flour very highly. Both types are doctored before sowing in some families (*icibyalilo*), and must be protected from contact with sex. In the old days a man had to purify himself after intercourse and wait three days before sowing the Kaffir corn. The crop is also considered to be injured by contact with death. 'People say: A hot person (i.e. a person who has not been ritually purified after a sex act) should not spoil the Kaffir corn; and a new death, it must not spoil it either.'[1] In the old days Kaffir-corn seeds were rubbed with a piece of dough, which had been made with water heated in the tiny marriage pot used to purify a chief mourner after the act of ritual intercourse with which he removed the taint of death from his family or village. This dough was thought to protect the seeds, as it contained elements of heat from contact with sex, and of cold from contact with death, and hence inoculated the crops against both dangers. Many of these beliefs are dying now, but the tribal sacrifices of the Bemba still coincide with its first-fruit ceremony (cf. pp. 374–8); its flour is used to scatter over the dead body of a chief, and his corpse cannot be buried until the cycle of the Kaffir-corn harvest is at an end. The flour is used to fill the sacred basket in the chief's relic hut. At one point in the girl's initiation ceremonies she lays her head on *amasaka* seeds. For all these reasons, the Bemba grow Kaffir corn whenever they can, and Citimukulu plants it definitely for ceremonial purposes. He went out himself with his sons to reap it during my visit and called me specially to watch the process. He kept saying it was 'good' (*cawama*) for a chief to grow Kaffir corn.

Two other old crops of the Bemba are handled ritually, but are

[1] *Baleti bukabe teti buonaule masaka: ne mfwa mbishi tekuti ionaule masaka.*

no longer at all important as food. These are the *mumbu* potato just described and the little cucumbers, *amankolobwe*. First-fruit rites and sowing ceremonies are still performed for both, although they are not grown universally. First-fruit rites are done in the case of maize, but its cultivation is evidently not considered as interesting, by a long way, as that of the Kaffir corn. The cycle of its planting and harvest is not an important rhythm in the agricultural year, and the Bemba do not value the crop as food very highly, as we saw. It is just a subsidiary crop and nothing more.

Legumes are a necessary relish, but I never heard of their cultivation described with special interest, and since these are usually planted a few at a time, like garden vegetables in Europe, there is no such thing as a bean or pea harvest as a communal activity. The cowpea is the legume crop with the greatest historic interest. First-fruits and sowing ceremonies are performed for it, and a sauce made of *ililanda* is used to pour daily over the chief's dead body while it is being dried and preserved. The common *icilemba* bean is the most used as food, and these seeds, from their variegated colours, are used to decorate the clay images used in the girls' initiation ceremony. Pumpkins and gourds are an old Bantu crop, and among the Bemba, as elsewhere, rites of first-fruits and sowing are performed over them. Women speak of their cucurbit crops with special interest. They watch the gourds form, laugh and talk about their different shapes, and carry curiously formed vegetables to their friends to see. These plants ripen, too, in the hunger season, and hence their coming is hailed with delight.

Cassava and sweet potatoes are the easiest of all crops to grow and should appeal to the Bemba on that account, but the people apparently despise them as food (cf. pp. 52–3), however unjustifiably. Cassava is associated with no sort of ritual whatsoever. The natives who were encouraged to grow these root crops in increased quantities during the locust raids apparently diminished their planting after Government pressure ceased.

(c) *The Sequence of Crops.*

The next point of interest for discussion is the length of time the Bemba are able to use their land. It is evident at once that they have no conception that the fertility of a garden can be more or less permanently maintained by means of a fixed rotation of crops, whether or not they could succeed in doing so on these soils. They use their old millet gardens (*ififwani*) for as many seasons as they can, because they believe that the soil of a garden that has once been thoroughly burnt gives a higher yield than that prepared in any other way,[1] e.g. by hoeing into mounds (cf. pp. 302–4). In these gardens they plant a sequence of crops, generally according to very sound principles. But after four or five years it no longer pays them to go on cultivating the same *icifwani*. Its yield has fallen rapidly; it requires digging up into mounds each year with a good deal of labour; and its fence has probably rotted away and requires renewing. Moreover, since each gardener is clearing a new patch of ground in the bush each year for his millet, he soon has more *ififwani* available than he has the labour to cultivate,[2] and hence he allows the oldest field to relapse into forest again.

It is not strictly accurate to call such a four- or five-year sequence of crops a rotation, since the series is not repeated and the motive of the native in alternating different crops is quite different from that of the European farmer. The latter tries to maintain the fertility of his land by planting the second year a crop that restores to the soil some particular constituent that has been exhausted in the first, that makes different demands on the soil from the preceding one, or that has some other improving effect on the soil. The Bemba farmer is not at all concerned with preserving the resources of the land, of which he has an ample supply. He merely wants to get as much food as possible from the ground with the least labour. As a purely subsistence farmer, he must plant every year each of the crops he needs to live on, even if he knows that the yield of any one may be low in the particular circumstances, and his small force of labour often makes the question of the work involved in each operation the decisive factor. Thus, though clever cultivators actually know a certain amount about the properties of the soil, and though the traditional crop sequences sometimes seem to conform to our own scientific principles, yet the practical exigencies of the moment—the desire for a particular crop or the absence of male labour—are often the predominating factor. In fact, it is motives of this kind that seem

---

[1] Natives say that cassava roots grown in an old burnt garden are bigger than those on their village mound gardens, and also that the maize and Kaffir corn grow taller.

[2] Cf. tables opposite: also p. 397.

Showing Gardens Cultivated by Two Owners during Residence on One Village Site
(Kasaka, near Shiwa Ŋandu)

FAMILY A: KASAKA

	Bukula 1	Kakumba 1	Bukula 2	Kakumba 2	Kakumba 3	Bukula 3	Kakumba 4	Kakumba 5	Bukula 4	Kakumba 6	Kakumba 7	Bukula 5	Kakumba 8
1928	Millet	Millet (mwangwe) Peas	..	..	..	..	..	..	..	..	..	..	..
1929	Ground-nuts	Peas	Millet	Millet (mwangwe) Peas	Millet (mwangwe)	..	..	..	..	..	..	..	..
1930	Millet (mwangwe)	Peas	Ground-nuts	Peas	Millet (self-sown) Beans	Millet	Millet (mwangwe) Peas	Millet (mwangwe) Peas	..	..	..	..	..
1931	Beans	Abandoned	Millet (mwangwe) Beans	Gives to son-in-law Abandoned	..	Ground-nuts Millet (mwangwe)	Millet (self-sown)	Millet (self-sown) Peas	Millet	Millet (mwangwe)	Millet (mwangwe)	..	..
1932	Pigs destroy	Abandoned	Beans	Abandoned	..	Abandoned	Monkeys destroy	Millet (self-sown)	Millet	Millet	..	Millet	Millet (mwangwe)
1933	Pigs destroy	Abandoned	Potatoes	Abandoned	..	Abandoned	..	Monkeys destroy	Millet	Millet	Millet (mwangwe)	Peas	Gives to son-in-law Millet

FAMILY C: CABELUKA

	Bukula 1	Bukula 2	Bukula 3	Bukula 4	Village Beds
1929	Millet	..	..	..	..
1930	Ground-nuts	Millet	..	..	..
1931	Millet (mwangwe)	Ground-nuts	Millet	..	..
1932	Beans	Millet (mwangwe)	Ground-nuts	Millet	..
1933	Monkeys destroy	Beans	Millet (mwangwe)	Monkeys destroy	..

Bukula = New-burnt garden.
Nkungwila = Millet sown in 2nd or 3rd year alternation before rains.

Kakumba = Small accessory burnt garden.
Mwangwe = Quick-growing millet.

It will be seen that each owner makes a new millet garden each year. In 1928 their main crops come from *Bukula* 1 and in 1929 from *Bukula* 2, and so on till 1933. After two years each gets also a smaller supply of millet from the third year alternation after ground-nuts, or peas, i.e. from *Bukula* 1 in 1930. *Bukula* 2 in 1931, &c., in the case of Family A. A quick-growing millet from the owner's small accessory burnt gardens, Family C having insufficient male labour to cut such additional gardens. Obviously each owner has an increasing number of gardens under cultivation each successive year, till it comes to the point when he cannot plant the lot for want of labour, e.g. Kasaka sowed his smaller gardens, *Kakumba* 1, 4, and 5, for three years only, and *Kakumba* 2 for two years, and *Kakumba* 6 and 7 he left fallow for a year. In 1931 and 1933 he lent small gardens to his son-in-law. The main gardens both he and Cabeluka planted four years running unless prevented by the raids of monkeys or wild pigs. The table also explains why a woman deserted by her husband has a supply of millet in the third year, but none after that.

to weigh with the Bemba. For instance, it is their usual practice to plant a legume after a grain crop (the usual millet, ground-nut, millet, beans sequence described below. This principle is, in effect, a rotation. But most Bemba do not follow this sequence for the same reason as the European farmer. Some of them claim that the second crop actually improves the soil and increases its *umufundo* or richness, but others merely say that they plant the legume because they cannot sow millet—their first need—two years running, except in special circumstances. I heard one educated native say that he had lent his old millet garden to a friend in his absence 'so that he can plant ground-nuts there and I shall come back and find the soil enriched'. But others explained the practice by saying that ground-nuts grow specially well in a newly burnt garden, or that they should be planted after millet, as they are a low-growing crop and hence self-grown millet from the year before can spring up in between and be reaped as well. More commonly still, informants answered me, 'I plant ground-nuts because a man with children must have many ground-nuts. When they cry for food in the hunger months, the mother can roast them a handful of nuts instead of porridge.' Or simply, 'because I want ground-nuts as well as millet'. When each family is entirely dependent on what it grows for what it eats, and there is no organized system of exchange, agricultural efficiency in the sense of the highest yield of any crop per acre can never be the gardener's first and only objective, and I was constantly impressed by the difference between the rules of cultivation explained to me and the variety of other motives—such as shortage of labour, a sudden increase in the mouths to be fed, a desire for a particular crop, or a late start in cultivation—any of which might determine the sequence of crops actually planted.

(i) *The usual sequence.* The most common sequence of crops in the areas I visited was as follows:

1st year	.	.	Millet
2nd year	.	.	Ground-nuts
3rd year	.	.	Millet

and this is the answer usually given by a native when he is asked what he plants each year. This sequence gives an alternation of the staple grain crop with a legume and provides the Bemba with the two chief foods he needs. The fourth and possible fifth year of cultivation varies.

Before planting the ground-nuts,[1] the straw of the millet is burnt in the dry weather in October (*ukuoce mpimbili*) and the soil hoed very lightly. When the nuts are ripe the following year (May–June), the whole plant is pulled up and the soil left fallow till September when the third-year crop of millet, known as *nku-ngwila*, is planted in the dry weather before the rains (*ukupamina*). The people only expect to get half as much grain from their third-year gardens as from their first, but they need the extra grain, and the crop ripens more quickly than the main sowing, as it has been planted earlier.

This *nkungwila* crop is of interest as an example of a change in cultivation, possibly due to contact between one African people and another, before the coming of the white man. Two old men told me that 'at the time of the birth of my first child', i.e. thirty or forty years ago, the *ififwani* gardens used to be abandoned after the ground-nut crop had been reaped, and the owner merely came back to dig up the self-propagated nuts (*shyamakoka*) the succeeding year. The Bemba seem to have learnt from the Lungu and other tribes to the west, that it is possible to get a second crop of millet from the one garden, and now this custom is almost invariably followed. 'Hunger taught us' is the expression usually used.[2]

In the fourth year the soil of the *icifwani* is thoroughly dug up by being raised into mounds. In this year a variety of alternatives may be followed. The most usual is to plant beans or some other legume crop, and then to allow the soil to revert to bush. But if the soil is good the Bemba will follow the legume with Kaffir corn, and perhaps after that with sweet potatoes, which are believed to grow anywhere and to require no attention. This makes a sequence of six years, i.e. millet; ground-nuts; millet; beans alone or with sweet potatoes; Kaffir-corn; sweet potatoes, and gives the alternation of grain and legume three times. The *nkungwila* millet may also be followed by Kaffir corn and then by beans—a sequence I saw practised near Kasama.

The five- and six-year sequences used on good soils show that the Bemba are perfectly capable of using their environment to its best advantage when they have the opportunity to do so, and

---

[1] Ground-beans are occasionally planted instead of ground-nuts in suitable soil, but no other legume to my knowledge.

[2] *Nsala yatufunda.*

that they may not be incapable of adapting their present cultivation
to a new system of habitation. The longest sequence of this sort I
had described to me was on very rich, red loamy soil at Kampamba,[1]
near Malole mission, where the alternation was stated to be as
follows:

1st year	.	.	Millet with cucurbits
2nd year	.	.	Ground-nuts
3rd year	.	.	Millet with cucurbits
4th year	.	.	Kaffir corn
5th year	.	.	Peas
6th year	.	.	Beans
7th year	.	.	Fallow
8th year	.	.	Ground-nuts
9th year	.	.	Millet with cucurbits
10th year	.	.	Kaffir corn

(ii) *Millet–cassava sequences*. Alternatively, the Bemba may
prefer to follow their third-year millet with a root crop, or to plant
cassava and millet together the first year. By this method very
little work is needed, since the cassava crop stays in the ground
two or three further years and requires no further attention.

(iii) *Millet–Kaffir corn sequence*. The Bemba also alternate
millet with Kaffir corn. The simplest method is to sow a few
seeds of the perennial Kaffir corn (*sonkwe*) broadcast with a handful
of millet. Both crops are repeated together the first year, and the
second year the *sonkwe* will spring up again with the ground-nuts
subsequently planted with it, and the third year it will sometimes
be allowed possession of the garden with any self-propagated
ground-nuts that may come up. The sequence is thus:

1st year	.	.	Millet and *sonkwe*
2nd year	.	.	Ground-nuts and self-propagated *sonkwe*
3rd year	.	.	*Sonkwe* and self-propagated nuts
4th year	.	.	*Sonkwe*

No further work of mound-making is required.

But where the soil is good enough to grow the annual Kaffir corn
(*amasaka*) the Bemba plant it in preference to other foods, since
they like the flour made from it. It can be sown in an *icifwani* after
millet, and may be planted two years running on good soil. It is

---

[1] This sequence struck me as so unusual in a tribe of shifting cultivators
that I returned a second time to the village to verify it.

sown broadcast the first time and planted on mounds the second.
Thus in 1934, on rich red loam five miles from Kasama, I heard
the following sequences described:

1st year . . .	Millet
2nd year . . .	Kaffir corn (broadcast)
3rd year . . .	Kaffir corn (on mounds)
4th year . . .	Millet
5th year . . .	Sweet potatoes
6th year . . .	Kaffir corn

In the same year in another Kasama village I met a different
variation of this sequence:

1st year . . .	Millet
2nd year . . .	Kaffir corn (broadcast)
3rd year . . .	Millet
4th year . . .	Kaffir corn (on mounds)
5th year . . .	Beans

This shows that two grain crops may be planted running by the
Bemba on good soil.

(iv) *Double millet sequence.* It is very rare for the Bemba to
attempt to get two crops of millet running, but I saw a case where
this sequence had been tried, unsuccessfully, near Chief Makassa's village, and heard of it as being fairly common in Chief
Kaporye's country. In both instances the soil was described as
being 'strong red earth' (*ua nkanka sana*), and in both the second
crop of millet was sown broadcast after burning the straw of the
previous year, and lightly hoeing the surface of the soil. The
alternation was as follows:

1st year . . .	Millet with pumpkin and gourds
2nd year . . .	„ „ „
3rd year . . .	Beans or sorghum sown on *mputa*

Native agriculture is often described as a simple stereotyped
procedure, but these different sequences show the number of
alternative forms of cultivation from which the Bemba has to
select.

(*d*) *Sequence of crops on the village beds.* The village beds are
also used as long as possible. In fact it is the exhaustion of this
soil rather than shortage of trees in the neighbourhood which
decides a headman to move to a new site. In the first year the
Bemba, according to their fundamental belief in the value of

burning soil, pile up branches on the small strip of ground allotted
to them near the village, if there is sufficient brushwood to do so, to
make a tiny seed-bed for millet (*akakumba*) in this way. They also
dig up long ridges (*amolua*) and cover these with brushwood which
they fire before planting cucurbits. But, apart from these few
fertile patches, the native must rely on mound-making to cultivate
his village beds.

It is in these beds that the Bemba gardener has his hardest
proposition to tackle. A man who does not like the soil of
his burnt garden can cut a new one elsewhere, but the strip
allotted to him near the village cannot be altered. He must find
some crop to suit it or go without. The ground round a village
often varies considerably. For instance, at Kacenja, near Shiwa
Dandu, only two out of nineteen cultivators were able to grow
cassava, while another had been experimenting for the last four
years without success. One owner had six mounds on which
cassava flourished out of about three hundred on which it was
poor.[1] In another village, Mungulube, near Chinsali, the soil to
one side of the village was a good rich black loam (*uafina*,
uatikana), and on this soil Kaffir corn seemed to have been
grown three years running; but on the other side the earth was
sandy and light (*uanguka*) and here the same crop was stunted
after sowing a second year.

For all these reasons it is difficult to speak of a definite sequence
of crops on the village beds. A man digs up a certain number of
mputa on his *ulukolo* the first year—'the mounds of the inaugura-
tion of the village' (*mputa shya nsokwela*). Next year he takes more
ground into cultivation, and so on till the fourth year. Some he
leaves fallow from want of labour for the hoeing or mound making,
or shortage of seeds, and others he cultivates with different crops
according to his individual judgement. Lastly, when the village
moves, he can return and gather sweet potatoes or any crop he
may have left there as requiring very little labour and spreading
very fast. The land-tenure map (see Appendix) shows a series
of strips taken into cultivation in this way, and the whole appearance of the village beds is like a patchwork of different crops in
the early rains—an overgrown jungle in the late.

The most common sequences can be divided into those that
begin with a legume crop planted on the new turf mound and

[1] Cf. pp. 283–4.

those with root crops. In good red loam I saw most commonly the following sequence:

1st year .	.	. Beans
2nd year .	.	. Kaffir corn and pumpkins
3rd year .	.	. Kaffir corn and pumpkins
4th year .	.	. Fallow, or complete remaking of mounds before more Kaffir corn
5th year .	.	. Kaffir corn

The same sequence was also found with sweet potatoes substituted for pumpkins.[1] A simpler sequence is: beans followed by maize and sweet potatoes, for as many years running as possible,[2] and the sweet potatoes are then left to ramble as they please till the village moves. Another common sequence is:

1st year .	.	. Cassava and sweet potatoes
2nd year .	.	. Cassava and sweet potatoes
3rd year .	.	. Cassava dug up and mounds remade and more cassava planted

On poor soil I also saw:

1st year .	.	. Sweet potatoes
2nd year .	.	. Sweet potatoes and maize
3rd year .	.	. Maize
4th year .	.	. Sweet potatoes

or

1st year .	.	. Beans
2nd year .	.	. Sweet potatoes
3rd year .	.	. ,, ,,
4th year .	.	. Tobacco and pumpkins

The Bemba use of old house-sites for cultivation has already been described (p. 282), but since these sites (*ifitantala*) are often cultivated for two or three years running, this method of using refuse soil must be mentioned again under the heading of sequence of crops. The cultivation itself is simple. It consists of waiting till the house has decayed (one rainy season) and then breaking up the

[1] Kacienja and Shimusenga, near Shiwa Dandu, 1933. At Mungulube, a mixed Bisa and Bemba village, near Chinsali, millet was sown the fourth year on a seed-bed formed by flattening out the third-year *mputa*, and it was followed by Kaffir corn again, 1933. This was specially good soil, described as 'heavy, sticking together', and one that does not get cold quickly; one that is warm and gives off smoke'.   [2] Seen at Kungu, near Kasama, 1934.

Y

rubble of the walls and digging it into the ground till it is soft. The following year the house-site (a rough circle of about fifteen feet in diameter) is hoed over and maize and pumpkins sown on it, as long as the soil remains fertile, after which tobacco or sweet potatoes take its place. This intensive use of old village-sites is likely to have increased importance in urban areas where the villages tend to shift very little. For instance, round Kasama the villages tend to move a quarter of a mile or so from one site to the other—and they make up for want of new land by growing maize, pumpkins, and tobacco—all plants needing rich soil—in ground where their old houses have rotted. The size of the maize plants grown on these *ifitantala* looks as though the increased use of this old practice would be a very successful one as long as the people do not want to build permanent brick houses and thus rob themselves of the use of this refuse soil.[1]

The map in the Appendix shows how the village Kampamba shifted from one site to another contiguous one and continued to cultivate its old house-sites, and the example given below will illustrate the use of the *ifitantala* more clearly.

Mound cultivation in a modern village. I give the following description of mound cultivation in a particular village for several reasons. First, it happens to show clearly the variations in the soil often found between the different strips round one village, and hence the degree of experimentation that is necessary when cultivating the village beds. Secondly, it shows the degree of individual variation in efficiency that exists, and this is specially marked in a modern village of the type described. Thirdly, in this village the people were actually making an effort to adopt fixed cultivation, and their methods of adaptation are of interest in that respect.

Kungu Village, near the Government Station at Kasama (visited March 1934), had remained fixed in the same spot for ten years, i.e. twice as long as the average Bemba village. Natives admitted that much of the garden soil was bad, but declared they did not want to leave the present site because it lay along a good bicycle path to Kasama, three miles off, where twenty-two out of the twenty-eight taxable males in the village were at work, and where it was possible to find a sale for vegetables and milk to

---

[1] There are of course other reasons in favour of the brick house—a raised standard of living, &c.

Europeans,[1] and beer to Africans resident in the town.[2] The houses had, therefore, been rebuilt twice since the founding of the village in 1924, but one site was only a hundred yards or so from the other. A third re-building was being planned during my visit on a site also in the near vicinity. Hence it is likely that this village may remain fixed for a period of twelve years, instead of the usual four or five.

The soil round this village varied tremendously. Some of the cultivators were gardening on a strip of light, sandy soil covered with scrub, and of these nine failed completely, even though four could probably have produced better results by hoeing more thoroughly. In a series of newer gardens, thirty-three gardeners were cultivating a different type of soil round the present village. Of these thirty-three, eighteen had made successful gardens— twelve on good soil, four on bad ground enriched through village refuse, and two because the owners, two elderly widows, 'had hoed so much that they managed to get food out of sand'. Ten gardeners had failed, seven through the poverty of the soil, two through not weeding sufficiently, and one because old potato runners had remained in the soil and were 'stealing the food of the maize'. Twenty-six other gardens had been made on better soil some distance away near the river-bed, and here the proportion of success was much higher. Thirteen of these gardens were on black loamy soil, and eight on the rich black mud of the river bank; two on a streak of clay; one on sand and two on the edge of an old village site. Of these twenty-six gardens, nineteen were successful, six were still being tried, and only one was a failure—said to be due to insufficient hoeing. On the other hand, those gardeners who were growing maize on the deserted house-sites of their village were nearly all successful. This maize was two or three feet higher than that on the surrounding village beds, and only two out of the fifteen disused house-sites were failures, due to want of judgement in sowing the patch too soon before the rubble of the old house had dissolved in the rain. Thus it will be seen that, of the total number of gardens, twenty out of ninety-two, or nearly twenty-two per cent., were unsuccessful, chiefly, in native eyes,

[1] Four inhabitants owned between them fifteen cows, nine sheep, six bulls, and three goats.

[2] The brewing of beer for sale is, though illicit, one of the few means of livelihood open to an elderly single woman, and many widows or deserted wives drift to the villages near the town for this purpose.

through the poverty of the soil or the wrong choice of crop, but also through bad gardening in some cases.

I do not know whether the rate of failure among these gardens was higher than that of the ordinary Bemba village. In native eyes it was so. Some gardeners definitely explained that they knew that some of the soil was exhausted, but they were continuing to dig there because they wanted to live near the environs of a town. They said that they could only succeed by leaving their village every two or three years and planting the disused house-sites, and their judgement seemed to be confirmed by the splendid crops of maize they had managed to get when cultivating these *ifitantala*. But other natives criticized the gardening of the inhabitants. They pointed out that some householders were using paid labour and that paid gardeners were 'slaves' who could not be trusted to work well. In at least four cases natives were paying men to dig their beds, while they worked in Kasama, one of these being a woman who had invested a large sum of money, acquired through the marriage of her daughter, in cattle and was paying two labourers thirty shillings each to dig her mounds on the proceeds of the sale of the milk.

I noticed myself greater individual differences in gardening efficiency in this and other villages near Kasama than in the bush communities.

In spite of these modern adaptations to urban life, the natives had acquired no new agricultural methods more fitted to a settled life, nor had they been taught any. The manure of cattle was thrown away unused. The village refuse was recognized to make the whole difference to the poor soil of some gardens, but it was never collected and spread. The only successful adaptation made by these natives was their use of the deserted village-sites for cultivation, the latter lying a few hundred yards from each other, with the more limited range of movement found among suburban communities.

As regards the efficiency of cultivation, I noticed in this and other villages near Kasama greater individual differences than in the bush communities. Several young men had planted their mounds so thickly with different crops that each seemed stunted. They laughed and shrugged their shoulders and said: 'We came back from the mines and thought, we are tired, let us rest now! Then we found that the time had passed for planting and so we said, "*Yangwe!* Hunger will catch us!" So we planted every seed at once.'

As a contrast to this inefficient cultivation, I found in these communities one or two natives more skilled in Bemba agriculture than any one else in the country. One cultivator, himself an artisan at work in Kasama, taught me more about Bemba agriculture than I learnt from any one else, and had a larger strip of land under cultivation than would have been possible in an ordinary village. He profited from his fellows' constant movement and lack of interest in their gardens. The few men who were paying labour were also making experiments on a more daring scale than would have been usual elsewhere. Lastly, several old women, entirely without support of male relatives, which would rarely have happened in an ordinary village, were hoeing with an energy thought frenzied by their fellows 'because of their hunger'. This individual variation in cultivation is, I think, characteristic of the modern Bemba community. It is not only that an individual household economy is appearing and with it inequalities in food consumption, but also here and there specialist gardeners, trying to make a success of village life instead of going to the mines. For instance, at Mubanga, six miles off, was a community of enterprising cattle-owners who had obtained permission in 1924 to build huts apart in the bush so that their small herds might not damage the crops of their neighbours. These two natives were plainly men of unusual initiative who had acquired knowledge of cattle-keeping during their travels down south, and had realised the money-making possibilities of selling milk to the small white community of Kasama. They were later joined by natives from elsewhere who wanted the chance to settle near Kasama, and the community was finally constituted a village by the chief, who appointed one of his sisters, Mubanga—a disreputable and unpopular old lady—as headwoman. She was joined by individualists of all sorts—those of the old régime and those of the new. Her adjutant, a middle-aged man who came from another village, was so much disliked that he had bought himself three goats in order to get the necessary permission from the Government to live outside the village. Near his small settlement was a native convicted of sorcery by the Hunting ordeal.[1] No one would have him in their village, so he borrowed five pounds from a well-to-do nephew at Ndola,

[1] Cf. p. 345.

bought cattle, and thus managed to acquire permission to 'build alone'. In 1929 a young tailor at work in a store at Kasama, who had spent some years in Southern Rhodesia with some relatives and had there seen maize cultivated on a large scale on a European farm, joined the community. He had saved money and built himself a four-roomed brick house a few yards outside Mubanga, with six huts around it for dependent relatives. He had then invested in a plough, with which he had put a field of about two acres under cultivation, and had planted maize European fashion. Mubanga village was, in fact, composed of a few individuals of unusual enterprise, much ahead of their contemporaries in outlook; two or three malefactors or unpopular persons living as outcasts near the European town under the cloak of the new economic practices; a successful prostitute, who was paying two men to work her garden for her; a more or less floating population of wage-earners; and a nominee of the Paramount Chief, who constantly tried to keep control over the town natives by appointing one of his own relatives to the position of headman or headwoman.

To conclude, my description of the Bemba attitude to their food-stuffs showed their entire dependence on one staple crop, millet, which they consider as an absolutely essential food, and which has a special social and ritual value for them. In their agricultural life, millet cultivation is the dominant activity. It absorbs their energies and enthusiasm and its demands are put before that of any other crop. Fortunately its cultivation is simple according to the Bemba method, even if the latter is now unsuitable owing to its complete dependence on male labour. The ground cleared for millet is used with a good deal of skill for the planting of other crops in subsequent years even though these old burnt gardens are no longer used to the full owing to decreased man-power.

In growing his subsidiary crops the Bemba show considerable knowledge of the properties of different crops and the use of soils, especially in their cultivation of the village beds. But here sociological factors often militate against successful agriculture. Historical tradition and the native's attitude to different crops determine their willingness to grow them. Village sites may be chosen and moved for non-economic reasons. Various psychological factors prevent the natives from putting their maximum effort into mound-cultivation, and shortage of labour and the breakdown of the tribal education system have pronounced effects. All these reasons prevent the agricultural knowledge of some of the older Bemba from being used with the best results. Some signs of the adoption of a more fixed habitation are seen in the villages round Kasama, where the people have shown considerable shrewdness in the use of their old village sites as a means of prolonging the fertility of the ground, and here modern economic conditions seem to have resulted in the appearance of the specialist gardener, who does better than his fellows in the bush, side by side with a mass of inefficient and indifferent cultivators.

The Adoption of Fixed Cultivation in Special Environments

An interesting example of the adoption of fixed cultivation in response to special environmental conditions was noted by Mrs. Gore-Browne among the Bisa on Cilubi Island, Lake Bangweolu, in November 1933. Here shortage of land on a small, rather densely populated island, and shortage of trees for the making of burnt gardens had caused a revolution in agricultural methods during a period of 15–30 years. Forest gardens were now cultivated continuously with a year's fallow every fifth year instead of the former shifting cultivation, and the staple crop had been changed. These people formerly grew millet after the Bemba fashion in burnt gardens and planted cassava with it. The history of particular gardens during the last sixteen years showed that cultivators had been able to use their land nine years running in the first instance, sowing millet with the cassava the first two years, then planting a succession of fresh cassava cuttings for three, redigging completely, and repeating the same sequence of cassava and millet in the subsequent four years. The ground was then left fallow for two years and by this time—the twelfth year of occupation—all attempts to grow millet were apparently abandoned and the people adopted a regular sequence of planting cassava, setting cuttings for three years running and following it with a ground-nut crop for the fourth year. After this they allowed the ground to lie fallow for a year, and then restarted the same four-year sequence.

In this way, the particular gardens visited had been kept in more or less continuous cultivation for a period of sixteen years. Under these conditions the Bisa have had to give up the use of millet as a staple crop entirely. They live upon cassava with a great deal of fish from the lake and a few supplementary foods such as ground-beans and peas grown on a small scale in special gardens made in the alluvial soil near river banks. They only plant millet for beer, and that on a neighbouring island with rich soil, and travel there by canoe two or three times a year to sow or harvest their crops, giving tribute to the local chief for the right to use the land. For the rest, as the first step in fixed cultivation in poor soil without manure, they make extensive use of deserted village sites as do the Bemba, and other local systems prescribe carefully the method of use of this valuable ground.

This instance shows that the native is perfectly capable of adopting some sort of fixed cultivation when environmental conditions compel him to do so. I do not know whether such an adaptation would occur among the Bemba with their far greater reliance on millet for their diet and their traditional interest in the crop, but I saw a case of conscious adoption of the Bisa practice by a Bemba village living near their border on a treeless plain on the banks of the Luansenshi River—1933, a year of locust raids. Here, the headman told me, the villagers had decided by common consent to give up their *ifitemene* for the first time in their lives 'because we have used up all the trees and we said "Well! then let us turn into Bisa now"', i.e. live on cassava. Such instances of the purposive adaptation of the customs of a neighbouring tribe, by a people living on their border, show that the hand of custom is not as heavy on the African as is sometimes imagined.

CHAPTER XVI

FISHING AND HUNTING

FISHING and hunting will be discussed only cursorily in these pages. It is, however, necessary just to touch on these activities in order to be able to complete the economic calendar of work.

Fishing Methods.

The Bemba cannot be described as a fishing tribe. As a food, fish makes one of their favourite relishes, and is reckoned nearly as great a treat as meat. They catch fish whenever they can, and very much appreciate dried fish, but such food is regarded rather as a sudden piece of luck than as a regular article of diet, and fishing itself in a greater part of the country is an amusing pursuit, particularly when undertaken communally, rather than a serious means of getting one's livelihood. Among the neighbouring Bisa, a fishing tribe living on Lake Bangweolu, each fish is known by name and referred to as such, and every child in the community is able to pick out the different sorts correctly from a heap. But among the Bemba, though different types are recognized by the older men, the rest of the natives just speak of 'fish'. The Bisa regularly dry fish and trade it over the country. They have a fixed system of prices and reckon each catch carefully in terms of financial profit. The Bemba, on the other hand, only sell fish occasionally, at certain seasons of the year, and then by a process of casual barter. Apart from those who live by the banks of big rivers they are indifferent boatmen and handle clumsily the paddles of the dug-out canoes at river fords. Along the Chambesi, Luansenshi, and other big rivers there are, however, definite fishing villages recognized by the natives as such. These villages remain fixed in one position year in year out. Here we find fishing by one method or another going on all the year round, a complex system of ownership of weirs and rights of use of ponds, and special fishing ceremonies such as are not found over the rest of the plateau. The inhabitants of these villages are definitely specialist fishermen, distinguished by name as *umulonga* (plur. *abalonga*) and considered very exclusive and even dour by the rest of the Bemba. The latter discuss the habits of these fishermen as though they were almost a race apart, although in reality they differ from other Bemba merely in regard to their fixed habitation, greater degree of intermarriage, and independence of their neighbours. It will be best to sketch fishing methods in general as they are practised all over the country, and then to describe the more complex type of occupation characteristic of these riverine villages.

Bemba methods of fishing, whether by trapping, netting, or poisoning, are only successful in shallow waters. For this reason fish are only caught easily during two seasons of the year: (a) *April and May*, i.e. at the end of the rains when the waters are falling on the flats and banks, and the fish may be caught returning to the big rivers from the smaller streams and backwaters, where they had gone to breed a few months earlier. (b) *September to November*, i.e. when the level of the water in the rivers has fallen to its lowest and trapping or netting is possible in the main body of the stream, and poison can be used in the smaller rivers. Fish may also be caught sometimes on their way upstream to breed in January or February. But in a river as big as the Chambesi fishing of one kind or another is practised all the year round.

The natives recognize no close season for breeding. Questioned as to why they wish to trap fish that are full of eggs or young fish that are undersized, they answer in some such terms as, 'Well, it is no use leaving the fish for some one else to catch, is it?'

(a) *Methods.*

1. *Fish poisoning.* The simplest method of catching fish is by the use of a stupefying poison known as *ububa*, which is obtained from the crushed leaves of a bushy plant (*Tephrosia*) cultivated especially for the purpose in any village near a stream.[1] Fish poisoning (*ukusungilo buba*) is a co-operative activity in which the whole village, men, women, and children, join, and which is quite unskilled. The whole village may go out together under the orders of the headman, or a group of villagers may plan their own expedition. The best time of year for such fishing is August to November, when the waters are at their lowest.[2] On the smaller rivers such fishing parties are

[1] Mr. E. B. H. Goodall in *Some Wemba Words*, 1921, states that *buba* is used as a collective term to cover all forms of fish poison collected from various roots and leaves, including the cultivated plant, *kowamushi*, and different forest trees and shrubs, but I only heard the name used for the former.

[2] I have known natives try to fish by this method much earlier, i.e. in July and August, but this will depend on the height of the water.

casual and light-hearted affairs, more like an English picnic than a
serious job of work. On one such occasion the company was about
twenty or thirty strong, men, women, and children,[1] and carried
provisions for a day or two's expedition as well as the baskets of
ububa and pestles to pound it. On the banks of the river it is common
to find remains of grass shelters used on previous expeditions,
and little hollows in the ground made by those who had pounded
ububa leaves there on other occasions. Here the women gathered
together in twos and threes, each with a heavy pestle, and stamped
the leaves in rhythm. Each trio was composed of near relatives,
three sisters, or a mother and daughters, any kinship group in
fact that had worked jointly at the cultivation of the *ububa*, and
had rights of ownership over it. The women sang special fishing
ditties while the men lay idly by and shouted the flirtatious
remarks that are typical of activities in which the two sexes co-
operate in groups.

When the baskets were filled with the crushed leaves they were
carried to the edge of the river. The first day of this communal
fishing demands special prayers to the chiefs of the land (*shyamfumu shye calo*) to open the season. They must be uttered by the
headman, often a descendant of the dead chiefs, and at any rate
appointed to his position by the present holder of the title. On this
occasion the headman was in a state of ritual impurity, so the
task devolved on his maternal grandson, a boy of ten, sexually
immature and therefore incapable of ceremonial defilement.

He was called on by the eldest man present by the honorific
plural *Ba*, and both gravely knelt on the grass with crushed *ububa*
in their hands. The old man recited the names of the dead chiefs
'the owners of the land', and then both threw a handful of the
crushed leaves into the stream. Every one stood a moment and
then the children plunged into the river with the big baskets of
ububa and began rinsing the contents to and fro in the water
(*ukusungila*). The height of the river only stood to the children's
waists, the ideal height for fish poisoning.

The *ububa* appeared to dissolve quickly in water since the whole
surface was green with it, but it took about half an hour to act on the
fish. In fact in some cases I was told the poison is put in overnight.

---

[1] Only the old people remain behind to watch the babies, and any menstru-
ating women, since the latter are believed to bring ill luck to the fishing, the
only Bemba activity which is subject to this common taboo.

The first sign of a fish floating stupefied to the top was greeted with shrieks of excitement. Men waded down into the stream and pronged each fish as it appeared with their fine barbed spears (*ukuela*) while the women caught them in baskets as they floated by. The men admitted that the women's method was more efficient but added, 'We men must not take fish like the women do. *Our work is to spike the fish with spears.*' Most of the village company returned to the village in the afternoon with eight fish of about $1\frac{1}{2}$ lb. between them, but laughing and contented with the day.

More serious *ububa* expeditions are made on the bigger rivers when temporary weirs are put up across a bend in the stream and fish traps set in these to prevent any stupefied fish being carried down the river. The fishers catch what they can with spears and baskets by day, and return next morning to look at the traps. In the valuable fishing pools near the Chambesi the territorial chief organizes fishing drives. Children use poison in tiny rivulets and catch small fish in them with traps.

2. *Fish traps.* The second common method of fishing is by trapping. Fish traps are set on the banks of flooded rivers with their mouths towards the stream to catch the fish when they leave the main body of the water in the breeding season, or reversed in the opposite direction to trap the young fish returning from the breeding places to the parent stream. They may also be set in specially constructed dikes or weirs. Trapping is the work of men alone.

The traps (*mono*, plur. *miona*) are of the simplest possible construction and similar to those commonly used by Bantu people, both in Central and South Africa. They consist of reed cones, either with an open end or with a circular disk with a hole in the centre plaited into the aperture to act as a kind of valve to prevent the escape of fish that have been sucked into the cone by the force of the current.

The different types include the tiny traps used by children, about two feet long and five inches in diameter (*tinto*), made by soaking split reeds in the stream for a day or so, tying them at one end, and plaiting them together with bark strands at intervals of about four inches in order to form a flexible cone which remains taut when the open end is fixed between two sticks (cf. diagram 1). They can only be used when the floods are beginning in February and March, and are set overnight by the boys whenever they can find some small eddying current among the grasses on the bank of a stream. They are also used by the girls in the dry weather, in

September, to catch small fish in rivulets sunk to about two feet wide on miniature fish-poisoning expeditions.

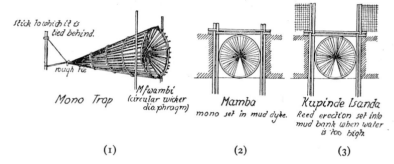

Mono Trap   Mfwambi (circular wicker dia phragm)

Mamba   mono set in mud dyke.

Kupinde Isanda   Reed erection set into mud bank when water is too high

Stick to which it is tied behind.

rough tie

(1)   (2)   (3)

The *mono* proper is between three or four feet long and about one and a half feet in diameter at the widest end which is closed with a valve (*mfwambi*). These traps are made of stouter reeds and must be more securely fixed by means of upright stakes at both ends (diagram 1), and the aperture sometimes concealed by grasses. These traps are set in reeds at the edge of some backwater or in small ditches in flooded flats. They are put out overnight and visited each morning. If any fish have been caught, the apex of the cone is simply untied and emptied out.

Any one can make a *mono* of this kind in a morning and set it where he pleases. But in fact the supply caught by this method is not a large one. They can only be set for a short period at the beginning of the floods and at the end. When the waters are rising swiftly they would be washed away.

3. *Traps set in dikes and weirs* (*ubwamba*, plur. *mamba*). A more serious method of fishing, and one practised only on the big rivers like the Chambesi, is to set the *mono* traps, in dikes (*amamba*) built about one and a half to two feet high of mud and grass sods, either parallel to the river banks, or else across tributary streams or backwaters near their junction with the main river.[1] The *mono* are set in gaps in the mud wall firmly held with wooden uprights and transverse rods (cf. diagram 3), and when the water has become too high in a backwater a reed construction is sometimes built on top of the mud bank to support the trap at a higher level (*ukupinde isande*).

[1] The big mud dikes built across the Chambesi flats near Molema were opened on 3 April 1933, and on the neighbouring backwaters in May.

Mamba are used (*a*) in backwaters of big rivers (*ifishiba*) in March; (*b*) on the flats about 400 feet from the river edge as the waters fall in April and May; (*c*) in the same dikes, with the traps reversed to catch the fish as they leave the main stream to breed in January, if the rain is not so heavy that it sweeps them away at once (*ukucilule mbelo*); (*d*) in the main body of the stream (*umulongo*) in May, in small rivers only.

Large numbers of fish are only caught by the trap method near the big rivers, but a sufficient number of small fish are picked up by the banks of streams to make a welcome variety in the diet.

4. *Weirs* (*icansa*, plur. *ifyansa*). *Mono* traps may also be set in weirs made of sticks and reeds placed across the big streams where there is a certain amount of current driving the fish into the traps (*uku milongo* or *ku mukuku*). These weirs include: (*a*) the permanent variety, such as are found on the Chambesi River in November and December; (*b*) semi-permanent weirs built to last for three years or so, or until the sand sifts up by the current; (*c*) temporary weirs built hurriedly to block up the current in a big river for a fish poisoning expedition, in which case traps are used. A much bigger variety of *mono* traps, about eight feet long and three feet in diameter, known as *banasabila* or *mumange* are used.[1] These weirs are in use in November and December until the crocodiles become a menace to the fishers. Thus the season is limited, but the method is very simple, and many of the larger varieties of fish are caught.

5. *Nets* (*amasumbu*). In the main body of a river natives catch fish by nets. Unlike the Bisa, who make about eleven different types of fishing net, the Bemba maintain that they only use one, with the occasional addition of small accessory nets (*akalenge*). The nets are made of twisted bark rope (*ulushishi*). The maker first digs up the roots of the *lwimbi* bush and hammers these out, removing the internal fibres. These he dries and then damps again, and finally frays off fine threads which are rolled together between finger and thumb into a very thin string. This latter is rolled on to a ball and used with a wooden threader to tat the net. It is said to take about three months to make a complete net, which is then four feet deep and twenty-five yards long, and sold for about three shillings. Nets are individually owned, and belong to men only.

The usual method of net fishing is known as *ukusoa*, the word

[1] I saw these used on the Luansenshi and Chambesi.

A trap set in a mud dike.

A Bemba fish trap.

Net-fishing in the Kalungu River—a small boy holds the bundle of net that is to be stretched across the river.

used for driving animals into a hunting net, and the process is in fact very similar. When the waters in the big rivers are low, either in September and October at the beginning of the rains, or in January and February at the end, the nets are stretched across the stream attached to grasses on either bank and kept up by a line of wooden floats (*mpepa*). They hang about three feet below the surface caught down to the bottom with stakes driven in by the foot if the stream is low. On a big river the fisherman, and one or two companions, sets the net and then paddles off down the bank in his canoe for about five hundred yards, turns, and then beats the water up to the net with sticks and shouting. The fish are driven into the net and either entangled in its meshes and pulled out by hand or else speared. The fishers then circle round and drive the opposite side of the net. On the bigger rivers this is a specialist activity, and two or three men set the nets together with a serious concentration of manner. They go out daily and bring back a dozen fish or so for eating or drying. In November big fishing drives are organized by the chief *Nkule* in the fishing pools over which he has rights. But in the smaller rivers (e.g. the Kalungu) I have seen young men playing at net setting in the same light-hearted spirit as that of the *ububa* fishers.

Other types of net-fishing are as follows:

(*a*) Setting the nets overnight (*ukutea ndala*), a method only suitable when the water has not fallen too low (July–October), and in still waters such as the backwaters (*ifishiba*) of the Chambesi near Molema, where neither currents nor crocodiles would sweep away the fish entangled in the nets before morning.

(*b*) Torch fishing (*ukusoe cenga*). This is a method practised in big rivers in December and January, i.e. when the waters are high. The fishers go out in threes and fours carrying flaming torches on the bows of their canoes specially lined with clay for the purpose. The fish come to the top, dazzled by the light, and are speared over the edge of the canoe or driven into the nets.[1]

(*c*) Beating the fish into small nets about one and a half feet long, deep set across flats to catch the fish, leaving the rivers to spawn, i.e. December and January. When the waters stand about three feet high on the flats, men and boys go out in bands, and drive the fish on foot, killing them with sticks or spears (*ukuela*). It will be seen that in the big rivers and their tributaries and

---

[1] I have only heard this activity described.

backwaters nets can be set by one method or another practically throughout the year.

Other methods. The Bemba also fish with hooks (*amaloba*) baited with fish and slung on a rope across a big stream, when the waters are low in August, but I never saw this done. Younger men say this method was introduced by the white people since they know that fish hooks are now only to be obtained at European stores. Older fishermen told me that, on the contrary, this type of fishing was practised from the earliest times, and that the Bemba 'always' knew how to make rough iron hooks for the purpose.

A few fish are said to be caught on the Chambesi flats when the floods are falling by means of plaited screens of grass (*uluangwa*) by which the women cut off small fish from the stream, but, indeed, when the waters are drying up at this season odd fish are caught here and there in all sorts of ways. I have often seen casual passers-by step off a raised pathway through fields flooded to a depth of six inches and catch fish of about $\frac{1}{2}$ lb. to 1 lb. in their hands in the grasses, or else spear them (*ukumela*).

To summarize, it can be said that the Bemba who live near the smaller streams of the district are for the most part unskilled fishermen, and rely on the low waters of dried up rivers, and flooded banks to catch a few fish at certain months of the year, but never get sufficient to dry or trade. They have no organized system of exploiting the resources of the rivers or definite leadership in this activity, but catch whatever they can during the breeding season, or before the fish are full grown.[1] In the regular fishing villages, on the other hand, the activity is almost continuous throughout the year. There are four or five different methods of fishing practised, and the men are universally employed in this pursuit. They value their reputation as skilled fishermen and know a considerable amount about the different types of fish caught. Though there is not sufficient fish caught to permit of regular trading, yet it is quite common for a man to be able to pay his 10s. tax by sporadic sales of dried fish.

6. *Fishing rights and ceremonies.* Fishing rights, like the rules of use of land, cannot be considered apart from the peoples' beliefs as to the spiritual ownership of food resources. The produce of

[1] How far the people are destroying their supplies of fish by this means does not yet seem clear. Cf. Report on the fish of Lake Bangweolu by C. K. Ricardo and R. J. Jones, December 1936.

rivers, like that of the bush, is thought to be under the control of the spirits of the land. To secure their blessing the people depend ultimately on their territorial chief, but actually, in the case of any particular expedition, on the headmen of the villages near the streams, whether these latter have succeeded to their title or have been directly appointed by the chief. Fishing ceremonies vary between village and village. The complexity of the magico-religious rites, the position of leadership secured by their performance, and the degree of definition of fishing rights depend directly on the economic value of the supplies.

Thus the headman of a village near a small stream offers prayers to the Land Spirits before an *ububa* expedition, as we have seen. But he is in no sense a leader in the enterprise, nor does his performance at the ceremony entitle him to special economic privileges.[1] Any stranger may join in a fishing party if he asks permission of the headman and gives him a fish or two from his catch. Each fish caught on such an expedition is the property of the man or woman who spears it, and, technically speaking, the headman or the owner of the *ububa* should get tribute from them. In the smaller rivers the supply of fish is so uncertain that most of these dues are not paid. *Mono* traps are set individually in the swamps without the accompaniment of any religious rite, apparently, and the setter of the trap may keep what he catches and put a conditional curse on the *mono*, if he knows one, to prevent fish being stolen. With net

---

[1] The rites performed at an *ububa* expedition vary in different villages. Molema, headman of one of the specialist fishing villages on the Chambesi, told me that in the old days spirit huts (*nfuba*, sing. *ulufuba*) to the *imipashi* in charge of the waters were built by the river and that the headman opened the season by throwing *ububa* into the stream, calling, 'Let them die! Let the fish that have rotted be white on top of the water' (*Fyafwa! Fyabola fyabute pa menshi tutu!*). This, he said, was to please the *imipashi* (*ukusekeshye mipashi*). When the first fish were caught three were put in the *ulufuba* for the *imipashi*. 'Nowadays,' he added, 'we are Christians. We do not build *nfuba*. We tie knots in the grass instead to imitate (*kupashyana*) an *ulufuba*. That is our sacred place (*E pa musumba!*) where we put the fish. A native of Shiwa Dandu confirmed this form of the rite. He said it was good to joke with the *imipashi* as men do with members of the opposite clan (*Banungwe*) and say to them after calling on them, 'You are the Mpende clan (*mpende* is a big fish that eats little ones, *mpepe*). You eat *mpepe*! (*Muli bene mpende!*) *Mulya ne mpepe!* This is the way men of the Crocodile rag with the fish clan, pretending they are going to eat them, and it is good to joke (*ukucena*) with the *imipashi* in this way. Also it is lucky to get a man who is a notorious drinker to throw in some *ububa* to open the season. Then the fish get drunk as he does. The man shouts, '*Uleke ikolwe bwangu bwangu!*' (May they get drunk quickly, quickly!)

fishing also, technically speaking, any man can set a net in the smaller rivers, but *de facto* few except the residents are able to do so for want of nets and canoes. Boats are individually owned, and though they may be borrowed, a man who takes a boat and catches fish in it or even kills meat on the opposite side of the river must share his luck with the owner.[1] It is rare to find more than one canoe in a village on a small stream. At the village of the Paramount, where there is much traffic over the Kalungu river, there are only two boats available for crossing and fishing. For this reason the inhabitants of fishing villages in practice have the monopoly of net setting.

In the specialized fishing villages the situation is changed. Magico-religious ritual becomes more complex and is closely associated with rights of use of the river.[2] When I spent some time on the banks of the Chambesi in the territory of Mwaba and Nkula, and even on the Kalungu near the Paramount's village, I constantly heard men being picked out as being lucky fishers, and the phrase 'an expert on boats' (*aleshibishyo bwato*) means not only a man who knows how to handle canoes, but who is reputed to have powerful fishing magic. Here also definite rites of prayer to the Land Spirits must be performed at the opening of the trapping and the netting seasons, and these are in the hands of economic specialists with magic powers (*icibinda*, plur. *ifibinda*) who are at one and the same time the most knowledgeable fishers, the leaders in co-operative enterprise, and the priests of the local deities.[3] This office is strictly hereditary in the line of the man first given the title by the original chief. I never saw any of the fishing rites of the Chambesi, but often heard them described as big gatherings of all the neighbouring villagers who assembled

[1] Large trees fit for boat-making are rare and must sometimes be fetched from a distance, usually after paying tribute to the chief of the district, nowadays 5s. per tree. To hollow out a canoe with an axe-head takes a man about two months, or a team of seven or eight men three weeks. The shaping of the prow head, which is merely pointed and not carved or ornamented in any way is the task of specialists who are paid about 3s., so that the whole process is an expensive one. It is characteristic of the present Bemba economic system that such boats have to be sold for about £1. 10s. in spite of the labour taken to make them. Why? 'Because a man in this country would not find more than £1. 10s.'

[2] Even the launching of canoes which is done in the smaller rivers without ceremony has its own special ritual on the Chambesi River (*ukusapiko bwato*).

[3] Specialist elephant hunters with magic powers are also known as *ifibinda*. The priests of local land deities are known as *shimiapepo*. The headmen of the fishing villages combine both functions.

first to watch the blessing of the traps and the weirs and later to invoke the help of the spirits at the setting of the nets on the big fishing pools (*ifishiba*). On both occasions the priest in charge asks those present if they have any grievance one against the other (*akantu pa mutima*), for the *umupashi* of an injured person might prevent the catching of fish by the rest. He then calls on the name of each of the Land Spirits, strikes the nets to bless them, and says, 'You, our spirits, now we are beginning to work, we people. Give us relish this year that we may eat and be satisfied.' It is important to notice that by the performance of such rites the *icibinda* definitely initiates the fishing season and synchronizes the activities of all the fishermen, and that these ceremonial duties are the basis of important economic privileges, which he maintains in spite of the overlordship of the territorial chief. This balance of interests between the local priest-headman and the chief produces a complicated system of fishing rights.

Permanent weirs are inherited in the matrilineal line and their ownership is often associated with the headmanship of fixed villages. The owner, besides his religious duties, allots trap holes in the weirs to different individuals who set their *miono* there. For instance, in one village the headman had divided the trap holes of a big weir between his sons and brothers, allotting two or three to each. Trap holes may be lent in return for a proportion of the catch, and in some cases a new-comer may obtain the right to build a small mud dike behind the main one giving tribute in return. Setting of nets arranged by casual agreement on the small rivers is strictly prohibited where fishing is valuable, unless the permission of the headman is obtained.

The *icibinda*, besides his right of allotting trap holes and giving permission to set nets, gets a proportion of the catch and also collects tribute for the chief. At one Chambesi village the headman (Molema) got one basket out of every three caught by each individual by the trapping method and two out of every three caught with nets. He sent to the territorial chief (Citimukulu) three baskets a year, two of these on the latter's special demand. In the case of some valuable fishing pools the territorial chiefs have secured special rights and can organize their own fishing expeditions (e.g. at Ca Kandwe, in Nkula's territory).

The sociology of fishing villages. Besides regulating the use of fishing resources this system of rights and ceremonies leaves its impression on the structure of the fishing villages. We have seen that the typical Bemba local unit is a loosely organized bilateral kinship group with a constant tendency to split into new communities. Among the fishing villages the value of the economic resources, and particularly the rights of ownership over the *ifishiba*, makes for fixed residence, although a very large village group would make cultivation difficult. New communities therefore divide off, but remain near to and closely attached to the old and under the same leader. Rights of inheritance of fishing weirs strengthen the cohesion of the matrilineal group since succession follows this line, and these Chambesi village communities are matrilineal lineage groups, localized in one district with their male members predominantly of one clan—a more formal kinship structure than usually found elsewhere in Bemba territory.

The headmanship of these villages obviously carries with it pronounced economic advantages. Such appointments are also a matter of great concern to the chief of the territory, who is dependent on the loyalty of these river headmen for his main supply of fish. It thus happens that the Bemba belief in the rule of matrilineal succession to village headmanships, and in the supernatural powers of the head of a local kinship group over the economic resources of a district, is sometimes in conflict with the territorial chief's conception of his own complete overlordship of the whole food supplies of the *icalo*. Under present-day conditions these interests seem equally balanced. The chief's right to appoint headmen in his district has been confirmed under the Native Courts Ordinance, and he does not scruple to use it. I have heard Citimukulu rating the villagers of one of the Chambesi communities, saying, 'You on the Chambesi, you! If you don't bring more tribute I shall chase you away and give the village to some one else.'

A similar attempt of the chief to secure control of valuable fishing resources is seen in the case of the fish-pool known as Ca Kabwe, belonging to the chief Nkula. This pool was originally in charge of two headmen, Sunga Kasawila, and Muŋwena, but the late Nkula chased them away on account of their 'pride' and installed his own brother in charge, merely keeping the hereditary headmen as *ifibinda* to carry out the necessary fishing rites at the beginning of the season.

But since the local clan group is composed of skilled fishermen who cannot in the last instance be replaced, the history of these riverine communities shows that their position is generally secure. The present structure of the Molema group illustrates this fact.

Some Chambesi villages. This group of fishing communities lies on the right bank of the Chambesi near the wooden bridge that used to carry the traffic from Chinsali to Kasama. Here the most important sources of the fish supply are (*a*) the main body of the river itself (*ku milongo*); (*b*) certain backwaters or ponds cut off from the main body of the river (*ifishiba*); (*c*) dikes or weirs built over the wide flats on the river banks. The first headman put in charge of these valuable fisheries was Mulilo, a member of the Lua clan, who was given control of the *ifishiba* at the time of Citimukulu Sampa, i.e. about three generations ago. He was succeeded by his maternal nephew on whose death the then Citimukulu (Ponde) put in a son of his own (the present Mukuikile) to hold the job. The latter failed. He was unpopular. He was an outsider among the Bena Lua. He was not a fisherman and could not perform the annual fishing rites. Temperamentally too he was described as a man who 'did not control his heart sufficiently to found a successful community' (*tatekelo mutima uakwe ua kumone cifulo*). He finally went off to take a job as a cook at Livingstone and the control of the fishing returned to the hands of the Lua clan, and two men in the direct line of matrilineal succession have succeeded to the office of Mulilo. With the growth of this community during four generations three other villages have split off, but have remained under the control of Mulilo. The first village to split off was given to Molema, a brother of the then Mulilo, who was appointed during the reign of Makumba, the first Citimukulu. Two other villages were given to Sampa and Kafoko during the present reign. In this group of four villages three of the headmen (Mulilo, Molema, and Kafoko) are own brothers, while Sampa, though actually their maternal nephew, ranks as their superior since he succeeded to the title of his maternal grandfather and hence became their *nalume*. In this case Mulilo is the senior and gives advice; Molema is the *icibinda* in the sense that he is the luckiest fisher; and Sampa actually utters the prayers during the fishing rites. I know no other case in which four Bemba villages remain united closely together, joining in common economic activities, acknowledging the leadership of one headman, and performing ceremonies to the ancestral spirits together. The value of the fisheries appears to have determined this form of social grouping.

Hunting.

Every Bemba is a hunter by desire and enthusiasm, but in actual fact game is not now very plentiful in the area—a situation for which the white people blame the black and black the white. Whether there has really been a considerable change in the supply of game since the coming of the European I do not know. White men certainly use more powerful weapons than the muzzle-loading guns imported by Arabs in the early days, and motor traffic through the country scares the buck near the main roads, but at the same time natives are not allowed to hunt elephant, hippo, and a number of the larger buck which were formerly available for them. It can only be said with certainty that hunting is a traditional activity which has its roots in the past, and that natives still look back to a golden age of plentiful game. Although meat does not now contribute largely to the people's diet, yet the Bemba still speak of hunting constantly, surround it with magico-religious rites, attach to it a special mythology, and spend a good deal of their time on it. It was interesting to note that in the copper belt many homesick recruits describing their tribal villages in glowing colours, ended with: 'And we hunt there every day'. In actual fact no Bemba does hunt daily or anything like it. The statement merely showed how their imaginations still lingered round their days of enjoyment in the village. Like the sportsmen of this country, they enjoy a day's shooting even if it brings little or no results, and I should prophesy that they would pursue an inedible animal with the same ardour and endurance as the European chases the fox.

The existence of specialist hunters and organized hunters' guilds has been described as characteristic of the Central Bantu, to which group the Bemba belong.[1] At present such guilds no longer exist in this area, although Melland has recorded their presence among the neighbouring Alunda.[2] Hunter magicians, that is to say skilled hunters with magic powers which give them rights of leadership or a monopoly over resources, exist as they do in many other Bantu societies,[3] and their position corresponds to that of the fishermen

---

[1] Cf. p. 18.

[2] F. H. Melland, op. cit., p. 267.

[3] Cf. Junod's account of the *maphisa* or specialist hunters of the Thonga, and the special villages of elephant and hippo hunters he also mentions, op. cit., vol. ii, pp. 59, 68. Also Doke, op. cit., pp. 321, 325.

magicians already described. Both are known as *ifibinda*. But naturally these specialist hunters are not common nowadays, since game restrictions prevent the killing of elephants—formerly their chief pursuit.

Every form of hunting has magic rites connected with it. Each hunter or setter of traps has his own charms (*ubwanga*) designed to make himself invisible, to draw the game to him, to slow its power of movement, &c. The animals themselves are thought to have magic attributes. Parts of their skin or bones are used as activating principles (*ifishimba*) in many charms or medicines, and many of them can only be hunted or killed after special ritual precautions have been taken to protect the hunter. All animals that attack or kill mankind are grouped in a special class known as *ifiswanga* (sing. *iciswanga*). These include the lion, leopard, cheetah, crocodile, hyena, or poisonous snakes, &c., and all these species are considered to have magic properties and to require ritual handling. Other animals are described as being *ifibanda* (sing. *icibanda*) or haunting spirits, or else are thought to turn into *ifibanda* when killed, and they are feared on that account. The bush-pig, bushbuck, hippo, rhino, eland and ant-bear are all *ifibanda*. Akin are the unlucky animals, e.g. those with the bottom teeth projecting or appearing first (*icinkula*, plur. *ifinkula*)[1] such as the zebra, the eland, haartebeest, or buffalo, which have no upper teeth in the middle of the jaw; the night owl (*ntiti mushi*) or the wild cat. None of these animals may be taken as tribute to a chief or eaten by a pregnant woman.

After killing one of the *ifiswanga* or *ifibanda*, the hunter must purify himself for fear the spirit of the animal will pursue him in dreams, bring him ill luck, or send him mad. This is also true of the elephant. The purification of a lion killer takes place at the chief's court and hereditary officials, the *Bamushika* (Kasenge and Cikutwe at Citimukulu's court), alone have the medicine required to wash the hunter.[2] But less elaborate rites are performed in the case of the leopard, crocodile, the caracal, and a bull eland with thick black tufts on its head. The ceremonies necessary after the killing of an elephant are described below.

[1] Children whose bottom teeth come through first are considered unlucky and are put to death.

[2] The *malaila* or war-song is also sung. I am indebted to Mr. T. Fox-Pitt and Mr. V. Brelsford for much confirmatory information on the magic properties of different animals.

All these rites, as well as the common charms for luck in hunting, show the intense emotional interest of the Bemba in this traditional activity, and their alternating sense of hope and fear in the pursuit.

Most types of hunting are non-specialist, and according to the Bemba system of land tenure, any commoner can hunt anywhere in his chief's *icalo* provided he is prepared to give tribute,[1] and except in the case of elephants there are no individual prerogatives over game based on supernatural powers as is the case with the fishermen headmen described. The chief methods of hunting are as follows:

(*a*) *Net-hunting* (*ukusoa*). This is one of the few communal activities of the Bemba and all the male members of the village usually take part in it. It is reputed to be the oldest method of hunting, and the Bemba places its origin in legendary times. They describe a mythical figure—Kampinda—who was sent by the High God, Lesa, with his wife NaMukonda to teach the old people (*bakalamba*) how to make and use nets. Kampinda is not the spirit of a chief like the other *imipashi*. He just came first (*ukutangila*) to teach the people, just as Luceleŋanga, another mythical hero, came to instruct the first doctors in the use of 'medicines'—a fact which seems to indicate that hunting and magic were reckoned the primary arts of this tribe. Small grass shrines are made outside many Bemba villages to Kampinda and his wife, and sometimes also to Mulenga, another hunting deity who is believed to wander up and down in the bush killing game for the people. Any animal found dead in the forest is said to have been struck by Mulenga. These three mythical characters are all spoken of with great affection and no fear. They are often called the *Bafundi*, or expert hunters.

Net-hunting also provides the oldest and most common form of divination, a preliminary test which can be carried out without the help of a specialist witch-doctor. It is almost invariably used at the present day to decide after the death of a member of a family whether the disaster has been caused by an avenging spirit of the patrilineal or the matrilineal line. If the right words have been spoken at the beginning of the hunt the sex of the animal first killed reveals the secret at once—a female shows that the mother's side is responsible, a male the father's. The method of hunting

---

[1] Not often exacted nowadays, except in the case of natives who live at the capital (cf. pp. 254).

Net-hunting. Bringing out the nets.
The nets stretched across the bush ready for a drive.

is the same as in the case of an ordinary hunt. The ritual variety is called *ukusoe libanda*, 'to drive evil spirits', and the former *ukusoafye*, 'just to drive'. The test can also be used to determine the guilt of a reputed witch or wizard. Again the words spoken, usually in secret in this case, when blessing the nets, convert the activity into a magic rite. A male animal killed means that *ubuloshi*, sorcery, is abroad.[1] Ritual hunts are also performed in some districts to test the probable prosperity of a new village site, and in this case a female animal is thought to bring luck.

The method of hunting is simple. The headman announces the expedition overnight, and early in the morning each man brings his own length of net (about 21 inches wide and 80 feet long) with a set of sharpened stakes forked at one end to support the top of the net. The nets are then stretched across the bush end to end to make a line some 600 feet long. Each owner stands behind his own net, concealed, if possible, by a tree. The children of the village are then sent out about a quarter of a mile into the bush to beat the game into the nets with boughs and staves. Any small buck which dashes into the net is hit on the head with an axe-handle or else speared. After the first drive the children make a detour and beat the bush on the opposite side of the net. The nets are then moved, and two or three drives of this sort may take place in a day. The whole performance takes place on a very small scale —five or six men are enough to conduct a net-hunt and big communal *battues* of game such as are described in South Africa do not take place, to my knowledge. Net-hunting is restricted to a definite season—the hot weather, after the bush has been burnt.

The rules governing the ownership of the meat are precise. The man who kills the buck has the right to the animal, but he gives a leg to the beater who first started the game. But in any case all the men of the village share in the meat meal, and usually eat it together. If there has been unusual success, such as the killing of five or six duiker in one day, the heads of the animals are cooked ritually at Kampinda's shrine. Hence the three clay cooking-stands often found near these small *nfuba*. In this case the wife of the headman cooks the meat and provides the porridge to eat with it, and the men and the children of the village eat together and dance and sing on the spot. I never saw this rite, but was told that it is still carried out in the Chinsali district at any rate.

---

[1] As also that animal of ill omen, the bush-buck—or *icisongo*.

Success in this form of hunting, as in other economic activities, depends on the ancestral spirits in charge of each strip of bush. These can give good or bad luck at will, and if invoked in the correct way will give an answer to their descendants' questions from the bush. The *imipashi* must be called overnight in the headman's hut and before the hunt begins. The people heap up the nets together and a child—usually one of the headman's grandchildren—strikes them with a twig of the magic trees *umufungo* and *umusangati* known as Kampinda's trees. The headman then calls upon Kampinda and his wife, next upon the dead chief of the district, and sometimes also on his own ancestors. I have a number of texts of this sort. For instance, before an ordinary hunt at Kasakatula village, the headman called, 'Kampinda, guardian of the bush, lead on in front of us with your wife NaMukonda. You pierce the undergrowth ahead of us, all you chiefs and you ancestral spirits. Go on light and bright ahead of us and let all evil branches lie down flat in front of us.' And at the same village when the people were carrying out a ritual hunt the nets were struck by the father of the dead child, who cried, 'We are looking for that which troubles us. If that which troubles us has come from your father, let it be a male animal killed. If it has come from your mother, let it be a female. Go on ahead of us.' There is no hunt of either sort in which the spirits are not addressed in some way or another before the nets are set up. Net-hunting is the commonest form of hunting among the Bemba and the least skilled. It has greater ritual importance than any other and on the whole produces more game (cf. figures given on p. 39).

(*b*) *Traps and pits.* Certain types of game and birds are caught in traps and snares. Any one can set such traps and the game killed becomes the owner's property. Trapping is not in any sense an organized or a specialized activity. A variety of such snares exists, but they are mostly found only in good game country, and even then they are only set from time to time. The most common is probably the *icitembo*, a running noose fixed over a small hollow in the ground and attached to a pliable sapling bent nearly at right angles by a rope caught round a notched stick in the ground and fixed by a transverse twig to form a delicate trigger, so that a buck, stepping in the hollow, releases the bent sapling, which immediately springs back to the upright position, pulling the noose tight about its leg. This snare is used for big game like roan antelope, and set to protect the millet gardens. The same principle is followed in small snares such as the *namwilindi*, used to catch moles and wild cats round the neck, or for birds. These snares are sometimes baited. Running nooses (*ifiselela*) are set in apertures made in barricades of branches. A log is then hung by a fine bark strand above the only opening in the barrier and attached to a delicate trigger on the ground. A wild pig that touches the latter as it brushes through the aperture releases the rope so that the log falls on to its head. Guinea-fowl are also caught in the same way. Stone traps (*ifiliba*) are used for tiny animals such as rats and moles, a big round stone being balanced precariously by a stick which the slightest touch is sufficient to dislodge. Small wild birds like parrots are caught by small boys who put lime on twigs on which a running noose has been set.[1] The Bemba also used to dig large staked pits (*amacinga*, sing. *ubucinga*), about eight feet deep, into which big game sometimes fell, but are now forbidden by the Government to do so on the grounds that a child might fall into such a hole and be killed. All trapping and snaring is carried out sporadically by the Bemba, and it is difficult to believe that this method produces much game. During three years' residence, admittedly not in particularly good game country, I never saw a buck caught in a trap, though I have occasionally been brought snared guinea-fowl. As far as I know there are no religious or magic rites associated with the setting of traps.

(c) *Duiker whistle* (*ichinyenye*). Hunters after duiker (*mpombo*) use a small duiker horn with a paper-like membrane, taken from a certain spider's nest, over the aperture. The hunter blows into the horn and produces a short, shrill scream which is thought to imitate the duiker's call. The animal is said to answer the whistle, and the instrument is universally believed in. Its negative results in my presence were always said to be due to the hostile influence of the wrong sex. These horns are doctored by successful hunters, who sell the medicine necessary for their use, and the new owner must address the whistle: 'I got you from X, a famous hunter, by purchase or as a gift (i.e. I did not steal you), so do your duty accordingly. I have rolled on the ground before the spirits, and before Lesa, begging him to give me of his cattle.'[2] The *icinyenye* is therefore definitely a magic whistle.

---

[1] T. L. Fox-Pitt writes: Pied wag-tails must be released, as they bring bad luck to the village. [2] I am indebted to the Rev. R. Macminn for this text.

(*d*) *Spears, bows, dogs, and guns.* The Bemba occasionally hunt in twos and threes with spears and dogs. Trained dogs are very valuable—about 10*s.*—and hard to buy. I never saw hunters go out with dogs, but I know that they are extremely skilful in throwing spears at a distance of about twenty feet, and that they sometimes kill small duiker in this manner. Bows and arrows are carried by very old men only and used to shoot at monkeys raiding gardens. A bow is handed down ceremoniously to a dead man's heir but is not often used in the hunt. It is the ambition of every native to own a muzzle-loading gun, which he can purchase for about 30*s.* and obtain a Government licence to use. Many Bemba still go to the mines for no other purpose than to earn the money for a gun, which seems to promise security and prestige in their old age. However, many of these guns are in fact more deadly to the hunter than to the quarry, since they are rammed with shot, slag iron, and rusty nails till the long-suffering barrels explode. It is unlikely that many buck are killed in this way.

European rifles are owned only by hunters employed by Europeans, or chiefs. The Bemba are said to be skilled trackers and think nothing of spending two or three days in pursuit of game. Game which is killed with a gun is the property of the shooter, to divide as he pleases, after he has given a portion to the nearest headman or chief. There is no special ritual attached to shooting, although the hunter may ask a blessing from the headman if he wishes, and in any case calls on his *imipashi* and carries magic charms.

(*e*) *Elephant hunters.* The Bemba elephant hunters were typical magician-specialists (*ifibinda*), i.e. they possessed both skill and the magic necessary to give them success. Elephants were killed formerly by the aid of weighted spears of specially heavy make by hunters known as *bashimunini*, with dogs and spears and large crowds of beaters by another type of hunter known as *bakalongwe*, or with guns traded from the Arabs by those called *Bafundi*. Nowadays elephant hunters only work for the Government or for certain big chiefs with special permission. The ordinary native is allowed to kill an elephant only when it is actually raiding his garden.

All elephant hunters were under the direct control of the chief in the old days, and he had the monopoly of the ivory so obtained. The chief summoned the hunters, but they were led by the *icibinda*.

This magician led out his followers when either he or the chief had 'dreamed elephants', after sleeping with their wives with special magic horns placed under the head of the bed. The party was blessed by the chief before leaving, and the *icibinda* carried his magic basket (*icipeshi*), containing charms and pumpkins cut up in small pieces, with him. He also prayed for the blessing of the spirits before the hunt and carried out the necessary magic ceremonies, both before the adventure began and after the animal was killed. Magic assumes a dominant role in this dangerous form of hunting, and both economic leadership and prerogative lies with the man who possesses the required charms. As in the case of fishing specialists, there is a balance of interest between the rights of the chief and those of the *icibinda*. The chief owned the elephants in his district, but he was absolutely dependent for ivory on his specialist elephant hunters with their magic powers.

An elephant hunt sometimes lasted two or three months and the people engaged on them, largely near relatives of the *icibinda*, seem to have been considered as almost specialists. When the hunt was lucky, the tusks of the elephant belonged to the chief, but the meat was divided according to special rule. I have heard it said that the heart, neck, hind legs, and intestines went to the magician, the front legs to the man who first struck the elephant, the back to the man who struck the second, and the chest to the hunter who was the third to wound the animal. Another informant told me that the leg, the liver, the heart, and the brain went to the chief, one front leg to the *icibinda*, and the others to the hunter who wounded the beast. One hundred hairs from the elephant's tail also had to be given to the chief.

Nowadays a few native elephant hunters go out as individuals at the behest of the Government or a chief. They own their own magic and win a high reputation in the community. It seems that a larger proportion of the meat now goes to the chief of the district, who no longer is able to keep the ivory for himself.

Besides the specialist magic of the *icibinda*, elephant charms are complex and of multiple forms. Charms to bring luck to the hunter are sold at high prices (£1 to £5). Sympathetic magic such as the spiking of the dung of the elephant to prevent him moving, or knotting grass across his path to stop his escape is common. Women can affect the fortunes of their hunting husbands by their fidelity or the reverse. Men who kill elephants must be purified by special medicines (*umufinsa*, *umusaka*, *katumbi*, *kaloɲansofu*, *umwenge*, &c.), and medicines are also placed on the head of the dead animal to prevent its *icibanda* returning to make the hunter mad. Further dangers await the man who sees the nerve of an elephant tusk before killing three elephants, and by this means becomes impotent. Such multifarious beliefs and rites could only be analysed properly in a treatise on Bantu magic, but they reflect the intense excitement of the people in the elephant hunt and all that pertains to it.

To conclude, hunting is the romance and delight of Bemba life, not a simple food-producing activity or even a very efficient one. The native hunts for food, but he hunts whether he gets game or not. Like other products of the bush, the supply of meat depends, in Bemba eyes, on the blessing of the spirits secured through the chief and hence it is subject to tribute, but the amount obtained is not sufficiently large for the development of complicated rights of economic ownership. Specialist hunters of the larger game existed, but few are still to be found. More magic surrounds the different forms of hunting than any other economic pursuit.

PART VI

ORGANIZING THE WORK

CHAPTER XVII

RELIGION AND MAGIC IN ECONOMIC LIFE

The Nature of Economic Ritual.

THE fundamental Bemba beliefs in the powers of their ancestral spirits have already been referred to constantly, whether in relation to their political organization, their system of land tenure, or their general attitude towards the production and collection of food. But the ritual of their ancestor worship remains to be outlined, and in particular the part it plays in their whole economic life. The Bemba pray, or offer sacrifices, at all the chief events of the agricultural year such as tree-cutting, sowing, and harvest. Formerly this ceremonial seems to have been unusually rich and complex, especially that performed at the Paramount Chief's court. Nowadays the rites are carried out with diminishing ceremony, by fewer people, and often with great secrecy, owing to severe discouragement from some of the missionaries in the area. But the beliefs associated with these rites still seemed to me to dominate the people's thoughts and to affect their agricultural efforts, while the ceremonies themselves, even when temporarily abandoned, were often resumed at times of ill luck or catastrophe. They had still to be reckoned as one of the most important sanctions of the chief's authority, and were hence unfailingly performed at the latter's court.

For all these reasons it is important for our special purpose to estimate the function of these magico-religious practices in Bemba economic life and, consequently, the effect which their lapse is likely to have on the production of food in the territory as a whole. In a tribe living at this particular level of development it is chiefly human energy and purpose which makes the difference between failure and success, and ritual has often been described as one of the chief means by which the courage and industry of a primitive people is kept at its height. This pragmatic aspect of magic and religion was first emphasized by Malinowski in his analysis of

Melanesian gardening and fishing.[1] Here he describes the series of magic acts which give confidence to the Trobriand fisherman embarking in a primitive vessel on a dangerous sea, or to the gardener about to start on the year's agricultural work. No less significant, in his view, is the function of an organized system of gardening magic in actually co-ordinating the activities of the whole community, since each individual waits for the appropriate ceremonial before beginning on his next agricultural task, and thus accepts the economic leadership of the gardening magician in charge. Radcliffe-Browne, in his study of a still more primitive community, that of the Andaman islanders, has also approached the question of ritual from a functional point of view.[2] He considers that the ceremonial associated with food production—the chief activity of each member of the society—not only impresses upon the individual the traditional tribal attitude towards this important pursuit, but also, as an additional function, gives a public affirmation of the unity of the group itself, a sentiment which is essential if successful economic co-operation is to be achieved.

Both these aspects of ritual seem to be apparent in the Bemba magico-religious system—the direct help which the rites give to the individual in his particular anxieties and difficulties, as well as their more indirect action in maintaining the confidence of the whole community and its sense of cohesion. From the purely economic point of view it is, of course, impossible to prove the pragmatic value of Bemba ceremonial in terms of increased agricultural output. Suffice it to say that in this area, as in the Trobriand islands, the rites seem to centre round those economic activities which give rise to the most doubts, fears, or anticipations among the people, itself a proof of the need they fulfil for each individual. For instance, the Bemba method of tree-cutting has been described as a pleasurable and exciting form of work, which the people consider very specially their own in contrast to the system of bush-clearing practised by neighbouring tribes. It is not surprising therefore that the annual *ukutema* ceremonies are reckoned as the most important of the whole year.[3] But this form

---

[1] Cf. 'Magic, Science, and Religion' in *Science, Religion and Reality*, edited by J. A. Needham, 1925, and *Coral Gardens and their Magic*, 1935.

[2] A. R. Radcliffe-Brown, *The Andaman Islanders*, 1922.

[3] I cannot find another instance of a bush-clearing ceremony in the literature dealing with the other Bantu peoples, nor have we sufficiently detailed material

of pollarding the trees is dangerous, if delightful, and the Bemba principles of land-selection by means of trees have been shown to be by no means infallible. Thus the gardener feels fear as well as keenness in approaching the tree-cutting. This emotional attitude is directly reflected in the rite itself. Every prayer I heard made on such an occasion contained some urgent request for safety for the tree-climber or for the blessing of the spirits on the selection of the new garden site. The people's attitude towards reaping is in striking contrast. When I asked an informant why the women did not pray before harvesting their millet, the idea seemed to him rather ridiculous. He merely laughed and said, 'Why should a person pray before reaping? Can a woman fall when she is standing on the ground? It is the man who climbs the trees who may fall. Let him call on the *imipashi* for help'—a clear expression of the different feeling of the community towards two essential economic activities.

Clearing the bush also marks the beginning of the new agricultural year when each gardener must plan the amount of ground he intends to cultivate. It is obviously important to the whole community that he should start his work with the highest ambitions and hopes. Here again it would be difficult to prove that the tree-cutting ritual actually does have this effect, except under modern conditions when it is possible to compare villages in which the rites are still observed and others in which they have been curtailed or abandoned. And I shall later give evidence to show that where chiefs were carrying out the traditional forms of worship, or had returned to them after a temporary lapse, the ceremony at the capital was the occasion of talk and enthusiastic comment in the surrounding district and, I think, really did act as a stimulus to further work.

Of the other important agricultural processes the firing of the piled branches is also considered an exciting moment in the economic cycle, but the act itself is, of course, not a dangerous one, nor is there much skill attached to it. It occurs, too, at the end of the hardest work of the season, and not at its beginning. We shall find that, though the firing of the branches is ritualized among the Bemba, the ceremony is a very simple one, and informants tend to omit it in accounts of the yearly cycle. Sowing ceremonies are still performed in all the chief's capitals, but they are tending to

from those areas to be certain whether the absence of such ceremonies is correlated with a less dangerous form of tree-cutting such as stumping, &c., or not.

disappear in other villages. In any case they are restricted to the subsidiary crops, and do not affect the staple millet. In some Bantu tribes these sowing rites seem to mark the beginning of the year's new activities and are thus treated as very solemn occasions, but among the Bemba the *ukutema* rites quite overshadow those at the *ukubyala*—the blessing of the seeds.[1] There are no hoeing or fencing rites among the Bemba. Both of these are arduous and important activities, but they depend upon human effort for their success and not upon luck. Harvest, in any agricultural community, is associated with complex emotions. The new food supplies bring delight, gratitude to the giver, and fresh possibilities of social life. The pulse of the village is quickened. Dancing, beer-drinks, and quarrels begin. The filling of the granaries makes the calculation of future needs inevitable, and the careless must be taught the tribal attitude towards the careful storing and handling of food. There may be a justifiable fear that the supplies will not last the rest of the year—an apprehension reflected among the Bemba in the many forms of magic of durability (*icibyalilo*) already described (cf. pp. 206–8). Thus it is not surprising that firstfruit rites in this, as in other Bantu societies, play an important part in the people's economic life and rival the tree-cutting ceremonies in their complexity. We can see from this analysis of the annual cycle how the ritual associated with each successive economic process depends on the nature of the particular activity and on the emotions of pleasure, doubt, or anxiety which are usually aroused by it.

How far the economic ritual of the Bemba actually synchronizes their activities is a question that is harder to answer. Formerly the people used apparently to wait to cut trees, to fire their gardens, or to sow until the chief had prayed for the ancestral spirits' blessings. Now they no longer do so in most commoners' villages, except in the case of the firing of the branches when there is a strong practical reason for their doing so (cf. p. 295). It must be remembered too that gardening is not in any sense a communal activity among the Bemba. The whole village does not work together in the millet gardens, and there would, therefore, be little

---

[1] It is interesting to note that among the Bisa of Cilubi Island in the Bang-weolu swamps, where tree-cutting has been abandoned, and a more or less fixed system of cultivation adopted, the bush-clearing rites have lapsed, but the sowing ceremonies seem to have gained correspondingly in importance.

value in a complete co-ordination of every stage of their labour. But, nevertheless, the fact that each process of cultivation is preceded by its appropriate ceremony does act, I think, as a sign to laggards that the season, whether of bush-clearing or of sowing, has begun.[1] Further, since religious prerogatives are invariably combined with political authority, whether in the case of the headman, the sub-chief, or the chief, economic leadership inevitably falls to the man who officiates as priest at these annual ceremonies.

But this list does not exhaust the economic functions of the Bemba magico-religious ritual. Where the belief in the supernatural influence of the chiefs over the land is such an integral feature of politico-economic life, any social mechanism by which this faith is publically expressed and confirmed, is of fundamental importance from an agricultural point of view. In such circumstances, to believe in the chief is to cultivate in hope and in the assurance that the land is sure to yield its utmost, and these annual economic ceremonials, all directly controlled by the chief and addressed to his own ancestral spirits, are the occasions when his supernatural power is made manifest.

The rites themselves with their insistence on a hierarchical grading of status, give a public expression, as we shall see, to the whole system of political values on which food-production, land tenure, economic leadership, and the exploitation of tribal resources depends. And the Paramount's ability to organize a series of large and imposing ceremonies at his capital is considered a sign of the supernatural power he is able to wield. In fact, as will be shown, some of the ritual performed by the Citimukulu seems to exist to demonstrate this fact alone.

It is an interesting reflection of the highly centralized political system of the Bemba that the people rely almost entirely on the help of their ancestral spirits, and in particular, of course, that of the *imipashi* of the chiefs of the land in order to harvest their crops successfully. Magic is, relatively speaking, unimportant in their economic rites. The native makes a clear distinction between the magic and religious rite. He keeps the term *ubwanga* to mean the use of charms, usually parts of trees or shrubs handled in a traditional

[1] Members of the White Fathers Mission have told me that in the area round their Missions the departure of preachers on their Christmas tour round the villages is often taken in the same way as a sign that the later sowing of millet should begin.

way[1] and prepared by a specialist *yanga*, from whom its use may be bought. *Bwanga* is used by the individual to protect himself from hostile forces, such as sorcery. He uses charms to increase the lasting power of the food in his gardens or granary (*icibyalilo*). He occasionally purchases counter-magic if he suspects a sorcerer of bewitching his millet store. Now and then I have seen charms put in gardens as a protection against birds or thieves. But, compared to some of the neighbouring tribes, the Bemba resort to economic magic rarely.[2] It is never used in tribal rites or by the chief in his capacity of priest of the tribe. It can never affect the productivity of the whole land as distinct from the individual garden. All public prayers and ceremonies are addressed to the ancestral spirits, and it is significant that the chief himself is not expected to use charms at all as far as his crops are concerned. 'Why should Citimukulu use *icibyalilo* like a commoner does?' said the official in charge of the chief's gardens. 'Hasn't he prayed to the chiefs of the land to give him food?' This statement seemed to me to be significant.[3]

This preliminary account shows us, I think, how the religious rites of the Bemba must have integrated tribal food production formerly and stimulated hard work. We must now proceed to a more detailed description of the ritual itself and estimate more exactly the part it still plays at the present day.

The spirit centres. The *imipashi* of the Bemba are approached in certain well-defined ways—calling on the names of the ancestors, usually at the same time spitting in the air (*ukupala mate*); prayers uttered by priests usually at one of the many shrines throughout the territory (*ukulumbula*)—and the offering of some material object such as cloth, flour, beer, chickens, sheep, or cattle to the spirits (*ukupepa*). The spirit centres at which the *imipashi* are invoked can be arranged in the order of their sacredness. They include:

[1] Often with the addition of a metal or part of an animal as an activating principle (*icishimba*).

[2] The neighbouring Bisa of Cilubi Island, for instance, invariably used protective magic against thefts in their cassava gardens, and Doke describes many of the same kind of charms among the Lamba (op. cit., pp. 294–5). Whether this greater reliance on magic is associated with a less powerful belief in the chief I do not know.

[3] The supernatural functions of some S. African chiefs differ in this respect, since the Zulu, Swazi, and Tschwana chiefs owe much of their power to the possession of rain magic, and many of the S. African chiefs are 'doctored' magically at the beginning of their reign and at subsequent ceremonies.

(1) *The individual's hut.* The hut of each householder is in a sense a shrine, since the spirits of his own ancestors and those of his wife are supposed to linger there, especially at dusk or in the early morning. The *imipashi* are addressed there at the birth, marriage, illness, or death of a member of the family or at any other event that concerns the group. In some areas a special calabash is reserved for the spirits, and beer is placed as an offering there overnight,[1] but I did not find any specially sacred spot in the hut reserved for the *imipashi*, as Smith and Dale describe among the Ila,[2] and as is common among some of the Southern Bantu. Objects to be blessed are placed at the head of the owner's bed as will be described.

(2) *Village shrines.* The hut of the headman is the centre of the religious life of the village, but in addition small shrines of grass about three feet high (*nfuba*) are built to the spirits. I have seen these standing outside some headmen's huts, although this is rare nowadays, or else outside the village, usually among the garden beds. They are still quite commonly built in the latter position since their presence is more easily concealed than when they are built in the village. There may be one, two, or even up to twenty-five of these small spirit huts built, usually one to the headman's own ancestors, and the others to the dead chiefs of the district. The headman of the village is always the officiating priest at these shrines.

(3) *Dead chiefs' villages (ifibolya).* The sites of dead chiefs' villages are honoured as spirit centres (cf. Chap. XIII). Shrines are built on them after the chief's burial and, though these fall into decay, they are rebuilt on special occasions as long as memory lasts.[3] The sites of villages made by the first Bemba chiefs or chieftainesses are famous ritual centres with big shrines about six feet high built on them (e.g. the Shrine of Katongo Mukulu on the Lubu River or that of Bwalya Cabala near Citimukulu's village). Others are only known by the local people. All are rebuilt at the time of a big ceremony at the orders of the chief of the *icalo*, and the grass around them cleared on less important occasions (*ukukungula*). They are in the charge of local priests (*bashimapepo*),

---

[1] This practice is more common where Bisa influence is predominant.

[2] Smith and Dale, vol ii, p. 166.

[3] Compare the custom of the Bangweolu natives of planting a tree on the site of the dead chief's hut.

usually descendants of the dead chief, and directly responsible to his living successor.

(4) *Natural phenomena (ngulu)*. Remarkable natural phenomena like big waterfalls or caves are also considered to be spirit-centres believed to have been inhabited by legendary personages, e.g. the cave under the Cishimba Waterfall near Cilubula, the Canga cave filled with bats near Kasama, a queer pointed stone in the river near Kapatu, warm springs at Mwamba Kambwale in Munkonge's country where women only may catch the fish, &c. Many of these sites are also associated with a form of snake worship, or are believed to be inhabited by a python. Battle-grounds or places where many people have been known to be killed, are also feared and believed to be haunted by spirits (e.g. Musonda Cinanda in the Chinsali district where a number of Arabs are said to have been slaughtered). All these *ngulu* sites are in charge of local *bashimapepo* acting under the orders of the chief.

(5) *Burial groves of dead chiefs (mwalule)*. It is characteristic of the centralized government of the Bemba that their big chiefs are buried in one place—Shimwalule in the Chinsali district— while the lesser chiefs and chieftainesses are buried in the grove of Bwalya Cabala near Citimukulu's village.[1] The great grove, a place kept with great secrecy and lying at about four days' walk from the capital, is said to have the greatest *imipashi* of the land. The priest in charge, the *Shimwalule*, is himself the burier of the Citimukulu, and is in a sense the ultimate authority in the whole spiritual hierarchy since he alone can sacrifice for rain,[2] or in the old days could pray for success in war.

(6) *Sacred relic shrines (babenye)*. The Paramount Chief, all the bigger territorial chiefs, and the most important *bakabilo*, possess relic shrines which are considered the ultimate source of their spiritual powers. These shrines are huts which resemble ordinary houses, but have their doors barred with logs or ivory tusks, and are kept with the utmost secrecy. They are hedged with taboos, and may only be entered by the chief, the 'wives of the relics' (*bamukabenye*), old women, descendants of the first chief's wives, and by the five most important *bakabilo*. They contain relics (usually stools) of the first holders of each particular title, by which the tribal spirits may be invoked. The most important religious rites of the Bemba are those by which a new Paramount acquires his

---

[1] Cf. pp. 240-1.　　　　　　[2] Drought is very rare in this area.

babenye, and so the right of access to his ancestral spirits. The ceremonies he performs at the relic houses are prayers for the benefit of the whole tribe. In the case of the economic rites, he initiates at the *benye* hut a whole series of ritual acts which are subsequently performed throughout the land.

Thus, even a study of the places where the Bemba spirits may be called and the persons who are able to invoke their help, illustrates quite clearly the dual function of the ceremonies first as ritualizing the individual emotions associated with each economic activity and next as sacralising the political structure on which the tribe depends. The commoner calls on his own ancestors inside his own dwelling on occasions which affect the welfare of his family only. The headman appointed by the chief does the same in the case of the economic processes which affect the welfare of the village as a whole. Nowadays he does not always wait to perform his own local ceremony till he hears that the *mfumu* has carried out his, but his chief can still be called the spiritual head of the district since the priests of the different *ngulu*, or those in charge of the dead chief's *ifibolya*, offer the prayers at these sacred spots at his orders. He not only gives them the command, but he provides the cloth, beer, flour, or animal sacrifices which may be required for this purpose from time to time. The Paramount himself has already been described as in supreme command of the supernatural resources of the whole tribal territory, and a series of sacrifices offered, first in his own *icalo*, but next at the orders of the territorial chiefs, at the spirit centres in their respective districts will now be described.

Special Ceremonial at the Citimukulu's Court.

Any economic rite, whether tree-cutting or harvest, can take three different forms at the Paramount's capital:

(*a*) The ceremony can be performed by the 'wives of the relics' at the *babenye* shrines of the chief, and in this case the rite is considered to affect the welfare of the chief and his own village in particular. It is his private affair more or less, and there is no spectacular ceremonial or large gathering of people at such times.

(*b*) A more complicated version of the ceremony takes place when the *bakabilo* assemble to purify the chief so that he may enter his own relic shrines with the 'wives of the relics' and the four senior *bakabilo*, and himself invoke the help of the tribal spirits there.

In this case the chief is praying for the welfare of the territory as a whole, and, for instance, at a tree-cutting ceremony, he is described as cutting 'the trees of the land' (*imiti ya calo*), as distinct from just cutting his own trees. This form of the rite was apparently not performed annually, even in the past. It involved the gathering of thirty or forty priests and councillors, with their respective retinues, and could only be undertaken when the chief felt certain of the loyalty of these hereditary officials and had the means of feeding such a large gathering during several weeks.[1] For instance, the present Citimukulu incurred for some years the hostility of his *bakabilo*, principally the Cimba, and hence was unable to carry out the full rite for some time, a fact which certainly diminished his authority. It seems clear also that the great chiefs of the past were able to vary the form of the ritual on such tribal occasions by adding particular ceremonies as special demonstrations of their power. The special tree-cutting and sowing rites described on pp. 366–74 are cases in point. Old men now describe such rites as having been introduced by such and such a chief, and count the number of times they have been performed.

(*c*) A still more elaborate form of prayer to the spirits is the series of sacrifices known as the *ulupepo lukalamba*—'big sacrifice' at which offerings of cattle, chickens, beer, hoes, or cloth are made at all the big shrines in the land.[2] This series of rites usually coincides with the first-fruit ceremonies, and in fact it would be difficult to feed a big gathering of officials except at harvest time. The special *ukusumata* (or 'tasting') rite for the Kaffir corn is first performed (cf. p. 378) and then the Citikafula, the *mukabilo* in charge of such sacrifices, should be sent with a basket of Kaffir-corn flour blessed at the relic shrines, and two oxen to the neighbouring shrines of Mulenga Porkili and Bwalya Cabala, the first royal ancestress. Here the beasts must be sacrificed and the flour scattered on the ground. This initiates the succession of sacrifices which are to follow. All the *bashimapepo* are called to the capital and are given cloth or chickens to offer at their local spirit centres, and messengers go to and fro between the different capitals to inform the territorial chiefs of the proceedings. They in their turn

---

[1] The poverty of the modern chief and his inability to get tribute labour naturally makes it more and more difficult for him to organize tribal ceremonies of this kind.

[2] According to the degree of respect to which the dead chief is due.

start to sacrifice at the sacred spots in their own districts. Only when the chain of sacrifices is complete the Bemba say *'Ulupepo luabuka mu calo'* ('The sacrifice has risen up in the land'). The organization of such ceremonies on the large scale of former days can have been no mean feat in a territory as large and as sparsely populated as that of the Bemba. Formerly even Nkula of Icinga, some 100 miles from the Paramount's village, 'prayed with Citimu-kulu', but a subsequent estrangement between the two branches of the royal house has resulted in independent action at the present day, although the Nkula was still obliged in 1931 to send to ask for Citimukulu's help in the arrangement of a sacrifice at the royal burial grove when Icinga was short of rain. Shortage of supplies, and in particular of cattle, for sacrifices make it impossible for the rites to take place on such a wide scale as formerly, and in 1931 Chief Mwamba offered a beast at the Ngulu cave at Cilubula without simultaneous action by Citimukulu.

Such tribal ceremonies have only been organized from time to time by the Bemba chiefs. The last Citimukulu, Ponde, reigned only a few years and 'did not sacrifice at all' (*tapepa*), while Makumba, the previous Paramount, ordered the *ulupepo lukalamba* twice, Sampa, his predecessor, three times, &c., and Citapankwa 'many times'. It seems to have been undertaken either when some unusual disaster, such as a drought or a small-pox epidemic, was affecting the whole tribe, or alternatively, when the Citimukulu was in a particularly powerful position and wanted to demonstrate his strength. This he did by showing his power to provide beer, food, and sacrifices for his whole territory, and commanding the loyalty of all his councillors assembled for the meeting. He was the *mwine lupepo*, the owner, or host of the ceremony, just as a man distributing beer to his friends is the *mwine ua bwalua* ('the owner of the beer'). The rite was also made the occasion of tribal council meetings (*ukuteke cilye*), and thus assumed great administrative importance as distinct from its political and economic function. To hold such a ceremony was a sign that the chief felt certain of his authority. No Citimukulu would undertake the *ulupepo luka-lamba*, I was told, until he had been firmly settled on the throne for some years and had built two or three villages. Successful chieftainship, like successful headmanship, is a position that must be built up gradually through the forging of personal ties, and of a Citimukulu who had not attempted the big sacrifice I was told

'He had not waited (lingered, dwelt) here long enough' (*Taba-kokwele kuno pakalamba*). The present Paramount's attempt, only partially successful, to organize such a sacrifice in 1934 illustrated well the sort of motives that seem to have operated. He had reigned about ten years and was about to build what he described as his last village.[1] He had achieved an uneasy reconciliation with his *bakabilo* after their previous discontent and was thus enabled to count on their support for the ceremony; and the plague of locusts that had been decimating the land for two or three years and the simultaneous fall in the price of copper which restricted employment for his people made him decide that the 'land was hard' (*icalo nacikama*) and that the tribal spirits were refusing their blessings as a result of some years' neglect. It was one of the occasions of return to ritual previously abandoned which I have mentioned above.

These alternative ceremonies at the big chiefs' courts show the extent to which their economic function is linked with, and even dominated by, the political. The rites are associated with agricultural activities and sometimes follow a disaster threatening the land's prosperity, but they have greater significance as demonstrations of the chief's authority and supernatural qualities, on which beliefs the successful cultivation of the land ultimately depends.

The Morphology of the Rites.

The form of all these annual economic rites is strikingly similar. The same elements appear in each successive ceremony. They evidently reflect the people's basic beliefs as to the supernatural forces that control them and a number of their fundamental concepts, such as that of the magic power of sex, of fire, or of water. The double nature of the rites, both as enlisting the help of the ancestral spirits in particular economic enterprise and also in stressing the political authority associated with the ownership and cultivation of the land, is also clear. All the rites include:

(a) *The invocation of the imipashi.* The officiating priest makes request for some particular aid such as protection from the danger

---

[1] He told me 'Because I am adult now (fully grown) we shall settle down in this village now. They (the *bakabilo*) shall teach me all the old ceremonies' (*Pantu ninkula. Tukekala ku mushi nomba. Bakamfunda fyonse fya kale*)—a sentence which expresses the Bemba conception that full supernatural powers are only acquired by the chief when he has reached age and success.

of tree-cutting, which is the individual concern of all those present, but he also stresses the omnipotence of the *imipashi* by asking them for such blessings as life (*ubumi*), fertility, health, and peace. The form of the prayers is interesting. There is no fixed formula laid down, but it is absolutely essential that the spirits should each be mentioned by name. By this means their help is invoked. At a tribal ceremony I noticed that Citimukulu always prayed with one of his senior *bakabilo* at his elbow to prompt him if he forgot one ancestral title out of the twenty to thirty dead chiefs to be called upon, and for a chief even to mention the names of his ancestors when walking to a ceremony was described to me as a form of prayer (*ukulumbula*). Headmen also call their ancestors by name when invoking them. Then again it is important that the dead should be named as having taught the particular activity upon which the living are about to engage, and this is especially the case at the tribal ceremonies. In fact one of the chief functions of this type of prayer, is, I think, to give traditional sanction to the gardening methods now practised and to confirm the people's belief in them by tracing their origin to the past. The words of one or two such prayers will illustrate what I mean. For instance, Mwamba, when invoking the *imipashi* at the beginning of his tree-cutting ceremony, prayed: 'We have come to you Great Mwambas.[1] It was you who left us the land. We beg for the power to work in it in the way you showed us you worked in the place from which you came (i.e. Lubaland). And we ourselves began to learn (i.e. how to cut trees) when we were still children, until at last we found we had learnt the way. We followed (lit. fell into) your words' &c. . . .[2] (Here follows the prayer for safety and success with the tree-cutting.) A similar reference to the *imipashi*, as teaching agriculture, was made by one of the 'wives of the relics', who told me she took first-fruits to the shrines of the ancestors with the words, 'We show the owners (i.e. of the food) who brought it with them from Buluba.'[3] All such prayers seem to give validity to the present methods of cultivation, and to pledge the ancestors to help descendants who are thus following in their footsteps. The form

---

[1] *Ba*—the plural of respect and also the plural indicating the number of dead chiefs.

[2] *Twaisa kuli imwe BaMwamba. Ni imwe mwatushile calo. Tulelomba uku-bomba imilimo, ifyo mwatulangile ifyo mwalecita uko mwatulile. Nga ifwe twata-lika ukusambilila twacili baice, twasuka twasambilila. Twaliponena amashiwi yenu.*

[3] *Tulelanga abene abafumine nafyo ku Buluba.*

of the prayer also emphasizes the right of the priest to officiate. He bases his claim to speak on lineage alone, and hence he usually calls the *imipashi* he is invoking by their kinship terms. For instance, some begin: 'You my mother's brothers and my grandfathers!' (*Mwe Bayama na Bashikulu!*); and I have twice heard a chief add a separate prayer to 'Our mothers' (*Banyinefwe*), that is to say, the ancestresses of the royal line. By such means the claims of the living on the dead are publicly stated, and also the rights of the headman or chief to the office he holds.

(*b*) *The blessing of the objects used.* Besides the initial prayers at the different ceremonies the chief object to be used in the subsequent economic activity, such as the axe for the tree-cutting or the seeds for the sowing, must be blessed. This is achieved by bringing it in contact with the magic power of sex. The axe or the seeds are given potency by being placed at the head of the bed (*ku mutwe*) on which the officiating priest and his head wife have intercourse on the night before the rite takes place. The magic effects of such an act are difficult to explain without a full analysis of the Bemba ideas on sex, procreation, and their contagious effects on fire, sacred objects, and on certain human beings. Suffice it to say that the sexual act is thought to make the body hot (*umubili uakava*) and 'bad' (*ukuba ne fibi*),[1] and that the individual is then thought unfit to approach the ancestral spirits or to have contact with any sacred object such as the chiefs' relics, unless he has been ritually purified. But, nevertheless, an act of intercourse between a man and his head wife, followed by this special purification, is the means by which magic potency is conferred on the object placed at the head of the bed, and in some inexplicable way the blessing of the *imipashi* themselves is thereby invoked. Natives, who were usually shy in discussing the magic aspects of sex, would give in explanation some such phrase as '*Ni kufunge mipashi*' ('It is to soften or propitiate the spirits'), and one added that the reason why the chief had such power of blessing the axe or seeds was 'because of his chieftainship' (*ubufumu*, the abstract principle of chieftainship). And of the object blessed, another informant stated that new qualities had been conferred on it 'on account of the chieftainship, because the chief lies on top of it' (*umulandu ua*

---

[1] A condition expressed by a number of technical terms such as *ukutetema* (to be ritually impure) or by euphemisms such as *ukuba na kantu* (to have some little thing wrong with you).

bufumu ico mfumu ilelalapo). The whole of this conception must be considered against the background of the people's belief in the supernatural powers of their chiefs, and the influence of his sexual capacities on the fertility of the land.[1]

(*c*) *The purification of the priest.* Since sex intercourse makes it impossible to approach the *imipashi* or to enter their shrines, the ritual purification of the officiating priest and his wife, after the blessing of the axe or seeds, is an essential act in each economic rite. It is one which is performed before every solemn prayer or sacrifice to the *imipashi*, before the founding of a new village, an inheritance ceremony, a death or the birth of twins, &c., either by the chief, the headman, or the commoner, as the case may be. In the case of a commoner or an ordinary headman, this rite of purification (*ukuwamya umubili*) is simple. The morning after the sexual act, the couple set on the fire the woman's marriage pot— a tiny clay pot made for her by her paternal aunt on her marriage —and they heat water in it. This the wife then pours over her husband's hands. Both then bathe in the river and return to the village, after which new fire must be lighted in the hut. Sex taboos are kept by the pair until the ceremony in question is over. In the case of the chief, and particularly the Citimukulu, this rite is, however, exceedingly complex. It involves the simultaneous ritual intercourse of the chief and the 'wife of the land' (*umukolo ua calo*), and the Cimba and the Cikutwe with their respective head wives in huts built specially for the purpose. Afterwards twelve or fifteen of the *bakabilo* must assist, each with his own hereditary part, in the purification ceremony and the lighting of the new fire. Without purifying his body the chief can never enter his *benye* house or use his powers over the land to the full, but the complication and expense of a rite which requires the simultaneous presence of so many officials is one of the reasons why the full ceremonial of tree-cutting or first-fruits described later is so rarely performed nowadays, when chiefs are impoverished and cannot always command the loyalty of their *bakabilo*.

(*d*) *The divination rite.* Except in the case of first-fruit rites, each ceremony, whether tree-cutting or blessing of seeds, is followed by some act of divination in which the intentions of the *imipashi* are revealed to their descendants. Here the element of individual doubt and uncertainty is apparent again. There are

[1] Cf. p. 249.

several methods of divination used. The blessing of the object is itself a preliminary test of the kind since the dreams of the officiating priest as he lies, with the axe or the seeds at the head of his bed, are taken as omens. 'When you have fallen asleep the *imipashi* come to you and you dream good things. If you dream bad things you will not succeed.'[1] The dreams of a chief on this or other occasions are very important for the land. But additional divination rites are sometimes added, particularly in the case of tree-cutting. Hunting ordeals commonly follow the tree-cutting ceremonies, especially in Bisa country, and Citimukulu sent out a man with a gun and a couple of cartridges to try the luck of the land after his *ukutema* ceremony in 1934. The people are delighted and unusually sure of success if a female animal is killed, and say, 'We have found a grindstone' (*twasange libwe*), while if a male animal is killed, that is nearly as good an omen and is described as finding an axe (the man's food-producing implement). If no animal is seen at the nets then the tree-cutting goes on, but without the same hopes of good fortune. 'We go to try to see if we are going to work well' is a typical description of the procedure, and the whole use of the divination rite reflects the anxieties and hazards of traditional agricultural processes already described.

The Economic Cycle.

This analysis of the main elements of the Bemba agricultural ritual must lead to a description of the individual ceremonies and the extent to which they were still performed:

(a) *The tree-cutting rite.* In old-fashioned villages the headman performs the tree-cutting ceremony with all the inhabitants of the village accompanying him. In modern communities he tends to do the rite alone, or with his near relatives only, while the rest rely on such magic charms as they possess for their protection, and are described as 'cutting trees anyhow' (*cikomekome*). The older form of the rite will be described, since it is still performed in however abbreviated a version in the majority of Bemba communities. In such settlements the headman, when he has decided to begin the clearing of the bush and fixed the site of his garden, calls the elders of the village and his own immediate relatives to

---

[1] *Nga mulala mipashi isuma iaisa, mwalota fisuma. Mulote ifishiweme, fishilungama.* (Bad dreams are those concerning snakes, lions, fire, &c.)

his hut in the evening. Here they sit on the floor in silence while he prays to the *imipashi* for blessing on the next day's work. Both in the six texts I collected during the course of actual ceremonies and in a number of others I took down from informants, the same requests were made. The spirits are asked to protect the tree-cutters when they climb, to give food as the result of clearing the bush, to free the people from illness, and to give them children and peace. Mwamba's prayer on the night before the ceremony is a good example: 'You, our Spirits, now we want food. You help us mightily to cut the trees with vigour. That is food! To-morrow I shall go and cut the tree branches. He who climbs the trees let the soles of his feet stick to the tree-trunk, and let dead wood fall to the ground only; and all the snakes that come out of hollow stems let them run into their holes; and so also the wasps that may swarm out of the tree. And then another thing! Those locusts that are here in the land, it would be good if you kept them far away, because if those locusts eat the food of we human beings so that there is nothing left to eat, then we shall all die of hunger. And then if we die of hunger, there will be no one left to praise you, you Spirits.'[1] Prayers said by an ordinary headman tended to be simpler, but made the same requests. All such rites of blessing are described commonly by the older men as 'begging for an axe' (*ukulombe sembe*).

During the prayers the headman's axe lies on the floor of his hut in the centre of the group of kinsmen. At night it is put at the head of his bed. In the morning the purification ceremony is performed by the headman and his wife before the village is awake, and then the same elders assemble in the hut to pray for further blessings on the day's work. After this the rest of the villagers gather together and the whole party goes off to the site of the headman's new *icitemene*. At this juncture the element of doubt as to the choice of the patch to be cleared is first manifested. The trees must be blessed as well as the axe, that is to say the produc-tivity of the soil must be assured by supernatural help as well as

[1] *Mwe mipashi, nomba tulefwaye cakulya. Mutwafwilishye ukukoma na maka. E kulya! Mailo nkesa kukuteme miti. Ulenina ku miti lukasa lukambate miti ne cileka conse cipone panshi ceka; ne nsoka shyonse shifume ku mpako, shingile kumendo; na malonda yafume ku miti. Kabili fimakanta filya fyaisa muno calo, cilingile ukuti mwafitandula ukutali, pantu fimakanta filya nga fyalya filyo fya fwe bantu, tapali cakulya. Ukuti bonse twafwe ku nsala. Nomba nga twafwa ku nsala tapali ua kumulumbula, mwe mipashi. (Mwamba's village, 13. v. 33.)*

the safety of the workers. For this purpose the first tree (usually an *umufungo* tree)[1] is ritually cut, preferably by a grandson of the headman, who sits on the ground meanwhile and again invokes the *imipashi*, in much the same terms as before. The chopping of the first tree with the blessed axe is the signal for the beginning of the work, and the villagers swarm up the trees shouting their *ukutema* cries (cf. p. 291).

A third invocation of the spirits takes place in the evening, when thanks must be returned to the spirits for their help. This ceremony is known in the capital as 'to return the work' (*ukubweshye milimo*), or 'to return thanks for the food-basket' (*ukulubulo lupe*), but merely as 'to ask a blessing' (*ukupala*) in a commoner's village. This time the spirits are told that every one is safely home from the tree-cutting. They are begged to continue their help during the year.

The following day is kept as a day of rest on which the spirits are supposed to come and continue the work begun by their descendants. I never met a native who genuinely expected to find additional cut branches on the ground next day, but many of them spoke of the custom in a reverent way, and only the chief, Mukuikile, something of a sceptic after many years spent as a cook in a European household in Livingstone, said outright with a quizzical smile: 'We say "Let the spirits cut the trees there" (i.e. on the site). But they don't ever lop off any branches. At least we have never seen it. They make fools of us! We have never been there when it happens.'[2] Nevertheless, the day of rest is generally kept, and in some parts of the country this day is used for the hunting test already mentioned.

At the capitals the tree-cutting ceremonies are similar to those in the villages, with the exception that the axe used for the ritual cutting must be forged new for the purpose, and that it must lie overnight in the chief's *benye* shrine instead of at the head of his bed. But the whole rite is, of course, invested with greater solemnity and pomp, at any rate when 'the trees of the land' are cut.[3] At the ceremonies I saw, both at Citimukulu's and at

---

[1] E. B. H. Goodall points out that *ukufunga* means to propitiate or bless (op. cit., p. 28).

[2] *Tuleti mipashi itemako. Nomba tabalelwishye miti. Tatumweneko. Baletucito bulwelelwele! Tatusangapo!* (Mukuikile, ix. 33.)

[3] The full ceremony at which the *bakabilo* are present and the *benye* shrines entered (cf. p. 360).

Paramount Chief going to tree-cutting ceremony. Tree-cutting ceremony, Citimukulu's village, 1933. Note the Chief in patterned cloth in centre and procession of villagers armed with bows and guns.

Mwamba's villages in 1933, I was impressed with the seriousness and reverence of the prayers offered by the chief on the night before the tree-cutting. Citimukulu sat inside one of his cere-monial huts with the most important *bakabilo* around him, his head wife opposite, and the new axe lying in one of the big court eating-baskets wrapped in the length of calico to be given to the spirits. The chief began suddenly to pray, calling out the names of about twenty ancestors, prompted by the Citikafula who sat next him. He asked for the blessing on the work and for peace and well-being. After the words had been said the *bakabilo* took the axe and cloth, and walked quickly to the *benye* shrines with four wrinkled old women—the 'wives of the relics' hobbling behind to unbar the log barricades of the sacred huts. They disappeared inside, followed by the chief *bakabilo*,[1] while the rest of the party crouched on the ground outside, clapping as a sign of respect. Then all returned to make obeisance on the ground outside the chief's hut, each *mukabilo* rolling on his back in turn while his ceremonial name was shouted by his fellows with more clapping of the hands. This alternating obeisance to the dead chiefs at the *beni* huts and to their living representatives in front of the royal dwelling is characteristic of all the Bemba court ritual.

Next morning, before dawn, the chief's big wooden war-drum (*icinkumbi*) began to sound, and his court-singers and praisers (*balukaluka*) stood up on the mound behind his enclosure shouting praise-songs and calling to the people. Every one gathered round excitedly. Citimukulu appeared from his hut with his ceremonial axe over one shoulder. He was hoisted on to a servant's back and set off down the path, while his wives knelt on either side giving the ululation salute. The rest of the party then set off at the double, drums going, rattles shaking, the blind singer wailing, and the children of the village running ahead shrieking with delight. The blessed axe was carried in front of the chief by one of his courtiers and his hereditary bow by another. It was a gay and animated scene. Citimukulu was greeted with shouts and obeis-ance at each group of huts we passed in a two-hour walk, or rather run. Once arrived at the tree-cutting site, a small sapling

---

[1] Technically speaking, only the Cimba, Munuca, Citikafula, Katenda, Mulombwelua can enter the *benye* shrines with the *bamukabenye*, but a quarrel between the Citimukulu and the Cimba had prevented the latter attending to purify the chief, and therefore the latter could not enter his own relic shrine, and the Munuca remained away as a sign of protest.

umufungo was quickly selected by the *bakabilo*, and Citimukulu sat down beside it praying yet again to the tribal *imipashi* by name and adding, 'Give us work! Let the axe cut cleanly through the trees (i.e. not slip). And the people let them not fall, no! May they not cut themselves with their axes! And then another thing, you great chiefs, now that the locusts have come they are eating the food. You help us! You chase them away!'[1] Then there followed a discussion with the local headman as to whether some other chief's spirit should be called upon, and the name of one of the first Mwambas (Amansenga), said to have died upon this very spot, was remembered. Then the prayers began again while Citimukulu's grandson knelt by the chosen sapling, axe in hand, waiting to chop: 'We have come to look for porridge. You help us with the work. May we all eat and be satisfied! May we fill our granaries to the brim. Now the locusts have come, you our ancestors help us. You the spirits of the land help us, you who died in this country. Let not the axe cut the people, and may their feet grip firmly onto the tree. To fall is bad! You our spirits, help us. May the food be crammed into our granaries tightly.'[2] As the words ceased, the royal grandson cut down the *umufungo* with a stroke, and the young men present began to climb the trees. They worked half the day, and returned in a triumphant, if weary, procession, the chief being greeted with the shouts used for returning warriors at his village outskirts, or the more usual salutation, *Mwakomene!* (i.e. 'You have cut').

In the evening the chief himself went to return thanks at the *benye* shrine to the beating of the *icinkumbi* drum. The *bamukabenye* opened the doors of the huts and sat each side of the specially raised door-step, while Citimukulu slowly lowered his great bulk to the ground and rolled on his back before his ancestors' shrine as his people do to him. This is the *ukulubulo lupe* or *kubweshya lupe*—the return of thanks. After it came the day of rest, filled in this instance with excited preparations for Citimukulu's move to

---

[1] *Tupeni milimo! Isembe ilungame mu muti! Abantu tekuti bapone, yo! Belakoma ne sembe. Kabili, mwe shyamfumu, nomba fimakanta fyaisa filelya fyakulya. Mutwafweko! Mufitamfye! . . .*

[2] *Twaisa ku kufwayo bwali. Mutwafweko milimo. Tuleikuta bonse! Tuleisushya amatala! Nomba fimakanta nafisa, mwe mipashi twafweko. Bashimatongo twafweko, mwe bafwile mwi calo. Isembe tailekoma bantu, no lukasa luleikata ku muti. Cakupona cabipa! Mwe mipashi yonse twafweko. Filepaka ku butala.* (Citimukulu, 3. iv. 33.) The present Citimukulu is not an eloquent man, and this prayer was much less poetical than some I heard uttered by Mwamba and the late Nkula.

the bush. This is a definite stage in the year's activities. The chief and his court move to temporary grass huts (*nsakwe*) built near the new *icitemene*, and here they live for a month or more, watching the garden-work, calling up tribute labour, and conducting the business of the tribe while seated at the edge of the garden site. Thus the phrase 'the chief has gone to the grass shelters' (*mfumu yaya ku nsakwe*) denotes a definite change in court life. In the old days a special official, Mulewa Cimfwembe, who was responsible for carrying the blessed axe to the tree-cutting ceremony, lived apart in a grass hut, keeping sex taboos, and levying dues on all the animals killed by the hunters in the neighbourhood, until the time came to fire the Paramount's gardens. He was described as 'watching the trees of the country' (*ukulindile miti ye calo*), and was highly rewarded by the chiefs for his services. But the Paramount's own move out into the bush seemed to me to have no ritual purpose, but rather an administrative one.

In the old days it can be seen that the *ukutema* rite at the capital must have had an important effect on the whole process of clearing the bush. With its sacred ceremony at the royal relic-house, its procession of drums and singers and tree-cutters into the bush, and its assembly of the notables of the district, the day must have given a terrific impetus to the work of the whole *icalo*. Besides this, it provided a large labour force for communal work on the royal garden and was associated with the transaction of tribal business by the *bakabilo* summoned to the capital. Even nowadays some of the inspiriting results of the rite can be seen, even though the ceremony seems to be a shadow of its former magnificence. The present Citimukulu's cutting of 'the trees of the land' in 1934, after a lapse of some years, certainly raised the enthusiasm and hope of the people. The ceremony was discussed in the neighbouring villages through which I happened to be travelling both before and afterwards. The statement that 'They' (the royal plural) had prayed, and that the chief was making big gardens this year, seemed to cause pleasure and to give encouragement. It meant fuller granaries at the capital, and therefore more food for the councillors and tribute labourers, but also, I judged from the reverent tone used, the coming of good luck—a return to the 'good old days' when the *imipashi* blessed the people, according to the popular legend, and everything went well.

As a contrast, it is worth considering conditions in the village of

Mwamba, the second greatest Bemba chief but one, who lives about ten miles from the white centre of Kasama, where his young men go to work. Here I also saw an *ukutema* rite, but only the old men participated. The boys looked derisively on while the chief made obeisance before his ancestors' shrines, and they only joined the subsequent tree-cutting reluctantly because they were interested by my presence and wanted to have the right to drink the beer provided for the workers on their return. These were youths who despised agriculture as a pursuit fit only for the old, and laughed at everything commonly known as 'the things of the past' (*ifintu fya kale.*) Their conduct distressed the old men exceedingly, and the comments passed with shrugs and in asides were instructive. They showed the complete association in the Bemba mind between the chief's political authority and his power of blessing. If Mwamba had been a 'great chief', the argument ran, he would have been able to control his men. That he was not showed that the spirits did not favour him and that the land had gone 'hard'. It was hardly likely that the royal garden would prosper, therefore, or, of course, the rest of the *icalo*. Elsewhere individuals still seemed to pray to the *imipashi* before tree-cutting, although some Roman Catholics have begun to cross themselves instead, or as well, but the integrating function of the chief's or headman's ceremony is evidently very much decreased.

(*b*) *Firing the gardens.* The firing of the piled branches, the next act of the economic year, is also ritualized, but the ceremonial is not public in any sense, either at the capital or in an ordinary village, and most commoners were unable to give me an account of what happened at the firing of the chief's gardens. In this instance they wait for the *mfumu's* signal to fire their gardens, but not for news of the ceremony performed then. The rite depends on the Bemba belief in the danger of contaminated fire, that is to say, fire that has been touched by any one ceremonially impure. If such fire is considered harmful to the life of a young child, or a chief, and a bar to any approach to the *imipashi*, it is not unnatural that the people should believe it necessary to light their branch piles with new fire, that is to say, made with fire-sticks or matches. A commoner whom I saw fire his gardens, brought matches, lit a torch of grass, spat into the air, and cried out, 'Now you fire burn well, and let us go in peace.'[1] A headman should purify himself

---

[1] *We mulilo ulepyafye cisuma! Tuende no mutende!*

Sacred relic shrine at Mwamba's village. Note the elephant tusks piled in front of the door.

Shrine built on the site of a dead chieftainess's hut. Mukukamfumu, 1931. Note the red cloth offering hung inside.

and light new fire in his hut before going out to fire his garden, an act for which the other villagers wait, but do not participate in. At the capital the headman of the village (*umwine mushi*), an official with entirely ritual functions and placed in charge of one of the chief's sacred fires, must extinguish his own fire overnight, borrow new fire from a second sacred hearth in the morning, purify himself with the aid of his wife, and go out with a glowing cinder of the royal fire to light the gardens. I never saw this rite carried out at the capital, and its privacy, as in the case of all ceremonial appertaining to the chief's fire, was stressed. The ritualizing of this particular economic process seemed to me to depend on the beliefs in the nature of fire and its sacred properties rather than on anything connected with the agricultural activity itself.

(*c*) *Sowing ceremonies.* Among the Bemba sowing ceremonies are insignificant compared to the tree-cutting rites. The staple millet seeds are not blessed at all, although they are doctored usually with the *icibyalilo* magic. Prayers are only offered to the *imipashi* in the case of subsidiary crops, and not by any means for all of these. Pumpkins, cow-peas, Livingstone potatoes, Kaffir corn, maize, and the *amankolobwe* are those usually given as the list.[1] Of course, the ritual may have been fuller in the old days. The Bisa and the Ushi describe a ceremony similar to those of a number of the Southern Bantu, in which the headman or the chief blesses or doctors handfuls of seeds given him by each of the women of the community, and these specially treated seeds are mixed with the rest to be sown. But among the Bemba I only collected one account of a rite of this sort. The *bakabilo* tell of a sowing ceremony at the Paramount's court following the special tree-cutting rite performed by Mulewa Cimfwembe in the old days (cf. p. 371). They say that after the latter had 'watched the trees of the land', and fire had been set to the royal garden, another hereditary official, the Kamenge, took his place to watch the freshly sown seeds until the ripening of the crop. He also kept sex taboos and lived apart in a grass shelter during this time. This act was known as 'watching the seeds of the chief'. It has evidently not been performed for two reigns at least. Another lost sowing

[1] Compare the list of crops for which the first-fruit rites are performed. It will be seen that Junod's suggestion that such rites remain associated with the older African crops is largely borne out (cf. p. 20), but maize is, of course, a more recent introduction, possibly included as it is sown and also ripens at the same time as most of the others listed above.

rite was connected with one of the most sacred of the Paramount's
babenye, a girdle made of the skin cut from the abdomen of a legendary figure, Mwase, said to have been killed for committing adultery with the Citimukulu's wife. It has now long since rotted
away, but living men tell of occasions when the relic was taken
from the *benye* house, bound round the waist of a young virgin, the
maternal niece of Munuca, the greatest *mukabilo*. The girl then
danced across the garden of the chief, scattering blessed sorghum
seeds broadcast, while the Citimukulu and his *bakabilo* followed
behind. This story, always told with great delight, seemed to me
a sign that the sowing rites must have had greater importance
formerly than at the present day.

Nowadays, the blessing of the seeds at a commoner's village is
done in typical fashion by standing them in a calabash at the end
of the headman's bed. In the morning, after the usual purification
ceremony, they are sown in the headman's garden, all the villagers
coming to help.[1] But I never saw such a rite performed myself,
and I noticed that some natives were doubtful as to which seeds
actually had to be blessed. For instance, of 10 informants, all gave
pumpkins in their list, 8 Livingstone potatoes, 7 Kaffir corn, 6
maize, 5 *amankolobwe*. At the capitals, however, the sowing rites
still persist. At Nkula's village in 1930 Kaffir-corn seeds in a huge
gourd were stood overnight in the *benye* house and were sown next
day on the chief's *mputa* by all the women of the village. The
sowing ceremonies evidently used to give the people a sign when
to start planting their crops, a matter on which skilled guidance
is often needed, but it is doubtful whether they were ever occasions
of big tribal gatherings of rejoicing as in the case of tree-cutting
or harvest rites.

(*d*) *First-fruit ceremonies.* Some form of first-fruits ceremony
seems to be performed in all typical Bantu societies, and in these
there are certain common elements recognizable. But the symbolism of these rites is often exceedingly complex, and varies
widely from area to area. The ceremonies also tend to become
the occasion of big tribal gatherings such as the army rites of
the Zulu since they inevitably occur at the plentiful season of the

[1] One informant told me his father, a headman, always blessed the seeds of
all the villagers and gave them each a handful to mix with their crops, but in
most instances now it seems that the headman merely blesses and sows his own
seeds. In Bisa districts, such as that near Shiwa Dandu, the original form of
the rite seems to be more often adhered to.

year. This combination of functions makes the question of inter-
pretation even more difficult.

Some writers have described the ceremonies as being essentially
a ritual which marks the change of the season and the beginning
of new forms of social activity. Thus Bryant calls the Zulu rite
umkosi, 'the stepping into the year', and Junod describes the
complex *luma* ceremonies of the Thonga as typical *rites de passage*.[1]
Of course, the harvest in any of these societies does actually mean
a complete change in ordinary village life, but among the Bemba
I heard no specific statement of this fact in any of the explanations
of the ritual, nor is there any great ceremony of public rejoicing
at the time except on occasions when a special harvest rite is
carried out at the capital, or when the *ulupepo lukalamba* has been
initiated. But the element of risk, thought to be associated with
the beginning of the new food-supply, is prominent here as it is
in other Bantu societies. The Thonga, according to Junod, consider that there is some magic danger attached to the eating of the
new grain, and the name of the ceremony—*luma*—comes from
ukuluma, 'to bite'. He suggests the taboo on the new food may be
due, in part, to fear of quarrelling—which is an actual risk when
beer starts to flow freely—or to a desire to avoid jealousy by preventing one man from beginning his new supplies before his
neighbours are able to do so.[2] The doctoring of the chief against
this danger of eating the new foods and the various rites designed
to remove the taboo on the new harvest occur again and again
throughout this southern area.

Among the Bemba I never heard a native state that there was
any magic danger attached to eating the new food, and the name
of the rite, *ukuposela* (to offer or place in front of some one), describes the essential element in their first-fruits—the recognition
of the prerogatives of chief and ancestral spirits which will be
described below. But it is evidently considered important that
each crop should be ritually treated immediately the first specimen
in any district ripens. There is no waiting till the end of the
harvest for the ceremony. In fact it is reckoned so necessary to

[1] A. T. Bryant, *Zulu–English Dictionary*, 1905; H. Junod, *The Life of a South
African Tribe*, 1929, vol. i, pp. 394–404.

[2] Cf. Junod, loc. cit., p. 394. *Report of the Commission on Native Law and Custom*,
1883, pp. 525–6 and 531–2. Cf. also M. Gluckmann, 'First-fruit Ceremonies of
South-Eastern Bantu', *Africa*, vol. xi, no. 1, p. 34, for stress on the danger of
quarrelling at harvest, and for other interesting interpretations of the Zulu ritual.

'offer' each crop as soon as it becomes edible that three separate
ceremonies are performed for the different new foods, rather than
that either should be postponed till the time of the main harvest.
Thus pumpkins, Livingstone potatoes, and maize, which are the
first to ripen, are offered to the spirits together, then *mwangwe*, the
quick-growing millet, then Kaffir corn, cow-peas, and *amankolobwe*.[1] Asked what would happen if a man began to eat his own
new crops before the ceremony had begun, most natives merely
said that it was bad to eat *cilyelye*, 'anyhow', i.e. without the right
ceremony or etiquette, but two or three added that a man would
be angry if he saw his neighbour eating new millet before he had
any himself, and that this would be bad. The Bemba thus express
a fear somewhat similar to that of the Thonga. But the ultimate
dread is evidently that of angering the spirits and not fellow men,
and older Bemba told me that failure to perform the ceremony
means that the land is 'hard', lions catch the people, snakes bite
them, and they fall off the trees, and that game becomes scarce—
all evils believed to follow an injury to the spirits or a failure to
give a living chief his due.

This brings us, I think, to another aspect of the ceremony which
is prominent in most Bantu first-fruit rites, that is to say, the
symbolic recognition of the prerogatives of the owners of the
land, the chief and his dead ancestors. In some areas the chief is
given special tribute at harvest, or beer is brewed for him when
he travels the country. Alternatively his rights are proved by a
ritual testing of the new food followed by his family, the tribal
councillors, or the elders, all tasting in order of precedence.[2]
Among the Nguni peoples the chief in his turn symbolizes his
function as the giver by breaking a gourd and scattering the new
food over the assembled peoples.[3]

Among the Bemba, this recognition of the rights of the living
or dead chiefs at the time of harvest is the central act of the ceremony. In fact one man, asked why it was bad to eat the new food

---

[1] Has this series of ceremonies any similarity to the distinction made by Kidd
between the little festival, when green crops are offered, and the great festival
which follows it when grain is ritually treated, among the S. E. Bantu? Kidd,
The Essential Kafir, 1925, p. 269.

[2] e.g. in Bechuanaland. Willoughby, *Soul of the Bantu*, 1928, p. 229: among
the Thonga, Junod, op. cit., vol. i, p. 394.

[3] Kidd, loc. cit.; T. Shooter, *The Kafirs of Natal and the Zulu Country*,
1857, pp. 26–7, 392.

without offering it to the dead, exclaimed: 'It is a crime. It is to steal';[1] and one of the 'Wives of the Relics' prayed at Mwamba's court: 'You Spirits, the people are eating your food gluttonously. They are eating your food without respect. We ask for mercy!...'[2] In the simplest cases, merely to show the new crop (*ukulanga*) to the headman is enough. This I saw done once when a handful of self-sown millet ripened early in the garden. It was not considered a real crop, but the woman who brought her basket to the headman said she did it 'just to show it because Lesa gave it to us. It was just a case of luck.'[3] In the case of the planted crops, however, the first head of grain to ripen or gourd that swells must be brought by its owner to the headman, and the latter blesses it in the usual way, places it at the end of his bed at night, and lastly carries it to the village *ulufuba* or spirit shrine, where it is given to the spirits. When the first new gourds are ripening it is common to see slices of pumpkin exposed in every tiny shrine when travelling from village to village. In the case of *mwangwe*, the headman's wife sometimes makes a dough (*umufuba*) of the new flour, and this is carried by a small boy to the *ulufuba*. All these are the rites known as *ukuposela*. At such ceremonies the priest apparently asks for nothing concrete. He merely, as he says, shows the food to the *imipashi* whose property it ultimately is, and tells them baldly that the food is now ripe. A prayer I heard was as follows: 'We have eaten the new food! May we go in peace! The new food is ripe now. We want to eat it now!'[4]

No tribute is given to the living chief at this time, although of course he gets more beer and grain at harvest time than any other. But the conception that tribute is due to the chief in virtue of his ownership of the land, seems to me to be reflected in the idea that ritual offerings must be made to the spirits at harvest time. The resemblance even extends to the belief that just as a man who gets an unusually good haul of fish or kills much game is bound to give a share to the chief, so when there is an unusually good harvest, it is necessary that a special offering should be made to the

[1] *Ni bupulumushi—Ni kuiba.*
[2] *Mwe shyamfumu! bantu balefunuka fyakulya fyenu. Nabalye fyakulya fyenu cilyelye. Twapapata!*
[3] *Kulangafye, ico Lesa atupela. Ni kushyukafye.* Self-sown Kaffir corn can be eaten without a ceremony among the Bamangwato. Willoughby, op. cit., p. 234.
[4] *Twalye cilyo cipya. Tuende no mutende? Fyakulya fipya mu calo. Tulefwaya tulye!*

spirits, and even when the foods of the bush—caterpillars, mushrooms, or ants—are very plentiful, a special *mukabilo* (Munuca)
performs an *ukuposela* ceremony to offer 'the owners of the land'
the fruits of the bush 'because they have given us a lot this
year'.

At the capital, according to the usual custom, the new foods are
exposed in the *benye* house instead of being placed at the end of the
headman's bed. They are afterwards cooked in the *kamitembo*,
the sacred kitchen (cf. p. 148), and then ritually tasted by the
chief, his children, and the *bamukabenye*. This is the act known as
ukusumata, 'to taste', as distinct from *ukuposela*, 'to offer'. It was
possibly done in commoners' villages formerly, but now only at
the chief's court.

A more impressive form of the *ukusumata* takes place at times of
great plenty at the capital,[1] when beer made from the new Kaffir
corn is ritually tasted by the chief and all his *bakabilo*—a symbolic
presentation of the hierarchical order of Bemba society. For this
special rite (*ukusumata masaka*) the *bakabilo* must be summoned,
and the chief purified. Beer is first brewed by the head wife in the
kamitembo, and after purification the Paramount and his wife sleep
here, keeping sex taboos till the beer is brewed. This is known as
ukulindilo musunga, 'to watch for the yeast'.[2] During this time flour
made from the new crop has been exposed in the *benye* house for the
blessing of the *imipashi*, and some of this is then sprinkled on the
sacred beer, to be drunk by the Paramount and the chief *bakabilo*
inside the *benye* house, and by the rest in order of seniority outside.
After this, the Munuca rubs some of the sacred flour on the chests
of the *bakabilo* present, and thus makes them free to celebrate
first-fruit rites of their own in their own villages. Later a basket
must be carried to the shrines of Kafula, a chief who died of small-
pox and was therefore buried alone near the present capital. If
liked, the *ulupepo lukalamba* can then begin. Such a ceremony is
obviously one of the elaborate alternative forms of the economic
rites described above. It was performed apparently three times in
Sampa's reign and three times in Cikwanda's. The present Citi-

---

[1] 'When the land is boiling over'—*Icalo calilabila*.

[2] Compare the function of the Mulemba Cimfwembe in 'watching the trees
of the land' and of the Kamenge in 'watching the chief's seeds'. The *cishiko*,
the lighter of the chief's sacred fire, has also to 'watch' the new fire when a
village is being built. There seems to me some protective power in the presence
of a man keeping sex taboos.

Harvest ceremony. Bringing beer to the chiefs. Npika district, 1933.
Note beer in gourd and man about to roll on his back to salute the dread
chiefs.

Shrines to ancestral spirits built outside a village.

mukulu tried to organize it again in 1933, but hunger forced his
wives to eat up the supply of Kaffir corn he had planted for the
purpose, and he was never able to collect sufficient grain to make
the beer.

(*e*) *Thanksgiving rites.* In Bisa districts a special rite of thanksgiving as distinct from the *ukuposela* is performed in August
to September or after the main millet harvest has been reaped.
This is known as *ukupelo bwalua kuli mfumu*, 'to give the (dead)
chiefs beer'. For instance, near Shiwa Dandu in August 1933
I found special fire-stands (*amafwasa*) had been built in the
open near three village spirit shrines especially for the heating
of water for this beer. The villagers gathered round the shrines,
men one side and women the other, and the headman began
to call on the chiefs of the land: 'You, Sir Matipa, Sir Maluma
Lubande, you, the owner of the chiefs of the Bisa. You know
your companions, all the other chiefs. Call them that they come
to drink our beer. We have come to pray for life. Make us go in
peace. We have brewed beer. We have brought it to you to honour
you. And then we beg for peace. May we eat food! We pray for
porridge. May the blood of animals be seen too! Save us from
the locusts'—a pause—'Now I have finished.'

After this the wife of the headman poured hot water on the big
gourd of beer standing by the spirit hut and she drank, afterwards
rolling on the ground in the royal salute 'because she was the
owner who brewed the beer' (*ni mwine ualongo bwalua*). She was
followed by the rest of the village in order of age,[1] and dancing and
singing began round the shrines, each performer rolling on the
ground as to a chief.

Such a ceremonial drinking at the spirit shrines may have been
much more common in all Bemba villages formerly. I have heard
of it happening after a hunt at the nets, and have seen gourd
beer-dippers lying in spirit shrines ready for a beer drink. But
in this Bisa district, harvest ceremonies of this kind are performed
to this day, and they are followed in some cases by a ritual hunt
to discover the will of the spirits.

All such harvest or first-fruit rites must be considered as a
means of sacralizing the gathering of the new harvest, encouraging
the community to handle the essential food supplies with reverence, or emphasizing, as Radcliffe-Browne would say, its 'social

---

[1] Except the headman, who may only drink in the village.

value'. But in Bemba society the ritual stress on the legal and political prerogatives of the chief is also prominent at the first-fruits ceremonies, and the harvest, as well as the tree-cutting, can be made the occasion of a big display of the Paramount's power.

(*f*) *Rain ritual.* Prayers for rain are rarely necessary in this area as the supply is usually ample, but when they occur the Citimu-kulu is alone responsible. I never heard of a territorial chief or a headman praying for rain, or an *yanga* asked to provide it by magic. The only means of obtaining rain is apparently to send an ox to the chiefs' burial grove in charge of one of the royal undertakers, and the ShiMwalule there sacrifices the beast at the shrine in the grove. One such sacrifice was apparently performed in 1930.

To conclude, the magico-religious rites of the Bemba were certainly an integral part of their whole economic system. The ceremonies gave an impetus to their ordinary agricultural activities, and enabled the chief to organize their efforts more effectively, and thus to support the whole machinery of tribal government. The performance of the ritual constantly emphasized the supernatural powers of the chief, both in his own person and by his right of access to the tribal spirits. On this deeply-seated belief in the attributes of their *mfumu*, economic incentives and the use of land ultimately depended. It is this faith which has been weakened nowadays with pronounced effects on the whole morale of the tribe, as far as agriculture is concerned. How far Christian ritual has taken the place of the old agricultural ceremonies I do not know. I have seen natives cross themselves before tree-cutting and sowing, and I believe that some missions hold church services for the blessing of the seeds, but it will remain a fact that the old Bemba ceremonial of ancestor worship put the control of the religious rites into the hands of the political and administrative authority of the tribe, while those of the Christian churches do not, and cannot, do the same, since no big chiefs have yet accepted Christianity.

CHAPTER XVIII

LABOUR AND TIME

I HAVE now described the chief economic activities of the Bemba—agriculture, fishing, and hunting—the pleasures and anxieties connected with them, and the body of empirical knowledge which guides the people in their work. But the whole question of food production has still to be discussed from the labour point of view. Where land is as plentiful as it is in this area, the amount of ground a man can cultivate obviously depends on the labour he can command, the annual sequence of his different activities, and the whole system of economic co-operation by which garden and other work is carried out. Less obviously, but equally certainly, production also depends on the people's economic rhythm, their habits of work, and their method of reckoning time.

Here I should say at once that my observations on the use of time by native cultivators are far from complete. It is difficult, of course, to calculate exactly the time and energy expended on any kind of work which is not subject to industrial conditions—regular hours, output, wages, &c.—but with primitive people who have no conception of a regular working day, and who do not thus calculate by fixed time units, the task is even harder. It would require a specialist study by some one familiar with the economic calendar and methods of work of the Bemba, who was able to concentrate on this particular problem by means of records of individual activities and daily diaries. This I was never able to do for long enough in any one place. I have, however, given such material as I have, both because of the practical importance of this subject and also because it is a sphere in which anthropologists have so far done very little work. I believe my observations on the division of labour, seasonal calendar, &c., are adequate, but the records of daily activities (Appendix, Table E) were only taken in two villages, and then for very short periods.

Division of Labour.

Briefly speaking, there is no specialization of labour in this area except on a basis of sex. Handicrafts—such as basket-making, iron-work, and pottery—are chiefly in the hands of a few individuals, who are reckoned to have special skill in this direction. Iron-work is definitely a hereditary craft, but such specialists are very few in number. None of these craftsmen or women are employed whole time. They merely take a day off now and then to ply their trade, whenever any one can be found to employ them. Our problem is therefore to study the organization of agriculture, hunting, and fishing rather than different crafts.

The sex division of labour has already been indicated in the descriptive accounts of the different activities. This information is given in tabular form below for the convenience of readers of this section.

Food Production

Men	Women
Tree-cutting. Sowing. Fencing. Hoeing. Hunting and fishing (nets, spears, and poisoning). Collecting honey.	Branch-piling. Sowing. Harvesting. Hoeing. Fishing (poisoning method). Collecting bush foods.

Domestic Work

	Cooking. Brewing. Fetching water. Mudding floors. Collecting firewood. Making salt and 'soda'.

Other Activities

Building huts and granaries (cutting stakes, mudding walls, thatching). Path-making and clearing. Making furniture, musical instruments, &c. Baskets. Fish traps. Mats (non-specialized). Ironwork. Sewing. Laundering. Barkcloth (formerly).	Hut-making (preparing clay for walls and whitewashing). Path-cleaning. Pottery.

It will be seen from this table that the only activities for which men are absolutely essential are: tree-cutting, fencing, house-making, hunting, and fishing; although the heavy hoeing should, properly speaking, be men's work rather than women's—that is to say, the men usually hoe up the grass and other roots (*ukusapike fisapi*) and the women follow and cover up the upturned roots with earth (*ukushikila*). It must be noted, however, that there is no strong taboo preventing a man doing a woman's work or vice versa, such as is common among so many primitive peoples. Women do not cut trees and hunt, because they are physically unfitted to do so,

and men do not willingly cook, because it is a woman's occupation.
On the other hand, men do most of the women's agricultural work,
when performing their tribute labour for the chief (including
harvesting and piling branches), and it is common to find a man
cooking for the chief when the latter is travelling through the
country, since by this means he avoids the dangers of impure
contact with his cooking-fire.   In the same way women try to
fence gardens now, however inefficiently, and near Kasama I saw
an emancipated woman mudding the walls of her hut instead of
a man. This conduct was thought amusing and rather daring, but
not definitely wrong. There is no doubt that the rigid sex dicho-
tomy of labour based on magic beliefs, which is characteristic of
some primitive societies, does not now exist among the Bemba,
and all the handicrafts, such as basket-making and mat-making,
could probably be taught to the women without much protest.

Organization of Labour.

(a) *The family.* The essential economic unit is the individual
household, since each husband makes a garden for each of his
wives and builds her a granary, but just as each family shares
supplies with the other householders in the matrilocal group, so
their agricultural labour is done in co-operation. This is particularly so as regards the big millet gardens. During the early
years of married life a young couple reckon to cultivate their
village beds more or less alone, but the parties of men who go out
together to cut trees or fence gardens usually consist of a father-
in-law with his sons-in-law, and possibly young sons or maternal
nephews under marriageable age. Young men like to work together, and therefore the men who have married daughters of the
same household often make gardens near each other. The size of
the group varies. In the old days it is probable that such a unit
included four or five men and some boys, allowing for the inclusion
of one or two slaves which was apparently the number usually
owned by a rich commoner. In an old-fashioned village of to-day
the team would be somewhat smaller, but would still include one
or two sons-in-law, either working on their father-in-law's garden
or camping near him in grass shelters at the tree-cutting season.
For instance, in the specimen village Kasaka, Malalo, head family
B, had an encampment of six grass huts, about three miles from
the village occupied by himself, his three sons-in-law, and two

sons, one a widower, and one whose wife's relatives lived a long way off (cf. Chap. X). But these groups, composed of two or three men, are becoming rarer, and it is common to find the old men making gardens single-handed for two or three deserted women relatives.

A woman's gardening group is usually composed of herself and her married and unmarried daughters, but as will be clear from Chap. VIII, her other female relatives tend to join up with her, especially under modern conditions. The husband's relatives (his mother or sister) occasionally co-operate also, but this is rare and would only be found in the case of older women of superior social status. A man would have to make his mother or sister her own garden in this case. The custom described as *ukupula* (Chap. IX) naturally provides for many additions, chiefly temporary, to the woman's gardening group.

The extent of co-operation varies, particularly among the men. In the old-fashioned villages you will still see a group of young sons-in-law working under the direct orders of their father-in-law, who is in complete charge of the selection of garden sites and the clearing of the bush. Where the sons-in-law are older, they would still make gardens near each other 'because our wives like reaping together', or in the case of pairs of young men who are close friends, they may like to work alternate days on each other's gardens for company (*ukuteme cima*). They say the work goes quicker so. In fact, a Bemba rarely works alone in a garden till middle or old age, and never likes doing so, nor works very efficiently under these conditions (cf. Chap. XIX).

(*b*) *The village.* The Bemba village may also be described as an economic unit. Certain tasks are definitely performed in the community. These include net-hunting, in which all the men of the village combine, and fish-poisoning expeditions joined by men and women. Joint work is done in clearing the village paths and in old-fashioned villages once a year on the headman's garden. The village is regarded as a unit for *umulasa* purposes, and its agricultural ceremonies and foundation rites are performed for the whole community.

Added to this, the working parties (*ukutumya*) described in Chap. IX in effect consist of all the able-bodied men or women respectively of the village. Thus the bigger the village the larger the force available for economic co-operation of this kind. The present tendency of building smaller and smaller settlements lessens the labour force in this way.

The economic leadership in the village, in so far as it exists, is in the hands of the headman. He directs joint enterprises, decides when the village should be moved, and chooses the new site in co-operation with the other elders. He is in charge of the communal rites, settles minor disputes between the villagers, and represents his people at the chief's court or the District Commissioner's office. He is responsible for the collecting of tribute, providing *umulasa* labour, and for any administrative duties the Government may charge him with, such as the catching of tax defaulters, &c. But there is no doubt that most of the Bemba headman's authority is derived from his position as head of a kinship group, and that he is respected as the grandfather, father-in-law, or maternal uncle of most of the inhabitants, as well as by virtue of his political status (cf. Chap. VII). Thus the power of a headman of an old-fashioned type of community, and in particular those of the *bakabilo*, is in striking contrast to the wavering authority exerted by those ruling over a modern village not definitely composed on kinship lines. For instance, Citikafula, one of Citimukulu's chief *bakabilo*, was headman of a village composed as follows:[1] 25 men, of whom 14 were close personal relatives of the headman (2 brothers, 4 sons, 3 grandsons, 4 maternal nephews, 1 cross-cousin), while the remaining members of the community had come from other villages to marry women at Citikafula's. There were 35 women, of whom 27 were near relatives of the headman (3 wives, 7 daughters, 6 grand-daughters, 6 sisters, 3 maternal nieces, 1 grandmother, and 1 mother-in-law). Hence nearly 75 per cent. of the men and women were members of the headman's own lineage group. In such a village he was able to get large gardens made for him by his younger relatives, strode about the settlement scolding householders with untidy huts, and organized the garden work by constant criticism and encouragement. Whereas Bwembya, a man of equal personality and a member of the royal clan, was headman of a village four miles from Kasama, that is to say, almost within a white township. His community was composed as follows: 52 men, of whom 5 were close relatives only (i.e. father, 1 brother, 1 maternal nephew, 1 brother-in-law, and 1 grandson), and 108 women, of whom 8 were near relatives (1 daughter, 2

---

[1] Using the kinship terms in their classificatory sense.

grand-daughters, 2 sisters, 2 maternal nieces, and 1 sister-in-law);
8 per cent. of the inhabitants only were thus closely related to the
headman, and 10 men were actually members of quite different
tribes.[1] Thirty out of the 52 men had joined the village with the
express purpose of finding work with the Europeans at Kasama
and not on kinship grounds at all. In a community of this type
Bwembya evidently found it impossible to control the activities
of his people, and they gave him little economic help in spite of his
royal rank. It is often stated that young men lose respect for tribal
authorities after working in the mines, and this is largely true, but it
must also be borne in mind that the tribal authorities are in charge
of groups of quite different composition from those of old days,
and they are asked to perform different functions of leadership.

(c) *The chief's leadership in economic enterprises.* There are
two aspects of the chief's functions as an organizer of labour. In
the first place, there are a number of activities he actually initiates
and co-ordinates, and in the second, his direction of his own
labour force and his accumulation of stores in the capital, sets the
pace for agricultural enterprise and forms the basis of the whole
economic system of the tribe.

We have seen that the chief actually sets the time for the firing
of the gardens, and that the performance of economic rites still to
some extent gives the signal for tree-cutting and sowing. The
knowledge that big gardens are being made at the capital, acts, as
I tried to show, as a stimulus to the undertaking of further work.[2]

Besides, it is difficult to realize, without living at the capital for
some time, the extent to which the *mfumu* directs agricultural
enterprises by advising or criticizing both the members of his own
big village and those of his *icalo*. Ultimately chiefs want food
produced in their district, because they then get plenty of tribute.
They express this fact quite frankly. A severe shortage also, as
I indicated, reflects on their supernatural powers, makes people
begin to grumble, and even in time threaten to leave.[3] From all
points of view, therefore, it is to the chief's advantage that the people
should cultivate efficiently. Their knowledge of cultivating processes, soil selection, and the best moment for planting is also

---

[1] Note the proportion of men to women in these villages: i.e. 25:35 and
52:108 respectively.

[2] Cf. p. 371.

[3] e.g. the charges made all over the country against Citimukulu during the
recent locust epidemic for failure to perform his ritual duties properly.

considerable. Even the most stupid or beer-sodden rulers seemed to discuss such matters with authority. The chief always selects his own site for tree-cutting in my experience. I have seen Citimukulu and Lucembe advise women as to whether their millet was ripe enough to reap, and Nkula upbraiding some of his people on two occasions, once for making village beds on unsuitable soil, and at another time for not fencing properly. He turned to me with a look as despairing as that of any white educator, and said: 'Look at them! They are working anyhow (*cibombebombe*). Is not that what hunger does?' [1]

Of their *icalo* as a whole the chiefs also know a great deal. The messengers who go about from village to village to fetch tribute labourers, or the headmen who come on business to the capital, report on conditions. I was amazed in fact to find how much of the conversation in a chief's hut concerned the whole organization of the food-supply, the exact type of soil in such and such a place, or the methods successfully used on it. Comments and criticisms are passed freely. The chief also knows when and where the rivers are in flood, and, in an incredibly short time, how many buck any travelling European has hit or missed. Thus his position at the capital, a place where people constantly come and go, his specialized knowledge of agriculture, and his personal interest in food-production, the latter at present correlated with the whole tribute system, gives the Bemba ruler opportunity to lead and influence the agricultural activities of the whole tribe. This fact may well acquire administrative importance if any new improved system of cultivation is ever discovered for this area.

In his own gardens the chief organizes the biggest labour force that exists in the country. To clear the bush on a large scale (*ukutema pakalamba*) means making a number of gardens in the case of a leading chief.[2] When cutting on a large scale, many gardens are made. For instance, in 1933 Citimukulu made gardens as follows:

Personal *mulasa* gardens: (1 big and 1 medium) = 3·2 acres (approx.)
Gardens for 16 wives: (11 medium and 35 small) = 8·5 ,, ,,
Gardens for 4 'brides of the relics': (3 medium
and 3 small) = 2·8 ,, ,,
Help over gardens for 4 courtiers, 1 blind singer,
2 widowed sisters: (gardens unmeasured)[3] = 3·5 ,, ,,
18 ,, ,,

[1] *Moneni apa! Balebomba cibombebombe. Te nsala?*
[2] This does not happen every year (cf. p. 215).
[3] These gardens were roughly paced round the edges. A big garden means

In 1932 Makassa made one big personal garden of about two and a half acres and medium gardens for five wives, two inherited widows from his predecessor, one widowed sister, and one deserted daughter. The amount of labour required during a nine-months' period for all the garden work of the Citimukulu plus the building of a new village has been given as 561 men and 329 women.[1] Mukuikile—a smaller chief—required 275 men-days for the cutting of his gardens, and 210 women-days for piling the branches.

In general, the *umulasa* labourers are supervised by the chief himself or one of his head officials, and the organization of this irregular labour force is one of the most important tasks he has to undertake, since on it his tribal supply of food depends.

Even though the *umulasa* labourers only work for the inside of a week, there are often as many as twenty or thirty men or women in the gardening team, drawn from different villages all over the *icalo*, so that the chief has not only the power to organize his own garden work but definite possibilities of instruction.

Work and Time Sequence.

From the main calendar of seasonal activities shown above, it will be seen that the season for tree-cutting, the hardest work of the men, is the cold time of the year, but this lopping of the branches can really be done at any time during the months from April until September when the forest fires which break out in hot weather might threaten to destroy the piled wood. The beginning of tree-cutting usually necessitates the movement of the whole family out into the bush, and thus makes a real break in the rhythm of daily life. During these cold weather months there are few other important food-producing activities for the men. For those who live on rivers, fishing on the flats begins in April and low-water fishing in July. The best months for net-hunting are hot weather at the end of this period. Basket-making and thatching must be done while the grass and reeds are still tall enough,

---

one more or less round, about 400 paces round; a medium one about 200 paces; a small one only 40 or so. Their area may therefore be calculated as follows:

      'Big' gardens—2½ acres approx.

      'Medium' gardens—7/10ths of an acre approx.

      'Small' gardens—1/40th of an acre approx.

    N.B. 4–10 acres of forest is needed according to the growth of trees and type of forest for one acre of garden. These approximations were made for me by Mrs. Gore-Browne.   [1] Cf. p. 258.

CALENDAR OF SEASONAL ACTIVITIES

Bemba months	English equivalents	Weather	Food-supply	MEN			WOMEN	
				Millet	Subsidiary	Other activities	Gardening	Other activities
Kabengele kanono	January	Heavy rain	Hunger month	..	Mound-digging and sowing	Fishing. Traps and nets set on flooded banks	Mound digging and sowing	Collecting mushrooms and caterpillars.
Kabengele kakalamba	February	„	Hunger month. Cucurbits ripe	Fencing gardens	„ „	Build houses (new village)	„ „	„ „
Kutumpu	March	Rain slackening	Subsidiary crops ripe	..	„ „	„	Harvest (maize)	Collecting caterpillars.
Shinde	April	Rains cease	Early millet ripe	..	..	Fish weirs set	Harvest (millet—early)	..
Kapepo kanono	May	Cold weather	Ample food-supply	Tree-cutting	..	„ „	Harvest (millet—main crop); Harvest (groundnuts)	..
Kapepo kakalamba	June	„	„	„	..	..	„ „ Piling branches	..
Cikungulu pepo	July	„ „	„ „	„ „	..	..	„ „	Collecting wild spinaches. Fish-poisoning.
Lipukutu lunono	August	Hot weather	„ „	„ „	Dry weather sowing	Fish-poisoning. Net-hunting begins	Dry weather sowing	„ „
Lipukutu lukalamba	September	„	„ „	„ „	„ „	Fish-poisoning. Net-hunting	„ „	Fish-poisoning.
Lusuba lunono	October	„	Less food	Firing gardens	..	„ „	..	Fish-poisoning.
Lusuba lukalamba	November	Early rains	Getting scarce	„ „	Mound digging and sowing	Fish-spearing and trapping on flats	Mound digging and sowing	Fruits.
Mupundu	December	Mid-rains	Hunger month	Sowing main crop	„ „	..	Sowing main crop	Collecting mushrooms.
Cinshi kubili	No English equivalent. The 13th month	„ „	„ „	„ „	„ „	„ „	„ „	„ „

i.e. before the hot weather, but otherwise a man should be able to finish his tree-cutting work by July or August and then to have a month or two more or less free. It must be noted, however, that the demand for European work on roads, &c., coincides with the tree-cutting months, since such labour has to be postponed till the cold, dry weather.[1]

The coming of the rains in October and November brings a complete change of programme. The softening of the ground means the beginning of the planting season, and the re-hoeing of village beds and the making of *mputa* on the *ififwani* should go on till February or March. There is fishing in the big rivers at the beginning of the rains, but not universally. At the end of the period (March) the gardens have to be fenced. Thus, apart from the tree-cutting season these months, November to March, should be the heaviest of the year. Whereas a garden has got to be cut if the staple crop is to be sown at all, the amount of hoeing done depends on individual energy and initiative, and since the hoeing months coincide with the season of scarcity, it is this work which tends to be skimped.

The women's work is more continuous throughout the seasons. During the cold weather months they have not only branches to pile but the harvest to get in. In the hot weather there is less garden work, but this is the season of brewing and the time when the women have the greatest difficulty in hunting for relish. In the wet weather their work is very similar to that of the men, since they also hoe and sow. In February and March the women have less garden work, but take time in going to and fro in their *ififwani* to collect the ripening pumpkins, then reap the early-maturing *mwangwe*, dry and beat it, and collect food from relatives &c. In general, these villages which rely chiefly on mound cultivation[2] are at their busiest at this time of year, while in the ordinary community it is not a heavy season.

The Rhythm of Work.

The Bemba, like many other primitive peoples, reckon the passage of time by the activities performed in it, rather than by

---

[1] In the early years of the copper mines (1930–1) the figures for voluntary labour rose to a peak during the rainy months, and fell during the times of the tree-cutting season.

[2] Cf. the description of cultivation in a typical village (Chap. XV).

any regular system of time intervals. The *umwaka* (plur. *imyaka*) is the name given to the complete cycle of climatic changes and economic processes which make up the year.[1] This is divided into thirteen months (*umueshi—imieshi*) which signifies moon, or the cycle of the moon (cf. table on p. 389). The names of these months are used with greater or less frequency according to the importance of the activities performed in them. The coming of each new moon is an important event in the people's life, since it affects very largely the tempo of ordinary activities. When the moon is full, laughter and talk go on late into the night and the drums sound for dancing. When the moon has waned, there is no other system of lighting and the people go early to bed. The days of full moon are also believed to be specially lucky and to be auspicious for the starting of any new activity. I noticed several times that the *bakabilo* of Citimukulu's court postponed important ritual acts, often at some practical inconvenience, until the nights were 'white, completely white' (*ukubuta tutu*), explaining in answer to my comment: 'We cannot work at such things in the dark' (*Teti tubombefyo mu mfifi*). The rhythm of the changing moons has thus a significance to the Bemba that it has lost in our society, and the appearance of the new crescent is greeted with delight and often with shouts from the children, but at the same time the calendar of months is rarely used as a method of calculating time or fixing the start of economic activities. Some months coincide with the change of season: *Shinde* (April), the change to the cold weather; *Lusuba lunono* (October), the beginning of the hot season; *Mpundu* (November), the coming of the rains and the time of the ripening of the *mpundu* fruit. In these cases the name of the month is used in daily conversation in planning activities. But in other cases the change of climate, i.e. windy season (*mpepo*) or the hot season (*ulusuba*) is referred to only, and there are several months in the year when, owing to the difficulties of working with a thirteen-months calendar, the ordinary native is not quite certain what the name of the particular moon should be.[2] The English child hardly notices changes in the moon, but learns to recite the months of the year

[1] The *umwaka* is a cycle of seasonal changes but it is never calculated by means of the stars, in which the Bemba seem to have little interest and never use as a means of reckoning time.

[2] In April 1934 I heard the chief's council discuss informally with the Paramount chief whether the moon that had just appeared was correctly *Kutumpu* or *Shinde*, and these learned men of the tribe took different sides on the question.

as an abstract sequence of names of which certain have an emotional significance as being a period containing a birthday or Christmas, but the Bemba child is delighted with the appearance of each new crescent and lives a more exciting life during the full moon. He only gradually learns at about 9 or 10 that certain of these moons coincide with particular economic tasks, and later still, as an adult, he is able to recite all the moons in order and to discourse wisely on the whole sequence of the calendar.

Before the coming of the white man, the Bemba had apparently no smaller subdivision of the month than the day. They have now completely adopted the English week, even in remote spots of the country where no one is working for a European. Every native keeps the Christian Sunday, known as the 'day of God', *nshiku ya Mulungu*, from which term the week itself is known as *Mulungu*, the word for God, and the days called the first, second, third, fourth, &c. (*pali cimo, pali cibili*, &c.). The conception of the week has been incorporated in Bemba economic life since it coincides with an adoption of the European rhythm of work and system of payment, and the acceptance for the first time of a time interval which is also a period of work. Wage-earners calculate their weeks of service, and chiefs who formerly called up tribute labourers when they were required now state their dues in precise terms, as for instance three days a week.

The Bemba word for night is *ubushiku*, and for day *akasuba*. In any one day the time is divided into three. Dawn is a fixed event (*bwaca*), and the period from dawn till midday is known as *ulucelo*. Midday, from 11 till about 3 o'clock, is called *akasuba*, the ordinary word for sun, and the period from 3 to 6, i.e. the time of sunset, is known as *icungulo*. Thus a man who wants to make an appointment with a friend does so to the nearest two or three hours, by telling him to come in the morning, at midday, or in the evening, and when acting as a witness at a legal court can place events in this manner, usually giving additional precision to his statement by raising his arm to point to the exact position of the sun in the sky at the time referred to, e.g. at 11 or 3, and adding, 'The sun was like this' (*kasubefi*).

It is hardly ever necessary to fix time in the night, but the natives speak of 'the middle of the night' (*pakati ka bushiku*) and will also reckon time by the number of turns they have made in their sleep, since these people apparently wake more or less regularly four or five times a night in order to shift their positions on their hard wood beds.

Thus it can be said that the Bemba method of reckoning time allows them to fix dates to the nearest year, season, month, or nowadays week, but it does not subdivide day and night into equal intervals, and in fact most of their activities do not need to be co-ordinated more closely than to the nearest day or half day. The conception of the equal time interval does not seem to occur to them in the ordinary course of life. Their days and nights are not in fact of equal length as ours are, with our independence of seasonal changes in light, dark, and temperature, and our regular routine of work. Bemba rise at 5 a.m. in the hot weather, but come reluctantly from their huts at 8 or even later in the cold season, and their working day is fixed accordingly. Meals are timed to the nearest two hours rather than to the minute, and night begins at any time from 8 o'clock on a chilly dark evening to midnight or later when the moon is full, and the people are tempted to stay out in the open. Nor does the work-time interval which dominates our activities and calculations exist for them. We, after all, can hardly conceive of time except in terms of energy expenditure and, to many of us, a fixed money value as well. But the Bemba in his unspecialized society does different tasks daily and a different amount of work each day. The diary of men's and women's activities given in Table E shows that in Kampamba the men were employed on five quite separate occupations (hoeing, hunting, chasing locusts, fencing, carrying, &c.) in the course of ten days, and at Kasaka, though the main work was branch lopping, yet various ritual observances, visits from friends or Europeans, interrupted the daily routine constantly. Domestic needs tie the women to certain daily tasks in this, as in other communities, but even then their garden work varies greatly from day to day. The working hours also change in what seems to us a most erratic manner. In fact I do not think the people ever conceive of such periods as the month, week, or day in relation to regular work at all. The major agricultural tasks have to coincide with certain seasons and moons, and that is all. A man says he has to cut trees between such-and-such climatic changes, but not that he has so many hours of work to get through, and daily work, which has become from habit almost a physiological necessity to many Europeans, only occurs at certain times of the year. The whole bodily rhythm of the Bemba differs completely from that of a peasant in Western Europe, let alone an industrial worker. For instance at Kasaka, in a slack season, the old men worked 14 days out of 20 and the young men 7; while at Kampamba in a busier season, the men of all ages worked on an average 8 out of 9 working days. The average working day in the first instance was $2\frac{3}{4}$ hours for men and 2 hours gardening plus 4 hours domestic work for the women, but the figures varied from 0 to 6 hours a day. In the second case the average was 4 hours for the men and 6 for the women, and the figures showed the same daily variation.

All these observations as to the African's conception and use of time are important in studying the relationship of black and white. There is probably no aspect of life in which the habits of both differ so fundamentally, and in both cases these habits are rooted in childhood training and a particular economic system. The Bemba have a 'sense of time' contrary to the usual European view, and it is fitted to guide them in the organization of their own activities, but it is ill-adapted to new routines and new economic values. A study of village life, therefore, explains many of the reactions of the Bemba to regular European work, particularly that on the mines. It surely also accounts for their desertions in the early days of employment, the utter exhaustion sometimes seen in new recruits at the end of a day's work, and the sudden desire of even the fully acclimatized native to return to his village and 'rest'—perhaps also the complete inactivity of many of such men returned to their villages on holiday. From the point of view of food production, too, it may account for the apparent inability of most natives to plan their work to obtain the maximum results, to calculate the labour required for any particular job, and lastly, to answer coherently the questions of an inquiring European as to 'how long' it takes to make a garden or build a fence.

Time taken on Particular Tasks.

I have sometimes been asked to estimate the time a Bemba man should spend each year in order to complete his necessary garden work. If this question could be answered precisely, the information would be extremely useful to those dealing with administrative problems such as the recruiting of native labour, the control of labour emigration, the optimum length of time natives should be encouraged to serve at the mines inside or outside the territory,

and the means by which they should be enabled to come and go
between mine and home. Unfortunately, however, the necessary
figures are particularly difficult to give. The Bemba has, as has
been seen, no 'normal working day' and no fixed size of garden
which he aims to cut. In his particular working conditions there
is a wide variation between the minimum time required for each
task by a man working continuously at it, and the average time
taken by natives working in their usual intermittent way and
responsible for a number of different occupations—gardening, fishing, house-building, &c. The former figure could be estimated
accurately I presume under experimental conditions: the latter
could only be determined by a series of records of individuals'
agricultural achievements in different villages all over the country
during a period of at least a year. Notes on the time taken to cut
a garden, fence, or hoe it by selected groups of natives, e.g. old,
middle-aged, or young, polygamous, or monogamous, &c.—if kept
by administrative officers or missionaries, would provide data for
calculating the time usually spent on different agricultural tasks.
Such figures I was not able to collect during the time I had available.

Another difficulty is to decide whether the time figures required
are those giving the minimum amount of male labour necessary to
use the land to the best advantage, or alternatively, that sufficient
to produce the minimum requirements of each domestic group.
The former figures could presumably be calculated at an agricultural research station, while the latter would have to be based on
some kind of assessment of each family's nutritional needs. I have
neither set of data at my disposal but give my own rough estimates
of the average amount of male labour required for Bemba cultivation as a stimulus to further investigations. My figures are based
on answers given by a number of informants to questions as to the
time taken over particular tasks, together with personal observations taken in a few villages where I stayed long enough to watch
the completion of different stages of garden work.

The most important tasks of the Bemba men are tree-cutting,
fencing, and hoeing. Elderly natives estimate that they would
take about one month working continuously to clear a good-sized
garden. A polygamist would need about seven weeks, as he would
make a big garden for his first wife and a smaller one for the second.
But the younger native would probably not work so continuously,
and would be more likely to spend six weeks making one garden.

Men usually ask for three months' leave to 'make a garden', but most of them treat their time in the village as a holiday as well as a gardening time. Thus it can be reckoned that for this, the most essential activity, the Bemba requires as a minimum four weeks' work, but usually takes two or three months a year interspersing this task with others.

Sowing millet is not a laborious process and a big garden can be planted in a day or two. Fencing, in those parts of the country where it is necessary, natives describe with rather a rare unanimity as the work of one month, thus making a minimum of two to three months' agricultural labour which can be done by men only.

Hoeing falls into a different category, both because this is a task that men and women do jointly, and also because there is every degree of individual variation in the amount done. To get good results a substantial amount of hoeing should be done, according to native theory, but to get some food out of the ground, surface hoeing only would be adequate (cf. pp. 303, 390). The main hoeing consists of the digging up of the old burnt gardens (*ifiti-meme*), but besides this, a man in a new village has to make new garden beds the first year, and should re-hoe the old completely every two or three years. He should weed Kaffir corn, burn the old legume stalks on the *mputa*, &c., for each of which tasks I have added one week. If labour is short or the people hungry, this last work is not done. I should estimate that the minimum of time a man should spend on hoeing and weeding would be one month, but to use the soil to the best advantage, two or three would be necessary, doing a little every day (cf. p. 308).

Other activities such as fishing, hunting, or handicrafts are sporadic, and probably the ordinary Bemba spends about a month a year all told on such work. To build a house would take a fortnight for a man working alone, but houses will last for three or four years.

To estimate the amount of male labour required annually, the reader should turn to the table given on p. 315. He will realize that each Bemba has three or four gardens to deal with annually, as well as his village beds. Thus the work can probably be listed as follows:

(*a*) Garden of present year to be = 4 weeks—during May–September. cut

Garden of present year to be = 4 weeks—during February–March. fenced

(b) Garden of last year to be dug = 2 weeks—during August–October.
    up for ground-nuts or other
    crop

(c) Garden of three years ago to = 1 week—during August–October.
    be burnt and prepared for
    third-year millet

(d) Garden of four years ago to be = 2 weeks—during October–Janu-
    dug into mounds for beans   ary.
    or other crops

    Total = 13 weeks as a bare minimum, of which 8 can only be done
    by male labour.

In the village beds the labour expended can be roughly estimated as follows:

(e) Digging of new village beds   = 2 weeks—usually during Decem-
    ber–February.

(f) Complete rehoeing of old beds = 3 weeks—usually during Decem-
    ber–February.

    Or light hoeing of old beds = 1 week—usually during Septem-
    ber–February.

(g) Burning, weeding, &c.   = 1 week—usually during Septem-
    ber–October.

    Total = 4–6 weeks.

The total time spent both in the main gardens and on the village
beds could thus be reckoned as a minimum period of 17–19 weeks,
of which 8 weeks—4 during the dry season and 4 during the wet—
can only be done by men. Probably, however, under ordinary
village conditions and combining other tasks such as house-
building, fishing, &c., the Bemba usually take 4–5 weeks longer to
produce the same results, making a total of 5–6 months' work.

How is the Bemba to find this amount of time under modern
conditions of migratory labour? He can clearly not produce the
optimum results from the soil, but merely the minimum amount
of food which will keep his family from destitution.

From the agricultural point of view the difficulty of the Northern
Rhodesia labour situation is the length of time for which the men
go to the mines and their lack of facilities for getting back to their
villages. Recruiting ceased in the area in 1930, and the men mostly
make their way to the mines (300–500 miles) on foot, or by bicycle.
The Rand mineworker signs up for an eleven months' contract
usually, with his return passage home automatically deducted from

his wages. But the Bemba has either to pay 35s. for a lorry passage home or he must bicycle or walk. The first is considered a prohibitive passage, except for the better-off native, and the second is only done when a man is really sick of the town and feels he must get home—say after two or three years or even longer. He cannot reasonably return every year for the three months' garden labour which we have reckoned as necessary with the present method of cultivation. However, it can be seen from the table on p. 315 that, if a man spent two years at home, he could make millet gardens and fence them in successive years. He could then spend two years at the mines, leaving his wife to plant the third-year millet. She would thus have some millet every year if her husband had facilities for returning again in the fourth year, but this is obviously only one of the minimum solutions described above. For an improved food-supply an alternative method to tree-cutting or greater ease of transport to and from the mines are required.

The Will to Work.

At the opening of this book I described Bemba diet as inadequate and variable, and their methods of gardening as primitive compared to those of their neighbours. In some of the succeeding chapters I have tried to account for the shortage in their annual and daily food-supply by describing the people's difficulties in preparing and producing different foodstuffs, or in their methods of handling, distributing, and storing them. We have still to ask one final question, and its answer is to be found scattered here and there throughout the book. Put crudely, it is the query which springs naturally to the mind of most Europeans living in this area, viz. 'If the Bemba go short of food so often, why don't they work a good bit harder and drink less beer?' Successive Government reports describe this tribe as 'poor agriculturists' or 'incorrigibly lazy',[1] and the traveller, gazing at ill-weeded gardens and broken-down fences, cannot resist the same type of comment. The average working day of a man has been estimated as only four hours, even though the women are undoubtedly overworked at certain seasons of the year, and I have given a good many facts to show

---

[1] e.g. the Government Report for Native Affairs, 1936, p. 47. 'Natives in this Province generally speaking strike one as singularly unenterprising and indeed downright lazy about the growing of foodstuffs.'

how intermittent the garden labour actually is. Few African
peoples probably work such regular hours as European peasants
do, but a number have been described as gardeners first and foremost, with all their hearts in their fields. Of the Bemba nothing
of the sort could be said. What makes them then unable or unwilling to garden more intensively, or to produce more food?

This whole question of incentives shows at once the extreme
complexity of the nutritional problem in human society, and leads
us to pass in review every aspect of food and food-production
already described—the people's diet, their eating habits, their
economic objectives, and the changes now taking place in their
life. The simple assumption that the shorter the food-supply the
more a man is willing to cultivate is obviously very short of the
mark. In fact, so-called 'laziness' may be directly due to diet
deficiencies, or to their more indirect effects on human appetites
or the will to work. Whether the intermittent character of Bemba
work is due to under-feeding or to some other physical cause such
as disease or the presence of parasites it is impossible to state
without further medical evidence. The Bemba dislike of regular
concentrated work may be due to some racial characteristic or
trait of temperament, as well as to upbringing. We do not know.
Suffice it to remind ourselves that their intake of certain foodstuffs
is about half that considered necessary for the mine-employees on
the Rhodesian copper belt, and that the native himself recognizes
the effects of the hunger season on his output of energy (cf. Chaps.
II and III). My own observations also convinced me that the whole
tenor of native life was less energetic when food was short, and
that certain gardening work, such as hoeing, which fell during the
months of shortage, was often hurriedly and carelessly done. But
of the direct results of any possible diet deficiencies in this area
we can at present say little more.

Indirectly, the nutritional habits of the Bemba are reflected in
their customs of work to a marked degree. Their methods of feeding from the days of infancy condition their appetites and digestive
processes, and shape their whole conception of what is normal and
inevitable in life. The adaptability of the human organism is one
of the perpetual surprises of comparative anthropology, and since
the Bemba are unaccustomed to regular or similar meals, they do
not feel the need of them or make a very resolute effort to get them.
To have too little to eat is not a shocking situation to any of them,

and therefore not a stimulus to exert their last ounce of energy to alter an intolerable state of affairs. Living at this particular economic level, other advantages sometimes seem preferable to a sufficiency of food. For instance, the immediate disadvantage of grinding and pounding to a tired woman may seem more obvious than the ultimate weakness she knows she will feel if she goes without her evening meal (cf. pp.˙ 104–5). In fact, paradoxically enough, it would seem as if the 'fatal resignation' commonly noted among primitive peoples could only be cured by giving them regular food! It was certainly true that the few Bemba whom I saw displaying energy and initiative in the adoption of new methods of European gardening, planting of vegetables, &c., were natives who were better off, in constant employment, or somehow removed from the feeling of insecurity which was the habit of mind of their fellows. All these observations throw light on a fact which first strikes the European as puzzling, viz. the evident absorption of the Bemba in their food problems, which they discuss so constantly and with such interest, and yet their apparent insouciance in arranging to secure better supplies. Whether or not the Bemba are lazy through physical inertia, it is certainly true that habitual insecurity robs them of continuous energy in planning their needs.

The direct cultural drives towards food production are even more complex. We have here to deal with the dominant tribal interests, the activities with which prestige is most clearly associated, and the ambitions of each individual member of the tribe. This question is important. We want to know whether the Bemba were always indifferent agriculturists, or whether their present attitude is something specific—the result of economic changes at the present day. Now this group is always described as a typical warrior people, and though Bemba tribal structure is not based on military organization as is the case among the Nguni peoples of South Africa (Zulus or Swazis) and to some extent the Rhodesian neighbours of the Bemba, the Ngoni, yet it is true to say that the dominant ambition of their chiefs was apparently military conquest. To this end they strove to build up armies of followers, and collected guns and cloth and slaves. Their authority depended on military strength, as well as the people's belief in their supernatural powers. If they made big gardens, this was never their only method of getting food, and the cultivation largely served their military objectives. Whereas some Polynesian chiefs regularly worked in their gardens and could not hope to succeed to this position unless they were expert agriculturists and craftsmen,[1] such a conception of chieftainship would be quite fantastic to the Bemba, among whom the royal clan definitely does not learn to cut trees, the chief male occupation of the tribe.

The same trend of thought seems to have dominated the interests of the tribe as a whole. Even now, when describing the past, the people constantly dwell on the fierceness of their chiefs, their military exploits, and the booty they were able to take from other peoples. In fact, *ubukali*, which may be translated 'ferocity' or 'ruthlessness', rather than bravery, is one of the few qualities I have heard admired in famous men of the past.[2] I noticed that if I ever criticized Bemba laughingly for their inability to carve or to make baskets as well as the surrounding tribes, and asked them what they thought they excelled in, the usual reaction was a throwing back of the shoulders and the word *ubukali* uttered with great intensity, 'But we were fiercer than all the rest. We made them give us tribute.' Gouldsbury and Sheane record that the Bemba of their day used to brag that they did not know how to hoe, for their only trade was war;[3] and though it is obvious that a people could not have lived on tribute alone, the boast is significant.

This tribal ideal is reflected in the Bemba attitude to industry itself. Talking to natives of the present day it is impossible to resist the conclusion that agricultural excellence is really not a trait which is much admired. To have food and beer is considered desirable and even essential to a man of high status, but it is always thought better that this food should have been produced by the labour of some one else. I never heard a young man being praised as a good gardener. The phrase *icilumba ca bulumendo*, the pride or arrogance of youth, may be said in tones of irritation when a young man refuses to hoe, but I think it is more often uttered with a kind of grudging admiration. In middle and old age the successful cultivator is thought well of, and without working he would probably be unable to build up a 'big house'. The word *umulimi* or 'good cultivator' exists and conveys approbation. But industry seems to be thought an unexciting virtue—an advantage or even

---

[1] Cf. R. Firth, *Primitive Economics of the N. Zealand Maori*, 1929, p. 164.

[2] Generosity and wisdom were the others.

[3] Gouldsbury and Sheane, *The Great Plateau of N. Rhodesia*, 1904, p. 24.

an essential in a prospective son-in-law, but not admirable in itself, or even a suitable attribute for a young man of spirit. I noticed that when I commented once on a woman who had put a whole stretch of ground under cultivation in one day, that the two young men with me shrugged their shoulders with the kind of pity we usually reserve for obsessional cases. 'Yes! poor woman. Grubbing away all day like a dog!'

This difference between the behaviour of old and young is, I think, the crux of the whole question from a practical point of view. In pre-European days there was a complete change of ambition between the youth and age. The young boy, under the system of matrilocal marriage, had no individual responsibility for gardening. He was expected to cut trees, but his main way of advance in life was to attach himself to a chief or to a man of rank and not to make larger gardens or to collect material goods. He often went on border raids or foraging expeditions. He did not expect to work in earnest until middle age, when his children were 'crying from hunger' and he had settled down. Nowadays we saw in concrete cases the immense difference between the regularity of work done by the old and young. This is partly due to the new insubordination of the boys, but partly also to a perpetuation of an old tradition. In our society youths and adolescents have, roughly speaking, the same economic ambitions throughout youth and early manhood. For most there is the same continuous incentive to make more money from year to year. Among the Bemba this was not so, any more than it was among such warrior peoples as the Masai of East Africa with their regular age-sets. Each individual was expected to be first a fighter and later a cultivator and the father of a family. In modern Africa there is often the same break between the employment of the young and the old. Many writers have pointed out that service at the mines has been substituted for the old warrior service of the young man. But there is of course this difference, that the Bemba goes away to the mines for far longer than he went to war, and that he is not able to settle down continuously in middle age. He has to pay tax until he is past working. He is not free to take his position at home as a father of three or four children and a leading citizen as he did in the old days at the end of his warrior period. Nor is there any reason for him to settle down to become an efficient cultivator.

Thus the answer to our question is, I think, definite. Before the coming of the white man, the warrior type was more highly valued than the good gardener in youth, and modern migratory labour has wiped out the stage in which the one would normally have passed into the other. In the absence of stock or other material possessions, the idea of accumulation never existed, nor the habit of organized trade, and with the present shortage of money-making possibilities in this area and the lack of a cash crop, the introduction of European currency did not act as a new incentive to agricultural work, rather the reverse.

Another difficulty inherent in the Bemba system of gardening is the absence of any definite units by which success can be measured or effort reckoned—a fact I have already stressed in descriptions of their methods of calculating quantities or assessing needs. The size of a Bemba garden is not fixed. The labour force of a family varies from month to month. The people are not in the habit of calculating the size of their field or its yield, the time it would take to clear the trees on it, or the amount of grain annually produced. Nor does the particular staple crop used lend itself to accurate measurement of this kind. I found that, if I asked Bemba how much ground they intended to clear, old men had some conception of their future needs, but young men more often replied: 'How much shall we cut? Oh, we shall cut until our arms ache. . . . Till our strength is exhausted. . . . Until we want to go and work for the Europeans. . . . Or until laziness seizes hold of us. Will the garden give enough to feed us? We do not know. Perhaps it will.' These statements are perhaps more casual than would have been heard in the old days—that is impossible to tell—but, in any case, it is clear that with such a system of reckoning, success in food production depends very largely on leadership and a definite compulsion to work.

It is just this leadership which, as we saw, is no longer effective. The matrilocal kinship organization with the economic group which is based on it, is one that is breaking down rapidly in contact with European conditions. The drive behind agricultural production is largely associated with beliefs in the authority of the Bemba chief, sentiments that have been inevitably weakened by contact with Europeanism. The Bemba are still willing to garden if told to, as the experience of the Government during the recent locust raids has shown. When ordered to dig four hundred mounds of cassava, most natives complied, and when the order was rescinded they gave up the extra effort. At present, however, the chiefs have little incentive to give such orders, and shortage of agricultural staff makes it impossible for Europeans to exert the same leadership. Whether or not it will be possible for Europeans to take the initiative in stimulating increased agricultural production it is impossible to say, but I have sometimes been impressed by the surprise of natives that any white person should be interested in their cultivation and by the question of an intelligent chief, 'Why do the Government officers ask me about the history of the Bemba and their magic, and never about our gardens and the growing of food?'

The effects of absentee labour on food production have been constantly referred to in this book. Its results on gardening enthusiasm are not easy to summarize. It is, however, a fact that men who go back to their villages from the mines do so to 'rest', after what is for them unusual strain, and not to work, and the common assumption of the European that every month spent at home can and should be given to making new gardens is really unwarranted. It is difficult also for a native to maintain his interest in agriculture after staying at the mines for as long a period as two or three years. When working at Luanshya Mine myself, I noticed that young men on their first visit were definitely homesick, and that old men spoke gladly of the possibility of settling down; but it was obvious that a man who had already made two or three visits of a few years each had no longer the same interest in talking of village life.

The agricultural enthusiasm of natives who stay behind in their village is an equally important factor. The native habit of working in twos or threes with relatives or age-mates is important from this point of view. It means that the youths of a village tend to go together to the mines in groups of five or six for a year or two, thus leaving their home community with only three or four old men in charge. Thus, to say that 40 or 50 per cent. of the total male Bemba are away annually from the Territory gives a misleading impression. It seems to imply that each village has half of its men present, whereas in fact some communities have plenty of male labour for a year or two while the others are so denuded of men that the remaining inhabitants tend to sink into apathy or leave the village to join a more flourishing community. Two or three energetic or enterprising natives seem to raise the whole tone of village activities. In the same way, the absence of most of the younger men leads to a crippling kind of depression. Any stranger arriving at a Bemba village will notice at once whether it is a thriving community in which plenty is going on, the huts well kept, and the people keen on their work. In fact, the dead appearance of villages with a large percentage of absent men is one of the most striking features of the country-side.

Thus the 'incorrigible laziness' of the Bemba is due to a whole variety of causes—their physique, history, tradition, the nature of their economic ambitions, their methods of planning their activities, and the type of virtues they admire, as well as changed social conditions over which at present they have little control. All these facts go to make the economic pattern of their daily life, and it is only by watching them at their food, in their gardens, drinking beer, or attending the chief's court that one can try to assess this people's 'will to work'.

To conclude, it is true that the foodstuffs of an African tribe are limited in certain directions by the environment in which it lives, but this work has shown in every chapter the extent to which a particular diet can be determined by purely cultural factors—the network of institutions that enable the people to produce, distribute, and consume their food, the different uses, economic and non-economic, to which edible objects are put, and the system of values that make them rate one food higher than another and work more or less hard to produce their annual supplies. These are the sociological aspects of the diet problem in Africa and other countries, and it is a study of these cultural determinants of food and feeding that can and should be included in a nutritional survey at the present time.

APPENDIXES

TABLE A

Chief Bemba Foodstuffs and Methods of Preparation

(The most common methods of preparation are preceded by an asterisk (*).)

English name	Native term	Methods of preparation	Native term
CEREALS			
1. *Finger millet* (Eleusine corecana)	*Amale*	1. *Flour made into porridge 2. *Flour made into thin gruel 3. *Flour made into beer 4. Flour made into a scone (for journeys only)	*Ubwali.* *Umusunga.* *Ubwalua.* *Icifuba.*
2. *Kaffir corns* (a) Sorghum spp. (b) Saccharine	*Amasaka* *Sonkwe* *Kancebele* *Icisale*	1. *Flour made into porridge 2. Flour made into beer 3. Whole grains boiled 1. Sweet stalks chewed	*Ubwali.* *Ubwalua.* *Umusaku.* *Imise.*
3. *Maize* (Zea mays)	*Nyanje*	1. *Green maize boiled on cob 2. *Green maize roasted on cob 3. Flour from green maize used for porridge 4. Flour from green maize used for beer (rare). 5. Grains pounded and added to water. This milky fluid boiled. It sets into a 'blanc mange' 6. Dried grains boiled and pounded 7. Dried grains boiled only 8. Very young corn boiled and eaten cob and all	*Ukunwenena (shya mituntumina).* *Ukuoca mu mapapa.* *Icimfumpa.* *Ubwalua* (rare). *Icisembwe* (rare). *Umunkuluto* (rare). *Shya miyeye.*
4. *Bulrush millet* (Pennisetum typhoideum)	*Ububele* (rare)	1. Ground into flour	
ROOT CROPS			
1. *Cassava* (Manihot utilissima)	*Kalundwe*	1. *Flour made into porridge 2. Roasted in chunks and dipped in ground-nut sauce	*Ubwali.*
2. *Sweet potatoes* (Ipomoea batatas)	*Icumbu* (plur. *Ifyumbu*) Eaten alone	1. *Boiled and eaten alone 2. *Roasted in ashes 3. *Dried potatoes (*fyafubululwa*) boiled with salt as relish	*Ukuipika.*[1] *Ukufumbika.* *Nsemwa.*
3. *Livingstone potatoes,* Hausa or Finger (Coleus esculentus)	*Mumbu* Eaten alone	1. *Boiled and eaten alone 2. *Stewed with ground-nut sauce	*Ukuipika.*[1] *Ukusashila*
PULSES			
1. *Ground-nuts* (Arachis hypogaea)	*Mbalala* Relish Relish Eaten alone	1. *Pounded into sauce to add to relishes 2. Ground-nuts ground and cooked into a cake and stamped hard with salt. Lasts two months. Used as relish 3. Nuts heated on a potsherd 4. Ground-nuts eaten fresh	*Ntwilo.* *Icikonko.* *Ukusalula.*[2] *Muntomfwe.*

[1] *Ukuipika* merely means to cook with water.   [2] *Ukusalula* means to heat without water.

English name	Native term		Methods of preparation	Native term
		Eaten alone	5. Nuts heated, pounded, cooked with water and pounded into a gruel	Umuseswe.
			6. *Nuts heated, pounded, heated again until oil floats to top. Used to oil the skin	Amafuta ya Mbalala.
2. Beans (Phaseolus spp.)	Icilemba	Relish	1. *Fresh pods boiled without salt	Imifoba.
		Relish	2. *Dried seeds stewed to form a purée—salt added	Imintipu.
3. Ground-bean (Voandzeia subterranea)	Ntoyo	Relish	3. *Pods half dried and cooked with water	Muntomfwe.
4. Cow-peas (Vigna unquiculata)	Ililanda	Relish	4. *Fresh leaves stewed as relish with ground-nut sauce if possible	Umusalu.
5. European pea (Pisum Sativum)	Ntongwe	Relish	5. *Dried leaves stewed with native soda, and ground-nut sauce if possible	Umusalu.
		Eaten alone	6. *Purée of stewed dried beans or peas pounded into a cake, and cooked when required with very little water and salt	Icitata.
		Eaten alone	7. Fresh peas or ground-beans cooked in pod without water	Ukusalula nkwangwa.
		Relish	8. Dried leaves softened with native soda cooked on potsherd with salt and water	Ukusalula nkwangwa.
CUCURBITS				
1. Pumpkins (Cucurbita spp.)	Icipushi (plur. Ifipushi)	Eaten alone	1. *Boiled and eaten alone	
			2. Seeds heated in pot as relish	Nseko.
		Relish	3. *Fresh leaves stewed (cf. cassava leaves)	Icibwabwa.
2. Edible gourds (Lagenaria sp.)	Mungu (plur. Myungu)		1. *Boiled and eaten alone	
3. Cucumbers (a) (Cucumis sativus)	Icibimbi(plur. Ifibimbi)		*Eaten raw	
(b) Small cucumber (probably Cucumis ficifolius)	Amankolobwe	Eaten alone	1. *Boiled whole	
			2. Boiled to form a hot drink	
			3. Skins cooked with native soda	
MISCELLANEOUS				
1. Chillies and Capsicums (Capsicum annuum vars.)	Mpilipili		Used as flavouring to relish	
2. Solanaceous fruits (Solanum naumanii)	Mpwa	Relish	Stewed as relish	Ukuipika.
UNCULTIVATED PLANTS				
1. Wild spinaches (not identified)	Umusalu Relish Many varieties including: Pupwe, Candabemba, Lusakasuka, Kapalala, Cinsanki, Tata, Caonde, Kaboswe		1. *Fresh leaves stewed with ground-nut sauce and salt	Ukusashila.
			2. *Dried leaves stewed with native soda	Ukuipika.
2. Wild orchid (Orchis mabembo?)	Icikanda	Relish	1. *Stewed with ground-nut sauce plus salt	Icikanda.
			2. Dried into a cake with salt	

English name	Native term	Methods of preparation	Native term
3. *Edible fungi*, 30 kinds (cf. E. B. H. Goodall, op. cit., p. 122)	*Boa* Relish Relish	1. Stewed with ground-nut sauce 2. Stewed	*Ukusashila* *Ukuipika*
4. *Fruits*			*Mukola ua.*
(*a*) *Wild plums* (Anisophyllea sp.)	*Mfungo*	1. Eaten raw 2. *Made into a drink	*Mfungo.*
(*b*) *Loquots* (Uapaka Kirkiana)	*Several varieties: Masuku, Mupangwa, Mukokola, Musokobwe, &c.*	1. Eaten raw 2. *Made into a drink	*Ulumembwe.*
(*c*) *Mpundu fruit* (Parinarium mobola)	*Mpundu*	1. Eaten raw 2. *Made into a drink	
MEAT AND FISH			
1. *Game* (mostly buck, pig, wild pigeons, guineafowl, duck)	*Nama* (i.e. 'meat')	1. *Slow stewing 2. Roasted on sticks by fire (journey method) 3. Cooked dry on a potsherd	*Ukuipika.* *Ukusalula.*
Chickens (domestic) shortlegged = *Nkuku*	*Nkoko*	,, ,,	,,
2. *Fish* (cf. Report of C. K. Ricardo and R. T. Owen)	*Ilisabi* (plur. *amasabi*)	1. *Slow stewing 2. Cooked dry on a potsherd	*Ukuipika.* *Ukusalula.*
3. *Miscellaneous* Caterpillars	*Ifishimu*, 6 chief types: *Icipumi, Mumpa, Nsenga, Namusuluka, Mpumbata, Fitolo*	1. *Slow stewing with ground-nut sauce 2. Cooked dry	*Ukusashila.* *Ukusalula.*
Flying Ants	*Nkate*	,, ,,	,,
Locusts	*Amakanta*	,, ,,	,,
Crickets	*Nyense*	,, ,,	,,
SALT			
1. *Cibwa salt* (formula on p. 410)	*Umucele*	Used in cooking dried pulses, dried leaves, dishes cooked with ground-nut sauce, sweet potatoes, boiled	
2. *Grass salt* (not analysed)	,,	,, ,, ,,	
3. *European salt*	,,		
4. *Cooking soda* from bark of tree (not analysed)	*Ifishikisa*	Used for softening dried leaf relishes	

TABLE B

Composition of Bemba Foods

(*Kindly prepared by* DR. E. M. WIDDOWSON)

	Protein	Fat	Carbo-hydrate	Cal-cium	Phos-phorus	Iron	Source of figures
	gm.	gm.	gm.(per 100 gm.)	gm.	gm.	mgm.	
Beans, dried	23	1·8	60	0·15	0·46	10·5	Sherman, 1937.
Beans, haricot	21	0	46	0·18	0·31	6·7	McCance, Widdowson, and Shackleton, 1936.
Beer (per pint)	4	0·6	12	0·23	0·17	15·5	Analysis of Bemba speci-men. Also contains 27 grams alcohol.
Caterpillars (dried)	65	5·0	0	0·16	0·77	7·3	Analysis of Bemba speci-men.
Chicken (includ-ing waste)	13	4·8	0	0·01	0·13	1·0	McCance and Shipp, 1933.
Cikanda	1	0	9	0·14	0·02	1·2	As spring onion. Mc-Cance, Widdowson, and Shackleton, 1936.
Cow-peas (dried)	21	1·4	61	0·10	0·46	7·9	Sherman, 1937.
Cucumber	1	0	2	0·02	0·02	0·3	McCance, Widdowson, and Shackleton, 1936.
Fish, fresh	16	5·9	0	0·06	0·20	1·0	McCance and Shipp, 1933.
Fish, dried	32	11·8	0	0·12	0·40	2·0	Calculated from fresh fish.
Flour, maize	8	6·7	72	Trace	0·41	2·2	Analysis of Bemba speci-men.
Flour, millet	7	1·4	75	0·32	0·32	2·4	,, ,,
Flour, cassava	2	0·3	87	0·05	0·06	1·2	,, ,,
Gourds, fresh	Trace	0	1	0·01	0·01	0·2	As marrow. McCance, Widdowson, and Shackleton, 1936.
Ground-nuts	28	49·0	9	0·06	0·37	2·0	As peanuts. McCance, Widdowson, and Shackleton, 1936.
Locusts	8	7·9	0	0·16	0·77	7·3	Orr and Gilks for protein, fat, and carbohydrate. Caterpillar figures for calcium, phosphorus, and iron.
Leaves, fresh	3	0	1	0·14	0·04	2·2	Calculated from dried leaves.
Leaves, dried	26	0	11	1·44	0·37	22·1	Analysis of Bemba speci-men.
Meat, stewed	15	4·4	0	Trace	0·11	2·5	McCance and Shipp, 1933. ½ values to allow for gravy.
Meat, venison (roast)	30	6·6	0	0·03	0·29	7·8	McCance and Shipp, 1933.
Mpundu fruit	1	0	7	0·02	0·02	0·4	As apricot. McCance, Widdowson, and Shackleton, 1936.
Mpwa fruit	1	0	3	0·01	0·01	0·4	As egg-plant. McCance, Widdowson, and Shackleton, 1936.
Mushrooms, fresh	2	0	0	Trace	0·14	1·0	McCance, Widdowson, and Shackleton, 1936.
Peas, dried	22	0	50	0·06	0·30	4·7	,, ,,

	Protein	Fat	Carbo-hydrate	Cal-cium	Phos-phorus	Iron	Source of figures
	gm.	gm.	gm. (per 100 gm.)	gm.	gm.	mgm.	
Potatoes, sweet (including waste)	1	0	18	0·02	0·04	0·5	McCance, Widdowson, and Shackleton, 1936.
Potatoes, *Mumbu* or Livingstone	2	0	3	0·03	0·03	0·4	As Jerusalem artichokes. McCance, Widdowson, and Shackleton, 1936.
Pumpkin, fresh (including waste)	1	0	3	0·03	0·02	0·3	McCance, Widdowson, and Shackleton, 1936.
Tripe	18	3·0	0	0·13	0·13	1·6	McCance and Shipp, 1933.

Local (*Cibwa*) Salt from Mpika
(*analysed by McCance and Widdowson*)

Na	K	Ca	Mg	Fe	Cl	SO$_4$	Cu	Mn
		(Gm. per 100 gm.)					(Mgm.per100gm.)	
32·50	2·405	0·313	0·038	0·045	45·60	21·30	0·25	0·70

REFERENCES

McCance, R. A., Widdowson, E. M., and Shackleton, L. R. B., 1936. *The Nutritive Value of Fruits, Vegetables and Nuts.* M.R.C. Special Report Series No. 213.

McCance, R. A., and Shipp, H. L., 1933. *The Chemistry of Flesh Foods and their Losses on Cooking.* M.R.C. Special Report Series No. 187.

Sherman, H. C., 1937. *Chemistry of Food and Nutrition.* 5th edition.

Orr, J. B., and Gilks, J. L., 1931. *The Physique and Health of Two African Tribes.* M.R.C. Special Report Series No. 155.

TABLE C

Chemical Composition of the Diet of 3 Villages of the Bemba Tribe. Results expressed per Man Value per Day

Village	Family	Total protein grams per day	Animal protein grams per day	Fat grams per day	Carbohydrate grams per day	Calories per day	Calcium grams per day	Phosphorus grams per day	Iron milligrams per day
KASAKA:	A	67·0	16·9	16·7	426	2,293	1·96	2·20	20·7
(Hot weather season—	B	90·0	22·4	21·8	591	3,164	2·56	2·92	28·1
August, September,	C	52·0	14·3	14·4	304	1,685	1·43	1·62	15·8
October)	D	50·8	20·3	13·7	270	1,440	0·97	1·31	15·4
	E	57·6	21·1	19·3	314	1,725	1·27	1·55	17·2
Mean		63·5	19·0	17·2	381	2,061	1·64	1·92	19·4
KAMPAMBA:	A	32·0	o	16·7	160	941	0·76	1·33	10·6
(Wet weather season—	B	64·6	o	17·8	506	2,510	2·20	3·00	22·6
November, December,	C	52·0	o	11·6	455	2,181	1·83	2·14	17·9
January)	D	38·5	o	9·3	316	1,544	1·38	1·77	13·6
	E	39·0	o	13·7	296	1,508	1·29	1·68	12·8
	F	61·0	o	15·0	521	2,642	2·20	2·80	20·9
Mean		47·9	o	14·0	376	1,888	1·61	2·12	16·4
KUNGU:	A	18·6	o	2·2	144	686	0·79	0·69	7·6
(Hunger months—	B	35·0	8·4	5·8	194	993	1·20	1·11	12·7
February, March)	C	11·8	o	0·4	57	286	0·60	0·37	7·0
	D	26·6	7·9	2·1	220	1,029	0·78	0·88	9·4
	E	37·0	o	5·4	320	1,512	1·52	1·46	14·2
	F	10·9	0·6	1·5	80	388	0·46	0·45	5·3
Mean		23·3	2·8	2·9	169	816	0·89	0·83	9·4
Average results for the 3 villages, representing the diet of each village over 8 months of the year		50·0	10·2	13·0	327	1,706	1·45	1·70	16·1
Chemical composition of a typical European or American diet		100·0	50·0	100·0	400	3,000	0·68	1·32	15·0

Republished from *Africa*, 1936, vol. ix, no. 2.

TABLE D

Notes on the Structure of the Bemba Village

I. *Table showing the length of life of the Bemba villages of three big chiefs'
territories*, 1934.

> Citimukulu's territory (Lubemba): 160 villages.
> Mwamba's territory (Ituna): 69 villages.
> Nkula's territory (Icinga): 76 villages.

	Citimukulu	Mwamba	Nkula
	%	%	%
New villages (i.e. headmen appointed in reign of present chief)	29	49	42
Villages with 1 previous holder of headmanship	16	26	9
Villages with 2 previous holders of headmanship	10	14	18
Village with 3 previous holders of headmanship	40	10	13
Villages formed by remnants of 2 or more old villages. . .	6	..	15

It will be noted that the proportion of new headmanships created
by each chief in his own reign is just under half the total titles in the
case of the territorial chiefs, about 30 per cent. in the case of the
Paramount chief.

The striking difference between the number of old titles to headmanships in Citimukulu's territory and those of the other two chiefs,
i.e. 40 per cent. as against 10 and 13 per cent. respectively, is due to the
concentration of the hereditary councillors of the tribe (*bakabilo*) who
must inevitably be headmen for social, political, and ritual reasons,
in Citimukulu's district.

II. *Table showing the proportion of commoner headmen to those of royal
blood*, and hence the political powers of the chief.

	Citimukulu	Mwamba	Nkula
	%	%	%
Number of commoner headmen .	49	42	42
Number of hereditary councillors or priests, acting as headmen .	30	6	17
Number of descendants of wives of early chiefs acting as headmen .	3	..	..
Number of chief's relatives acting as headmen	19	41	33
Number of headmen from other tribes	..	10	10

It will be noted that the number of commoners given positions of authority is under half the total number in each territory. The far greater number of chief's relatives holding office in Mwamba's country is due to the number of surviving descendants of the previous Mwamba (Mubanga Cipoya) an extremely powerful ruler, who put his relatives in charge of villages all over the country.

(a) In the case of Citimukulu, the chief's relatives consisted of: Brother of the chief, 1; sisters, mothers, or maternal nieces of the chief (*banamfumu*), 7; sons of the chief (*bana ba mfumu*), 10 (9 men and 1 woman); grandchildren of the chief (*beshikulu ba mfumu*), 9 (8 men and 1 woman); relatives in law (*bukwe*), 3 (2 men and 1 woman).

(b) In the case of Mwamba, the chief's relatives consisted of: 1 brother, 1 sister; 11 ranked as 'children of the chief', 3 of the present Mwamba, 3 descendants of sons of the past Mwamba, and 5 of the penultimate Mwamba (5 women and 6 men in all); 7 were grandchildren, 4 descendants of other royal lines; and 3 descendants of the wives of former Citimukulus.

(c) In the case of Nkula, the chief's relatives consisted of: 1 brother and 2 sisters, 5 'children of the chief', 4 grandchildren (1 woman), and 4 relatives in law, and 9 descendants of other royal lines.

III. *Details showing kinship composition of typical villages.*

(Only adult members of the village are noted. Such terms as brother, sister, grandchild are used to indicate own brother and sister as well as the classificatory extension of these terms.)

(a) A village composed of the headman's own *ulupwa* (the bilateral group composed of near relatives of both sides of the family, plus affinal kinsmen).

e.g. *Cikutwe*, a young *mukabilo* of Citimukulu's territory (1934).

Relatives of the present headman, including matrilineal group: 1 mother, 4 mother's brothers and wives, 2 sisters and husbands, 2 maternal nieces (deserted), 2 daughters (one married), and 3 grandchildren (1 male and 2 female) with their spouses.

Others: 2 married brothers temporarily resident; and 2 deserted wives, relatives of the headman's wife.

Relatives of the past headman:

Remains of *matrilineal group*: 1 maternal niece (widowed), 3 grandsons (married), 2 granddaughters (married).

Remains of *matrilocal group*: 2 married daughters and husbands, and 1 son (married) temporarily resident.

(It will be noted that Bemba make a difference between the kinsmen of the present and past headman. Both groups are really kin to the present headman, since the title is hereditary, but the first are closer connexions to him than the second, and the distinction is made between those men and women who actually joined the community on his account and those who originally belonged to the past village.)

(b) *Two villages composed of the family group of the headman plus that of one or more other bakalamba (great ones)*, i.e. contemporaries, men who have remained in the village after the death of the previous headman, or those temporarily members of the community, while they are gathering a sufficient following to enable them to build a village of their own.

e.g. *Pambalasa*, near Chinsali (1930).

Relatives of headman:

Matrilocal group: 2 wives, 2 married daughters and husbands, 2 married daughters (husbands away), 2 married grandsons, wife's maternal niece (deserted).

Matrilineal group: 1 mother, 1 married sister and husband, 1 maternal niece (deserted), 1 maternal nephew and wife.

Others: 2 married sons and wives.

Relatives of a mukalamba. ShiNconi, husband of headman's maternal niece (i.e. still living in his wife's village, but in his middle age become head of a group of his own), 1 mother, 2 married sisters, 2 brothers (married to Pambalasa's daughters), 1 brother also married into the village.

Relatives of a mukalamba. ShiMulenga (awaiting permission to form a village of his own) and head of a following, i.e. 2 wives, 1 mother, widowed wife of father, 4 married sisters, 3 married maternal nieces, wife's brother, 3 unmarried maternal nephews. (With this following ShiMulenga formed a village in 1931.)

Kacienga, near Shiwa Dandu (1931 and 1933).

Headman's *matrilocal group* composed of his wife and 7 married daughters and their husbands; the mother and deserted sister of one of his sons-in-law, and a married sister of his wife's.

Two bakalamba, distant connexions of the former headman, each with his own small following composed of 2 married daughters and their husbands.

(c) *Village formed on a basis of common purpose.*

Mulenga, near Nkula, 1933. The village of an *ngulu*, i.e. man possessed by a chief's spirit and able to heal people through his knowledge of medicines and powers of clairvoyance. In this instance the kinship structure was hardly apparent, since so many strangers had joined Mulenga in order to get his blessing (many of them barren women hoping to secure children through the blessing of the spirit).

Fishing in the neighbouring river, Cambesi, was also lucrative. The community was composed as follows:

The headman's relatives: 2 married daughters and husbands, 2 wife's sisters (deserted); 1 maternal niece (married), 1 maternal nephew (married), 1 female cross-cousin (deserted), 1 son (married).

Strangers: 9 married couples some temporarily and some permanently part of the community, and 3 deserted wives.

This made the total male and female relatives of the headman, 12, and the total number of strangers, 21, an unprecedented state of affairs in an ordinary village.

Cf. also the two villages analysed on pp. 385–6.

INDEX

(N.B. *Native nouns have been written for convenience sake without prefixes.*)

Agriculture, adaptations of, to urban life, 322–7; adoption of new methods in, 19, 205, 275, 317, 322, 327; attitude to different crops, 311–13; attitude to gardening, 309, 398, 401–2; burning of gardens, 19, 288–301; choice of garden sites, 267–71, 278–80; cultivation of ground-nuts, 301–2; cultivation of millet, 288–301; cultivation of subsidiary crops, 302–11; effects of climate on, 33; estimation of yield from, 205, 289; fencing, 297, 396; firing gardens, 294–6, 354, 372; fixed cultivation, 270, 282, 327–8; harvesting, 299–300, 309; hoeing, 304, 396; individual differences in, 324–6; incentives in, 291–2, 351–4; lack of incentives in, 105, 209, 400–2; manuring, 282, 300; methods compared to other tribes, 19–21; modern changes in, 402; mound cultivation, 243, 302–10, 317; old house and village sites used for, 273–4, 281, 321–2; ownership of gardens, 185; piling branches, 293–4; seasonal calendar, 388–90; sequence of crops, 313–22; shifting cultivation, 19, 282, 289; size of gardens, 289, 387; soil selection, 283–7; sowing, 296, 301–7; success or failure in, 323–5; time taken over tasks, 396–8; tree-cutting, 19, 288–93; wasteful methods of, 289; weeding, 289, 301, 308. *See also* Ritual, Land.

Ancestors, *see* Chief, Magico-religious beliefs, Ritual.

Ant-hills, soil of, 281.

Anthropologists, approach to diet, 8, 10; approach to agriculture, 229; observational methods of, 10–14; preservation of material of, 13.

Ash, importance of, in agriculture, 19, 279, 289, 304.

Axe, uses of, 21, 290.

Bafilolo, see Court officials.
Bahima, diet of, 5.
Bakabilo, see Councillors.
Barotse, origin of, 17.
Barter, *see* Exchange.
Beans, *see* Legumes.

Beer, average consumption of, 81; brewing of, 97–9; composition of, 78, 409; craving for, 59; drinking customs, 77–80; frequency of brewing, 80, 164; in modern communities, 81; nutritional value of, 76; payment for communal work in, 146–7; ritual relating to, 80; social value of, 77; tribute of, 252, 377.

Bemba, affinities of, 15–17, 28–30; crops of, 20; dietetic theory of, 50–4; geographical position of, 15; history of, 15–17; language of, 11; material culture of, 21, 27, 100–1, 209–11; militarism of, 22, 400–1; mode of life, 16–21; population density of, 18; social structure of, 23–6; temperamental characteristics of, 28–30, 268, 271–3.

Bemba country, access to, 32; boundaries of, 30–1; climate of, 32; geographical details of, 29–33; rainfall, 32–3; types of bush in, 31.

Bisa, comparisons with, 17, 29, 38, 43, 76, 93, 187, 226, 327, 353, 356.

Boa, see Mushrooms.

Bryant, A. T., 375.

Budgeting, difficulties of, 88, 151–2, 201–2. *See also* Housecraft, Counting, Measurement.

Bwali, see Porridge.

Bwalua, see Beer.

Caterpillars, attitude to, 57, 60; collection of, 104, 232; in diet, 38, 41, 48; ownership of, 188; preparation of, 95.

Cattle, *see* Domestic animals.

Cassava, attitude to, 52; cultivation of, 20, 302, 307; food value of, 66, 93, 409; ownership of, 186; poisonous properties of, 93–4; preparation of, 93–4; sequence of millet and, 318; storage of, 84.

Charms, use of, 355–6; in hunting, 343–9. *See also* Ritual.

Chickens, *see* Domestic animals.

Chief, ancestral spirits of, 25, 188, 234, 240, 248–9, 339, 357–8, 363; burial ritual of, 240–1; district of, 243; duties of wives of, 78, 138, 148, 151; economic ambitions of, 213–16, 401; economic leadership of,

215, 295, 349, 386–8; expert knowledge of territory of, 387; favours of, 211–14; fixity of village of, 277–8; following of, 211–13; food supply of, 215; gardens of, 189, 215, 291, 297, 361, 387; hierarchy of, 24, 243; as land owner, 244–8, 260–2, 265; military powers of, 25, 257, 401; officials of, 24, 147; payment of labour by, 147, 151, 259, 263; political powers of, 110, 212, 246, 278, 340; present economic position of, 25, 252, 255, 259, 261, 263–4; provision of food by, 141, 147–51, 261–4; ritual enhancing importance of, 359–62; sacred kitchen of, 148; sanctions for authority of, 248–51, 260; sex powers of, 149, 249, 359, 364–5; supernatural powers of, 25, 248–51, 261–2, 355, 364; tribute labour of, 144, 243, 256–62, 267; tribute paid to, 138, 147, 251–5, 377; villages of, 18, 239–42; wealth of, 214–15.

Cilemba, see Legumes.
Citimene, see Tree-cutting.
Citimukulu, *see* Chief.
Civilization, *see* Modern changes.
Clothes, craving for, 216–17; European, 27, 216; in old days, 27, 211, 219.
Cooked food, labour paid for by, 142–4; symbolism of, 127–8.
Cooking, education in, 105–7, 125, 132, 202; methods of, 90–7; publicity of, 99, 199; ritual cooking, 148, 345; number of dishes known, 59–60, 406–8; seasoning, 96; teams for, 125–7, 130–4, 191, 203; time taken over, 100, 102–4; vessels used for, 90; women too tired to do any, 72–4, 104–5, 168–9.
Counting, method of, 203–4. *See also* Budgeting, Measurement.
Councillors, districts of, 243; distribution of food to, 141, 147, 262–4; duties of, 24, 359–62, 365, 369, 371, 378; villages of, 278.
Court officials, 147, 211–14.
Crops, attitude to different, 311–13; cultivation of subsidiary, 302–10; estimation of amount of, 206; list of, 20, 406–8; origin of, 20; ritual connected with, 311–13, 373–4, 376; protection of, 297; sequence of, 307–8, 313–22; sale of, 274; soils suited for different, 280, 318–21.
Cucumbers, *see* Cucurbits.

Cucurbits, attitude to, 47, 53, 310, 313; cooking of, 95; cultivation of, 305; origin of, 20; ownership of, 186; ritual connected with, 313, 373–4, 376–7; storage of, 84.
Curses, conditional, 187–8; by land spirits, 188.

Diet, anthropologists' approach to, 8–10; Bemba theory of, 50–4; calorie intake, 39–40, 411; characteristics of primitive, 1–14; composition of, 37–41; daily intake of, 39, 78, 83; deficiencies in, 1–2, 35–40, 42; effect of European contact on, 3–4, 72, 81, 153; difficulties of primitive research in, 5–10, 123; diseases due to, 1; effect on energy of Bemba of, 36, 37, 42–3, 50, 399; Elmolo, 5; fat in, 34, 38–9, 49, 66; fish in, 39; government scale of, 40; growing interest in primitive, 2; importance of millet in, 37–8; in hunger season, 35–7; legumes in, 38; Masai, 5; meat in, 7, 39, 56–9; on mines, 3, 40; monotony of, 59–60; salt in, 39, 96, 164; seasonal changes of, 41–3, 73, 160; Somali, 5; variations in, 41–2, 74, 153, 165, 169, 175, 178–83; vitamins in, 38, 39, 76, 84. *See also* Cooked food, Food.
Digestion, native theories as to, 51–2; troubles recognized as caused by food, 54.
Distribution, by chief, 147–50, 261–3; education in, 195–202; effect of, on tribal dietary, 151–3; kinship obligations of, 108–9, 127–30, 135–41, 185, 188, 193, 200; modern changes in, 153, 195; of meat, 141; political importance of prestige conferred by, 135–6, 147, 198; supernatural sanctions enforcing, 199; tribal, 150–3; in typical village, 165, 177–83.
Doke, C., 243, 246, 342, 356.
Domestic animals, attitude to, 7, 63–4; Bemba lack of, 18, 210, 323; exchange of money, 195; tribes owning, 17.
Drinking customs, beer, 76–81; water, 75. *See also* Beer.

Eating customs, chief meal, 72–4; catering groups, 122–3, 151, 165–77; education in, 71; etiquette at meals, 75; European, 6, 71; frequency of meals, 72–3, 75; rate and manner of eating, 75–6; meal-times, 73,

PRINTED IN
GREAT BRITAIN
AT THE
UNIVERSITY PRESS
OXFORD
BY
JOHN JOHNSON
PRINTER
TO THE
UNIVERSITY